complete yoga aromatherapy tai chi and massage

A step-by-step guide to spiritual and physical well-being

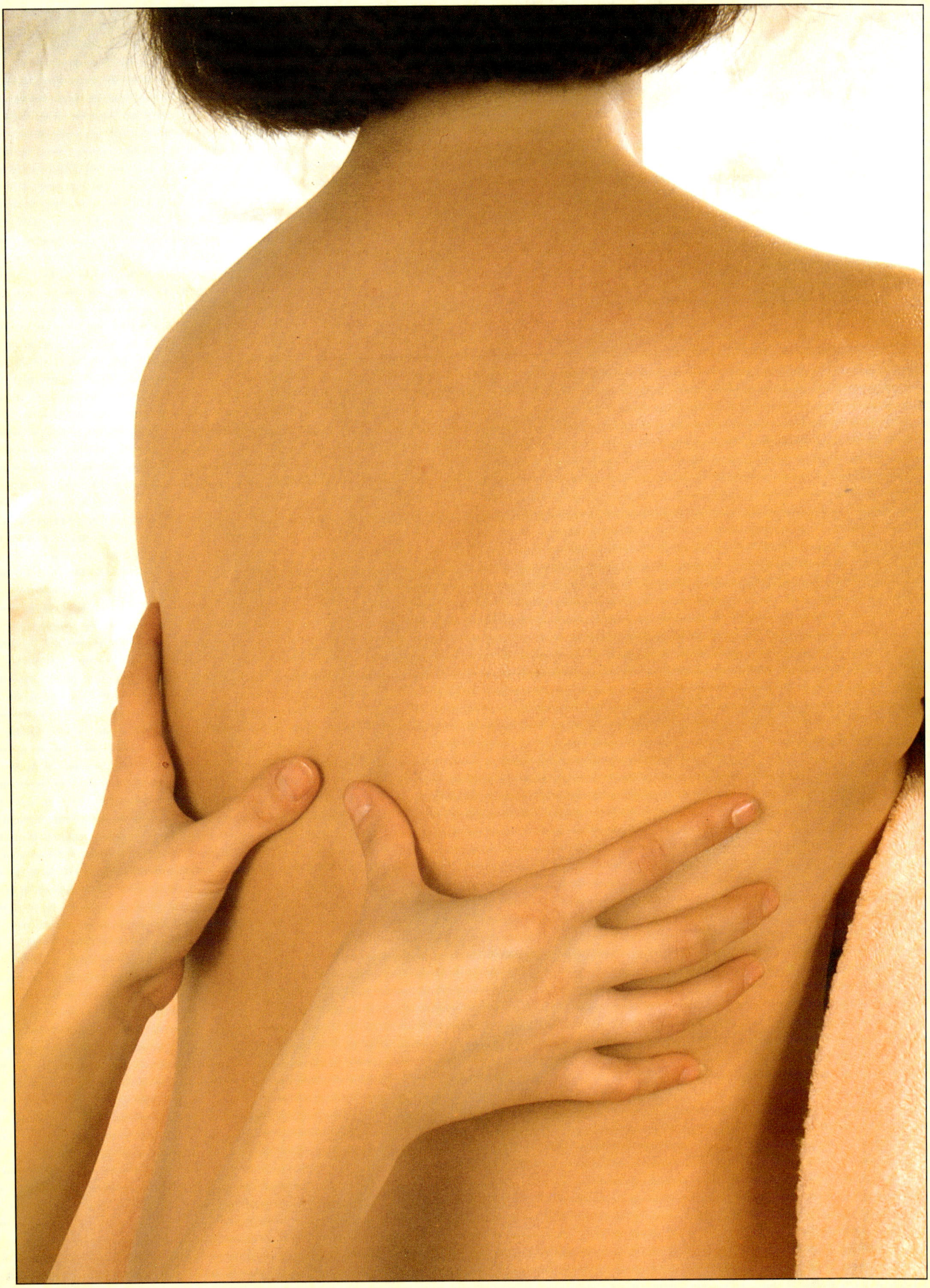

complete yoga aromatherapy tai chi and massage

A step-by-step guide to spiritual and physical well-being

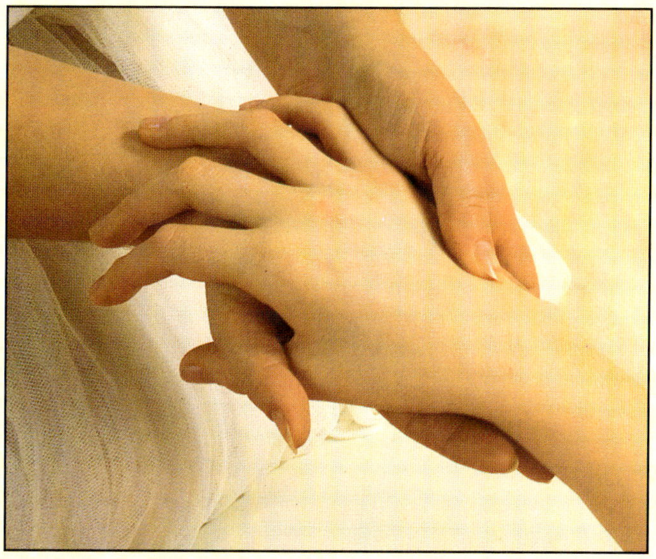

Carole McGilvery Jimi Reed Michèle MacDonnell
Paul Tucker Mark Evans John Hudson

HERMES HOUSE

This edition is published by Hermes House

Hermes House is an imprint of Anness Publishing Ltd
Hermes House, 88–89 Blackfriars Road, London SE1 8HA
tel. 020 7401 2077; fax 020 7633 9499; info@anness.com

A CIP catalogue record for this book is available from the British Library.

Publisher: Joanna Lorenz
Project Editors: Elaine Collins and Emma Gray
Photographers: Sue Atkinson, Don Last and Dave Jordan
Photographic Assistant: Kirsty Wilson
Additional photography: Michelle Garrett, Simon Bottomley and Alistair Hughes
Designer: Kit Johnson
Additional layouts: Balley Design Associates, David Rowley, Lillian Lindblom and Ian Sandom
Artwork: Raymond Turvey, King & King
Illustrations on pages 162 and 163 by Michael Shoebridge

The majority of this book was previously published as
The Encyclopedia of Aromatherapy, Massage and Yoga

1 3 5 7 9 10 8 6 4 2

ACKNOWLEDGEMENTS

The authors and publishers would like to thank the following for their valuable contributions to the book:

Nina Ashby, Andrea Ashley, Richard Good, Angela Inverso, Clive Ives, BKS Iyengar, Kay Kiernan, Lisa Myhill, Rachel Stewart, Eve Taylor, Karin Weisensel and Janice Welch for advice and contributions to the text.

Michaeljohn, The Bluestone Clinic, Clarins, The Ragdale Clinic, Henlow Grange and Grayshott Hall for providing advice, expertise and personnel.

Avalon Aromatic Candles, The Body Shop, Boutique Descampes, Clarins, Cosmetics to Go, Culpeper, Decleor Ltd, Futon, Gore Booker, Knickerbox, Kobashi, Nice Irma's, Pineapple Dance Studio and Purves and Purves for providing equipment, clothes and products.

Andrea Ashley, Mary Atkinson, Alison Barry, Nichola Clare, Laura Cream, Max Collins Wolff, Karen Flynn, Richard Good, Angela Inverso, Clive Ives, Tabitha Jackson, Maya Jacobson, Colette Keogh, Kerry Le Surf, Sophie Marks, Lisa Myhill, Maria Nuccio, Sue Paterson-Jones, Anna Rand, Rachel Stewart, Michelle Thomas, Karin Weisensel, Janice Welch and Karen Wilding for appearing in the photographs.

PICTURE CREDITS

The Ancient Art and Architecture Collection: pp.11 it, 100 and 101.
A-Z Botanical Collection Ltd: p.244 ml.
The Bridgeman Art Library: p.8 t b.
French Picture Library: p.11 ib.
Garden & Wildlife Matters: p.251 tr.
Picturepoint Limited: pp.9 and 10–11.
Tony Stone Images: pp.242 bl, 243 bl, 245 tr, 246 tl br, 247 tl br, 248 bl, 249 t and 251 bl.

PUBLISHER'S NOTE

The reader should not regard the recommendations, ideas and techniques expressed and described in this book as substitutes for the advice of a qualified medical practitioner or other qualified professional. Any use to which the recommendations, ideas and techniques are put is at the reader's sole discretion and risk.

Contents

AROMATHERAPY

The pure essences of aromatic plants have been prized for thousands of years for their health-giving properties and heady scents. Discover the ancient art of aromatherapy, refined over the centuries, and learn how to harness the therapeutic powers of essential oils in a relaxing, restorative massage that combines the sense of smell with the healing value of touch. Use the beneficial properties of the oils to treat common ailments, promote good health and emotional well being, and to enhance every aspect of your life. These potent, volatile essences are nature's gift to mind and body.

AN ANCIENT ART

The value of natural plant oils has been recognized for more than 6000 years, for their healing, cleansing, preservative and mood-enhancing properties, as well as for the sheer pleasure of their fragrances. Today, these properties are being rediscovered as we look to the wisdom of past eras and civilizations to restore the balance that has been lost in modern-day life. Stress, pollution, unhealthy diet, hectic but sedentary lifestyles – all these factors have adverse effects on our bodies and spirits. The art of aromatherapy harnesses the potent pure essences of aromatic plants, flowers and resins, to work on the most powerful of senses – smell and touch – to restore the harmony of body and mind.

SECRETS OF THE OILS DISCOVERED

The origins of aromatherapy can be traced through the religious, medical and social practices of all the major civilizations. It is likely that the Chinese were the first to discover the remarkable medicinal powers of plants around 4500 BC. However, it is the Egyptians who must take the credit for recognizing and fully exploiting the physical and spiritual properties of aromatic essences. From hieroglyphs and paintings we know that aromatic preparations were used as offerings to the gods. Furthermore the natural antiseptic and antibacterial properties of essential oils and resins, particularly cedarwood and frankincense, made them ideal for the purpose of preserving corpses in preparation for the next world. The discovery of remarkably well-preserved mummies up to 5000 years after their preparation is a tribute to the embalmer's art.

By around 3000 BC priests who had been using the oils in religious ceremonies and embalming rites became aware of the usefulness of their properties for the living, too. Closely guarding their secrets, they became the healers of their time, mixing and prescribing "magic" medicinal potions. Use of essential oils gradually permeated all levels of society as cosmetics and perfumes became widespread.

From Hippocrates we know the Greeks had some awareness of the therapeutic properties of the oils and their value as sedatives and stimulants was certainly recognized. The Greeks and Romans used aromatics widely in rituals and ceremonies and the oils played an important role in the rise in popularity of baths and massage and body-culture generally. However, with the fall of the Roman Empire the use of essential oils died out in Europe.

Left: The personal use of perfume was widespread in ancient Greece and Rome. The Roman girl in this portrait (from around AD 350) carries a small pot of aromatics.

Right: From the tomb of the Noble Senedjem, ancient Egypt. The cones of unguent worn on the heads melted in the heat, waxing and scenting the hair and body.

This Milesian container for perfumed oils is fashioned in the form of a Siren, a sea nymph of Greek mythology. It dates from around 525 BC, when Miletus was one of the principal Ionian seaports.

The art flourished elsewhere, though, particularly in Arabia, where Avicenna was the first to distill rose essence around AD 1000. Arabia became the world's centre for production of perfume, importing raw materials from Egypt, India, Tibet and China, and trading their products internationally.

With the Crusaders the art of perfumery was reintroduced to Europe around the twelfth century. Records show that aromatics were used as protection against the plague and the lower incidence of death among perfumiers suggests they were to some degree effective. The fifteenth century saw the rise of the great European perfumiers, and their wares were widely used to disguise body smells and ward off sickness. By the seventeenth century the aphrodisiac properties were certainly well recognized, and with the work of the great herbalists, such as Culpeper, the therapeutic properties also started to be recorded, laying the foundation for modern-day aromatherapy.

The Modern Renaissance

The term "Aromathérapie" was first used in 1928 by a French chemist, René-Maurice Gattefossé, to describe the therapeutic action of aromatic plant essences. His work was taken up by Dr Jean Valnet who found the essences' remarkable regenerative and antiseptic properties effective for healing the wounds of World War II soldiers.

The application of aromatherapy to beauty therapy and health care was pioneered by Marguerite Maury in her influential book, *The Secret of Life and Youth.* She also developed the method of applying the oils through massage.

Today there is a world-wide revival in the art of aromatherapy and contemporary research is beginning to understand the scientific foundations of the oils' properties and applications, discovered by trial and error over thousands of years.

ESSENTIAL OILS

The vital element in any aromatherapy treatment is the pure essential oil. These oils are very different from the heavy oils we use for cooking; they are concentrated essences, much lighter than water and highly flammable. They evaporate quickly, so they are usually mixed with other ingredients to trap their effectiveness. Because they are so concentrated, essential oils are measured in drops.

ESSENCE

This is a natural living substance: the "living" element of a plant which is captured and capsuled. It is a delicate operation. For instance, certain petals and leaves must be picked at exactly the right moment, or the quality of the oil is affected. Only the purest essences are used in aromatherapy so that the therapeutic properties are maximized and the effects are predictable.

Essential oils are extracted from an array of plant sources – petals, leaves, seeds, nut kernels, bark, stalks, flower heads and gums and resins from trees. Apart from their sensuous vapours, which provide the fragrance in many perfumes, they can be used in the bath, smoothed over the body, and used in the myriad ways described in this book.

Because of their small molecular structure, essential oils can penetrate the skin more effectively than vegetable oils, which only lie on the surface. Used medicinally over the centuries, essential oils have now become an established "alternative" natural therapy which can assist in the treatment of almost every type of ache and pain, as well as smoothing away the stress and strains of modern life.

HOW THEY WORK

Essential oils are composed of tiny molecules which are easily dissolved in alcohol, emulsifiers and, particularly, fats. This allows them to penetrate the skin easily and work into the body by mixing with the fatty tissue.

As these highly volatile essences evaporate they are also inhaled, thus entering the body via the millions of sensitive cells that line the nasal passages. These send messages straight to the brain, and affect the emotions by working on the limbic system, which also controls the major functions of the body. Thus in an aromatherapy treatment the essential oils are able to enhance both your physical and psychological well-being at the same time.

Each oil has a distinct chemical composition which determines its fragrance, colour, volatility and, of course, the ways in which it affects the system, giving each oil its unique set of beneficial properties.

METHODS OF EXTRACTION

Distillation

The Egyptians stored their raw materials in large clay or alabaster pots. Water was added and the pots

Main picture: Field of lavender, Drome, southern France. French lavender produces the finest quality oil, with a fruitier and sweeter aroma than English lavender, which has a camphorous undertone. It takes one ton (one tonne) of plants to yield about 20 lb (9 kg) of essential oil.

Inset top: Egyptian relief showing perfume-making, from the fourth century BC. The large alabaster pot (a "linge") was filled with flowers, herbs and water, and then heated. The aromatic vapours would saturate a cloth stretched across the pot's opening.

Inset below: Art meets science in the skills of the perfumier, blending a subtle new fragrance from the hundreds of essential oils at his disposal.

heated so that steam rose and was pushed through a cotton cloth in the neck of the jar. This soaked up the essential oil which was then squeezed and pressed out into a collection vessel. The same principle remains in use today as high-pressure steam is passed over the leaves or flowers in a sophisticated still often using a vacuum, so that the essential oils within them vaporize. When the steam carrying the essential oil passes through a cooling system, the oil condenses and can be separated easily from the water.

Maceration

Flowers are soaked in hot oil to break down the cells, releasing their fragrance into the oil which is then purified and the aromatics extracted.

Enfleurage

This is the method by which flower essences, such as jasmine, neroli and rose, which are more delicate and difficult to obtain, are extracted. Flowers or petals are crushed between wooden-framed, glass trays smeared with a greasy animal fat until the fat is saturated with their perfume.

Pressing

This is a simple method of squeezing out, literally, essential oils from the rinds and peel of ripe fruit, such as orange and lemon, into a sponge.

Quality Control

Once the flowers and plants are harvested they are usually processed and stored quickly to preserve the freshness. Climate, soil and altitude can all affect the character of an oil. French lavender, for example, is famous for its rich aroma but, like wine, the quality can vary from year to year.

Always buy pure and natural essential oils as synthetic clones or adulterated oils do not act on the body in the same way and many of the beneficial properties are lost. The best quality oils may be expensive but they are always worth the extra cost.

USING ESSENTIAL OILS

You can soak and splash in them, feed your skin, sensually smooth them all over, or simply breathe in their wonderful aromas. The pleasure and versatility of aromatic oils make them one of nature's kindest gifts. Essential oils contain the active ingredients of a plant in a highly concentrated and potent form. They therefore need to be treated with care and should never be applied directly to the skin undiluted. However, there are many ways of dispersing their fragrance and utilizing their therapeutic properties, and most methods do not require any special equipment.

Inhalation
Steam inhalation is an excellent method for treating respiratory problems, colds and so forth, but should not be used by asthmatics. Add 6–12 drops to a bowl of steaming hot water. Place a towel over your head and breathe deeply. This is also a great way of deep-cleansing the face.

Therapeutic Massage
This is the classic aromatherapy treatment, triggering the body's natural healing process by using lymphatic massage and essential oils to stimulate the flow of blood and lymph fluid. The aromas also act upon the emotional centre in the brain (the "limbic" system) which governs the way we feel.

For massage use a 1–3 per cent solution of essential oil to base oil.

Fragrancers
These attractive pots, also known as diffusers or vaporizers, are simple to use. Fill the top china bowl with water and add a few drops of essential oil on to the surface. The candle in the pot underneath heats the water, slowly releasing the natural fragrance of the oil into the room.

Stand the burner on a plate or tile, not on plastic surfaces.

Decorative fragancers for diffusing essential oils.

3–6 drops of essential oil are sufficient, depending on the size of the room. It is also possible to buy battery-driven fan vaporizers which blow air through oil-impregnated pads, which can be changed to suit the mood.

Baths
Run hand-hot water and then add 5–10 drops of the essential oil to suit your mood. Close the door, keep in the vapours, and soak for 15 minutes. For sensitive skin it is better to dilute the oil in a base oil first, like sweet almond, apricot or peach kernel. Essential oils can mark plastic baths if they are not dispersed thoroughly. Wipe the bath straight after use.

Foot Bath
Refresh tired feet by adding 4–5 drops of peppermint, rosemary and thyme to a large bowl of hot water. Soothe with lavender.

Hand Bath
Soothe chapped skin by soaking in bowl of warm water (not hot) with 3–4 drops of patchouli or comfrey before a manicure.

Shower
After soaping or gelling, rinse well. Dip a wet sponge in an oil mix of your choice, squeeze and rub over your whole body while under a warm jet spray.

Sauna
Add two drops of eucalyptus or pine oil per 1/2 pint (330 ml) of water and throw over the coals to evaporate. These are great cleansers and detoxifiers.

Jacuzzi or Hot Tub
Relax by adding 10–15 drops of sandalwood, geranium or ylang-ylang, or simply bubble over with the stimulating effects of pine, rosemary and neroli.

Room Sprays
To make a room spray blend ten drops of essential oil in seven tablespoons of water. One tablespoon of vodka or pure alcohol added to the solution will act as a preservative but this is optional. Shake well before filling the sprayer.

Pillow Talk
Perfume your pillow with 2–3 drops of oil. Choose a relaxing oil to unwind or one for insomnia if you have sleep problems. For a different mood, try an aphrodisiac like ylang-ylang or be extravagant and use rose or jasmine, the two most expensive pure oils.

Perfumes
The finest perfumes are traditionally blended from pure essential oils, particularly the flower extracts, though these days synthetic aromas tend to be used, particularly for cheaper perfumes. The art of the perfumier is subtle and skilled, and difficult to emulate at home as it is hard to find a medium to use as a substitute for alcohol. If you have a favourite oil or blend of essences you can use it all over in a body oil (three per cent solution), or make a very concentrated blend (25 per cent) to dab behind ears, knees and on wrists and temples.

Pomanders
Hang porous corked bottles in the wardrobe. The essential oil is absorbed by the clay and released slowly. Fill with the fragrance of your choice: try melissa or bergamot, or cedarwood to keep away moths.

Pot Pourri
Add a few drops of an appropriate flowery or spicy essential oil to refresh tired pot pourri, or make your own.

Handkerchief
The most portable way of using essential oils. Add 3–4 drops to a handkerchief and inhale. Useful for treating colds or headaches, or for clearing your head at work.

Shoe Rack
Freshen the cupboard with lemongrass. Deodorize shoes with two drops of pine or parsley oil.

From the top: perfume bottle, pot pourri and oil lamp.

Humidifiers
You can add your favourite oil to the water of a humidifier or improvize by adding five drops of essential oil to a small bowl of water placed on top of a radiator.

Ring Burners
Use the heat from light bulbs to release perfumed oils. Small ring burners, usually made of porcelain or aluminium, sit over the top of the bulb. Add a few drops of essential oil, and the heat from the bulb will gently vaporize the essential oil.

Wood Fires
Sprinkle drops of cypress, cedarwood, pine or sandalwood over the logs to be used about an hour before lighting the fire and then burn them to release your favourite aroma.

Scented Candles
Wax candles can be bought ready-impregnated with essential oils and are a delightful way of fragrancing a room. Or you can add a few drops of essential oil to an oil lamp for the same effect.

Compresses
Soak a clean cotton cloth (such as a face flannel, handkerchief or small towel) in $^1/_4$ pint (160 ml) warm water with 5–10 drops of essential oil. Squeeze out and lay across the area to be treated. Cover and leave until cold. A useful method for sprains, bruising, headaches (place the compress across the forehead) and hot flushes.

Body and Facial Oils
These can be used on a daily basis to nourish the skin. Use a one per cent blend of essential oil to carrier oil for the face and a three per cent blend for the body.

BLENDING AND STORING

Essential oils are the basis for all traditional aromatherapy. Each one has a particular fragrance and properties and the art of blending them harmoniously combines the skills of the perfumier and the pharmacist. Although two essences may have a similar smell or property they may not necessarily mix well together. One essence can overpower the other. For example, frankincense and ginger, both heavy smelling essences, give an overpowering, unpleasant smell when combined, whereas lavender and rosemary happily marry together. In general it is best to use a maximum of three oils in a blend so there is less chance of detracting from their individual qualities.

Assemble bottles of different sizes for storing appropriate quantities of blended oils. Funnels and droppers ensure accurate measurements and help prevent spillages.

THE ART OF BLENDING

Essential oils are highly volatile substances which should be handled, mixed and stored with care and used sparingly. Spillage of one particular oil can overpower a whole room and adversely affect young children and animals.

The power of aromatics is quite subtle. Never try to sniff or smell a pure essential oil straight from the bottle. Place a drop on the side of a glass and become a connoisseur: sniff, consider and take notes if you wish.

MIXING

Base oils play an important role in carrying and diluting highly concentrated essential oils, which are only used in small quantities measured in drops. These base oils dilute the pure essentials, inhibiting the evaporation rate and – since they spread evenly and easily over skin – encouraging quick absorption of the therapeutic oils into the skin.

When mixing, use a glass, porcelain or aluminium bottle and check that you have the correct amount of vegetable carrier oil before adding the recommended drops of essentials with a dropper or pipette for accurate measurements. Mix well and label the bottles clearly.

If you accidentally spill any, wipe up instantly with a paper tissue and dispose of it outside as the smell will be overpowering.

STORING

Dark glass bottles with stoppered caps are used to store essential oils. At home, keep them in a cool dark place, stand them upright, and always out of sight and touch of children. Never store essential oils in plastic bottles: both the oil and the bottle will perish. Oils will keep for at least a year if properly stored, although citrus oils may have a shorter life.

CARRIER OILS

Base oils are normally extracted from nuts or seeds and each has its own particular quality. Sweet almond oil is probably the best all-purpose carrier oil because it is neutral and non-allergenic. It can even be used for massaging babies. Walnut acts as a co-ordinator and balances the nervous system; sesame is ideal for stretch marks; apricot kernel, peach kernel and evening primrose oils are all good for cell regeneration. Walnut and evening primrose oil help alleviate menstrual problems including pre-menstrual tension. Wheatgerm acts as an anti-oxidant and will help preserve a mixture.

These oils are all rich in nutrients, and are ideal for most dry and sensitive skin types. The most important thing when buying these basics is to check that they have been naturally processed and not chemically treated. Cold-pressed is best.

AROMATICS

Aromatic oils extracted from flowers, fruits, leaves, barks, resins and roots have been used throughout the centuries for their healing properties and marvellous fragrances. Hundreds of essential oils are used today in such industries as food, cosmetics, pharmaceuticals and perfumery. Modern-day aromatherapy uses a much smaller selection, but the range of aromas and applications is nonetheless remarkable. This section is a connoisseurs' guide to thirty-five of the most popular, versatile and safe oils. Get to know their individual characters, their origins, their therapeutic values and discover your own favourites. Lavender, geranium and rosemary are excellent all-round oils and provide a good basis for any collection. Rose, though expensive, is also well worth the investment if you would like to explore the benefits and delights of aromatherapy.

BASIL

Ocimum basilicum

Origins Basil was used in baths and body massage by ancient Greek nobles for its fragrant perfume. The Egyptians used the aromatic fragrance in their offerings to the gods and also mixed it with essences of myrrh and incense to embalm bodies. In India it is believed to offer protection to the soul and is sacred to the Hindu gods Krishna and Vishnu.

Description Native of Africa and the Seychelles and now grown as a popular culinary herb in Europe, it can grow up to three feet (90 cm) in height and has small white flowers. The essence is distilled from the leaves and is a light greenish-yellow with sweet green overtones.

Therapeutic effects Ideal as a nerve tonic, to lift fatigue, anxiety and depression. Also good for bronchitis, colds, fever, gout and indigestion, and reputed to soothe snake bites.

Uses Inhalation, baths and massage. It has both hot and cold qualities. When used in the bath or smoothed over the body it has an invigorating effect – great for sluggish skin and pepping up circulation. Combined with other oils such as thyme it also acts as a powerful antiseptic.

Cautionary note A powerful depressant if over-used. Also best to avoid during pregnancy.

Bay

Pimenta racemosa

Origins Roman emperors wore sprigs of bay, known as *Laurus nobilis* (Roman laurel), not only as a sign of wealth, but to ward off evil spirits. Greek priestesses chewed the leaves for their soporific effect, and after gastronomic banquets it was chewed as a breath freshener.

Description Popular as a culinary herb, bay is an attractive evergreen shrub whose shiny leathery leaves produce clusters of yellowish-green flowers in spring. The spicy-smelling oil is extracted from the leaves and is yellowish-brown in colour.

Therapeutic effects As a pulmonary antiseptic, it helps relieve bronchitis, colds and flu. Also used to aid digestion and sleep, to soothe rheumatic aches and pains, and as a general tonic.

Uses Inhalation, baths and massage. Widely used in perfume and exotic bath essences for its uplifting effects.

Benzoin

Styrax benzoin

Origins In the Far East the gum from the benzoin tree was one of the main ingredients used in incense to drive away evil spirits. The compound tincture is highly potent, pharmaceutically used in friar's balsam and as a fixative in perfume.

Description The benzoin tree is cultivated in Borneo, Java, Malaysia, Sumatra and Thailand. Like the rubber tree, its gum is taken from the bark by making a deep incision in the trunk. The gum is dark, with reddish-brown coloured streaks. These pigments contain the fatty oils which exude a delicious aroma similar to vanilla.

Therapeutic effects Valuable for treating urinary infections, it has a warming, relaxing, action suitable for respiratory conditions such as bronchitis, coughs and colds. Also effective for relieving skin conditions, and for gout.

Uses Inhalation, massage and in cough medicines. This is an energizing oil which can be used in one of two forms: simple tincture or compound – the former is not so toxic and is preferable for skin conditions.

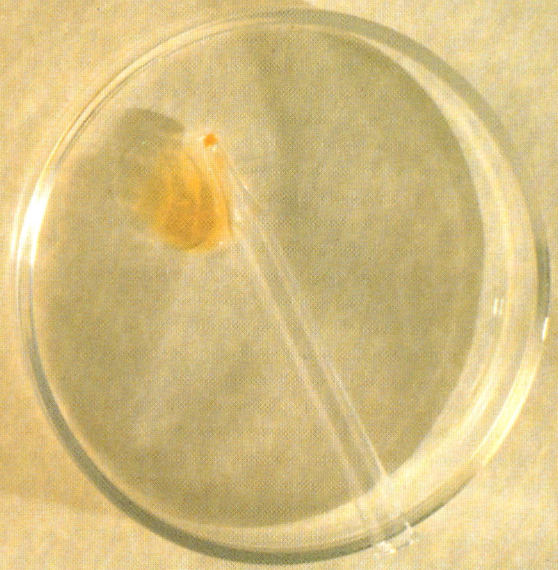

Bergamot

Citrus bergamia

Origins Native to Morocco, it wasn't until bergamot rooted in Italy that its essential properties were recognized.

Description The bergamot tree belongs to the same family as the orange tree and the essential oil, as in most citrus varieties, is expressed from the fresh peel of the fruit. The oil is emerald green in colour, and smells spicier than lemon but with a similar, citrus quality. The odour is familiar from its use as a flavouring in Earl Grey tea.

Therapeutic effects Has a powerful uplifting and refreshing action. As an antiseptic it has proved effective in the treatment of mouth and skin infections, and sore throats. Can lower fever, and help with bronchitis and indigestion.

Uses Bergamot blends well with most essences and is a popular top note in perfumery. Along with neroli and lavender it is a main ingredient in eau-de-Cologne and is commonly used in toiletries to refresh and relax. In massage it can stimulate or soothe depending on the oils with which it is mixed.

Cautionary note In concentrations above one per cent it can irritate the skin. Also, even though it is sometimes added to commercial suntan agents to stimulate melanin production, it must never be used in home mixtures for tanning purposes.

Cedarwood

Juniperus virginiana

Origins Cedarwood oil, similar to sandalwood, was used by the Egyptians in the embalming process. It was highly prized for its antiseptic properties and so became an important ingredient in cosmetics. Originally it was made from the beautiful Lebanon cedar, but, over-felled for furniture, this is now very scarce, and the red cedar is primarily used in its place.

Description The cedar is grown in North Africa and the USA for its highly valued, fragrant wood. The clear, syrupy essential oil is extracted by steam distillation of waste woods. The odour of the oil is reminiscent of wooden pencils.

Therapeutic effects Used for skin complaints such as acne, alopecia, dandruff and eczema, and respiratory problems, especially bronchitis and catarrh. Also acts as a diuretic for help in urinary infections.

Uses Inhalation and massage. Increases sexual response. Blends well with cypress, juniper and rose.

Cautionary note Will irritate the skin in high concentrations.

Chamomile

Alternative spelling: Camomile

Anthemis nobilis

Origins The Egyptians thought this was a sacred flower and dedicated it to the Sun God. It was used in ritual ceremonies and medicinally to stop fits and fevers.

Description Chamomile species grow throughout Europe, North Africa and are often found growing wild. They have fine, feathery leaves with tiny white or yellow-centred daisy-like flowers. The pale blue oil is extracted from the flower and has a slightly apple fragrance which blends well with rose, geranium and lavender.

Therapeutic effects Particularly noted for its anti-inflammatory and sedative properties, it is excellent for childhood ailments (whether in children or adults!) from peevishness to earache. Also used for allergies, anaemia, burns, dermatitis, diarrhoea, fever, indigestion, insomnia, menstrual and menopausal problems, rheumatism, toothache and ulcers.

Uses Certain chamomile species are used for herbal infusions, but the oil is used in body, bath and hair products for its anti-allergenic properties. Use in dilute form for children.

Cinnamon

Cinnamomum zeylanicum

Origins The Chinese believed that no remedy or treatment was complete without cinnamon. It is one of the oldest spices known – used by the Egyptians, Romans and Greeks, and it was also mentioned in the Old Testament.

Description Grown in the Far East, East Indies, and China, cinnamon has a distinctive hot, peppery aroma and taste. The twigs and leaves are picked and distilled to produce a sweet, pungent and bitter aromatic oil, which is a dark yellow-brown in colour. Its warm, spicy essence is often used in perfumery.

Therapeutic effects Useful for fatigue and depression, it is also a tonic for the respiratory and digestive systems, especially useful for coughs, colds, flu, stomach ache and diarrhoea. An aphrodisiac, it may also help impotence.

Uses Inhalation and massage. Burn to prevent the spread of flu virus, or add bark or oil to spice up a pot pourri. To relieve muscular spasms use in a compress or massage.

Cautionary note Use only in very low concentrations or under professional advice.

Comfrey

Symphtum officinale

Origins Herbalist Nicholas Culpeper wrote in his medicinal scripts in the seventeenth century that this herb 'helpeth those that spit blood or make a bloody urine'. The root boiled in water or wine was drunk to help solve all internal problems, inwardly healing wounds, ulcers of the lungs and to help the flow of blood.

Description Normally grows wild near damp watersides. Comfrey has large hairy leaves which can irritate the skin if touched. The stalk grows to three feet (90 cm) high with pale purplish flowers. The leaves and roots are used in herbal decoctions but the oil is extracted from the leaves and stalks.

Therapeutic effects Containing allantoin, a cell regenerator, comfrey oil is particularly valuable for the treatment of wounds and skin disorders, including eczema, psoriasis, athlete's foot and torn muscles. Helpful, too, in treating stretch marks and for menopausal and menstrual problems.

Uses Massage and compresses.

Cypress

Cupressus sempervirens

Origins Egyptians used this wood to adorn their stone coffins along with using the oil for its medicinal properties. In France it is traditionally planted in graveyards.

Description A tall, conical, evergreen tree, it originated in the East but is popularly grown throughout the Mediterranean area, especially in Algeria and southern France. The essence is obtained by the distillation of the leaves, twigs and cones of the tree. Clear, pale yellow or green, it has a refreshing, spicy fragrance, reminiscent of pine-needles.

Therapeutic effects Most noted for its astringent and antispasmodic qualities, it can be used for circulatory conditions, colds, coughs, flu, haemorrhoids, menstrual and menopausal problems, varicose veins and whooping cough. It also acts as a sedative to soothe nervous tension.

Uses Inhalation, baths and massage. Use in compresses for swelling or rheumatism or in the bath as a muscular tonic. Its astringent properties make it suitable for use in cleansers for oily skin.

Cautionary note Not to be used by anyone who suffers from high blood pressure.

Eucalyptus

Eucalyptus globulus

Origins One of the tallest trees in the world, it originated in Australia and later grew in Tasmania, China, USA, Brazil and the Mediterranean. There are something like 200 species.The Aborigines may have been the first to use it medicinally.

Description The silvery, blue–green leaves produce a pale yellow oil which has a cool, camphorous smell. The fresh leaves give a rich yield of highly potent essence, one of the most versatile in aromatherapy.

Therapeutic effects The principal constituent of the oil is the antiseptic eucalyptol. Combined with its anti-inflammatory properties, eucalyptus oil is particularly helpful for asthma, bronchitis, flu, sinusitis, skin infections, rheumatism and sores. It can also reduce fever, is a strong diuretic, and its head-clearing qualities are well-known.

Uses Baths, inhalation and massage. It has a cooling effect on body temperature, reduces fever and is also a remedy for muscular/rheumatic aches and pains. It is widely used in cold and cough medicines and rubs. Use in the bath to relieve cystitis or on a handkerchief to clear the head.

Fennel

Foeniculum vulgare

Origins The ancient Greeks and Romans advocated the strongly flavoured fennel seeds to give them strength, to ward off evil spirits, kill fleas, and sweeten the breath.

Description These graceful perennial plants are found in Europe, often by the sea, and have delicate bright green feathery foliage. Their bright tufts of yellow flowers attract the bees. As a herb, the fresh leaves are particularly valued for fish dishes whereas the seeds, which smell like aniseed, are used in liquorice. The sweet oil, which has a similar smell, is extracted from the crushed seeds.

Therapeutic effects Noted as a diuretic, and a mild laxative, fennel has been found effective for colic, constipation, digestive problems, kidney stones, menopausal problems, nausea and obesity. It is also often helpful for increasing milk yield during breast feeding.

Uses Massage. The sweet aromatic oil is mainly used for flavouring medicines to help flatulence and indigestion. It is a constituent of gripe water, and can be infused in teas.

FRANKINCENSE

Boswellia thurifera

Origins Frankincense (also known as olibanum) and myrrh were the first tree resins used as incense by the Egyptians. They were burned to clear the air in sickrooms and during religious ceremonies to drive away evil spirits. They ranked alongside precious stones as a valuable commodity and, according to the Bible, were offered by the three Kings to celebrate the birth of Jesus Christ. The gum comes from a small tree grown in Arabia, Africa, and China. It was first brought to Europe in the late seventeenth century.

Description To make the gum a deep incision is made in the tree trunk where the resin exudes in tear-shaped globules which harden on contact with air. The essence is spicy, with camphor undertones, but becomes lemony when mixed with myrrh.

Therapeutic effects Has an uplifting effect and aids concentration. Helpful as an expectorant in cases of bronchitis, coughs, colds and laryngitis. Reputed to preserve a youthful skin, eradicating wrinkles.

Uses Inhalation, baths and massage. Inhale to release catarrh, or relax with a few drops in a bath or body massage oil to warm, relax and meditate. It is often combined with myrrh, and blends well with essences such as basil and sandalwood.

GERANIUM

Pelargonium adorantissimum

Origins The geranium originates in Africa and was not brought into Europe until 1690. It was used in ancient times as a remedy for tumours, burns and wounds.

Description Widely grown throughout Europe, it reaches around two feet (60 cm) in height. There are hundreds of different species cultivated for their pretty flowers, but only the aromatic pelargoniums (the ones that smell lemony when the leaves are pinched) give rich yields of the sweet yellowy-green essential oil. This is distilled from the leaves, stalks and flowers.

Therapeutic effects Unusually, it is both sedative and uplifting, and so invaluable for treating nervous tension and depression. Also used for circulatory and skin problems, especially wounds. Use in a footbath for chilblains.

Uses All uses. A popular ingredient in perfumes for its sweet, fresh, floral essence, the geranium is also therapeutically massaged or inhaled for its relaxing yet refreshing qualities. It can blend well with most other essential oils.

Hyssop

Hyssopus officinalis

Origins Ancient alchemists used the powdered leaves and roots as a purgative and in ointments to spread over the stomach to combat worms. Small doses taken internally were mixed with honey to clean the mucous matter from the intestines or with crushed figs to loosen the bowels.

Description A small herbal perennial, hyssop has long stalks with narrow leaves and blue flowers. The oil, extracted from the leaves and flowering heads, is used in perfumes and liqueurs, including Chartreuse.

Therapeutic effects Hyssop is used for disorders of the cardiovascular system, and as it is both stimulating and sedative, it can regulate blood pressure whether high or low. It has powerful effects on the respiratory tract, for bronchitis, coughs and colds, and is also used for skin disorders.

Uses Massage and inhalation. It is also used in cough mixtures for bronchial conditions.

Cautionary note Use only in extremely small quantities. Do not use during pregnancy.

Jasmine

Jasminum officinale

Origins An ancient favourite of the Arabs, Indians and Chinese, jasmine had a wide variety of uses including perfuming the body, scenting rooms and flavouring herbal teas. It was introduced from Persia to Europe in the sixteenth century.

Description The *Jasminum grandiflora* species is a small bush, native to the East Indies and Egypt and cultivated in southern France, Spain, Algeria, Morocco, India and Egypt. Its delicate white flowers produce a honey-sweet floral bouquet with fruity undertones. The deep red oil is produced by *enfleurage*, and has an intense rich, floral fragrance that is warm and exotic. It is one of the most important and expensive extracts, along with rose, used in perfumery.

Therapeutic effects Jasmine is a mood enhancer, lifting anxiety and depression. An aphrodisiac, it has a reputation for the treatment of both frigidity and impotence. It will also relieve menstrual cramps and is soothing to inflamed or irritated skin.

Uses Inhalation, bathing and massage will all exploit its warming and relaxing qualities. Also makes a delightful uplifting perfume or room fragrance.

JUNIPER

Juniperus communis

Origins Grown in North America, Asia, Africa and Europe, this small shrub with aromatic leaves and berries was popular as incense to burn in religious ceremonies and to purify the air and ward off the plague.

Description An evergreen bush with thick branches and narrow needle leaves, juniper produces small yellow flowers and small purplish-blue berries. Both the berries and leaves have a strong aromatic fragrance, similar to pine-needles, but the oil is extracted from the berries by distillation, producing a pale yellow essence.

Therapeutic effects Diuretic and antiseptic, it is especially effective for the urinary tract and an excellent treatment for cystitis and water retention. Use for acne, colic, coughs, dermatitis, eczema, flatulence, rheumatism and skin ulcers.

Uses Inhalation, baths and massage. The oil is a great stimulator and, like cypress and pine, makes a refreshing bath oil. Massaged on the skin it stimulates the circulation.

LAVENDER

Lavendula officinalis

Origins Lavender comes from the Roman word "lavare" meaning to wash. It was one of most favoured aromatics used by the Romans in their daily bathing rituals. Both the Greeks and Romans burned lavender twigs as a room purifier to ward off the plague. It was brought to Europe by the Romans.

Description A shrubby plant with woody branches and long narrow leaves, it has purple-blue flowers on long spikes. After cutting, the plants are dried and steam-distilled.The essential oil is clear to pale yellow in colour with a strong aroma.

Therapeutic effects Its sedative and tonic effects make lavender a great balancer of the nervous and emotional systems. Excellent for migraine. As an antiseptic it can be used for many skin conditions and infections of the lungs, digestion and unrinary tract. Extraordinarily versatile.

Uses Inhalation, baths, room spray, massage and most other uses. Use as a cold compress or place a few drops in boiling water and inhale for headaches and migraine. A warm towel wrap will soothe nervous exhaustion. A late-night lavender bath will help combat sleeplessness.

Lemon

Citrus limonum

Origins Early seafarers stocked up with fresh lemons before a long voyage to help prevent scurvy and to purify the ship's drinking water. Its astringent and antiseptic properties were fully appreciated in the first aid kit and used to treat cuts, bruises and insect stings.

Description The lemon tree, which has white–pink flowers and bright yellow fruits, is cultivated in most Mediterranean countries, Brazil, USA, Argentina, Israel and Africa. The pale yellow oil is expressed from the rind and peel of the fruit and has classically been used in perfume for its intense, sharp, citrus-fresh aroma. The essence becomes cloudy, and deteriorates over time, if not properly stored.

Therapeutic effects Lemon is highly antiseptic and astringent, and so is naturally used for skin complaints including boils, warts and veruccas. Also good for lowering blood pressure, colds, digestive problems, fever and gallstones.

Uses Inhalation, baths and massage. Lemon, as with most citrus oils, is a good cleanser inside and out. Use in skin-care preparations for oily skin. Evaporated in a fragrancer it will help colds and act as an insect repellent.

Lemongrass

Cymbopogon citratus

Origins This sweet-scented grass was mainly used to season food in India, the African Congo, the Seychelles, Indonesia and Sri Lanka. Its main constituent, citral, was discovered to be a strong, cleansing antiseptic, and used to deodorize clothing and footwear. Dried leaves were burned to keep the mind alert.

Description Lemongrass is a tall-stemmed, grass-like tropical plant. Its oil is steam-distilled from the fresh or partly dried grasses, and has a refreshing, lemony smell. It is used in low-cost citrus soaps, perfumes and cleaning agents.

Therapeutic effects Through its anti-bacterial action, it is good for skin complaints, sore throats and respiratory problems. Also effective against headaches.

Uses Inhalation and massage. For the active work-out enthusiast, lemongrass is the ideal cooler and deodorizer. It can help alleviate athlete's foot and its refreshing fragrance acts as an energizer. Massaged or breathed in, it tones the heart and works on the digestive system. The oil will also repel insects.

Marjoram

Origanum marjorana

Origins The Greeks grew marjoram for use in their perfumes and herbal potions. They prescribed it as a medicinal antidote and to purge the system.

Description This popular perennial plant is one of the classic culinary herbs, and is grown world-wide. The amber-coloured essence is extracted by steam-distillation from the fresh and dried leaves and flowering tops. Its warm and slightly spicy aroma is often used in masculine fragrances.

Therapeutic effects A warming agent, able to relieve spasm, it is particularly valuable for treating the nervous system. Use for anxiety and insomnia, but also for arthritis, asthma, bronchitis, circulatory problems, constipation, headaches, menstrual problems, muscular strains and rheumatism.

Uses Inhalation and massage. It blends well with bergamot, lavender and rosemary. In bath and body oils it gives a warm, relaxing feeling. Steam-inhaled or smoothed over the sinuses and temples, it can relieve colds.

Cautionary note Do not use in early pregnancy. Do not use in high doses as it can have a narcotic effect and is also known to curb sexual drive.

Melissa

Melissa officinalis

Origins The Greeks and Arabs knew the properties of melissa and in the sixteenth century the Swiss physician Paracelsus hailed it as the "elixir of life".

Description Mostly a native of Europe, it is also cultivated in North America. Better known as sweet balm or lemon balm, it is a bushy perennial of the mint family. The aromatic oil smells like lemons and is extracted from the leaves by distillation.

Therapeutic effects Long known as an uplifting and calming cure for "melancholia", its tonic, antispasmodic properties make it effective too in the treatment of allergies, colds, diarrhoea, hypertension, menstrual problems, migraine and stress headaches, nausea and palpitations.

Uses Inhalation, baths and massage. The essential oil helps lower blood pressure and remove tension. Add six drops to the bath water. Melissa calms the body and mind, yet lifts the soul: an oil to dream with.

MYRRH

Commiphora myrrha

Origins The Egyptians and the Greeks prized myrrh as a precious commodity. It was used by both civilizations in worshipping their gods, celebration rituals, cosmetics, perfumes and herbal treatments. The Egyptians combined it with frankincense for embalming and purification purposes.

Description A small tree, rather like a bush, myrrh is native in Arabia, Somalia, Ethiopia and other North African countries. Although the leaves are aromatic it is the resin which is distilled to produce the viscous, yellow essential oil. It has a warm, lightly spicy, sweet smell.

Therapeutic effects Anti-inflammatory and expectorant, myrrh will ease bronchitis, catarrh, coughs and colds. Good too for digestive problems, infections of the mouth and throat, and skin conditions.

Uses Inhalation and massage. It is used in pharmaceuticals and perfumery. In aromatherapy, because of its cooling effect, it blends well with camphor and lavender.

NEROLI

Citrus aurantium

Origins Neroli is believed to have been discovered by the Romans. In 1680 it was used to scent the bath water and gloves of Anna Maria Orsini, Princess of Nerola, who brought the fragrance into fashion amongst the Italian aristocracy.

Description Neroli oil is better known as orange blossom. It comes from the white blossoms of the bitter orange tree which originated in China but also grows in Egypt, Morocco, Algeria, USA, Italy and southern France. The pale yellow oil is expensive to produce since it takes approximately one ton (one tonne) of flowers to extract just 2 lb (1 kg) of oil. These are hand picked as they are just about to open and then distilled. Its powerful, wonderfully uplifting, floral fragrance is reminiscent of lilies and is extensively used in eau-de-Cologne.

Therapeutic effects An excellent sedative and anti-depressant, neroli counters anxiety, hysteria, shock and palpitations, and combats insomnia. It is helpful for dermatitis and dry skin, pre-menstrual tension and menopausal problems.

Uses Inhalation, baths and massage. Use in the bath or as a body oil to alleviate the symptoms of pre-menstrual tension and generally improve circulation, or just for the benefits of its delightful fragrance and relaxing properties.

ORANGE

Citrus aurantium (bitter orange),
Citrus sinensis (sweet orange)

Origins China was the first home of the orange tree and the fragrant qualities of sweet and bitter orange oils have long been prized for culinary, cosmetic and medicinal use.

Description The sweet and the bitter oils are similar and both are extracted by cold pressing of fresh orange peel (it is only neroli oil which is extracted from the blossom). The bitter and sweet oils range from yellow to brown in colour and are used extensively for their fresh top notes in perfume.

Therapeutic effects Refreshing but sedative, orange is a tonic for anxiety and depression. It also stimulates the digestive system and is effective for constipation. Its antiseptic properties work well for mouth ulcers.

Uses Baths and massage. These essential oils, rich in vitamin C, are used widely throughout the food and cosmetics industry in products ranging from bath and body oils to chocolate-orange confectionery.

PARSLEY

Petroselinum sativum

Origins A lot of folklore surrounds the parsley plant. It was a medieval belief that it grew in the garden only if the man or woman of the house was "honest". When chewed, it would keep away the devil or, as later discovered, reduce bad breath.

Description Native to Asia Minor, it is now found all over the world. The common parsley is cultivated for its culinary uses and essential oil properties. The highest content of oil comes from the ripe seeds but the leaves are also used in distillation. It has a warm, herbaceous, spicy smell and is used in many herbal perfumes and cosmetic products.

Therapeutic effects A diuretic, useful for kidney and urinary problems and water retention. Also high in vitamin A – essential for healthy hair, skin, teeth and eyes; and iron – for the blood and liver, and during menstruation and menopause.

Uses Massage. It blends well with fennel to help combat excessive water retention when massaged over the body. In conjunction with lemon and rosemary it can help clear toxins in the liver and kidneys. In general, a good oil to help calm the nervous system.

PATCHOULI

Pogostemon patchouli

Origins Along with rose, jasmine, sandalwood and basil, patchouli was one of the favourite perfumes used in India, and shawls and blankets were impregnated with this rich oil. It is an aphrodisiac, and became very popular again in the 1960s for this reason.

Description The oil is extracted from the dried, fermented leaves of the small shrub and emits an intense, woody, sweet-spicy, balsamic odour. It improves with age and is used as a fixative in perfume.

Therapeutic effects Patchouli is an astringent, and is useful for scalp and skin conditions including dandruff, acne, eczema and scars. It has an uplifting effect for depression and anxiety, and can help alleviate fluid retention.

Uses Inhalation, baths and massage. Small quantities will have a stimulating effect; larger doses sedate. Often worn as a perfume and used for an exotic, sensual massage.

PEPPERMINT

Mentha piperata

Origins The Egyptians used this aromatic herb in flavouring wine and food and valued its menthol content. Culpeper recorded in the seventeenth century that it was the herb most useful for "complaints of the stomach, such as wind and vomiting, for which there are few remedies of greater efficacy".

Description The leaves of peppermint are shorter and broader than spearmint with larger spikes of purple flowers. A British classic, it has spread throughout the world. The almost colourless peppermint oil is distilled from the whole of the partially dried plant and has a strong refreshing fragrance.

Therapeutic effects Excellent for the digestion, as a decongestant, and for skin disorders. Use for colds, flu, flatulence, headaches, indigestion, nausea, toothache and sunburn.

Uses Inhalation, baths and massage. Peppermint oil is still used in gripe water to settle upset stomachs. A few drops on a handkerchief can alleviate headaches and symptoms of sea and travel sickness, as it is refreshing and invigorating. It makes a refreshing skin tonic or bath oil in the summer because of its cooling properties. Used in a footbath it can help sweaty, smelly or tired feet, or in a compress to relieve hot flushes.

Cautionary note For skin complaints do not use in a concentration of more than one per cent as it can cause irritation.

Pine

Pinus sylvestris

Origins The Scandinavians have traditionally used pine in the sauna or steam bath for its refreshing and antiseptic qualities.

Description This species of conifer grows wild all over Europe, North America and the USSR. General pine oil comes from the heart of the wood but the best essences are distilled from the pine needle. The oil has a fresh fragrance with a resinous woody undertone.

Therapeutic effects Acts as an antiseptic, and is particularly valuable for treating the respiratory tract, for bronchitis, catarrh, colds and sinusitis. Will also help relieve cystitis, arthritis and muscular aches and pains.

Uses Inhalation, baths and massage. Widely used to give coniferous fragrance in household products and in some masculine perfumes, this oil is popularly used throughout the cosmetics and pharmaceutical industries in balms, body rubs, soaps and bath oils. The oil can be used as an antiseptic deodorizer (add a few drops to freshen shoes) and in saunas or hot tubs for its invigorating steam.

Rose

Rosa centifolia, Rosa damascena

Origins The rose has been loved for its fragrance at least since Roman times, when it was used in garlands, scented baths and perfumes, often in ostentatious public displays. But the rose has its private uses too: Cleopatra reputedly carpeted her bedroom in rose petals to aid her seduction of Mark Antony.

Description The Damascena rose is cultivated in Bulgaria. The flowers are picked at dawn and the yellowy-brown oil is extracted within 24 hours. It takes approximately five tons (five tonnes) of blossoms to produce just 2 lb (1 kg) of oil – not surprisingly one of the most expensive in the world. Centifolia roses, also yielding a richly fragrant oil, are cultivated in France, Algeria, Morocco and Eygpt.

Therapeutic effects An aphrodisiac and mood enhancer, rose is a general tonic and fortifier, useful for circulatory problems, constipation, headaches and mental fatigue, menstrual and menopausal problems and skin disorders.

Uses Baths and massage. One of the least toxic of all essences, it is particularly good for older, drier, skins, and is useful for pot pourri or to perfume bed linens and underwear (add a few drops to the final rinse).

Rosemary

Rosmarinus officinalis

Origins First favoured by the Egyptians, rosemary was popular with the Greeks and Romans who believed it symbolized love and death. During the plague it was burned in public places and worn around the neck for its antiseptic qualities.

Description A small shrub, it grows to around three feet (90 cm) high, with grey–green leaves and pale blue–white flowers. The clear oil is steam-distilled from the flowers and leaves, and has a powerful, warm, woody aroma.

Therapeutic effects A good stimulant, especially for the circulation and memory. Also helps alopecia, bronchitis, burns, colds, dandruff, diarrhoea, flatulence, headaches and obesity.

Uses Inhalation, baths and massage. Inhale from a handkerchief to clear headaches and fatigue. In massage it stimulates the lymphatic system.

Cautionary note Use in low concentration, as excessive doses may bring about epileptic fits or convulsions. Do not use in early pregnancy or if you have high blood pressure.

Sage

Salvia officinalis, *Salvia sclarea* (Clary sage)

Origins A sacred herb, its properties were used by the Egyptians to help cure infertility in women. The Chinese have used it medicinally for centuries.

Description The many varieties of common sage are all shrub-like herbs with rough, wrinkled leaves. The oil is distilled from the dried leaves and has a powerful, fresh, spicy fragrance with a hint of camphor.

Therapeutic effects A tonic, particularly renowned for regulating menstruation, it can also help relieve arthritis, bacterial infections, throat infections and water retention.

Clary sage (*Salvia sclarea*) is also used for its sedative and euphoric effects, and in treating insomnia, anxiety and depression, as well as menstrual and menopausal problems. It has a spicy fragrance, rather more floral than common sage.

Uses Bathing and massage. A sage bath helps muscular aches and the effects of prolonged stress or mental strain.

Cautionary note In high doses, sage can overstimulate and should be avoided by anyone who suffers from epilepsy. Both sage and clary sage should be avoided in early pregnancy.

Sandalwood

Santalum album

Origins In China, India and Egypt sandalwood was used in perfumes and cosmetics. It has also been prized by furniture makers, and in India many of the temples were built with this lovely wood. Worshippers also covered their bodies with its essence, along with rose, jasmine and narcissus.

Description The evergreen sandalwood tree grows to a height of up to 30 feet (8 metres) in Indonesia, South East Asia and in particular East India. The syrupy, balsamic oil is extracted from the roughly chipped and powdered wood by steam distillation. It has a rich, warm, woody odour. It is used as a fixative in perfumes and gives the lingering classic base notes in many expensive fragrances.

Therapeutic effects Sandalwood's sedative properties are good for treating depression and tension. It is also an expectorant and anti-spasmodic; useful for bronchitis, coughs, nausea, cystitis and skin complaints. Regarded as an aphrodisiac.

Uses Inhalation and massage. Apply in a warm compress to revitalize dehydrated skin. Blends well with neroli and rose. Massage enhances its soothing effects.

Tea Tree

Melaleuca alternifolia

Origins The antiseptic properties of the tea tree were discovered centuries ago by the Aborigines of Australia who used it medicinally for treating sunburn and many bacterial/fungus infections, from ringworm to athlete's foot. It was known as an antidote for venomous snake bites.

Description A native of Australia and Tasmania, it is often referred to as the swamp tree. It produces white hanging flowers on a long spike, but the pale green oil is extracted from the twigs and leaves, which have a strong aromatic odour. The oil itself has a camphorous smell, reminiscent of eucalyptus.

Therapeutic effects A strong disinfectant and antiseptic, it is ideal for skin complaints including athlete's foot, burns, cold sores, mouth ulcers, verrucas, thrush and warts. Also effective for many respiratory complaints.

Uses Inhalation and baths. It can be used to kill fleas on pets but is more commonly used as a deodorizing/antiseptic foot bath. Dab on cold sores. Inhale to alleviate laryngitis and bronchitis. Diluted in water, it can be used as a mouthwash (not swallowed) to soothe ulcers.

THYME

Thymus vulgaris

Origins The ancient Egyptians incorporated the essential oil of thyme into their embalming fluids. The Greeks drank a herbal infusion of the leaves after banquets to aid digestion. Culpeper considered it a great lung strengthener and a remedy for shortness of breath.

Description This common low-growing wild herb has dark green leaves, woody stalks and small pink flowers. It is cultivated throughout the Mediterranean, Algeria, Yugoslavia and in Egypt for culinary and pharmaceutical uses. The oil is extracted from the whole flowering herb by steam-distillation and has a pungent, sweet herbaceous smell. It is an important component in colognes and herbal perfumes.

Therapeutic effects Helps fatigue and anxiety, but best known as a natural antiseptic for treating coughs and infections of the respiratory tract. Good too for rheumatic aches and for skin problems such as sores and swellings.

Uses Massage and baths. When added to a bath, its invigorating effects help revive tired muscles.

YLANG-YLANG

Cananga odorata

Origins A tropical tree, its first medicinal uses were to treat malaria, soothe insect bites and generally fight infections. Its antiseptic qualities were appreciated but it was also recognized as an aphrodisiac and a tonic to the nervous system. In the past, the flowers were mixed with coconut oil to perfume and condition the body and hair.

Description A native of Indonesia and the Philippines, the ylang-ylang tree reaches a height of 60 feet (10 metres). The yellow flowers are freshly picked in the early morning and the oil extracted by steam-distillation. It has a narcotic, floral-sweet, jasmine-like aroma which adds warmth to perfumes.

Therapeutic effects A great relaxer (if used sparingly) and highly recommended for anxiety, depression, insomnia and frigidity. It also has benefits in treating high blood pressure and skin conditions.

Uses Baths and massage. This oil can soothe away all forms of stress when used as a bath oil or massaged onto the body. Its lasting fragrance is often used in facial and skin preparations, pot pourri and pomanders. It blends well with bergamot, melissa, sandalwood and jasmine.

OILS FOR COMMON PROBLEMS

KEY

R Relaxing oil
S Stimulating oil
U Uplifting oil

Some oils have more than one of these properties, tending to balance or normalize the emotions and bodily systems.

CAUTION

This chart is a general guide only. For the treatment of persistent problems, seek the advice of a qualified aromatherapist. Chronic conditions should be referred to a medical practitioner.

Never mix more than three oils in any one treatment as the synergistic effects are less predictable. Do not exceed the proportions of essential oil to carrier oil suggested in this book.

The following oils should not be used during pregnancy:

Bay · Basil · Clary Sage · Comfrey
Fennel · Hyssop · Juniper
Marjoram · Melissa · Myrrh
Rosemary · Sage · Thyme

Oil	Key	Acne	Anxiety	Arthritis	Athlete's Foot	Blood pressure: High	Low	Body odour	Bronchitis	Cellulite
Basil	R, U		❀						❀	
Bay	R			❀				❀	❀	
Benzoin	S			❀				❀	❀	
Bergamot	R, U	❀	❀							
Cedarwood	R	❀							❀	
Chamomile	R	❀	❀	❀						
Cinnamon	R						❀			
Comfrey	R				❀					
Cypress	R		❀					❀		❀
Eucalyptus	S	❀		❀					❀	
Fennel	S									
Frankincense	R									
Geranium	R, U		❀							
Hyssop	R, S					❀	❀		❀	
Jasmine	R		❀							
Juniper	R, U	❀	❀							❀
Lavender	R, U	❀	❀	❀	❀	❀		❀	❀	
Lemon	S	❀				❀				
Lemongrass	S	❀			❀			❀		
Marjoram	R		❀	❀		❀			❀	
Melissa	R, U		❀			❀				
Myrrh	S								❀	
Neroli	R		❀					❀		
Orange	U		❀			❀				
Parsley	S									
Patchouli	R	❀	❀		❀					❀
Peppermint	S						❀	❀	❀	
Pine	S			❀				❀	❀	
Rose	R		❀	❀						
Rosemary	S						❀			❀
Sage	S		❀	❀			❀		❀	
Clary Sage	R, S		❀			❀				
Sandalwood	R	❀	❀						❀	
Tea Tree	S				❀				❀	
Thyme	S		❀						❀	
Ylang-Ylang	R		❀			❀				

Water retention									❀				❀			❀	❀								❀			❀		❀	❀					
Warts																	❀	❀									❀							❀		
Varicose veins									❀							❀		❀	❀								❀			❀						
Travel sickness																	❀																			
Throat infections				❀						❀		❀	❀				❀	❀	❀			❀									❀	❀	❀	❀		
Stress						❀							❀				❀			❀	❀						❀						❀			
Sinusitus										❀							❀						❀					❀								
Sexual problems					❀		❀						❀		❀											❀			❀			❀	❀			❀
Rheumatism		❀				❀			❀	❀						❀	❀	❀		❀			❀					❀		❀					❀	
Pre-menstrual syndrome	❀					❀			❀				❀			❀	❀				❀		❀						❀	❀	❀	❀	❀		❀	
Obesity									❀		❀															❀				❀	❀				❀	
Nausea	❀										❀						❀				❀						❀		❀				❀			
Muscular aches							❀	❀	❀	❀							❀			❀								❀		❀	❀					
Mental fatigue	❀															❀					❀							❀		❀	❀	❀			❀	
Painful periods						❀		❀	❀						❀	❀				❀	❀								❀			❀				
Irregular periods						❀										❀	❀				❀								❀	❀	❀	❀				
Menstrual problems (general)	❀					❀								❀		❀	❀				❀								❀	❀		❀			❀	
Menopausal problems						❀		❀	❀		❀		❀				❀	❀			❀		❀	❀					❀		❀	❀				
Insomnia					❀	❀			❀			❀		❀			❀			❀			❀						❀			❀	❀			
Influenza	❀						❀		❀	❀				❀														❀						❀		
Indigestion	❀					❀										❀	❀	❀	❀	❀	❀	❀		❀			❀			❀						
Hormonal regulation						❀							❀								❀			❀												
Headache	❀					❀				❀							❀		❀	❀	❀						❀			❀						
Hayfever						❀				❀											❀								❀							
Haemorrhoids									❀													❀					❀						❀			
Flatulence				❀		❀					❀			❀		❀	❀	❀									❀			❀		❀			❀	
Fainting	❀					❀											❀										❀			❀						
Eczema					❀	❀		❀	❀				❀	❀	❀	❀						❀				❀							❀			
Diarrhoea						❀	❀		❀	❀			❀			❀	❀	❀			❀	❀					❀									
Depression	❀			❀		❀			❀				❀		❀		❀		❀				❀	❀		❀			❀	❀	❀	❀	❀			❀
Dandruff					❀								❀			❀	❀	❀								❀				❀			❀	❀		
Cystitis			❀	❀					❀	❀						❀									❀			❀			❀		❀			

THE ESSENTIAL MASSAGE

An aromatherapy massage using essential oils is a therapeutic treatment for both mind and body which works mainly on the nervous system. Aromatherapy is both holistic and practical in that it helps to protect the body's life-saving immune system and energize or stabilize emotions. It is often called the "sensual science" because it combines the powers of touch with the sense of smell. More effectively than any other massage, aromatherapy can either relax or stimulate the body and mind. The highly potent essential oils penetrate the body via the skin and are also inhaled as the massage progresses.

SETTING UP

Any massage is relaxing but you can enhance the experience by following a few simple steps to help create the right mood.

An aromatherapist uses a massage bench, but at home you can work comfortably on a cushioned floor or a futon (Japanese mattress). An ordinary bed is not really firm enough. Prepare the floor or surface with a large cotton sheet covered with a bath towel. You should also have to hand a pillow, a large wrap-around towel for the body, and a warm blanket or even a hot-water bottle by the feet.

RELAXING YOUR PARTNER

Additional touches help to establish a calming atmosphere. You could fragrance the room with a burner, using a relaxing oil, and switch on some background music: play instrumental tracks, as voices can distract any train of thought.

The room temperature should be warm. Once the oils are gently massaged in, the whole body responds by slowing down and, although the skin may feel warm to touch, the body feels colder. It is important to keep your partner comfortable, so offer to cover parts that are not being worked on if you think your partner may be getting cold. Being at ease with one another is an important part of any treatment.

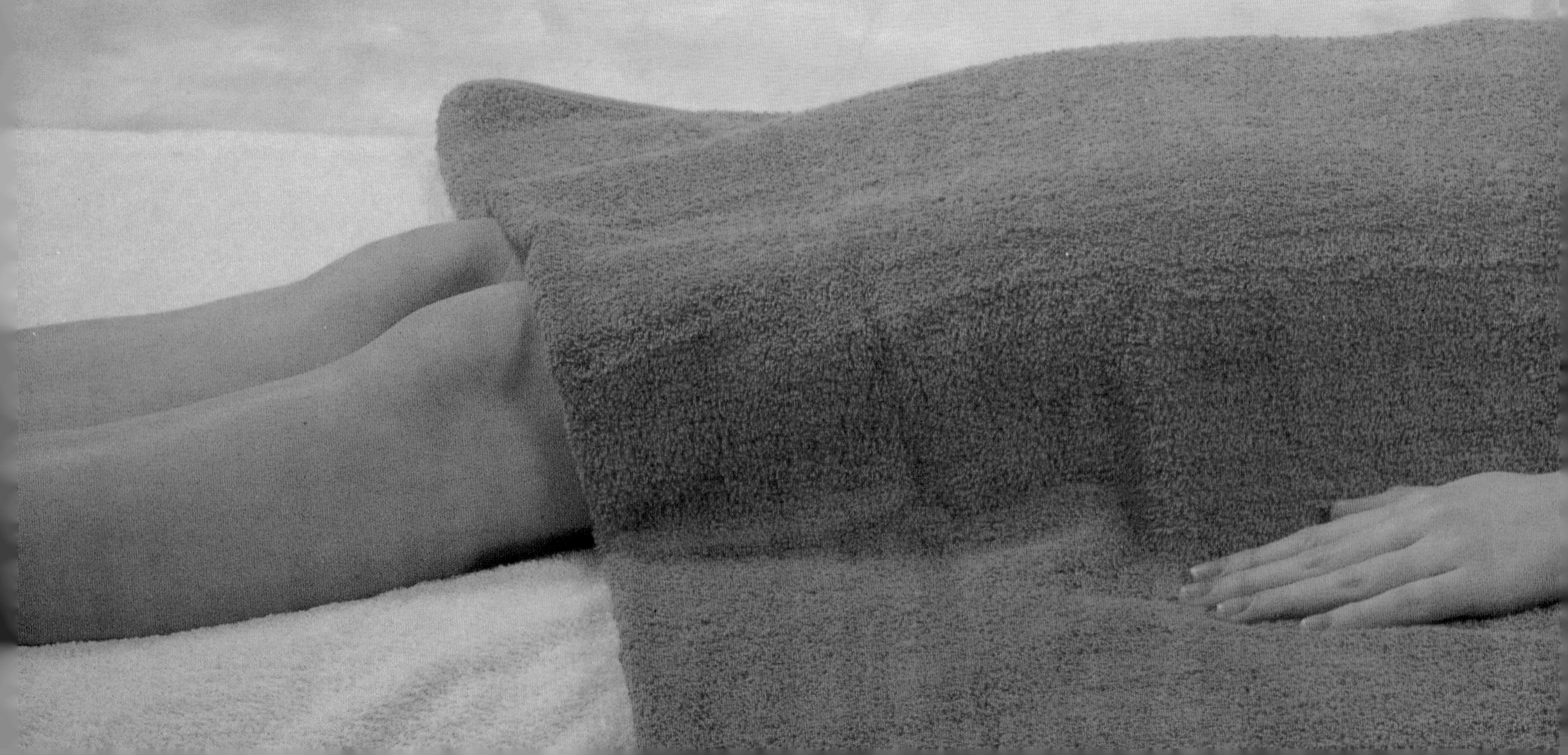

Choose a room which feels like a comfortable retreat: draw the curtains, switch on the heater and dim the lights. In aromatherapy, it is important to be able to switch off from everyday noises and that means the television, the telephone, or traffic zooming by, so close the window and shut off the rest of the world.

ABOUT THE TREATMENT

A complete aromatherapy massage takes just under an hour from top to toe. It is important to find out before massage about physical aches and pains, in particular back injuries, recent operations or whether the person you are massaging is in an "emotional" state of mind at the time.

GIVING THE MASSAGE

- Make sure you have read through the step-by-step instructions several times to familiarize yourself with the sequence. You don't want to keep stopping to refer to the book.
- Try out the movements on parts of your own body to get a sense of how the strokes should feel and how much pressure to use.
- Massage movements should be slow and gentle to help relaxation and eliminate tension which tightens the muscles.
- Remember that the movements should flow into each other. If you find you have missed out a step or gone on to the wrong part of the body, don't panic. Finish the part you are working on before going back to it, or leave it out altogether, rather than interrupting the flow of the massage.
- When you give the massage, make sure *you* are relaxed and comfortable, as well as the person you're working on, or you will transmit your own tensions to your partner and it will not be an effective massage.
- Try to maintain contact with your partner's body as much as possible; even as you move into a different position try to keep a hand on the body.
- When massaging different parts of the body keep the areas not being worked on covered with a large towel or blanket. The heat helps the body to absorb the oils.

CHOOSING THE ESSENTIAL OIL

Aromatherapists never start a massage immediately. In order to provide the most effective treatment, the therapist has to ascertain the state of mind and body of the individual, and establish whether there are any specific problems to attend to. Is the problem physical? Is it mental? Is it a combination of both? To help them to treat a wide variety of complaints, aromatherapists have many oils at their fingertips, but they never mix or use them until they have worked out a prescription for the receiver's individual needs.

Mixing the oils is a trained art, yet there are simple recipes you can use at home to deal with specific problems from muscular aches and pains to headaches and stress. With potent essential oils it is far better to use less, rather than more, so if in doubt, start the massage technique with a base oil like sweet almond and add two or three drops of just one essential oil. Lavender, rosemary and geranium are good all-purpose oils, or use chamomile for particularly sensitive skin.

APPLYING THE OILS

Keep the oil in an easy dispenser or bowl so you don't have to worry about lids during the massage. But keep the oil covered in some way as essential oils will quickly evaporate.

- Always warm your hands before applying oils.
- Some therapists recommend warming the oil in your hands before applying it to the body as a courtesy to the recipient. Others advise against this on the grounds that it hastens evaporation of the essential oil and that the oil takes on your own energy rather than your partner's.
- If the part of the body you're working on is particularly hairy or the skin is very dry you will need to apply more oil.
- Keep your touch light and sensitive. Remember that your hands are the main channel of communication.

- If the recipient's back is stressed in any way, place a pillow under the knees when lying on the back, and under the pelvis when lying on the stomach.
- Wear loose comfortable clothing to give the massage, so your movements are not hampered.
- If oil is accidentally spilt on clothing, dab off quickly with a tissue. It will soon evaporate, but it may leave a stain so rinse out clothing in warm soapy water.
- For complete relaxation avoid chatting during the massage: play music if you don't like silence. But do encourage feedback from your partner – you must be told if something doesn't feel good.
- Ensure that the person you are going to work on is given the following set of guidelines.

Receiving the Massage

Before the Massage

- Have a cool shower or wash before a massage. Do not soak in a hot bath, or the oils will immediately seep into the skin.
- Don't use an underarm deodorant or body spray during the treatment, as this will block the effect of the oils.
- Don't have a large meal just before an aromatherapy massage as the body's systems will have to work too hard at digesting to be thoroughly relaxed.
- Don't drink alcohol before a treatment.
- Don't have a massage if you have flu or a fever or any serious condition (*see* Cautions). Wait until you are over the worst and then let an aromatherapy treatment help restore your system's balance.

After the Massage

- Drink a glass of still water immediately after a treatment.
- Lie still for at least five minutes before getting up.
- Don't bathe or shower for at least twelve hours after a treatment to allow the oils to be absorbed by the skin and begin the all-important work of detoxifying the body.
- Drink plenty of water for the rest of the day as the kidneys will be active in eliminating the toxins.
- Avoid alcohol for at least 12 hours after the treatment to give the body a chance to detoxify thoroughly.

THE MASSAGE STEP-BY-STEP

Following your assessment, select the oils you are going to use and blend 10–15 drops of your chosen oils with four tablespoons of base oil.

The massage starts with your partner lying face down, with the back uncovered and the rest of the body covered with a towel or light blanket.

ESTABLISHING CONTACT

Take a few moments to create a bond of communication with your partner and to prepare yourself for the massage. Focus or "centre" yourself by becoming aware of your whole body and its role in giving the massage, and letting go of outside concerns to concentrate on the task in hand.

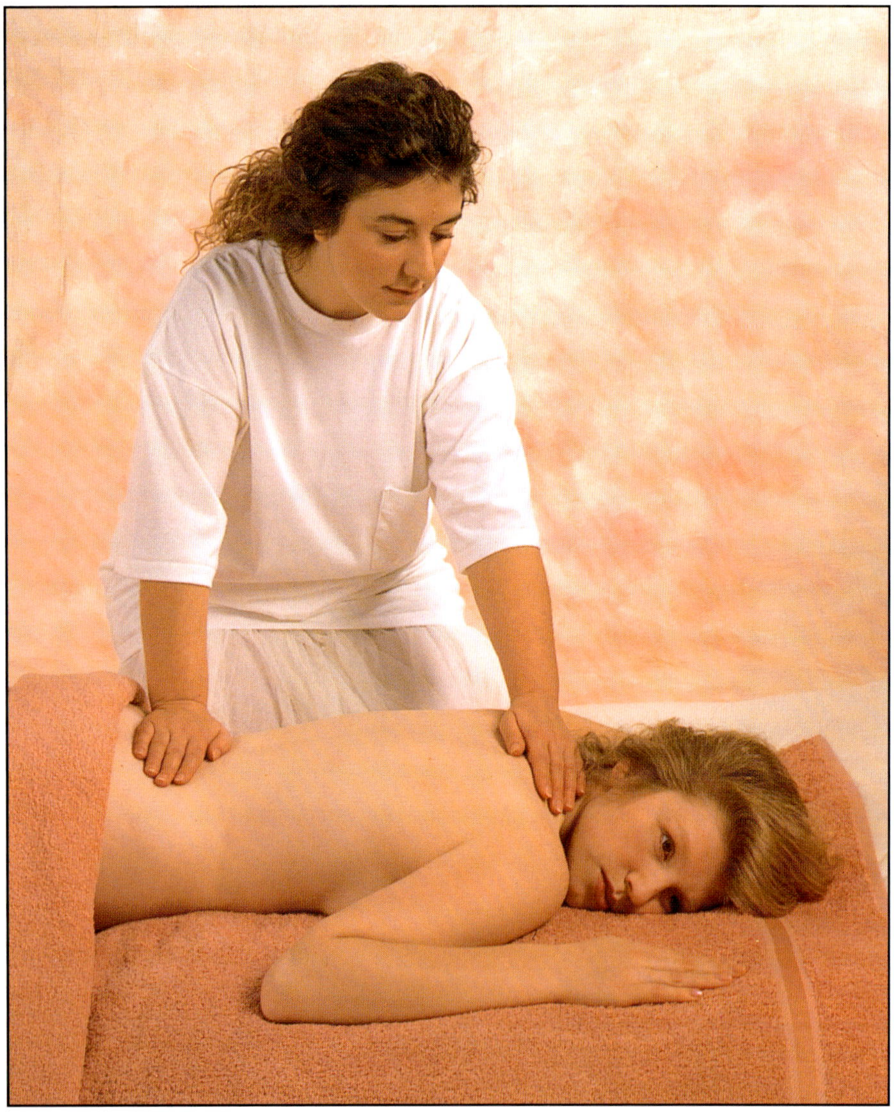

Left: With your partner face down, rest one hand lightly at the base of the neck (the occipital bone) and place your other hand on the lower back (the sacral area). Hold the position for a count of 20, while you focus on your breathing and clear your mind. This is carried out with dry hands.

CAUTIONS

Aromatherapy is an holistic therapy in that it works on the person as a whole. Though it is an excellent way of treating minor ailments, stress and negative emotional states, it is not a substitute for conventional medical treatment. If symptoms persist, always consult a medical doctor.

Never attempt to treat the following conditions:

- cancer
- progressive neural disorders
- heart conditions
- advanced asthmatic conditions
- post-operative states
- severe varicose veins
- very high blood pressure
- epilepsy

For oils to avoid during pregnancy *see* Pregnancy Treatments.

THE LEG

EFFLEURAGE (SMOOTHING STROKE)

This is a smooth, sliding movement which soothes the skin and distributes the oil. Always worked in the direction of the heart, effleurage *improves circulation, lymph flow and the function of the muscles. It is used between movements throughout the massage to provide continuity and to prepare a new area with oil.*

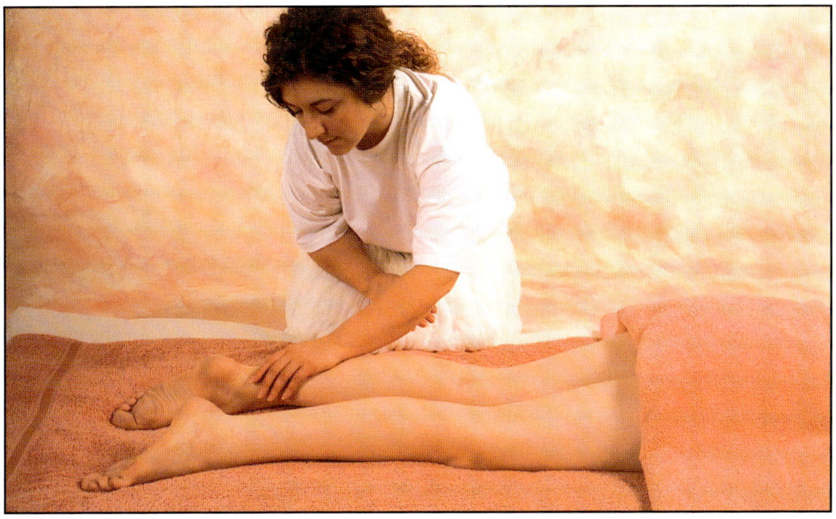

1 Seated to the side of your partner, begin with one hand at the heel, brushing in an upward, sweeping movement to the buttock ridge and sliding round to the thigh.

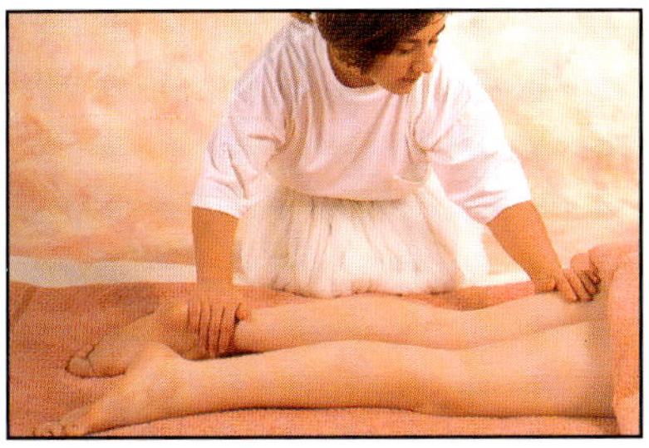

2 As the first hand comes round the thigh, place the other hand at the heel and brush with an upward sweep, ending at the back of the knee.

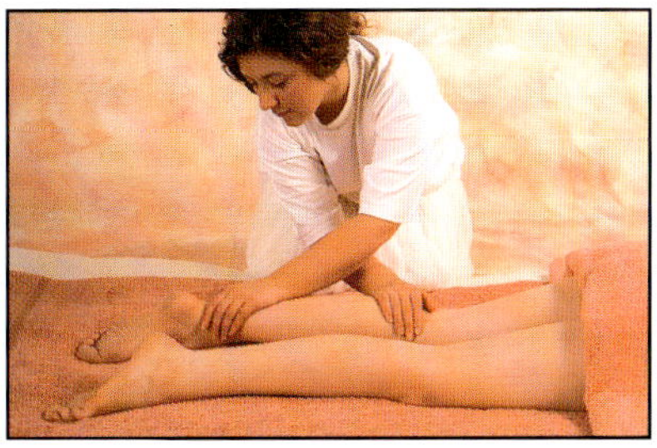

3 As the second hand comes off, cross the first hand over and begin the movement again from the heel up to the thigh.

Repeat the sequence about six or seven times, keeping the movements continuous and flowing, and then repeat on the other leg.

ANKLE THUMBING

The ankles are an important centre of energy, and this movement helps to relieve congestion.

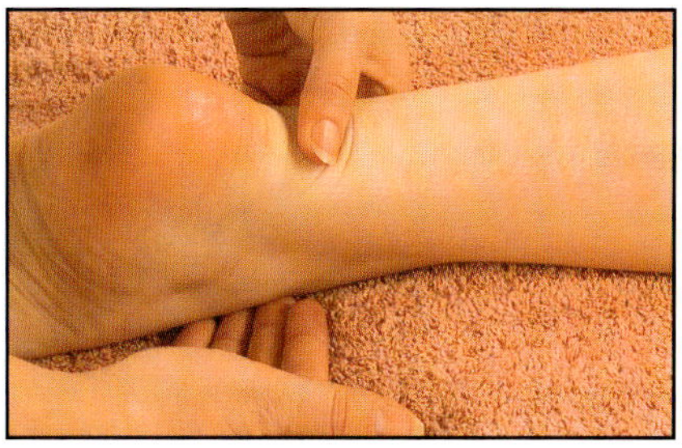

1 Sitting at your partner's feet, cradle one ankle gently with your hands, allowing the thumbs to sit naturally above the heel.

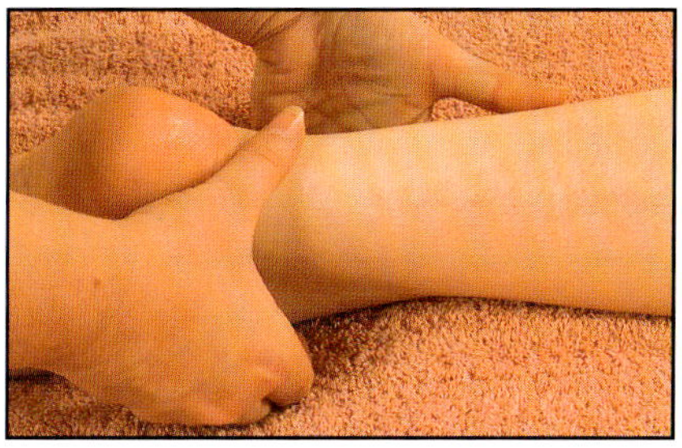

2 Keeping the rest of the hand still, apply a light pressure with the thumb as it brushes in an upward and outward movement.

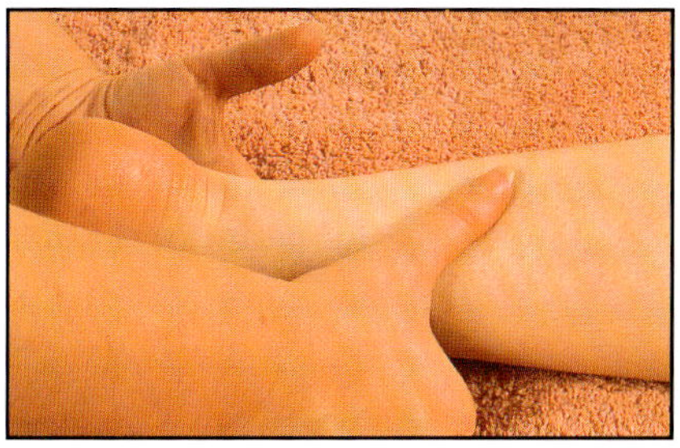

3 Repeat with alternate thumbs, continuing in a rhythmic sequence for about 30 seconds.

FLUSHING

Flushing drains the lymph channels and stimulates the circulation. This movement should not be used on anyone with severe varicose veins.

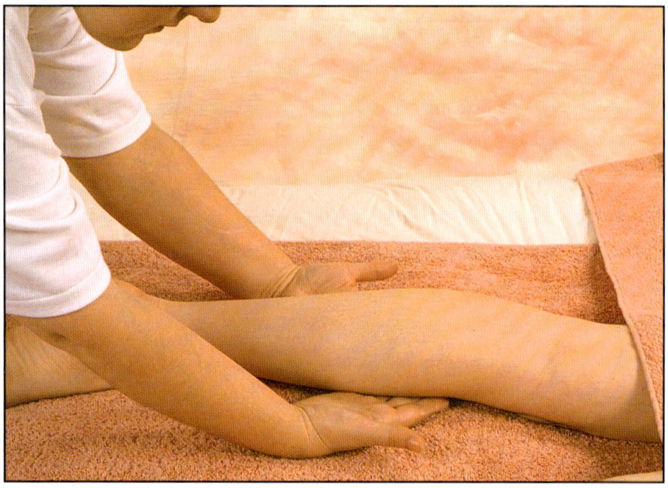

1 *Sitting at your partner's feet, gently slide the thumbs up the middle of the leg, ending at the back of the knee.*

2 *Slowly bring the hands back down to the ankles by brushing down the sides of the calf muscle, taking care not to drag.*

Repeat the movement five or six times.

KNEADING

Move back round to the side of the leg for this movement. It is particularly effective for relieving tension at the back of the legs.

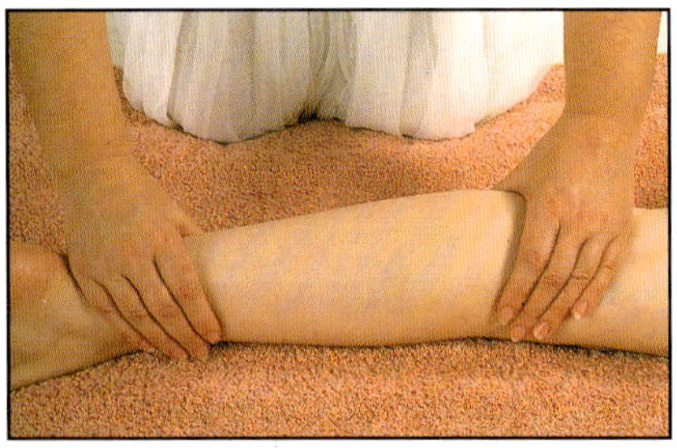

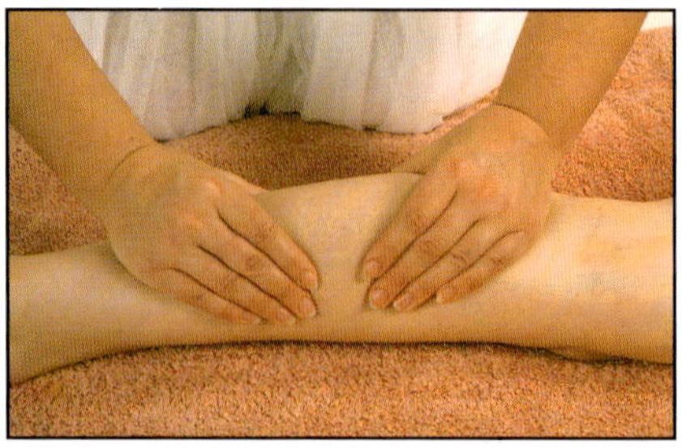

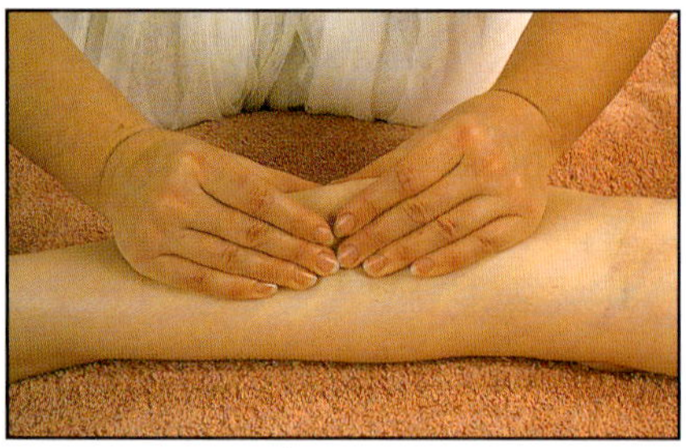

1 *Place the hands gently on the calf, one at the top and one just above the ankle.*

2 *Grasp the calf muscle firmly with both hands and slide them toward the centre of the calf, lifting the muscle.*

3 *Using gentle pressure, knead the area by bringing the fingers and thumbs together and raising the muscle further.*

Continue kneading for about 30 seconds.

WRINGING

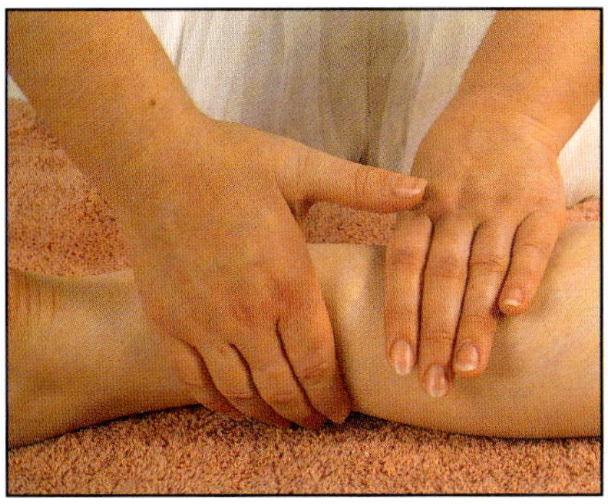

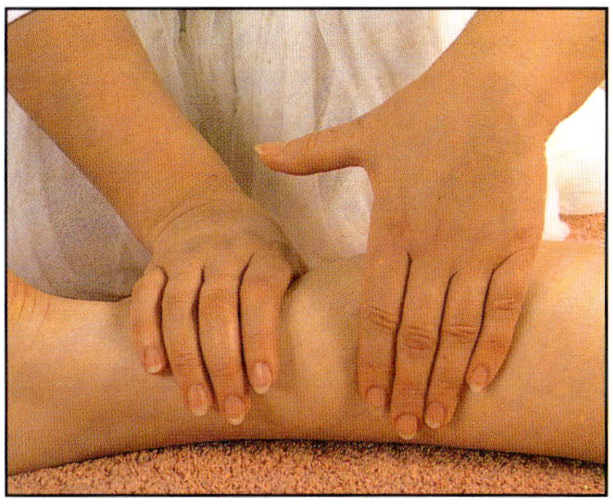

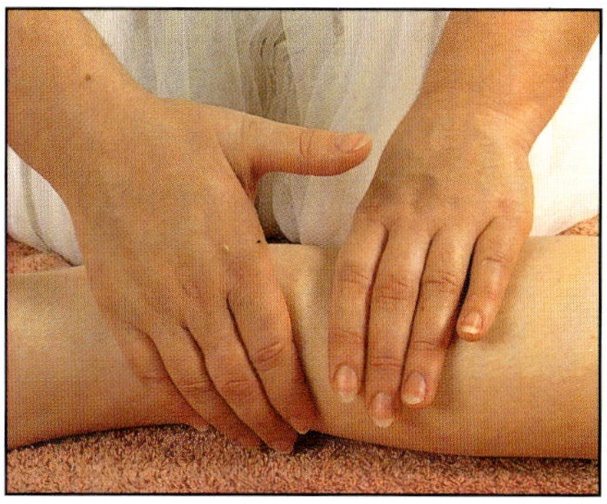

1 *Place the hands on opposite sides of the calf, just above the ankle. Gently glide the hands past each other so the heel of one hand is pushing away from you while the other hand is pulling.*

2 *Keep the thumb of the pulling hand raised so the thumbs don't collide as they pass each other each time.*

3 *The hands alternate the pushing and pulling as you work all the way up the calf and down again. The pressure should be firm but gentle.*

Clear these movements by flushing through again from ankle to back of knee.

THUMBING THE KNEE

This is the same action as the thumbing performed at the ankle base. It is helpful for people who suffer from cold feet as it stimulates the circulation.

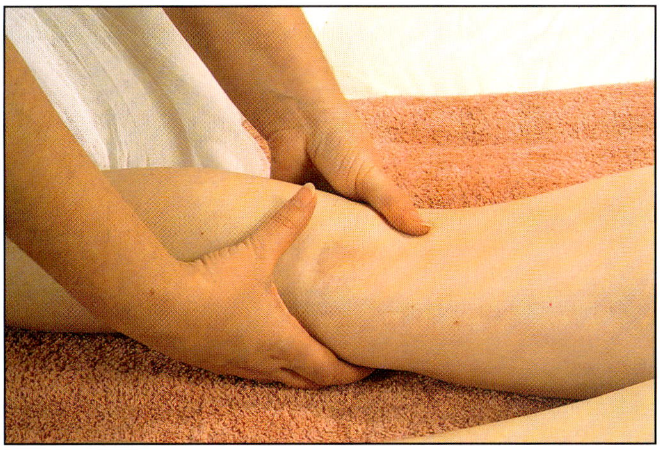

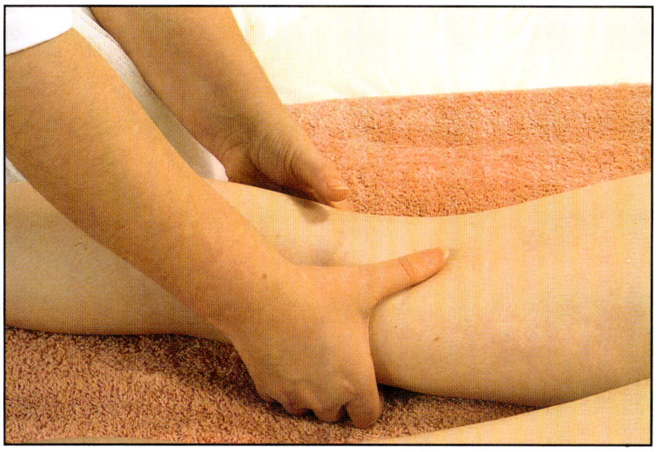

1 *Cup the hands gently around the knee, allowing the thumbs to sit naturally on the fleshy part at the back of the knee.*

2 *With the same thumbing movement used on the ankles, brush one thumb upward and outward, covering the full width of the knee, and follow immediately with the opposite thumb.*

FLUSHING

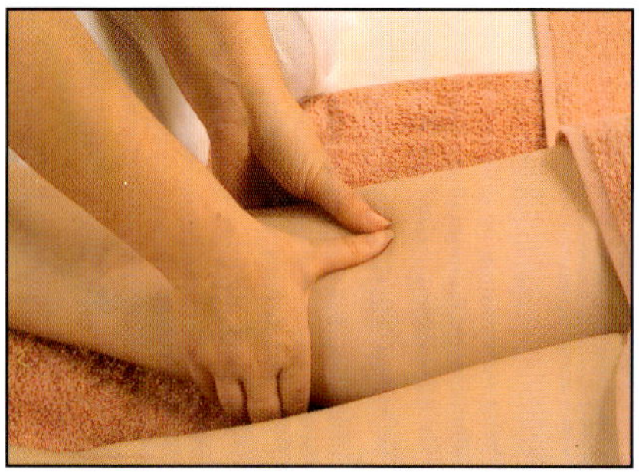

Flush through with the thumbs together from the back of the knee to the top of the thigh.

WRINGING

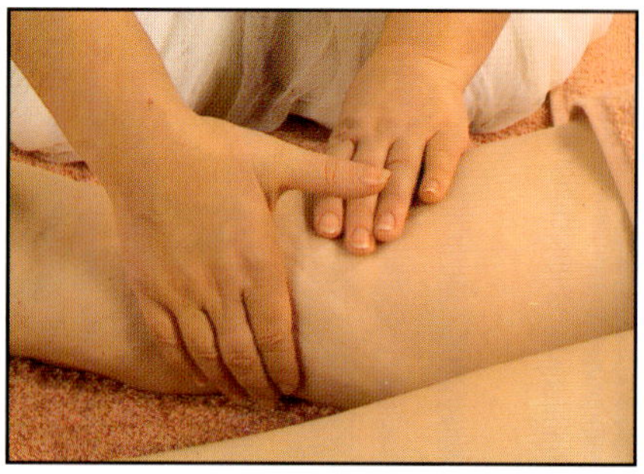

Wring the leg from the knee to the top of the thigh with the same action as used on the lower leg.

THIGH PUSH

This knuckling movement is very effective for breaking down cellulite, helping to disperse the fatty tissue and improve the circulation.

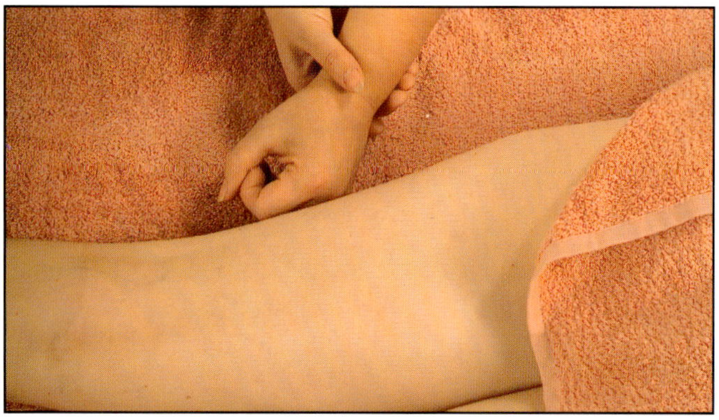

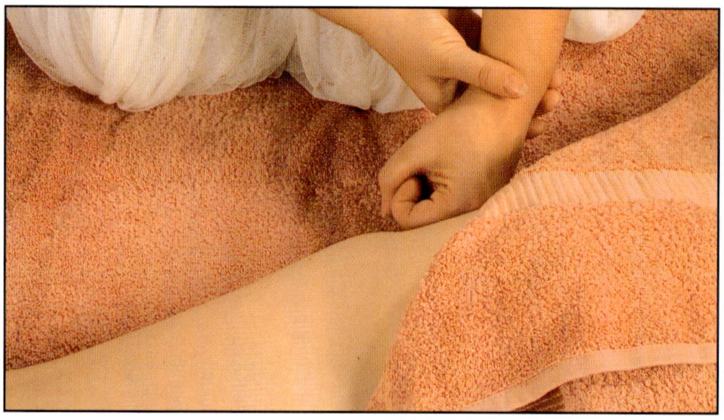

1 *With the supporting hand wrapped around the wrist of the working hand for stability, place the clenched fist on the side of the thigh, just above the knee.*

2 *Drag the fist slowly up the side of the thigh toward the hip bone. This is not a heavy action – all you need is gentle pressure.*

Repeat five or six times, working slightly different parts of the thigh each time.

Finish the leg massage by repeating the opening effluerage *movement and then repeat all the steps on the other leg.*

Cover the legs with towels before proceeding to the next stage. An extra blanket or hot water bottle at the feet might also be appreciated.

BACK MASSAGE

The back carries a lot of strain and these relaxing movements are often the most appreciated part of the massage. Don't be tempted to use too much pressure: it is better to keep the strokes broad and flowing.

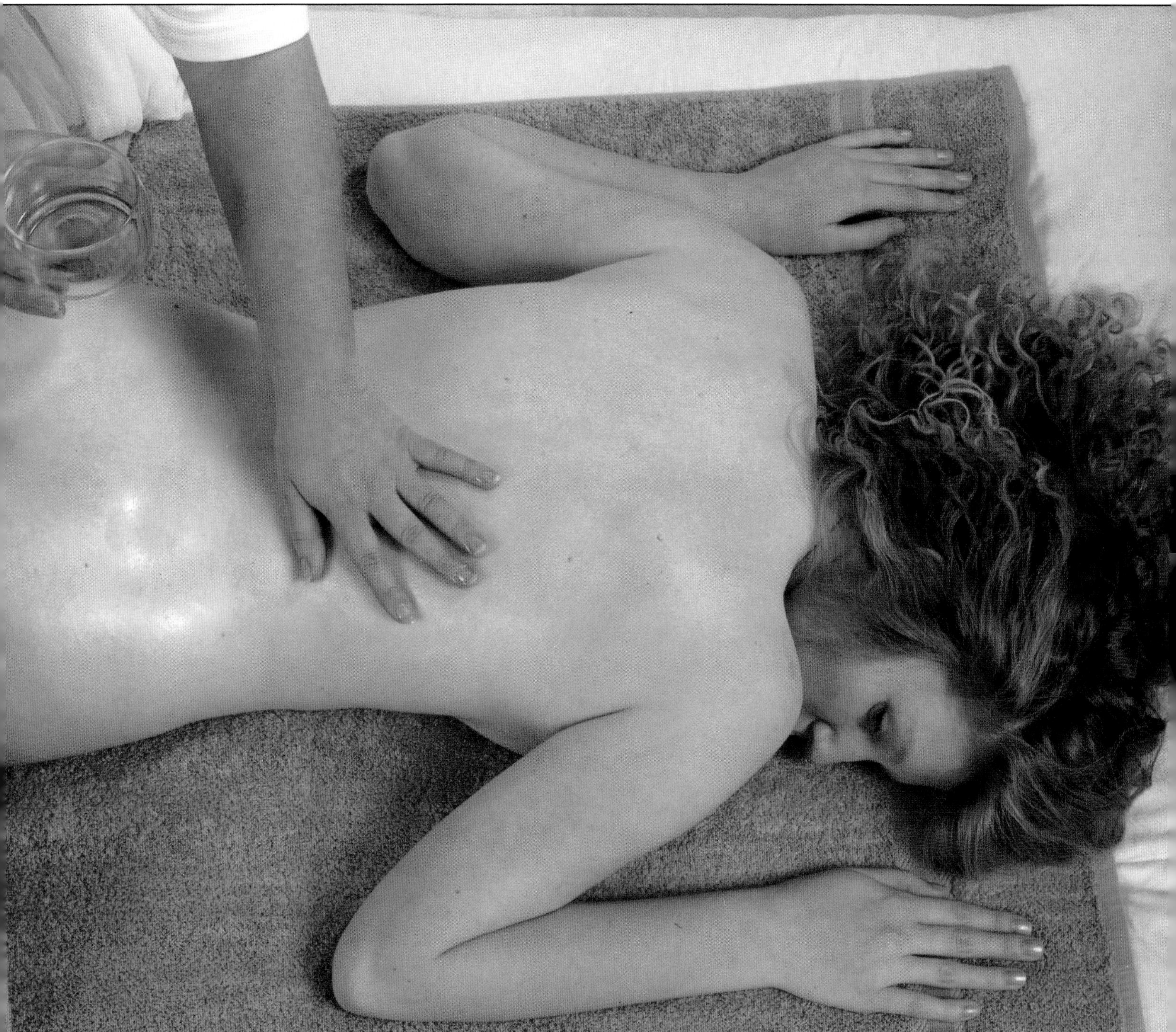

Seated to the side of your partner, apply oil evenly over the back with smooth upward strokes, following the direction of the lymph flow.

FIGURE-OF-EIGHT

This sequence loosens the tissue all over the back and helps to stimulate blood and lymph flow, and relieve tension.

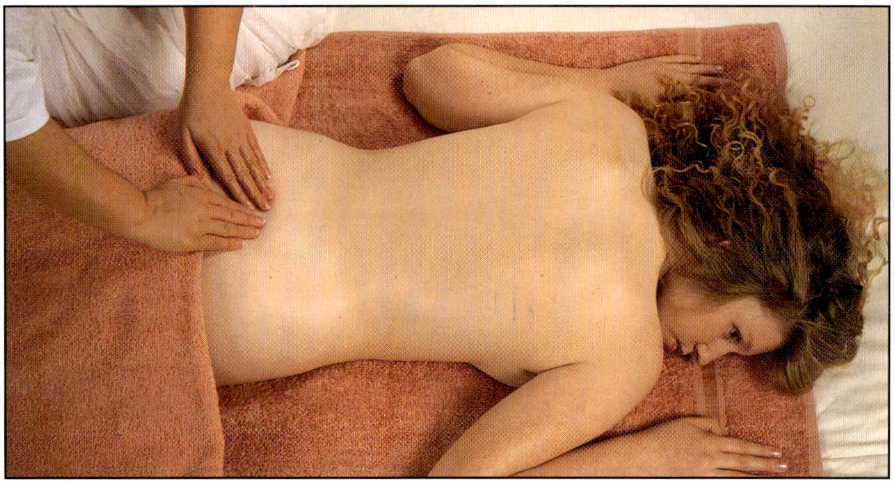

You should be kneeling level with the buttocks, facing the head so that you can lean into the movement and reach the shoulders without straining.

1 *To begin this large sweeping movement, place both hands on the lower back, just above the base of the spine, fingers pointing toward the head.*

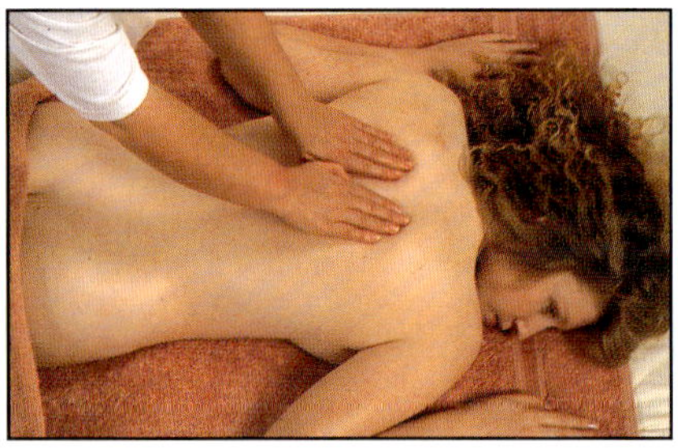

2 *Slide both hands all the way up the sides of the spine to just below the base of the neck.*

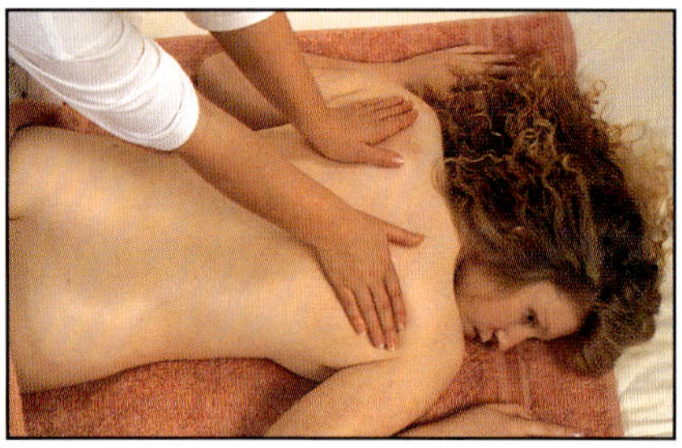

3 *Move the hands out around the shoulders and in toward each other across the upper back.*

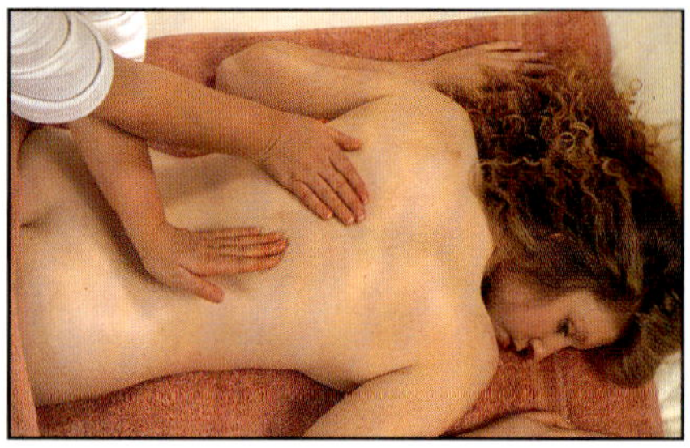

4 *As the hands pass each other, cross the right arm over the left and continue gliding.*

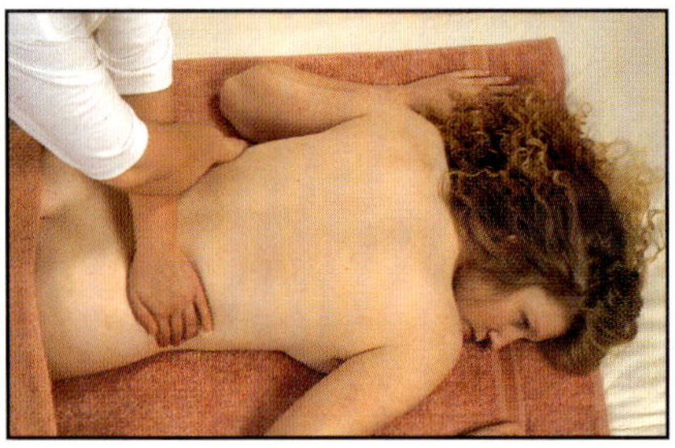

5 *With arms still crossed, reach down around the waist.*

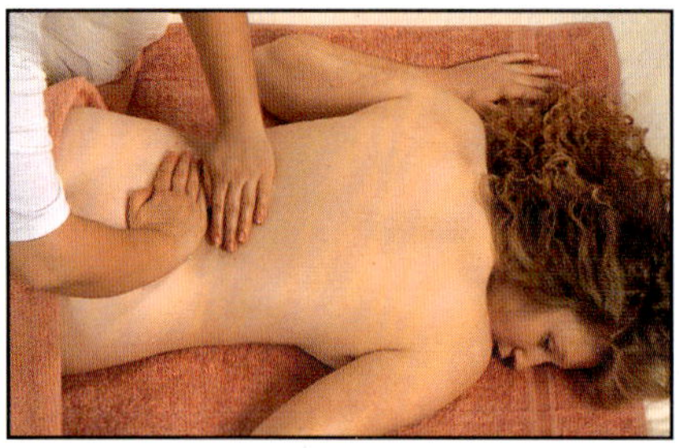

6 *Pull the flesh up firmly around the waist and then gradually release the sides as the palms glide to the middle of the lower back and pass each other.*

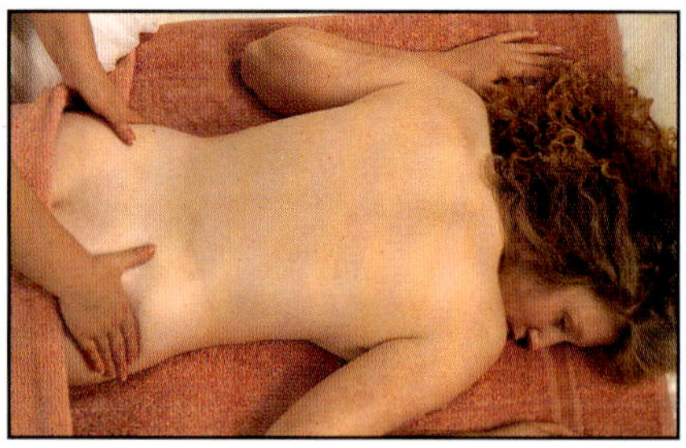

7 *Continue the movement by sliding the palms out around the hips and complete the figure-of-eight by returning the hands to the starting position.*

Repeat six times, always keeping the movements broad and flowing.

FANNING

This action works on the nerves along the spine and helps to disperse the fluid that accumulates in the back tissue as a result of tension. The effect is wonderfully relaxing.

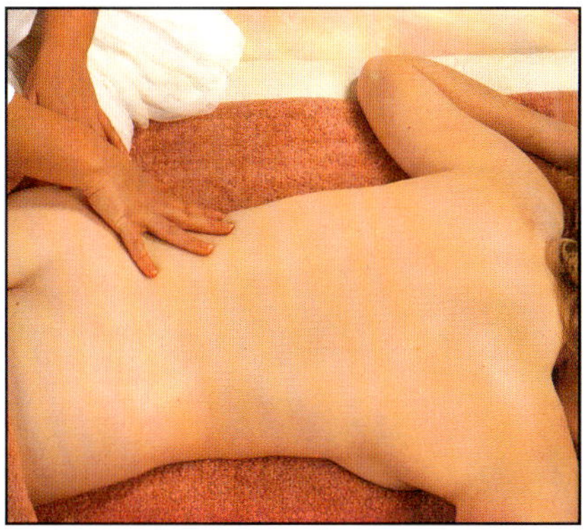

1 Place one hand on the lower back, at the base of the spine. The fingers should be splayed open, with the index finger pointing to the side of the spine.

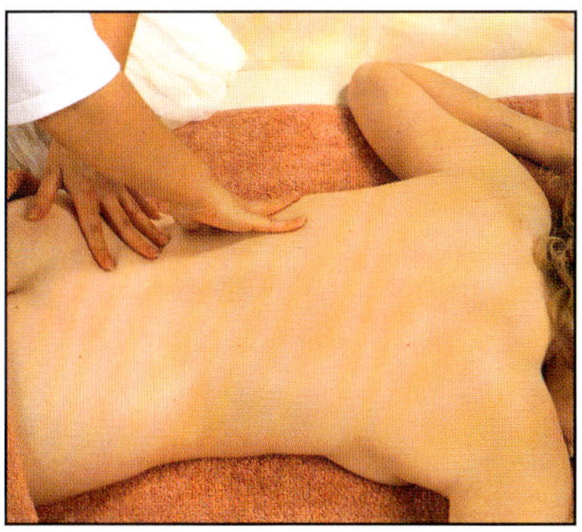

2 Fan the hand round in an upward and outward motion away from the spine. The other hand follows on the same side as the first completes the movement. Work all the way up the side of the spine, alternating hands.

Repeat the steps four or five times before moving round to work on the other side of the spine.

BUTTERFLY SHOULDERS

Before being given an aromatherapy massage, always wash off any anti-perspirant or deodorant. This is particularly important for this movement as it drains the lymph towards the major lymph glands in the armpits – the axillary glands. This movement relaxes the shoulder and disperses tension.

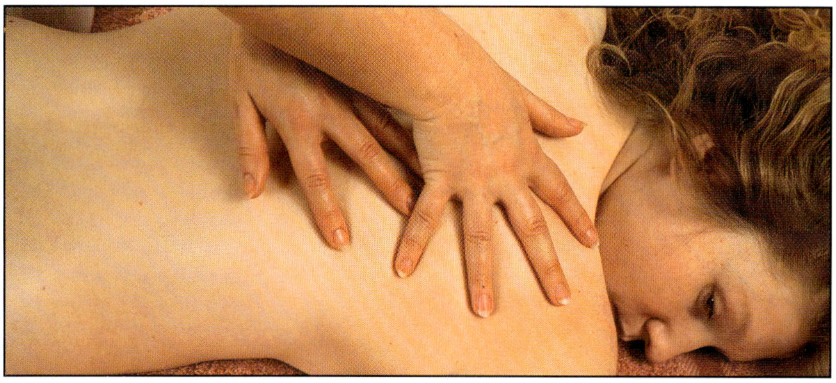

1 Place one hand at the bottom of the shoulder blade (scapula) with fingers splayed and the second hand poised to follow on the same side.

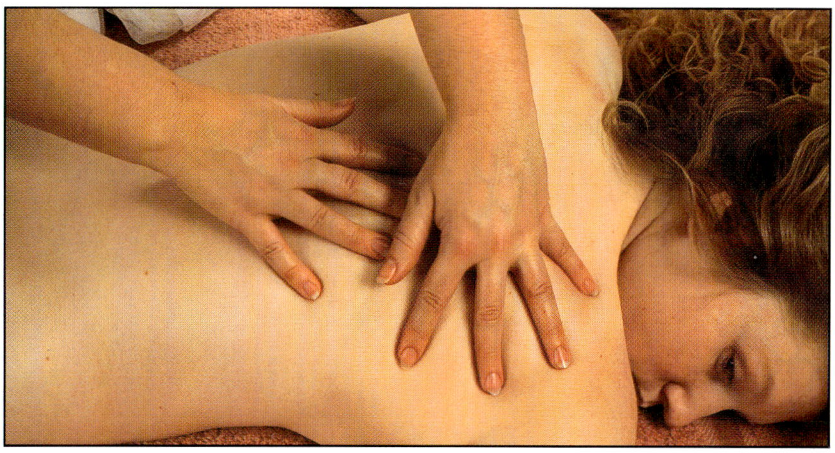

2 Brush the hand up and out in a smooth fanning movement. Follow with the second hand, work all round the shoulder blade and out over the shoulder, toward the armpit.

Repeat the whole movement four times, then work on the other shoulder.

FOREARM SWEEP

Kneeling at the side of your partner, turn the head away from you.

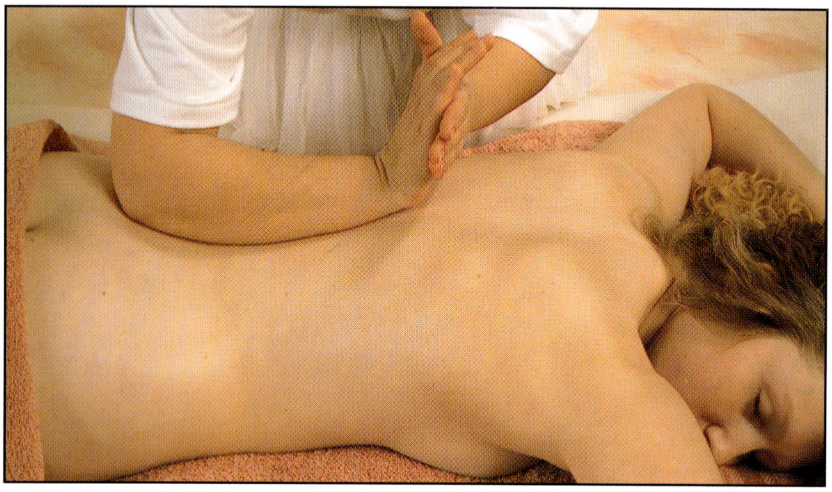

1 *Place your forearm alongside the spine with your elbow just above the buttocks. Clasp the working hand with your other hand for support and stability.*

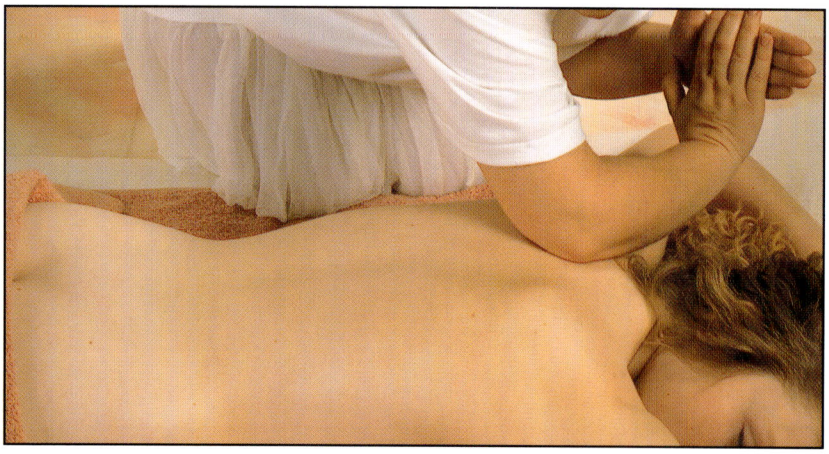

2 *Using the flat bone of the forearm (the ulna), slide all the way up the side of the spine to the top of the shoulder ridge.*

Lift the arm off gently and repeat twice from the beginning.

Then turn your partner's head and work on the other side of the spine, using the opposite forearm.

DRAINING

Sit to the side of your partner, facing across the back.

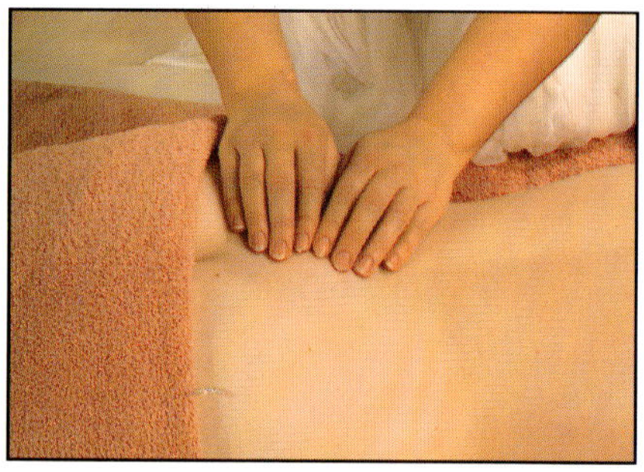

1 *With hands together and palms raised, place the fingertips at the side of the spine, just above the coccyx (tail bone).*

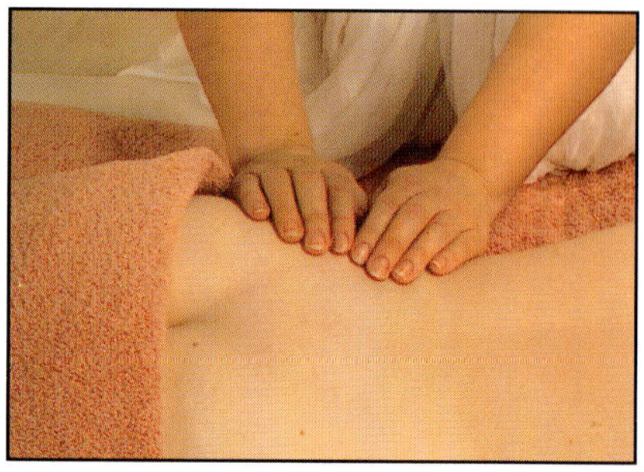

2 *Keeping the fingers together, pull them toward you down the side of the back.*

Repeat the movement all the way up the spine, ending at the base of the neck so the final movement pulls across the shoulders toward the glands in the armpit.

Repeat with the other side of the spine. You can work the opposite side without changing your position by reaching across and brushing away from the spine, or you can move around your partner and repeat as above, if it feels more comfortable.

KNEADING THE NECK

This gentle petrissage *movement releases tension and helps disperse the fatty deposits that can build up in this sensitive area.*

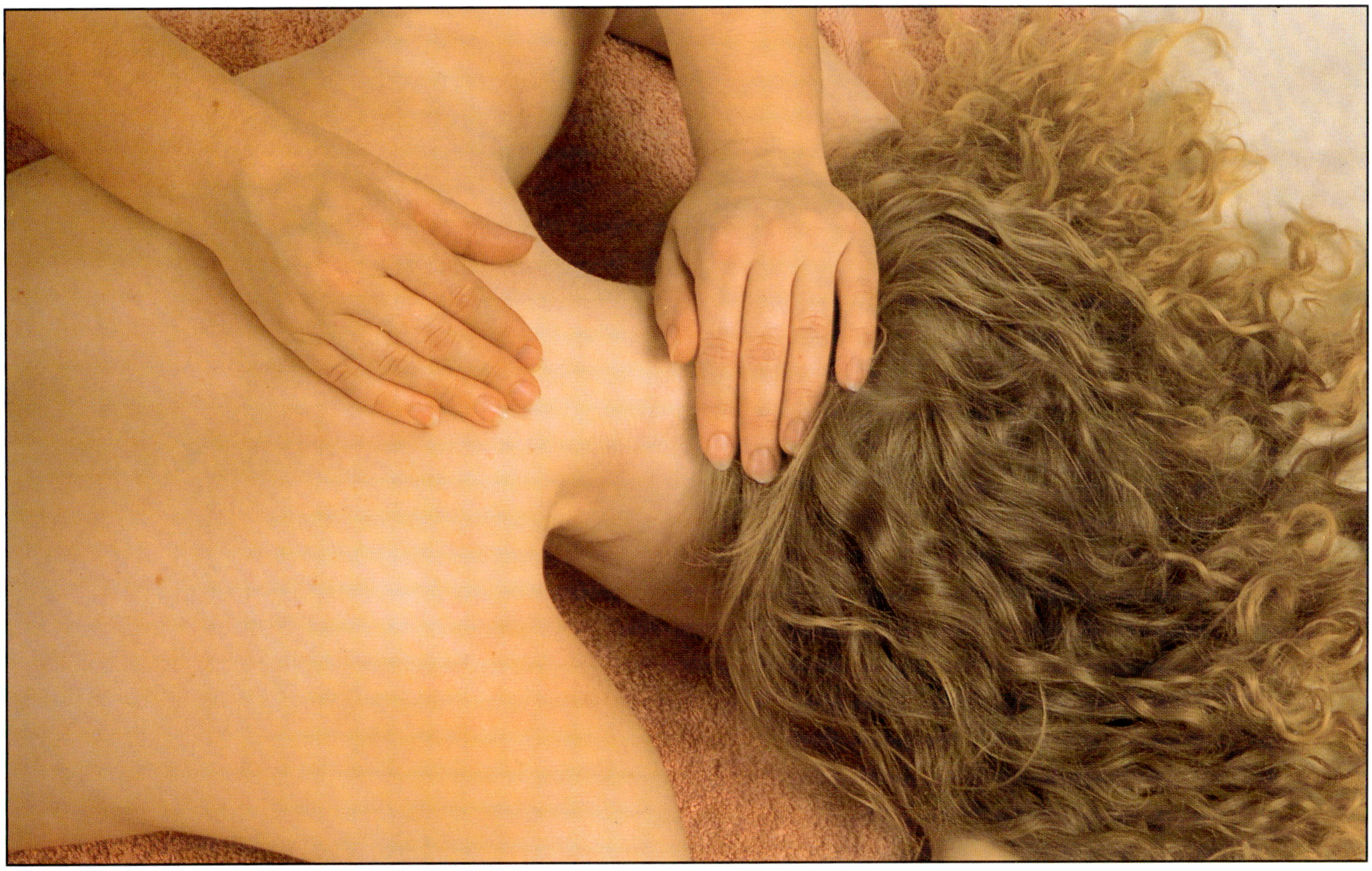

Your partner should rest facing down with forehead on hands, so that you can work your fingers into the base of the neck. Smooth the hair away from the neck.

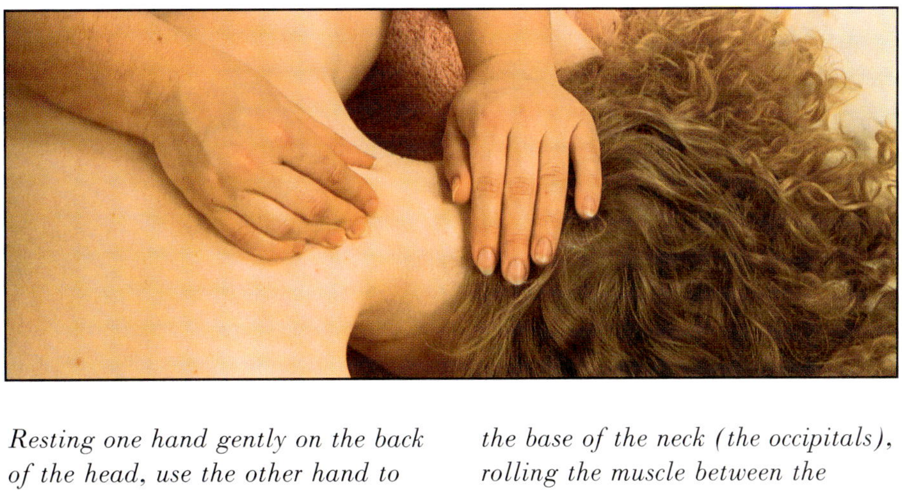

Resting one hand gently on the back of the head, use the other hand to pull up and knead the muscles in the base of the neck (the occipitals), rolling the muscle between the thumb and the other fingers.

FRONTAL MASSAGE

Help your partner to turn over onto their back, and ensure he or she is comfortable. Provide cushions or rolled towels for any parts that need support, such as behind the legs or neck. Cover the body up to the neck with a towel or blanket to keep your partner warm.

SPINAL STRETCH

This movement is not suitable for people suffering from severe back problems, though it helps relieve minor aches and stiffness.

1 *Seated at your partner's head, place the hands to the sides of the neck, palms up, with the middle fingers lifted, to prepare for the movement.*

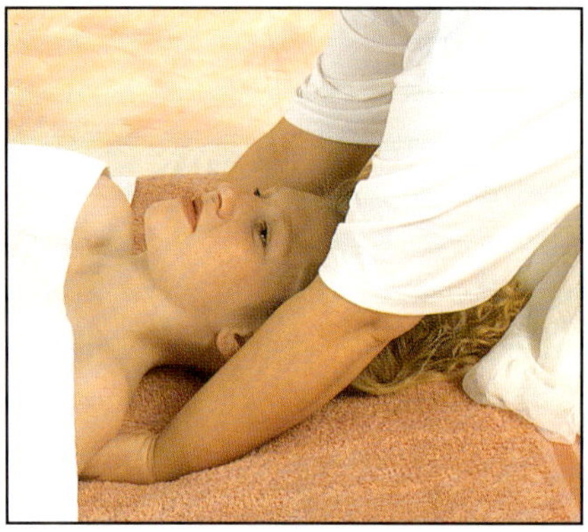

2 *Slide the hands underneath the back, just between the shoulder blades so the middle fingers are pressing on either side of the spine.*

3 *Gently lift the torso so the rib cage rises, maintaining the pressure from the middle fingers.*

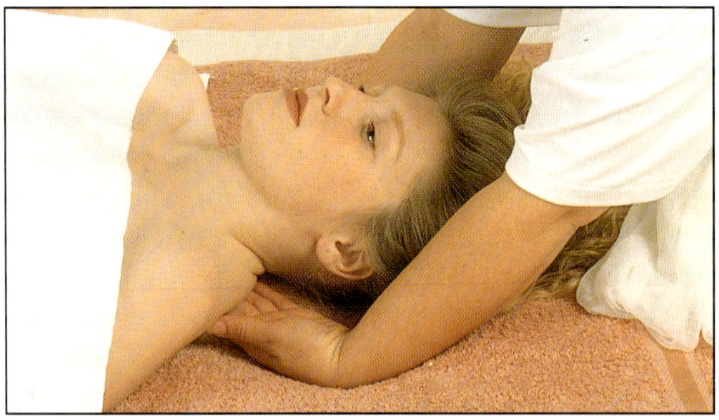

4 *Slowly pull your fingers up the sides of the spine. When you reach the top of the neck, hold for a count of two and then release. Repeat three times in all.*

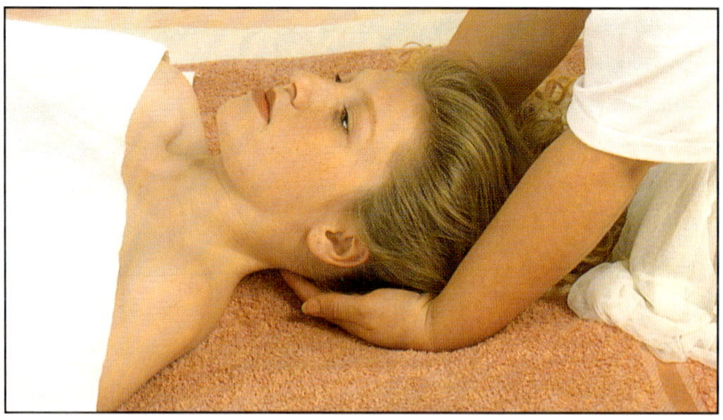

5 *Finish the movement by cradling the head gently with both hands.*

THE FACE

This treatment is a great boost to the circulation, and the complexion will improve with each treatment.

Seated at the head, prepare the face for the massage with a simple refreshing cleanser, using upward and outward strokes. Apply a small amount of facial oil to the face and neck with flowing movements.

TAKE CARE

Even when diluted, essential oils are extremely potent so work carefully around the eye area. If the oil accidentally makes contact with the eye, apply a few drops of pure sweet almond oil to dissipate it. Never wash the eyes with water.

FOREHEAD STROKE

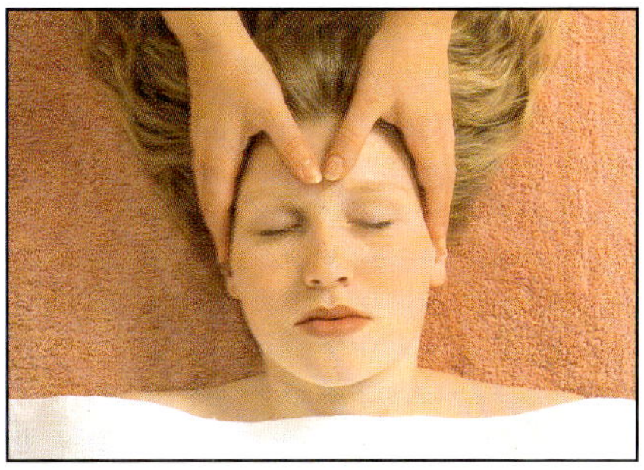

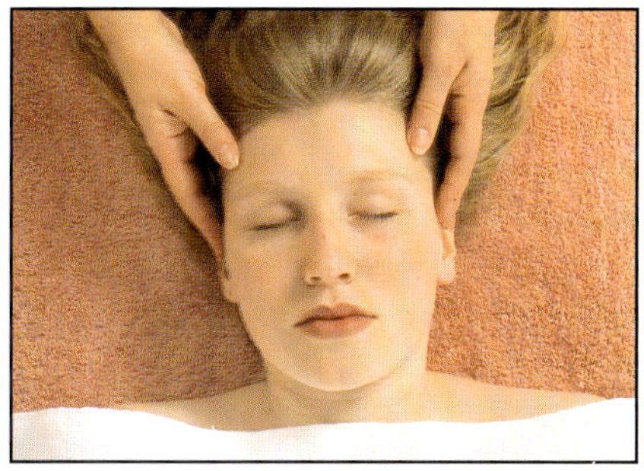

1 *Rest your thumbs on the centre of the forehead, just above the eyebrows, with the palms supporting the sides of the head. The stroke should be kept light and sensitive as the facial skin is very delicate.*

2 *Slowly draw the thumbs out toward the temples and down to the sides of the ears. Repeat the stroke several times, moving the starting position up a little each time until you reach the hairline.*

DRAINING THE CHEEKS

This sequence of raking movements stimulates the lymphatic flow in the face, improving the complexion, clearing the sinuses and releasing tension.

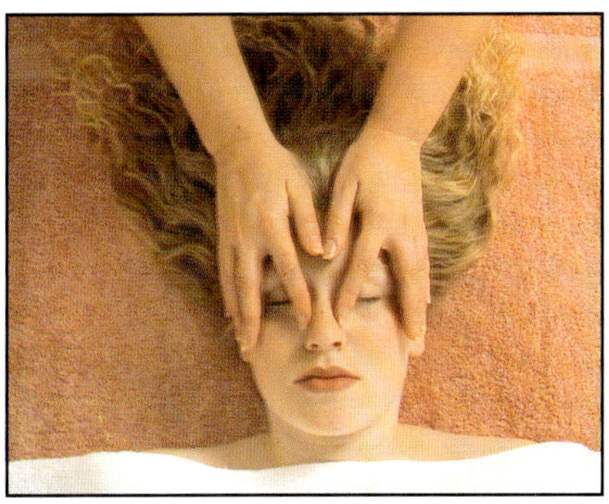

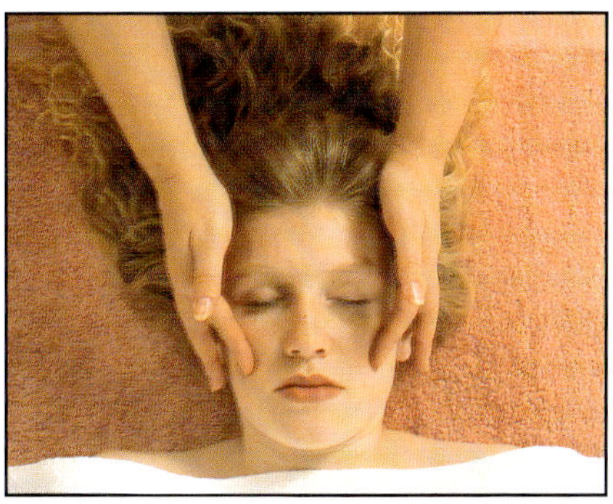

1 *Place the index fingers on either side of the nostrils and hold for a count of five.*

2 *Slide the fingers out and down to the ears. Lift the fingers and replace by the nostril. Sweep in a slightly narrower curve to reach the jawbone just below the ears.*

3 *Repeat with successively smaller curves, ending by tracing the laughter lines around the mouth, downward to the sides of the chin.*

CHIN MASSAGE

This not only tones the jawline, but also stimulates the energy points that govern the stomach and small intestine.

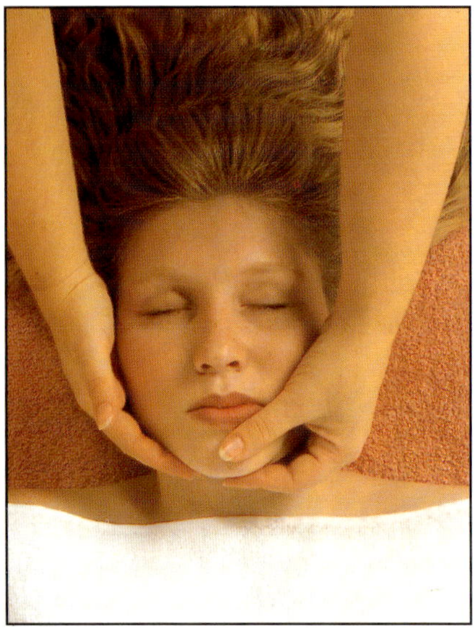

1 Place the thumbs on the chin, allowing the rest of the fingers to cradle the jaw.

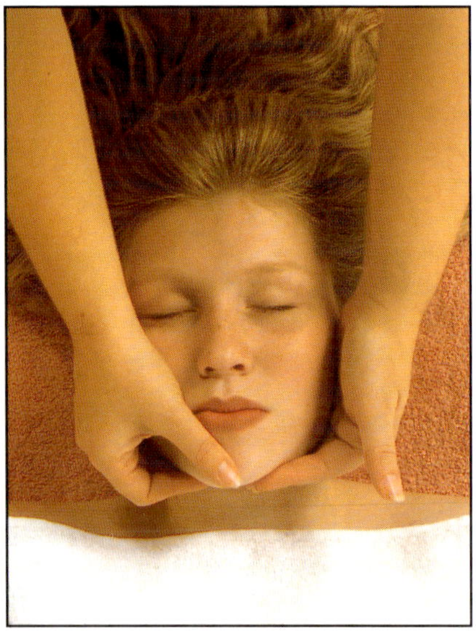

2 Brush alternate thumbs down and outward, with a light stroke. Repeat the movement six or seven times with each thumb.

NECK SWEEP

This is an extremely soothing stroke which improves the tone of the muscles as well as flushing the neck.

1,2 Above and right: Apply a little facial oil to the neck, upper chest and shoulder areas using the flat of the hand. Gently brush down with the hand from the side of the ear out to the shoulder, using a broad sweeping stroke to cover the area.

3 Repeat the movement working round the front of the neck, down from the chin to the top of the chest, and then sweep from the other ear to the shoulder.

The sequence of sweeps round the whole neck should be repeated three times.

FANNING THE SHOULDERS

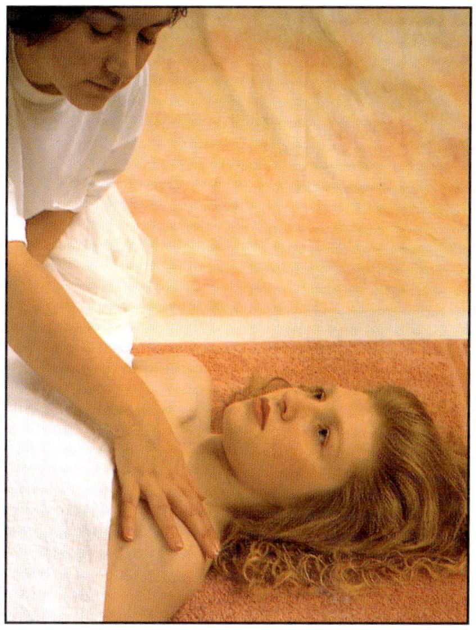

1 *With fingers spread, brush with the flat of the hand across from the breastbone and out over the shoulders.*

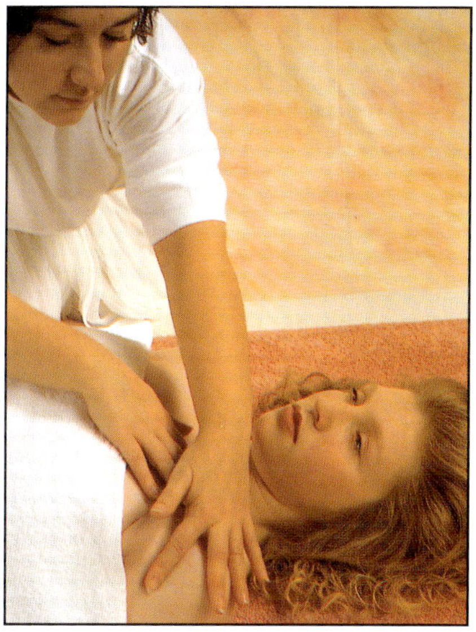

2 *The second hand follows closely behind the first, so they are draining simultaneously toward the armpit.*

Repeat twice before moving onto the other shoulder.

STOMACH AREA

ABDOMEN

1 *Left: Apply a little oil evenly over the stomach. Place the palm of a hand on the centre of the abdomen.*

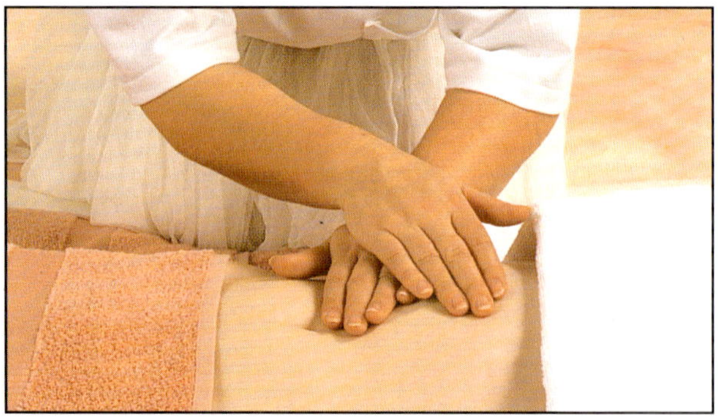

2 *Work the area with tender circular movements, always in a clockwise direction.*

Repeat with the other palm. This movement aids digestion.

RIB-CAGE SWEEP

This movement helps to cleanse the stomach and spleen by pushing the lymph away from these areas.

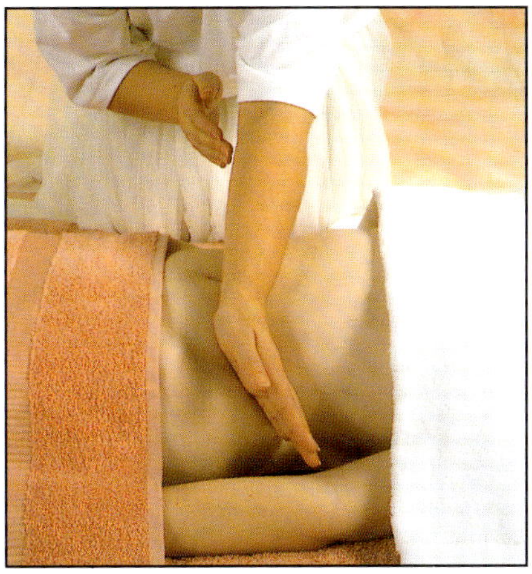

1 *Starting with the outer edge of the hand placed at the centre of the rib-cage, sweep away from you, following the line of the ribs with a long sweeping movement out to the waist.*

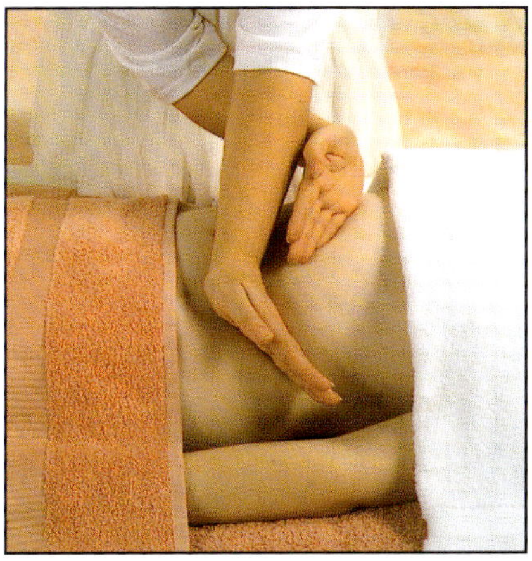

2 *As the first hand finishes the movement, the other hand follows on the same side.*

Repeat the movement with both hands six or seven times and then move around the body to work the other side of the rib-cage.

WAIST PULLS

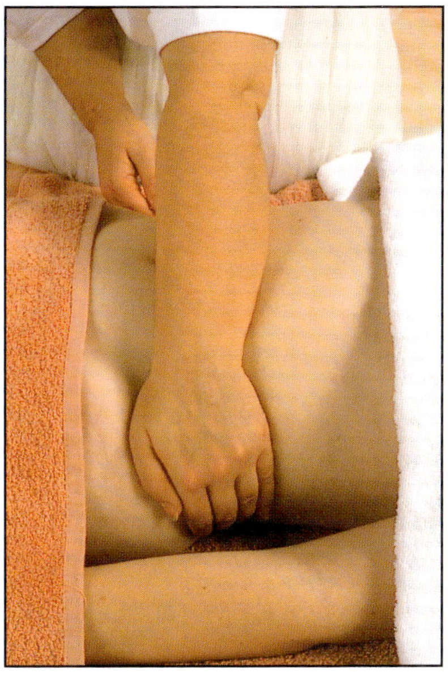

1 *Reach across your partner, placing a firm grip round the waist with one hand. Reinforce your grip by placing your other hand on top of the first hand.*

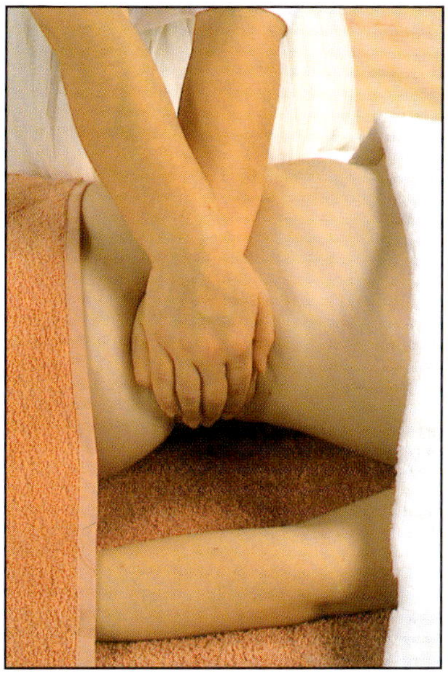

2 *Lift the waist by pulling your partner's body-weight toward you, then gently release while sliding the hands around the hipbone. This cleanses the liver and gall bladder.*

3 *Complete the movement by sliding the hands across and around the pelvis, draining toward the major glands in the groin. Be careful not to dig with the fingers as this is an extremely tender area. Keep the pressure light and even over the whole hand. This is particularly beneficial for women who suffer from menstrual problems.*

Repeat five or six times before moving round to the other side of the body.

FRONT OF LEGS

EFFLEURAGE

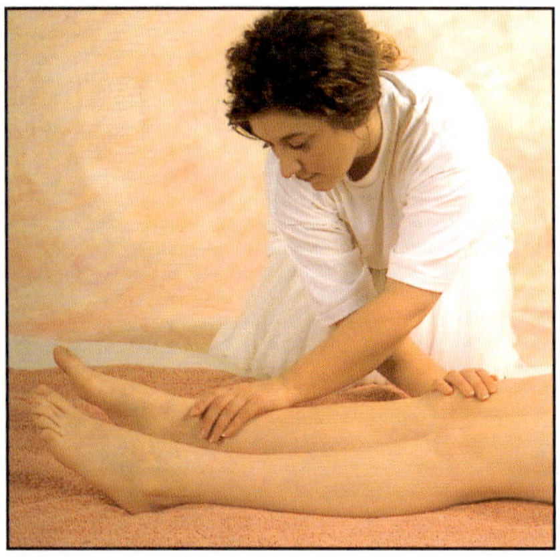

Apply oil to both legs using an effleurage *movement working up from the ankles, as used on the back of the legs.*

Repeat the effleurage *strokes sequence several times to ensure an even distribution of oil.*

LEG STRETCH

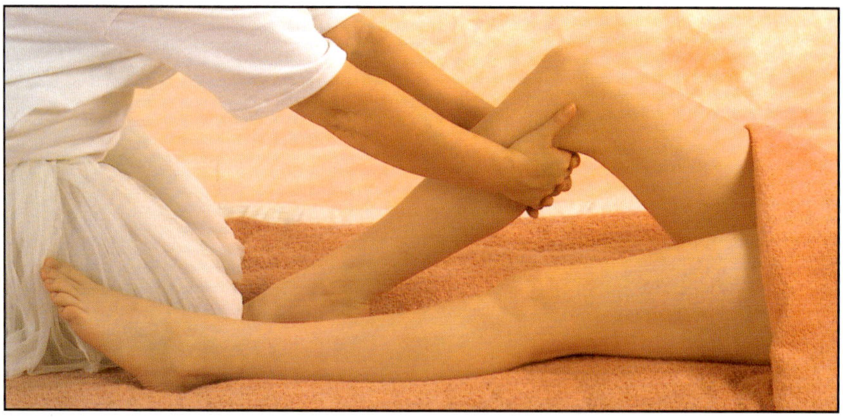

Supporting the leg at the ankle and behind the knee, bend the leg up and place it in line with the shoulder.

Clasp the hands around the back of the knee. Ask your partner to inhale deeply, then pull the calf muscle toward you.

Hold for a slow count of three. As your partner breathes out, release the pull on the calf.

Repeat the whole movement three times, then gently lay the leg down and repeat the stretch on the other leg.

ARMS AND HANDS

EFFLEURAGE

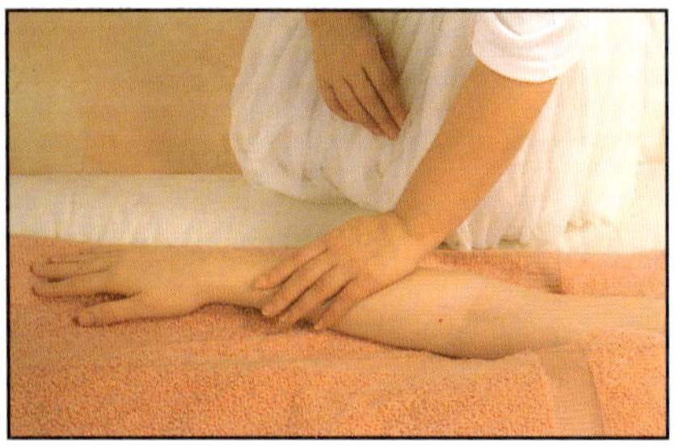

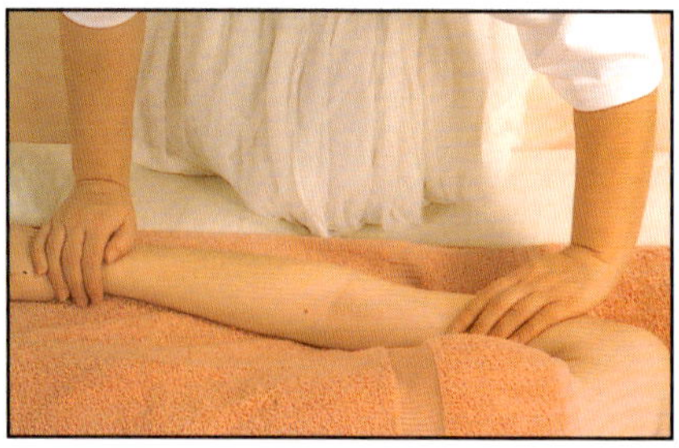

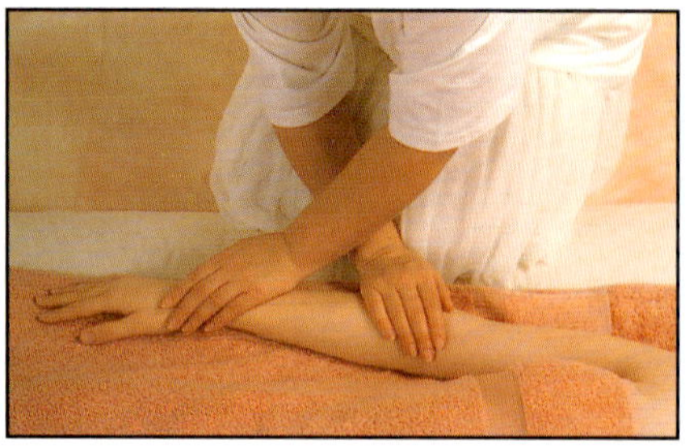

1 *Seated to the side of your partner, move the arm slightly away from the body. Apply the oil by sweeping from just above the wrist, up to the shoulder and round.*

2 *As the first hand comes off the arm, the other hand starts at the wrist and sweeps upward to the gland sited in the elbow joint.*

3 *The first arm crosses the second as it reaches the elbow and again sweeps from wrist to shoulder.*

Repeat six or seven times.

You can follow the effleurage *with flushing to the inside of the arm, using the same movements performed on the leg, working from the wrist to the elbow.*
Before going on to the second arm, massage the hand of the first arm.

HAND MASSAGE

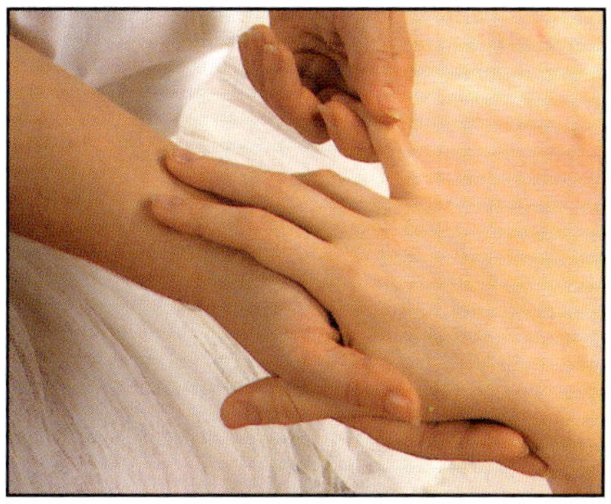

2 *Pull back to the fingers, gently massaging the joints between your thumb and forefinger as you draw towards the tips. Finish with a slight pull to the finger to stretch it out.*

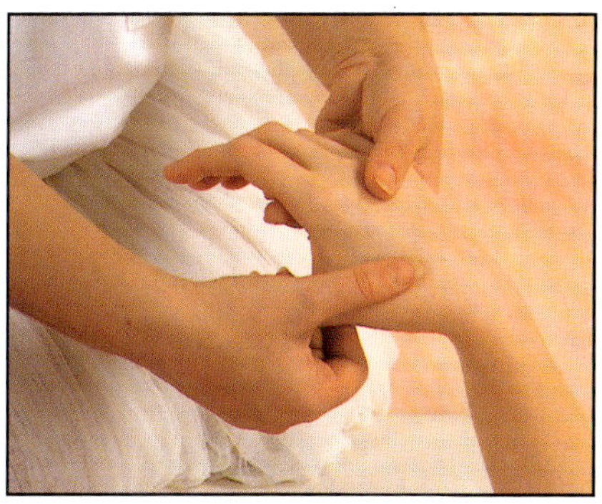

1 *Resting your partner's hand palm down over your own palm, use small brushing movements with your thumbs to work upward between the joints of the fingers toward the wrist.*

3 *Repeat with each finger, finishing with the thumb.*

Now repeat the movements on the other arm and hand.

To finish the massage, cover your partner to the neck, check he or she is warm and comfortable, and leave to rest for a minimum of five minutes (up to 15 minutes is preferable). Upon returning, help your partner to sit up carefully and offer a glass of water.

PREGNANCY TREATMENTS

Pregnancy can be one of the most exciting and fulfilling times of a woman's life. The joy of bringing another human being into the world creates a tremendous feeling of contentment and anticipation, but it is also a time of great physical and emotional upheaval. Together with the ever-important trio of exercise, good diet and rest, essential oils can play an important role in helping a woman cope with the stresses of nine months of pregnancy, the pain of labour and post-natal recovery.

COMMON AILMENTS

Surging hormone levels and changes in your swelling body can bring a host of discomforts, many of which can be alleviated by aromatherapy treatments and other simple steps.

Backache
The lower back region takes a lot of strain during pregnancy, and will benefit from a firm massage with four drops each of lavender and sandalwood in two tablespoons of base oil. Six drops of lavender in the bath will help to soothe away the aches.

Morning Sickness
Eat little and often during the day, avoiding junk food and heavy meals late at night. Choose fresh foods which are free from preservatives or chemicals. Try herbal tea infusions such as chamomile, peppermint or orange blossom, which are good for the digestion.

Heartburn
Avoid heavy meals and particularly rich, spicy foods. Peppermint tea infusions help, and you can rub the solar plexus with a blend of two drops each of lemon and peppermint essential oils in one tablespoon of base oil.

Spoil yourself with the luxurious and relaxing scent of rose for body and facial oils, to keep your spirits up during pregnancy.

Sore Breasts
These need extra care and attention during pregnancy as they expand. Use a gentle massage oil with rose and orange, three drops of each in one tablespoon of sweet almond oil; or if breasts are swollen, make a cool compress using rosewater and place over the breasts while having an afternoon rest. Sweet almond oil on its own is excellent for sore, cracked nipples during breast-feeding. Never use pure essential oils on the breasts during this period as they can easily be transferred to the baby while feeding.

Constipation
Make sure your diet contains plenty of fresh and high fibre foods and drink plenty of still water. Tension can also be a contributory factor, so try a relaxing bath with three drops of lavender and four drops of rose. Massage your abdomen and the small of the back with a blend of four drops of chamomile or orange in one tablespoon of base oil.

Sleep Problems
In the last few months of pregnancy, with the baby kicking and other discomforts, it is often difficult to get a good night's sleep. A relaxing bath with neroli and rose is soothing, and you can add ylang-ylang for its calming, sedative effect – a maximum of eight drops in total. Two drops of rose or lavender on the edge of the pillowcase will help induce sleep.

Stretch Marks
When the stretched skin returns to the body's normal shape it can leave tiny jagged scars. A daily massage around the hips and expanding tummy, using five drops of lavender in one tablespoon of jojoba, wheatgerm or evening primrose oil, will help keep skin smooth and supple. Start around the fifth month of

pregnancy and continue after the birth until you return to your normal weight.

Swollen Ankles
These can be reduced with a cool to warm footbath of benzoin, rose and orange. Add two drops of each directly to the bowl or mix with one tablespoon of base carrier oil such as sesame seed. Rest with feet raised on cushions or pillows.

Varicose Veins
During pregnancy the blood flow to the legs is often slowed down, causing the veins to dilate. Two drops each of cypress, lemongrass and lavender, mixed with two tablespoons of apricot kernel base oil, can be smoothed gently over the legs for relief. If veins are prominent then one of the best oils for the circulation is geranium, though this should always be very dilute for use in pregnancy. Add four drops to the bath or to one tablespoon of carrier oil to massage the leg with upward movements. Do not work directly on the veins or apply too much pressure to the leg.

Labour

To create a relaxing atmosphere in the labour room, use a few drops of lavender in a fragrancer, or try rose, neroli or ylang-ylang to fortify you as the labour progresses. Any of these oils can be used in a massage blend for the lower back to help with contractions. If labour is progressing slowly, try marjoram as a massage oil or compress across the abdomen to stimulate contractions.

After the Birth

The "baby blues" often occur around the third or fourth day after childbirth, though some women can suffer a more severe form of post-natal depression for up to a year. A bath of jasmine and ylang-ylang will help you feel better, or use a body oil of chamomile, geranium and orange (5 drops to two tablespoons of sweet almond oil), which is a good mix for hormonal imbalance.

To ease any perineal pains, a bath with lavender is soothing. Tea tree can also be added, since this is a powerful antiseptic and helps heal internal wounds and stitches.

CAUTIONS

The following oils should be avoided during pregnancy (particularly the first five months) because of their strong diuretic properties or tendency to induce menstruation:

Bay · Basil · Clary Sage · Comfrey Fennel · Hyssop · Juniper Marjoram · Melissa · Myrrh Rosemary · Thyme · Sage

Use all essential oils in half the usual quantity during pregnancy and take extra care in handling them. Ensure that the oils you are using are pure essential oils, as adulterated blends or synthetic oils can sometimes have less predictable effects.

If you have a history of miscarriage you could also avoid chamomile and lavender for the first few months, although in general these are excellent oils for pregnancy.

Because of their potentially toxic nature and strong abortive qualities the following oils should *never* be used except by a qualified aromatherapist, and must be avoided during pregnancy:

Oreganum · Pennyroyal · St John's Wort · Tansy · Wormwood

Recommended Oils for Pregnancy
Chamomile · Geranium (in low doses) *· Lavender · Lemon · Neroli Orange · Rose · Sandalwood*

PREGNANCY MASSAGE

These simple touch massage movements can help to relieve many of the stresses and discomforts of pregnancy, and the back massage is particularly welcome during labour. The basic essential oil massage is modified in various ways to take account of the pregnant condition.

- Check the box on the previous page to find which oils are suitable and which are to be avoided.
- Use a lower concentration of essential oil to base oil; $^1/_2$–1 per cent is ideal.
- Keep strokes lighter than usual.
- In addition to the steps suggested, you can incorporate a facial and gentle breast massage.
- It is particularly important to observe the rest period after the massage and to help your partner get up gently.
- The positions you work in need to be adapted for a pregnant woman, as she cannot lie out straight on her front or back and needs to be well supported.

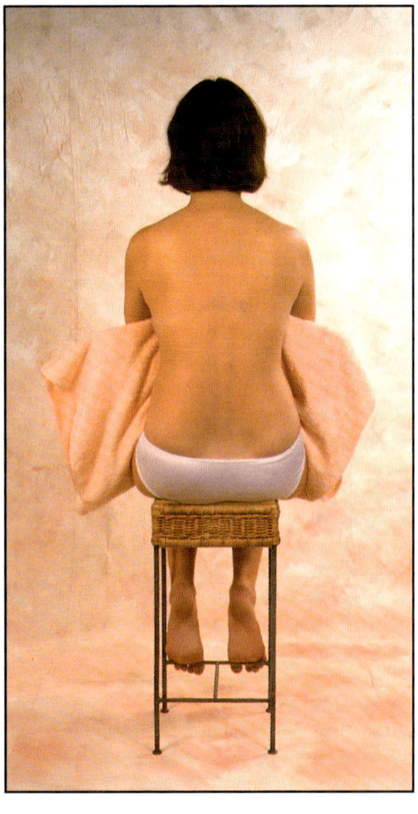

THE BACK

After about the fourth month of pregnancy it becomes uncomfortable to lie on the stomach, so work with your partner sitting up with a towel-wrapped pillow or back of a chair to lean over for support.

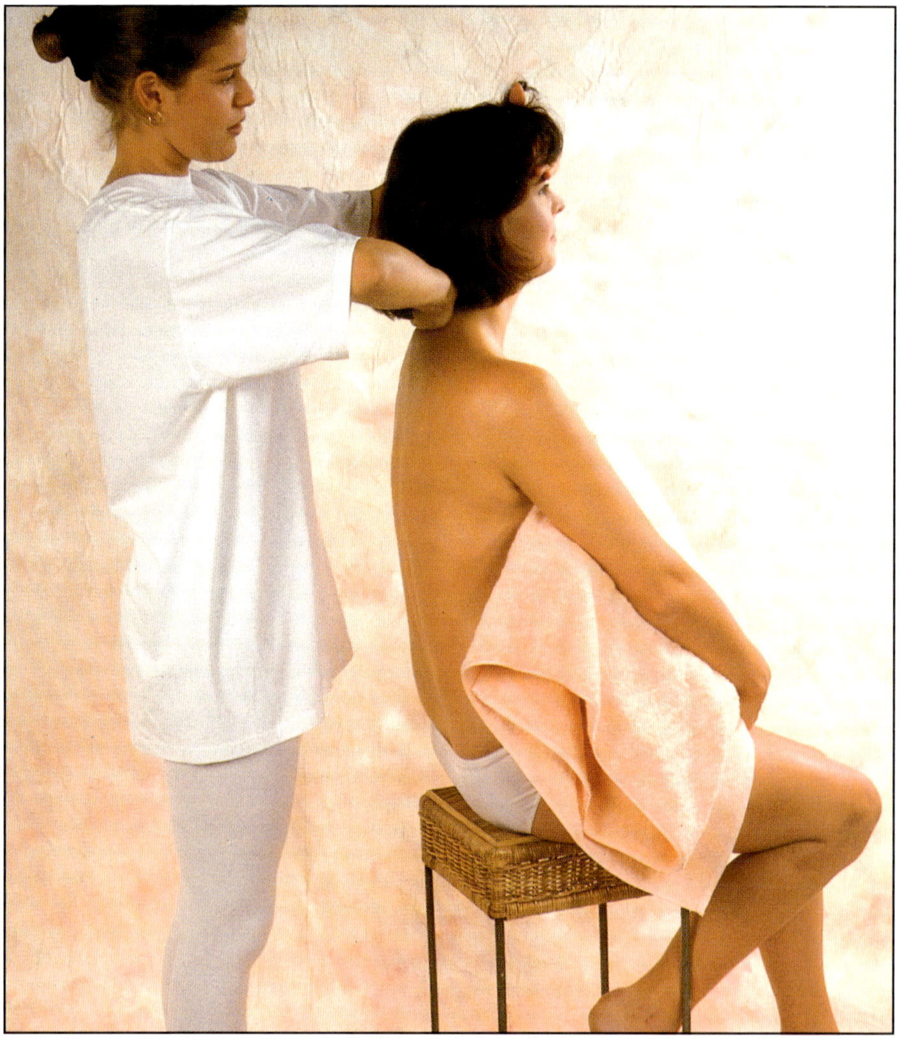

1 *Make sure your partner is comfortable and place your left hand over the forehead and the palm of your right hand across the back of the neck. Hold for a few moments and then release.*

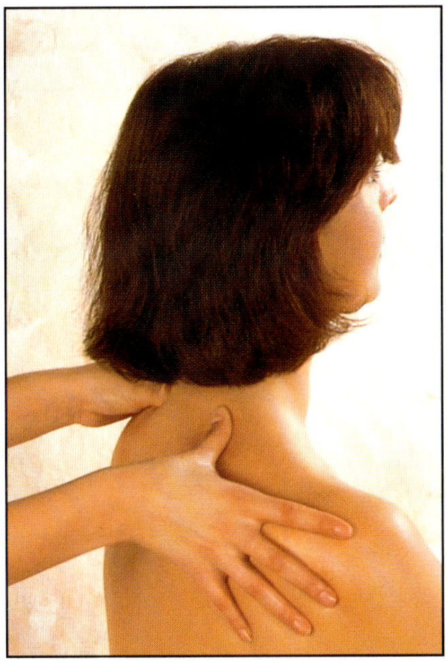

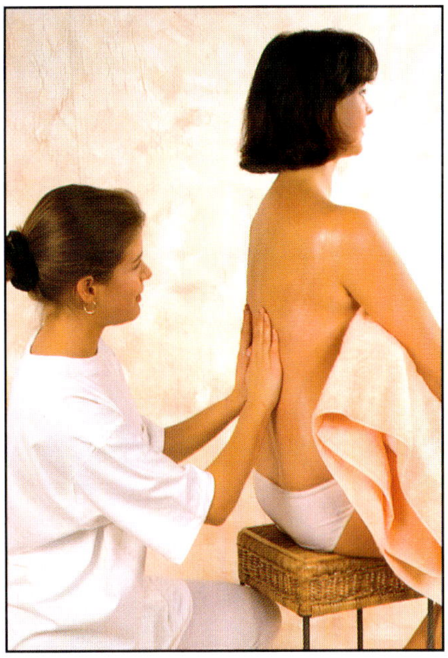

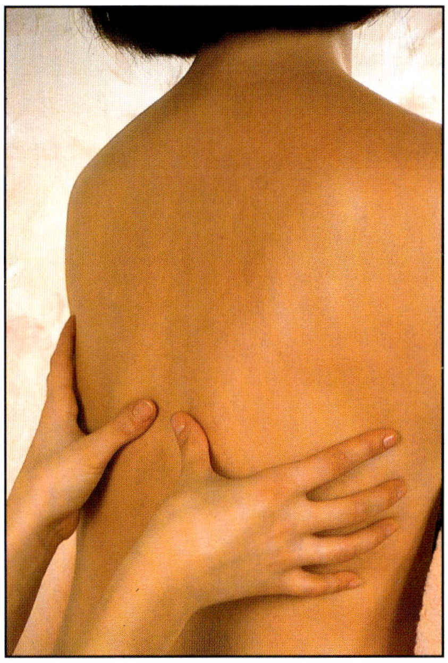

2 *Apply a little oil to your fingers and using a slight but gentle pressure, softly massage each side of your partner's neck and shoulders, kneading mainly with the thumbs. This will help to relieve the tension often caused by the weight of enlarged breasts.*

3 *Stroke the oil evenly over the back and begin an* effleurage *movement (a soothing, stroking motion with two hands, moving up the sides of the spine and out over the shoulders). Repeat several times to establish a rhythm and relax your partner.*

4 *Using the thumbs, work upward on each side of the spinal column from the lower back to the neck to help release congestion along the spinal nerves. Repeat four times. Clear the movement by sweeping up the back using the calming* effleurage *stroke.*

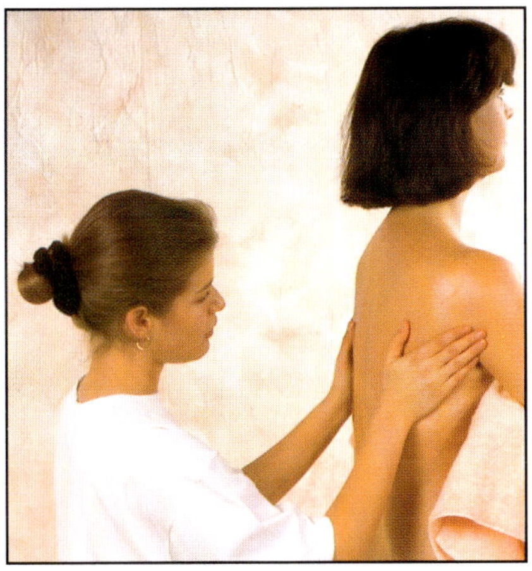

5 *Starting from the centre of the back, begin working up and outward across the width of the back with superficial* effleurage *movements. Repeat the movements several times until your partner is relaxed. This will help to stimulate the circulation and has a soothing effect on the nerve endings.*

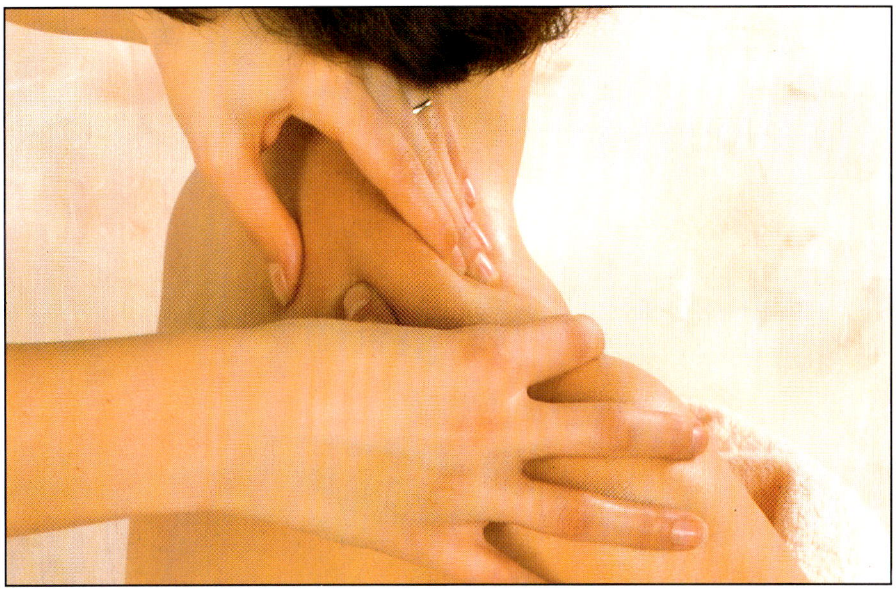

6 *Using a double-handed movement, press down and then gently lift the muscles to the side of the neck, rolling with the thumb, and then release. Work out from the neck across the shoulder, and then repeat across the other shoulder. Performed slowly with rhythmic movements this is very relaxing and will alleviate stiffness.*

THE ABDOMEN

For a pregnant woman, the weight of the uterus can constrict important blood vessels if she lies down flat on her back, so provide plenty of pillows, cushions, bolsters or rolled towels to support your partner behind the back, under the neck and knees and anywhere else she needs to feel comfortable.

1 *Below: It may seem alarming to massage the abdomen during pregnancy but, providing the strokes are light and careful, it is safe and relaxing for mother and baby. Gentle massage all over the abdominal area can be very soothing and is beneficial for relieving the stretched feeling often experienced during pregnancy. Apply oil evenly over the area to help feed the tissues and lessen the possibility of stretch marks.*

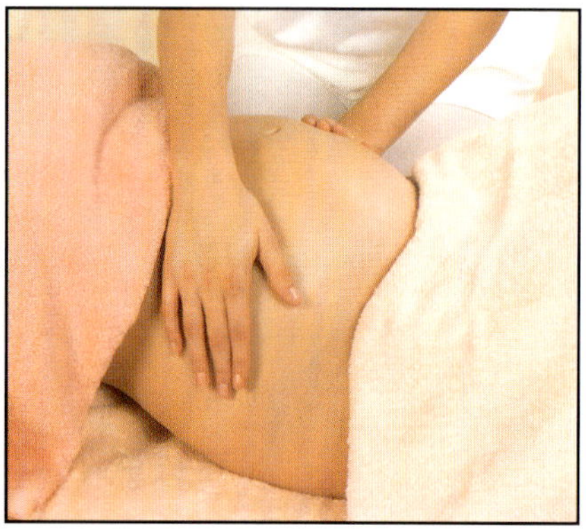

2 *Using the flat of your hands, carefully glide them up from either side of the waist, lifting your hands off as they reach the navel, and then start again. Continue to stroke the area with a light, soft touch, working over the whole of the abdomen to soothe and calm.*

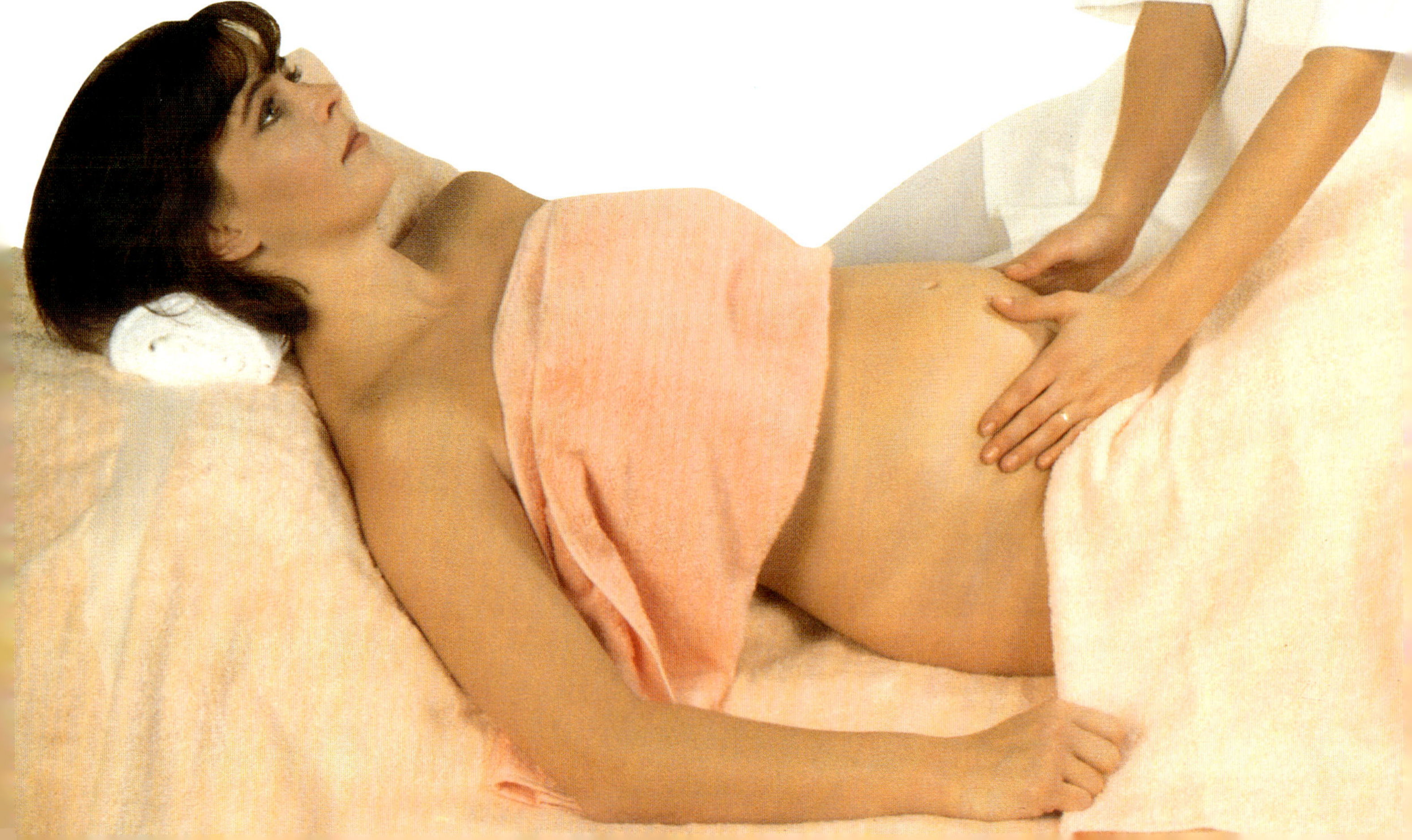

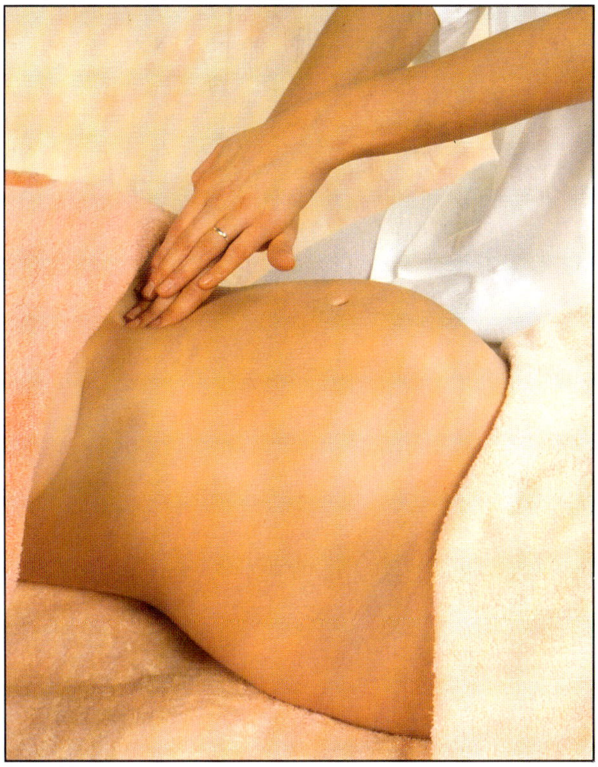

3 *After a minute of gentle circular movements, place the fingertips of your left hand on the higher section of the solar plexus region and cover with your right hand. Rest both hands for a moment and then release to help alleviate stress.*

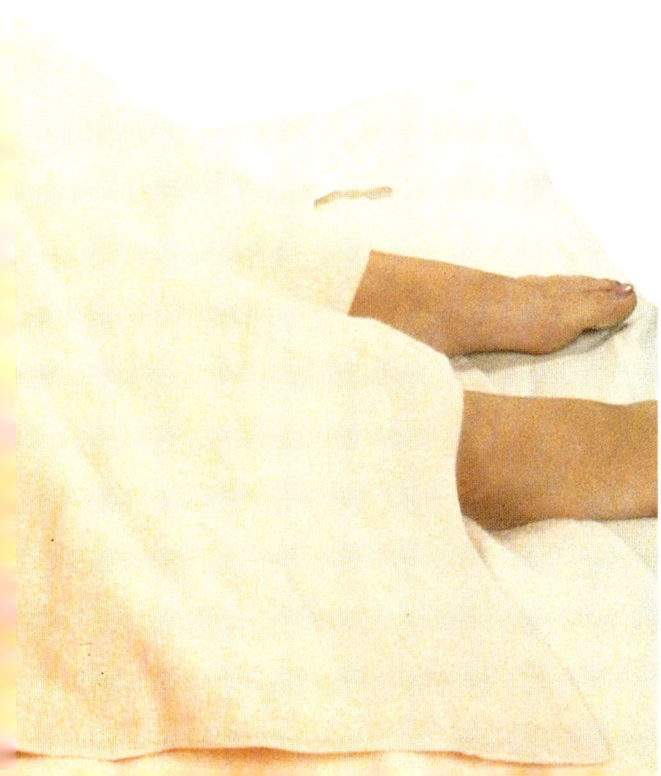

LEGS

Make sure your partner is comfortable, with the knees supported by cushions.

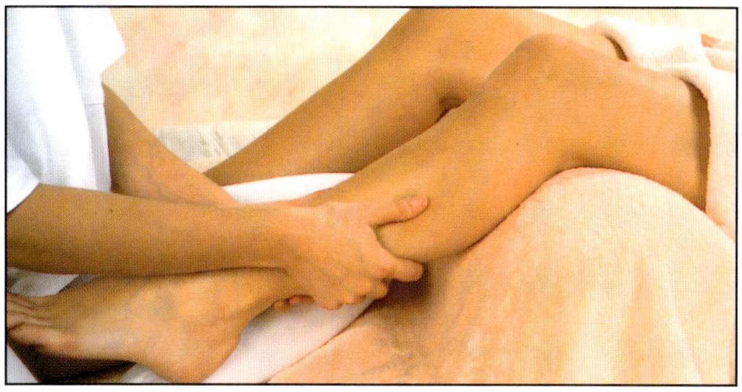

Begin gently stroking the leg with an effleurage *from the ankle to the knee, smoothing up the shin and then glide around the calf.*
It can help to relieve the swelling, varicose veins or cramp which afflict many pregnant women. Do not use any heavy movements to the legs and avoid any reflexology movements to the feet, though gentle stroking around the ankles may well be appreciated.

TO FINISH

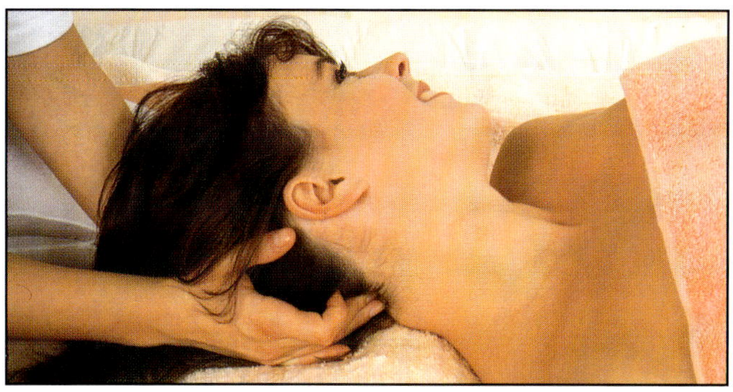

With both hands positioned at the back of the neck, apply light circular pressures to the cranium (skull) with your fingertips working in an upward direction to help release tension.

End the massage by smoothing the hair away from the neck and forehead, releasing all the negative energy. Allow your partner to rest for 15 minutes and then help her to get up very gently.

BEAUTY BASICS

Looking good starts with great skin, and aromatherapy can help you achieve this in various ways: the remarkable penetrative properties of essential oils make them excellent moisturizers, and the wide range of their properties means there is always the right oil for the right condition. For instance, rosemary stimulates the circulation and thyme help the cells to regenerate. As well as being stimulating to the lymphatic system, which helps cleanse the tissue that causes sluggish skin, essential oils can be used as part of your daily skin-care routine and to treat specific problems such as acne.

FEED YOUR SKIN

Skin needs to be fed and nourished – inside and out. Healthy diets can keep the body in shape but to keep skin in peak condition it needs to have a ready supply of valuable vitamins and minerals. Many factors can drain the body of this valuable resource – canned and over-processed foods, caffeine, alcohol, nicotine, sunlight, central heating, carbon monoxide and habitual drug taking. The effects of these can build up and attack the skin so from time to time you need to give it a break.

A one-day fruit and vegetable diet is an excellent regime to adopt once a month to cleanse your body and give a boost to your system.

SKIN TYPES

Choose the right oils for your skin type and use them to blend your own cleansers, toners, masks and moisturizing facial oils. Remember that skin types can vary: skin may be drier in winter or summer or more prone to oiliness around the time of your period, and it can change several times between puberty and menopause. So review the oils you use to suit your skin now and vary them to meet the changing needs of your complexion.

Few people are blessed with normal skin and even those who are may tend towards dryness or oiliness at times. Letters in parentheses indicate what other skin types an oil is suitable for. D = dry, S = sensitive, O = oily, A = all skin types.

Oils for Normal Skin
Chamomile (D, S) · Fennel (O)
Geranium (A) · Lavender (A)
Lemon (O) · Patchouli (D)
Rose (D, S) · Sandalwood (D, S)

Oils for Dry Skin
Chamomile · Geranium · Lavender
Hyssop · Rose · Patchouli
Sandalwood · Ylang-Ylang

Oils for Sensitive Skin
Chamomile · Lavender · Neroli
Rose · Sandalwood

Oils for Oily Skin
Bergamot · Cedarwood · Cypress
Lavender · Lemon · Geranium
Juniper · Frankincense · Sage

Combination skin has an oily T-zone panel from the forehead down to the nose and chin area, and may be normal or dry elsewhere. Double up on the treatments, using oils for oily skin on the greasy patches and oils for normal skin on the rest of the face area.

CLEANSERS

Choose the correct essential oils for your skin type and blend them in with an ordinary unperfumed brand of cleanser, liquid soap, or tissue-off lotion/cream, and they will do nature's work of rebalancing the skin.

FACIAL STEAM

Add five drops of chamomile for a soothing steam or try lavender, peppermint, thyme or rosemary to stimulate; comfrey or fennel for their healing properties.

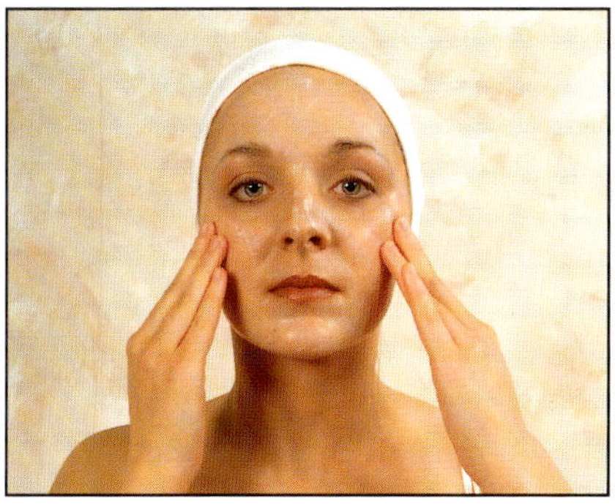

Above: Cleanse the face, paying particular attention to the oilier areas.

Above right: For a facial steam, boil the water, cool slightly and add the oils. Steam for five minutes.

Toners

Essential oils are the gentlest way of toning up. Rose water for normal or dry/sensitive skin or witchhazel for oilier skins are ideal bases for fresheners. These can be applied with cotton wool or for a more refreshing tone, sprayed on to the face.

Herbal tea infusions are also ideal toners. Boil a cup of water and infuse chamomile, marigold, rosehip or nettle teas (you can use herbal tea bags if you can't get hold of the herbs), add two drops of orange or lavender oil and leave to cool. Oily skin benefits from juniper or lemongrass whereas drier skins would appreciate rose or sandalwood.

Facial Oils

Well-moisturized skin is soft and supple, reflects a healthy glow and ages less quickly. Younger skin only needs light conditioning whereas older skin needs specific nourishing treatments. Most moisturizers soothe and sit on the surface of the skin, but essential oils, with their fine molecular structure, work their way through from the surface to the inner dermis (the skin's deeper regenerating layer). Mixed with the correct amount of base oil, these pure essentials do not clog up pores on lubrication: they are light enough to be absorbed spontaneously by skin.

Use two tablespoons of base oil and add six drops of essential oil (maximum of three different oils) to suit individual needs.

Masks

Both clay and oatmeal are ideal ingredients for any face mask. A natural powdered clay is fuller's earth, which can be mixed into a paste with hot water. Cool and then add yogurt for a smoother consistency. Similarly, finely ground oatmeal can be mixed into a paste and left to cool. Add 15 drops of essential oils to suit your skin type per cupful of paste. Smooth on to your face, leave to dry slightly and then sponge off. For particularly dry/sensitive skins add one tablespoon evening primrose base oil to give a more moisturizing mask. When applying, avoid the eye area.

EYE TREATS

While relaxing with a face mask on, close the eyes and cover with cotton pads soaked in rose water, or soothe with two slices of fresh cucumber.

ACNE

Because of their anti-bacterial, anti-inflammatory and rebalancing properties, essential oils are ideal skin treatments for acne sufferers.

It is often a mistake to scrub oily skin over-zealously: this only activates the sebaceous glands which in turn produce more sebum. If you suffer from pustular acne then avoid excessive facial steams which may spread the condition: use a mask instead. Often it is better to opt for a daily sensitive-skin type cleanser and moisturizer, adding two drops of juniper, which is stimulating and antiseptic. Opt for a deeper clay-type mask treatment once a week, adding a couple of drops of juniper, which is healing, soothing and tightening, or eucalyptus which is anti-inflammatory, antiseptic and antibiotic. Increase your intake of vitamin E, which is a great skin healer.

BROKEN VEINS

These small, red, spider-like thread veins often appear on the surface of skin around the cheek area. They are broken capillaries and seem to affect those with a delicate or fragile skin type. Hot and cold elements, along with stimulants such as alcohol and caffeine, can often trigger this condition. To treat it at home the secret is to protect the skin from losing excess moisture and to give it extra essential oil treatments using parsley, geranium, chamomile, rosemary or cypress in a heavy base oil.

COLD SORES

Cold sores are small blisters on the lips or surrounding area which are caused by the virus herpes simplex. It normally lies dormant in nerve cells but can surface following a simple cold or flu. Any lip sore that persists should be treated medically but for the common cold sore a dab of undiluted tea tree oil will help.

ODD SPOTS

If prone to occasional spots then mix one drop each of neroli, lemon and lavender in one teaspoon (5 ml) of base oil and treat just the affected area. For a single spot use a cotton bud and dab on one drop of undiluted sandalwood.

FACIAL MASSAGE

Massage helps the skin to absorb oils and creams easily. Give skin a clear start with our step-by-step facial.

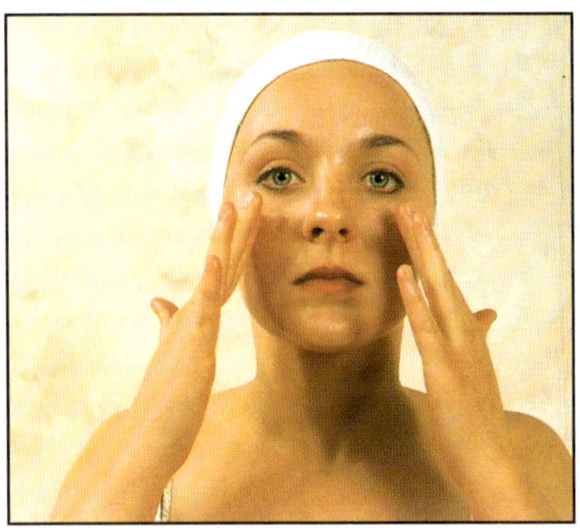

1 *Pour a small amount of blended oil into the palm of your hand and gently apply all over the face, avoiding the eyes.*

2 *With the back of your hands, gently tap the skin around the jaw-line and underneath the chin to stimulate the skin cells.*

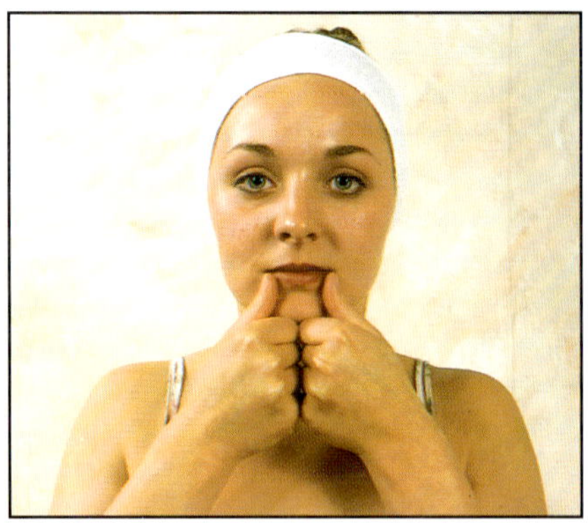

3 *Apply small circular movements to the chin area, using your thumbs, to tone, help circulation and eliminate toxins.*

4 *Make an "oooh"-shaped mouth. Massage either side easing out fine lines.*

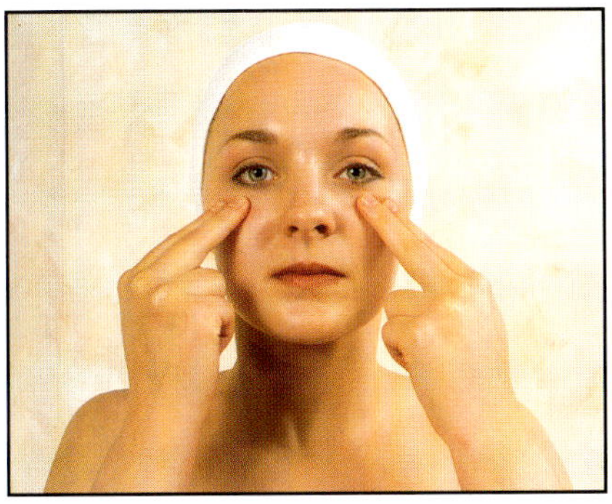

5 *With your fingertips, press along the top of the cheekbones and massage outward up to the temples to release toxins.*

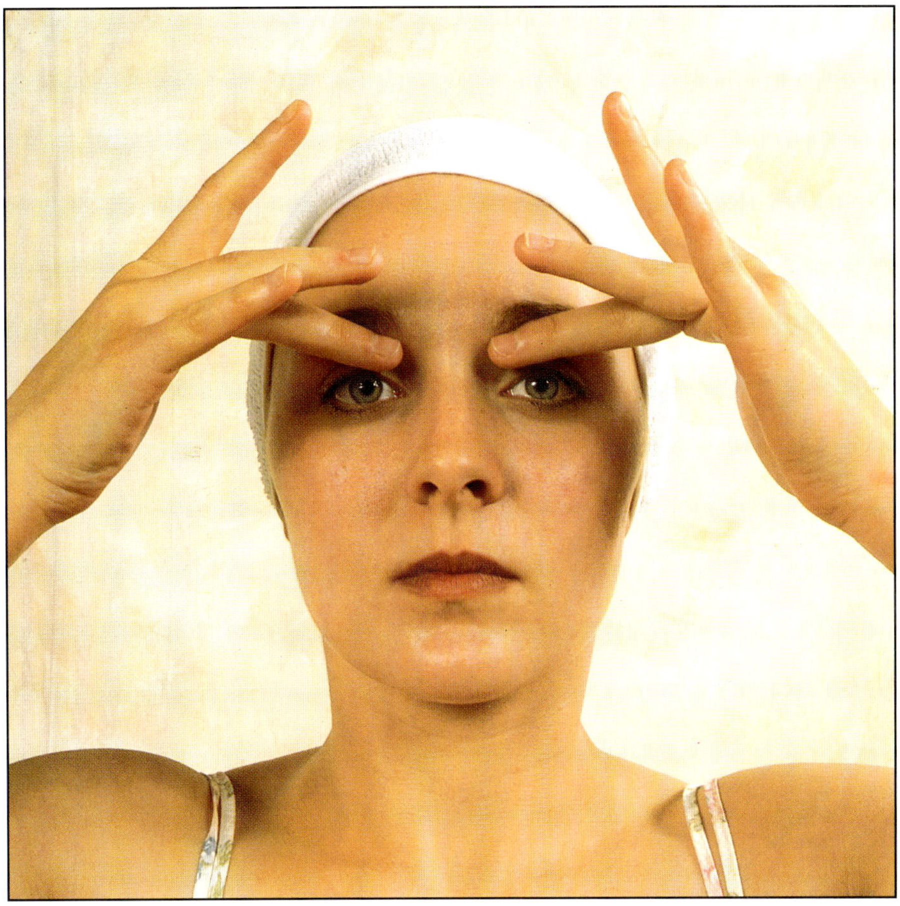

6 *With the middle fingers, apply pressure to points above the bridge of the nose and underneath the eyebrows. Hold for five seconds and smooth across from the inner to the outer corners of the eyebrows and continue up to the temples.*

7 *To relieve tension, apply firm pressure at either side of the temples, and rotate backward.*

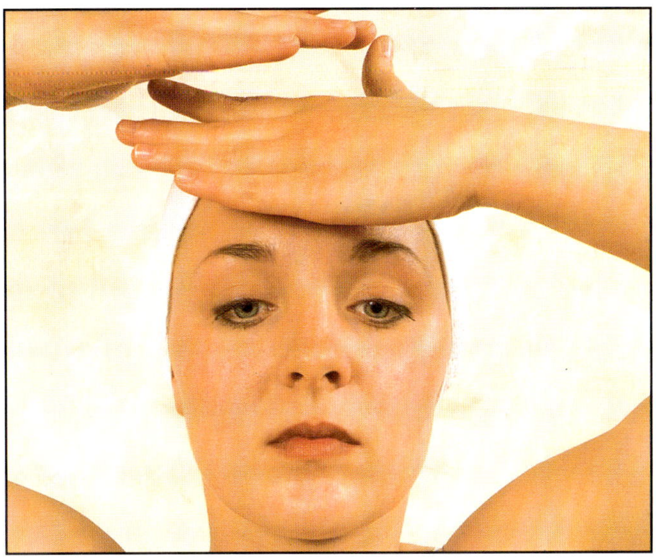

8 *Stroke up the forehead to the hairline with the palms of the hands, smoothing out fine lines.*

HEALTHY HAIR

Hair can define your image and style but it is also a mirror of your health. Emotional or physical problems can soon result in a lack of bounce or shine. Keeping hair in peak condition is a combination of caring for it on the surface and nurturing it from inside with a well-balanced diet.

SCALP MASSAGE OILS

Dry hair is rough to touch, thick in texture and dries out at the first sign of heated rollers or tongs. Avoid chemical colourants and perms and opt for shampoos and conditioners with jojoba and almond oils. Hot oil treatments allow essential oils to soak in easily and condition the hair. After massaging warm oil into the scalp, wrap the head in a warm towel and leave on for half an hour.

Oils for Dry Hair
Rose · Sandalwood · Ylang-ylang
Lavender · Geranium

Greasy hair tends to look dull, lank, lacks body and won't hold a style. Central heating and environmental elements aggravate the condition but it can stem from a hormonal imbalance. Check your diet and avoid harsh degreasing shampoos. Clean brushes and combs weekly. Plastic brushes are better for brushing through as bristle continually stimulates the scalp. Choose light conditioning rinses to detangle but try a scalp massage to regulate the oil-producing sebaceous glands.

Oils for Greasy Hair
Basil · Eucalyptus · Cedarwood
Chamomile · Lemongrass
Cypress · Sage · Rosemary

Normal hair is glossy with plenty of natural body and bounce. An occasional hot-oil scalp treatment

will keep it looking good and growing healthily.

Oils for Normal Hair
Geranium · Lavender
Lemongrass · Rosemary

Combination hair has ends that are dry or normal and the roots are greasy. Avoid using hot appliances near the scalp and keep the ends regularly trimmed and conditioned. Use a scalp treatment with oils for greasy hair but don't comb through to the ends.

How to Mix
Base oils Choose from sweet almond, apricot kernal, avocado, jojoba, evening primrose or sunflower.

Essential oils For one scalp treatment, choose up to three oils and use five drops of each for two tablespoons of base oil (for very long hair you may need more oil). Warm the blended oils by placing the container in a bowl of boiling water, and then massage into the scalp. Wrap with a hot towel, leave for 15 minutes and then shampoo.

HAIR PROBLEMS

Dandruff
There are two types: dry and the more common oily. It's not catching! It can be caused by factors such as chemical body changes, stress, poor eating habits or wrong application of hair products. Both flakey and dry scalps can be treated with essential oils. Use special dandruff shampoos and conditioning rinses and treat the scalp by gently massaging with oils to suit. Use a base oil formula with patchouli and tea tree. For a dry, itchy scalp try cedarwood and lavender.

Grey Hair
Grey hair is more porous and needs extra conditioning, particularly if it is chemically treated or coloured. Use a scalp formula for dry hair adding essential oil enhancers like chamomile to lighten or sage to darken any discolouration.

Hair Loss
Hair coming out in handfuls is often due to a hormonal imbalance, stress or anxiety, so the first step is to learn to relax. Any unusual thinning patch should be looked at by a trichologist but, as a general remedy, use a scalp massage with lavender and rosemary oils.

SCALP MASSAGE

This is a wonderful way to condition hair, stimulate the scalp and relieve tension. You can use these steps to treat your own hair but it's even more relaxing if you can persuade a friend to help, especially if you've got long hair.

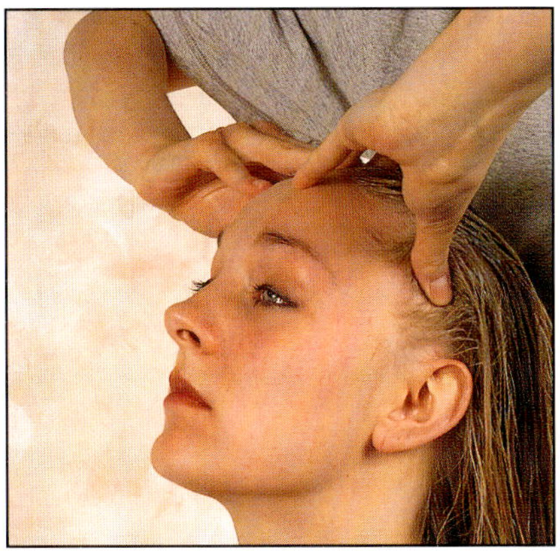

1 *Shampoo the hair and towel dry to absorb excess water. Comb through with a wide-tooth comb. Tilt your head back and pour some oil on to the hairline, massaging in with thumbs on the temple and fingers spread apart over the centre of the head.*

2 *Loosely run fingers and oil over the top of the scalp from front to back, lifting hair at the crown. Keep dipping your fingertips in the treatment oil to spread through the hair while massaging.*

3 *Massage the head with kneading movements. Grip and push (with fingerpads, rather than fingernails) against the scalp. The scalp should gently rotate against the skull. Concentrate on one area at a time, with the hands positioned on either side of the scalp.*

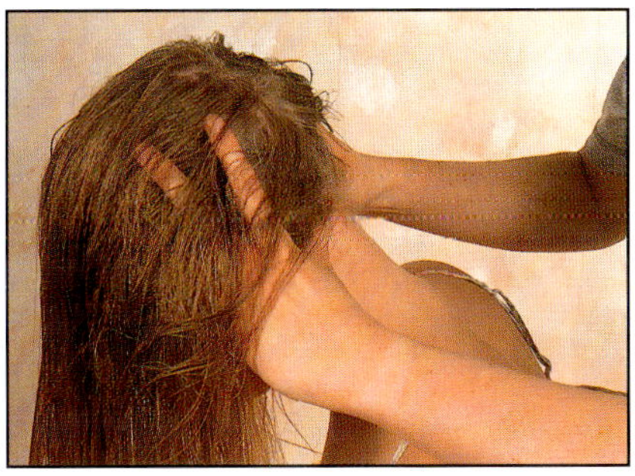

4 *Scalp massage works from front to back, from the forehead, frontal hairline, temples and sides, over the crown of the head to the base of the neck, following the natural flow of blood. If the scalp feels particularly tight then concentrate on areas where the scalp doesn't want to move. At the base of the skull, press firmly and push the whole scalp up toward the crown to release tension.*

5 *Pull any extra oil through the hair, working out from the roots to the tips. Make sure all the hair is well oiled, and then leave towel-wrapped for at least 15 minutes before shampooing.*

THE AROMATIC BATH

The relaxing and remedial properties of water and of massaging oils into the body were recognized in ancient Greek and Roman cultures, when bathing first became a daily ritual.

A bath with essential oils is one of the simplest and most effective aromatherapy treatments. It can be stimulating or relaxing, depending on the temperature of the water and whether you choose oils with uplifting or calming properties. In the bath, the therapeutic action of the oils is two-fold: they are absorbed through the skin, moisturizing the dermis and entering the circulatory system, and at the same time their aromas are inhaled, stimulating the brain and increasing your sense of well-being. An aromatic bath can detoxify the body, help problems like cellulite, joint stiffness, general aches and pains, colds and headaches, tone and condition skin, and relieve anxiety and tension.

RUNNING THE BATH

Bath temperature and the time spent in the tub are important. A cooler bath is more stimulating and warmer water relaxes. Very hot water is damaging, however: it causes blood vessels and capillaries to expand and increases the heart beat. You should particularly avoid hot water if you have varicose veins, haemorrhoids, high blood pressure or are pregnant. A 15–20 minute soak is long enough before skin cells over-hydrate and swell with water. Wait until the bath is almost full before adding the oils, as they evaporate so quickly.

OILS FOR THE BATH

Essential oils are the best way of making a bath both aromatic and therapeutic. They sink into the skin easily and at the same time impart their lovely herbal or floral fragrances. You can add drops of oil directly to the bath and they will float on the surface in a fine film and evaporate, giving you the full benefit of their aromas. Or if you want to absorb them more you can disperse them through the water by mixing with a base carrier oil such as sweet almond, apricot kernel, jojoba or evening primrose (these rich base oils all nourish and rejuvenate the skin in their own right).

Mix a bath oil with a combination of up to three essential oils, five drops from each, in one tablespoon of skin-softening base oil. Choose oils with similar or complementary effects so they do not counter-balance one another.

THE RELAXING BATH

To calm yourself after a fraught day or to prepare yourself for a peaceful night's sleep, turn your bathroom into a private sanctuary. Keep the light soft if possible, or use an eye mask or burn aromatic candles. Plants create an oxygenated atmosphere. Support your head with a bath pillow, close your eyes and inhale deeply. Concentrate on your breathing, empty your mind and let the oils soothe away the stresses and strains. After a 15–20 minute soak, get out slowly and wrap yourself in a large, warm towel.

Oils for Relaxation
Basil · Bergamot · Cedarwood
Chamomile · Frankincense
Hyssop · Juniper · Lavender
Marjoram · Melissa · Neroli
Patchouli · Rose · Sage
Sandalwood · Ylang-Ylang

Although these oils have a predominantly calming effect some can also be used to stimulate the circulation and lymphatic system, in particular lavender oil and also bergamot.

THE STIMULATING BATH

Best for the morning to get you started or to revive you before an evening out. Keep the water fairly cool and use an invigorating bath mitt to rub down and stimulate the circulation. When you've soaked, rinse yourself with water as cold as you can bear, either by splashing directly from the tap (faucet) or shower, or by adding more cold water to cool down your bath.

As you get out, either slap yourself dry to make the skin tingle or rub yourself vigorously with a towel.

Oils for Stimulation
Cypress · Eucalyptus · Fennel
Geranium · Juniper · Lavender
Lemon · Lemongrass · Peppermint
Pine · Rosemary · Thyme

THERAPEUTIC BATHS

Oils for Dermatitis
Chamomile · Hyssop · Lavender
Oils for Eczema
Chamomile · Geranium · Hyssop
Juniper · Rosemary · Myrrh
Oils for Psoriasis
Bergamot · Chamomile · Lavender
Oils for Arthritis/Rheumatism
Chamomile · Eucalyptus · Juniper
Lavender · Rosemary · Thyme

SHOWERS AND COLD RINSES

Invigorating jets of water are ideal for getting the blood pumping and there's no need to forego the benefits of aromatic oils. Skin tends to be sluggish in the cold winter months but sloughing off dead top layers can help regenerate cells and allow moisturizers to be absorbed more easily. Showers are ideal for smoothing skin with exfoliating rubs using wet salt, a loofah or a mitt to slough off the top surface of dead skin cells. A dry friction glove or loofah is too harsh for most skins so soften first in warm water. Soft bristle brushes can also help to get the circulation going with gentle massage on problem areas like hips and thighs. To keep friction brushes and mitts fresh always rinse and hang up to dry.

Essential oils can be used under the shower: try a base oil mixed with invigorating essences and with a clean face-cloth or sponge, pour on the oils and rub all over the body in circular motions whilst showering. To clear the sinuses and help coughs and colds, sponge the chest with a mix of eucalyptus and peppermint oils. A cold-water shower after cleansing improves the circulation and tightens skin pores.

Start off your shower or bath routine by whisking off dead skin cells with a friction mitt. Moisten the palm of the mitt with warm water or softening oils such as sweet almond or evening primrose. Concentrate on outer thighs, working from the knee in upward circular movements across the buttocks.

AFTER-BATH BODY TREATMENTS

Moisturizing oils and lotions applied after the bath or shower help to nourish the skin, keeping it soft and supple. As we get older our skin dehydrates since the oil glands do not produce as much oil as in youth.

Apply a body oil all over the body, starting from the feet and working right up to the neck and tips of the ears. Avoid talcum powders which clog the pores and tend to have a drying effect.

BODY-OIL FORMULA

Essential oils sink beautifully into warm damp skin. For a lasting effect, mix the three chosen bath essential oils, five drops of each, in two tablespoons of base oil. If you want to make up a larger quantity of body oil, use a concentration of three per cent essential oil in base oil.

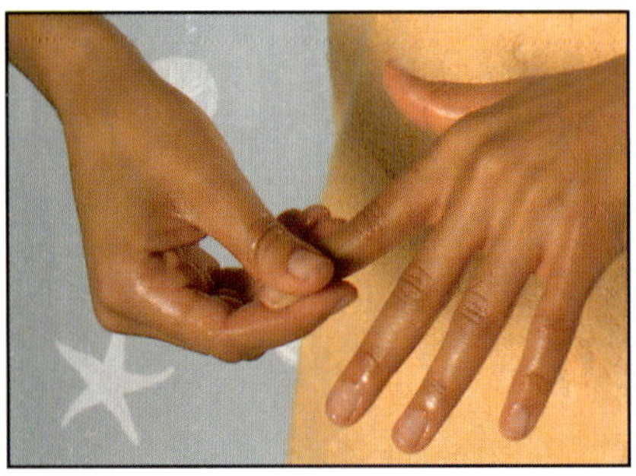

Above: Condition hands and nails with a simple finger-pulling exercise. Spread and stretch the fingers straight out; massage each finger with oils, working from the tip of the nails to the cuticles and up to each finger knuckle.

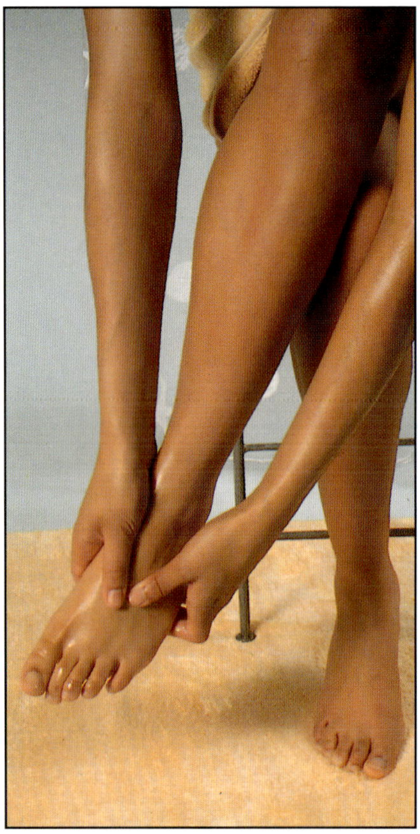

Right: Soften the feet after a bath by massaging between the toes and then working around the tougher skin and heel areas. Finish with sweeping movements all over to stimulate the circulation.

PROBLEM ZONES

Hands and nails take some rough treatment with everyday chores. The ideal time for a manicure or pedicure is after soaking in a bath when nails and skin are softened, making it easy to clean around the nail bed and to clip uneven nails without snagging.

Fragile or flakey nails benefit from a rich, nourishing treatment: rub them with apricot kernel, wheatgerm or jojoba oil. Restore hands with a soothing, moisturizing mix of one tablespoon of sweet almond oil and five drops each of patchouli, lavender and lemon.

Feet are often neglected until they hurt. Polish hard skin around heels and soles with a handful of damp salt or use a pumice stone. While in the bath, bend one knee, grip the toes and then work with the fingers massaging in an upward direction, from the toes to the heels and up the calves in order to stimulate blood flow and relax tired feet. Massage a body oil into the feet after a bath, shower or pedicure.

For a deodorizing and soothing footbath add three drops each of cypress and lavender to a basin full of water. Chilblains can be treated with a massage blend of three drops of geranium and a drop each of lavender and rosemary in one tablespoon of sweet almond base oil.

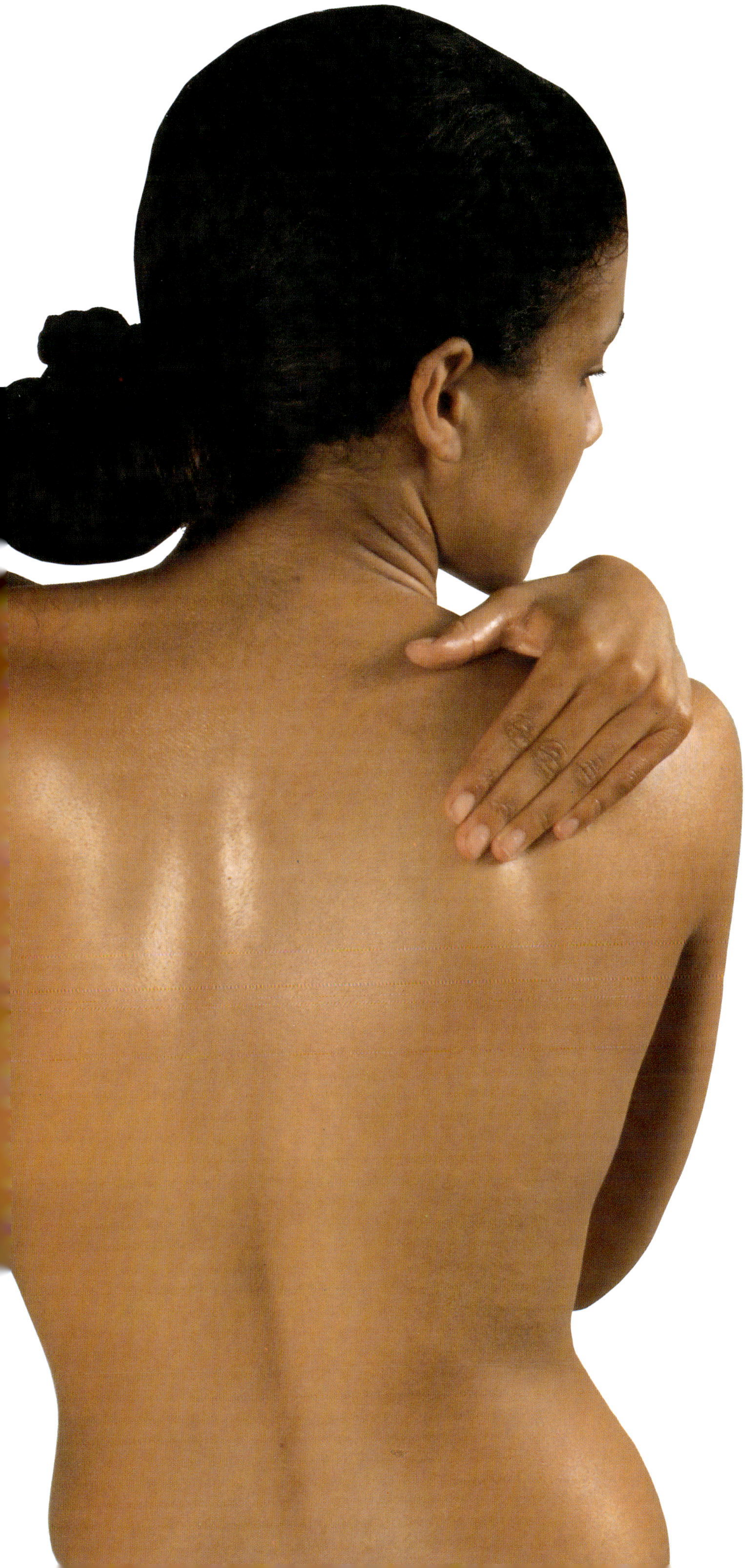

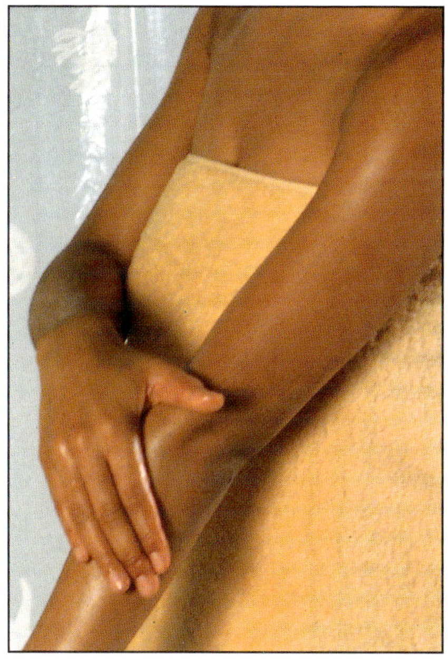

Above: Apply body oil to the arms with smooth upward strokes, concentrating on the elbows and upper arms where the skin is often rougher and drier.

Elbows can soon build up hard protective layers of grey, unsightly skin. A good softener for tough elbows is a sweet almond oil and oatmeal scrub. Mix three tablespoons of sweet almond oil with three tablespoons of fine oatmeal and mix to a paste with fresh milk or yoghurt. Smooth and rub over the elbows and any grey, goosey areas of skin around upper arms. Add six drops of fennel if arms are flabby. Another great elbow booster is the traditional recipe of cutting a lemon in half, squeezing out the juice and rubbing the elbows in the hollow of the lemon.

Left: When it comes to applying body oil, the back, neck and shoulders are often neglected because they are difficult to reach, but these are key areas for releasing tension and the skin needs to be nourished, so smooth as far as possible, or enlist the help of a friend.

IN THE REALM OF THE SENSES

The power of perfume to inspire romance has been known since the Babylonians, and perfume and flowers are still today the favourite gifts for lovers. Cleopatra's seduction of Mark Antony was carefully staged with a carpet of rose petals and rare and exotic scents in every conceivable form – even the sails of her barge were drenched in perfume to catch the breeze and announce her arrival.

The sense of smell is fundamental to our sensuality. Pheromones, chemicals secreted in human sweat, act as the most basic trigger to sexual attraction. The smells of flowers and plants are the plant equivalent of pheromones, irresistible to birds and bees and just as attractive to humans. We can use natural aromatic plant oils to relax, heighten our awareness, excite the senses and create a mood for love.

SETTING THE SCENE

Create a calming and sensual atmosphere with scented candles or a few drops of essential oil evaporated in a fragrancer or light-bulb ring. Dim the lights and turn up the heat.

Scent your lingerie or bedlinen by adding three drops of your favourite oil to the final rinse, or store them in drawers with aromatic bags or scented balls. Sprinkle drops of rose or jasmine on the pillows.

PREPARING YOUR BODY

Luxuriate in an aromatic bath or hot tub, or, better still, share it with your partner. After soaking, perfume your whole body with a rich body oil or use a strong concentration to dab pulse points such as wrists, temples and behind the ears and knees, and wait for your partner to discover these secret scented areas.

PARTNER MASSAGE

We are all sensual beings and yet at times we may need help to switch off from everyday concerns and tune in to our senses. The loving touch of partner massage is always enjoyable; it is relaxing and yet sensually stimulating – a total physical experience.

You can adapt the basic essential massage, using plenty of *effleurage* all over, deeper kneading for tense areas and light feather strokes with the fingertips to excite the surface of the skin. Avoid the lymph drainage movements as these are distinctly unerotic! Discover your partner's erogenous zones – explore the ears and feet and the inside of the forearms and thighs. Find some more. Be tender and loving, playful and creative – let your imagination guide you.

OILS FOR SEDUCTION

Most of the aphrodisiac oils combine well with each other, but be careful not to use too many together or they may clash and work against each other. Subtlety is the key to the art of seduction.

- *Clary sage* – sweet, sensuous and slightly intoxicating, but be careful as in high doses its sedative effect will inhibit sex drive.
- *Geranium* – a strong floral that both relaxes and uplifts.
- *Jasmine* – the heady floral fragrance boosts confidence and creates a luxurious atmosphere.
- *Neroli* – fresh and sweet, its fortifying effect helps overcome shyness and inhibitions.
- *Patchouli* – heavy and exotic, it is stimulating in small doses and heightens the senses.
- *Rose* – the quintessential oil for lovers. Rare and powerful.
- *Sandalwood* – woody, sweet and exotic with spicy undertones.
- *Ylang-Ylang* – the long-lasting floral scent gives a feeling of relaxed well-being, helpful for impotence or frigidity.

You can also try the warm, spicy exotics such as black pepper, ginger, cardamon, cinnamon or cedarwood, but be sparing with these as they can easily overpower.

Layer the scents by choosing just three or four and using them in different strengths and combinations for the room fragrance, bath, body oil or massage blend.

With a massage oil blended from floral and spicy aphrodisiac essences you can arouse the intimate senses of touch and smell simultaneously as you explore the skin and curves of your partner's body with strong smoothing strokes. Let the heady scents work their spell on the senses and emotions.

AMBIENT AROMAS

A lingering smell, whether pleasant or foul, is usually the first thing we notice when we enter a room, and it can strongly affect the way we feel. Fragrancing the home to cover unpleasant smells and delight the senses is an old tradition. For centuries the Chinese have suspended balls of jasmine flowers over the bed to clear the air and promote pleasant dreams, while posies of jasmine were handed to guests to refresh them on leaving banquets or dances. Lavender sachets placed in drawers and bowls of pot pourri to scent a room were particular favourites of the Victorians.

STUDIES AND OFFICES

Work-places are often stuffy and full of unpleasant smells, but if you work in an open-plan space fragrancing the whole area may not be a viable option. Inhaling a few drops of oil from a handkerchief is the most personal way of using a fragrance, or you can spray your immediate environment with a room spray, or add a couple of drops of oil to a cup of hot water on your desk.

Useful oils for the work-place are basil, rosemary, bergamot, lemon and melissa. Bergamot and lemon are particularly antiseptic, and lemon has the added advantage of helping efficiency. Basil stimulates a tired brain and rosemary is a great aid to concentration. Rosemary is also helpful in relieving headaches. If you are feeling overwrought try clary sage or juniper, but watch the dosage as too much will cause sleepiness.

LIVING ROOMS

The methods for fragrancing a room are many and diverse. Those that involve evaporating the oils, such as fragrancers/diffusers, water bowls, light-bulb rings and room sprays, are best for preventing ill-health, balancing the emotions and disguising unpleasant smells such as cigarette smoke or cooking odours. All these methods disperse the fragrance through a large space extremely quickly and effectively. For more lingering and subtle scents, blend your own pot pourri or, alternatively, use pomanders.

Rose, geranium, orange and lavender are pleasing and uplifting scents for a room, used individually or blended together.

For an exotic, intimate atmosphere use sandalwood or patchouli, or to unwind in the evening try geranium, lavender, sandalwood or ylang-ylang.

Perfumes for parties

Clary sage or jasmine will create a heady, "feel-good" atmosphere for a party, or use orange, lemongrass or neroli for a lighter, fresher touch.

For a festive blend choose from the spicier oils such as frankincense, cedarwood, sandalwood, cinnamon and orange.

BEDROOMS

Whether to ensure a restful night's sleep or to turn your bedroom into a place of passion, fragrancing the bedroom just before retiring will create an appropriate atmosphere. Rose, neroli and lavender are delightful all-purpose oils for the bedroom. Use lavender to freshen a musty spare room to make it welcoming for guests.

INSECT REPELLANT

Use tea tree, eucalyptus, melissa, lemon grass or the closely related citronella in a diffuser to keep insects at bay.

DISINFECTING

Vaporized molecules of any essential oil will neutralize airborne bacteria, but some – such as tea tree, bergamot, lemon, pine and lavender – are particularly antiseptic. Use these in a fragrancer or room spray. Pine, lemon and tea tree can be used on a damp cloth to disinfect surfaces in the kitchen or bathroom. Clear the atmosphere of a sickroom with bergamot, eucalyptus and juniper.

POT POURRI

To make your own pot pourri assemble fully-dried flowers, petals, herbs, leaves and other plant materials. There are no hard and fast rules about quantities and proportions, but an allowance of two or three tablespoons ground spices, two tablespoons orris-root powder, two teaspoons dried lemon, orange or lime peel, and six drops of essential oil to every four cups of dried plant material makes a pleasant balanced mixture.

If your pot pourri loses a little of its aroma over a period of time, it can be revived. Simply stir in another two or three drops of essential oil. And if the mixture loses its colour sharpness just stir in a few dried flowers such as miniature rosebuds, santolina flowers or tansy clusters.

Cottage Garden Mix

1 cup dried lavender flowers
1 cup dried rose petals
1 cup dried pinks (*Dianthus*)
1 cup dried scented geranium leaves
1 tbsp (15g) ground cinnamon
2 tsp (10g) ground allspice
1 tsp (5g) dried grated lemon peel
2 tbsp (30g) orris-root powder
3 drops rose oil
3 drops geranium oil

Mix ingredients together in a covered container, and set aside for six weeks. Stir daily to distribute the fragrances.

Woodland Mix

1 cup lime seedpods, or "keys"
1 cup cedar bark shavings
1 cup sandalwood shavings
1 cup small cones
1 tbsp (15g) whole cloves
1 tbsp (15g) star anise
1 stick cinnamon, crushed
2 tbsp (30g) orris-root powder
4 drops sandalwood oil
2 drops cinnamon oil

Mix ingredients together in a covered container and set aside for six weeks. Stir daily.

Ingredients which can be used to make pot pourri. From the left: dried rosemary, lavender, and bay leaves, dried ground orris-root powder, dried rosemary leaves, a selection of essential oils, ground cinnamon, dried chilies and cinnamon sticks, whole cloves, a blend of dried flowers, limes and lemons. The dried peel of citrus fruit is finely grated or chopped for use in the spice mixture.

THE STRESS FACTOR

Pressure can be stimulating, challenging and motivating, but if it builds up we may be left feeling unable to cope. Our response is often to deny the pressure and ignore the physical signs of stress such as fatigue, self-doubt, sleeplessness and headaches. If the symptoms and causes of stress are left untreated they will affect your general health and well-being, and can even lead to serious illness, such as ulcers, heart attacks and clinical depression, so it's important to start tackling problems at an early stage, before they erupt. De-stressing requires a positive tactical plan for learning how to cope and retain a balanced outlook on life.

Aromatherapy is a marvellous antidote to many of the problems associated with stress as it draws on the calming, relaxing, uplifting and restorative powers of particular essential oils, providing a natural and powerful alternative to tranquillizers, anti-depressants and other drugs. They can work to relax the nervous system and give it enough stimulation to rebalance and control itself, leaving you refreshed and ready to cope.

ANXIETY

Whether it's a temporary bout of nerves, caused by something like an impending examination or interview, or an ongoing response to a persistent problem, anxiety can be a debilitating response to stress. It prevents you from dealing effectively with a problem and makes you feel tense. Essential oils, when inhaled, stimulate the lymbic portion of the brain which is responsible for all our feelings of well-being and discontent. They can balance the senses before deep depression sets into a more serious state. Temporary anxiety can also trigger skin eruptions so watch your diet and boost levels of vitamins C and E and B-complex.

Anxiety can be alleviated with a combination of uplifting and calming oils.

Basil (uplifting) · Bergamot (uplifting) · Geranium (relaxing) Lavender (soothing) · Neroli (sedative) · Sandalwood (calming)

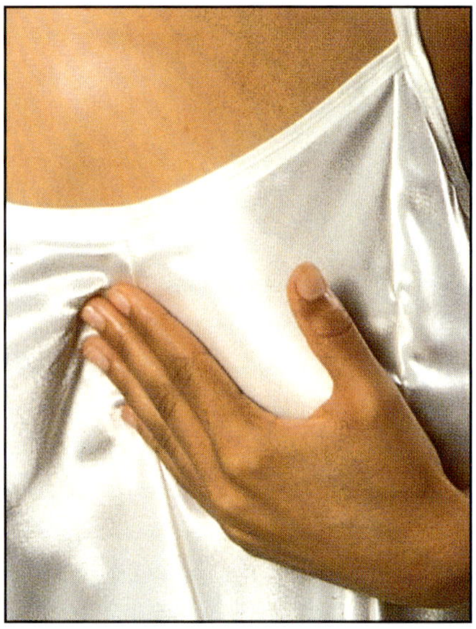

SOLAR PLEXUS STROKE

A marvellous way of unlocking tension by calming the main nerves that run through this area. Use your left hand (for calming) to stroke the solar plexus (located just below the breast bone) in anti-clockwise circles. Close your eyes as you do this and try to empty your mind. It can help soothe you even if you're clothed, but the effect is enhanced if you use a relaxing oil such as lavender or geranium. Try it while your bath is running, or when lying in bed before you go to sleep.

You can use the oils individually or mix them, using two relaxing oils to one uplifting oil. A good combination is basil, neroli and lavender. Stick to the same blend and proportions for bath and body, mixing five drops of each of the three oils in one tablespoon of base oil for the bath and two tablespoons for the body. All of the oils can be used individually in light-ring burners or fragrancers.

MILD SHOCK

This is a temporary form of stress, but the impact on the system can nonetheless be very strong, so a fast-acting remedy is needed.

Chamomile (calming) · Rosemary (stimulating) · Melissa (anti-depressant) · Neroli (relieves anxiety) · Peppermint (invigorating pain-reliever)

Use only two essential oils: both camphor and melissa work well individually with neroli, and peppermint has an affinity with melissa. Use a total of six drops in

$1^1/_2$ tablespoons of base oils, with smaller quantities of rosemary (for example, four drops of rosemary to six drops of melissa). For fast relief add four drops to a handkerchief and inhale.

Headaches

Often one of the first signs of stress and a regular affliction for many people. Cold compresses of lavender or geranium across the forehead provide pleasant relief. Add five drops of one oil to a small bowl of cool or warm water, soak a cloth in the water, wring out and lay it across the forehead. To help a headache caused by tension in the neck, try a sandal-wood compress across the neck. Scalp massage is soothing, or try the shiatsu headache relief steps.

Depression

The blues can hit us all from time to time, as financial, emotional or work problems hang over like a dark cloud. In the long term, if problems are not resolved, depression lowers the immune system, leaving you prone to a spiral of worstening mental and physical health. Essential oils can work wonders in lifting the spirits to prevent this.

Uplifting Oils
Bergamot · Cypress · Lemongrass
Rosemary · Sage

Soothing Oils
Chamomile · Geranium · Jasmine
Lavender · Marjoram · Neroli
Patchouli · Rose · Sandalwood
Ylang-Ylang

Start off with three soothing oils, and then drop one of these in favour of an uplifting oil to give an element of stimulation, and eventually introduce two

stimulating elements. Geranium, lavender and bergamot is a good combination. Use your formula for bath and body treatments.

Depression can be difficult to lift and if it persists you should consult a doctor or mental-health professional.

Mental Fatigue

When you feel near to exhaustion or cannot concentrate on one thing at a time because problems seem to be crowding in on you, listen to your body's warning signals. Take time to unwind (try a bath with any of the soothing oils listed for depression), clear your head with a walk or deep-breathing exercises, and then revive yourself with oils such as eucalyptus and pepper-mint. Rosemary is helpful in concentrating the mind and stim-ulating the body so that you can continue to work if you feel you really can't afford to take a break.

Insomnia

Sleeplessness is a common response to stress, as your mind and body refuse to let go enough to give you the rest that you need. Learning to relax has to be built into a daily pattern with a healthy diet, regular exercise, and a calming routine to wind down before bedtime. Try a milky drink or herbal tea last thing at night. Have a relaxing bath and massage, drawing on the sedative powers of up to three of the following oils:

Chamomile · Cedarwood
Frankincense · Hyssop · Lavender
Marjoram · Melissa · Neroli
Orange · Patchouli · Rose · Sage
Sandalwood · Ylang-Ylang

Breathing aromatic vapours in the bedroom helps to induce sleep:
Frankincense is warming and relaxing, and encourages tranquillity. Use in a fragrancer.
Lavender's relaxing quality can be harnessed by dabbing two drops on the edge of your pillow.
Marjoram has excellent soporific properties. Release in a light-bulb ring or fragrancer.
Neroli's wonderful floral fragrance is also sedative. Two drops on the pillow or in a fragrancer will help disperse unpleasant thoughts.

HEADACHE RELIEF

Headaches and migraines are common symptoms of stress. Follow these simple shiatsu steps to sweep away the tension, relieve pain and clear the head. The sequence is quick and easy to administer; it can be used anywhere and friends and colleagues will be grateful for the relief of their pain. You can perform some of the steps on yourself, though the healing touch of another's hands is more effective.

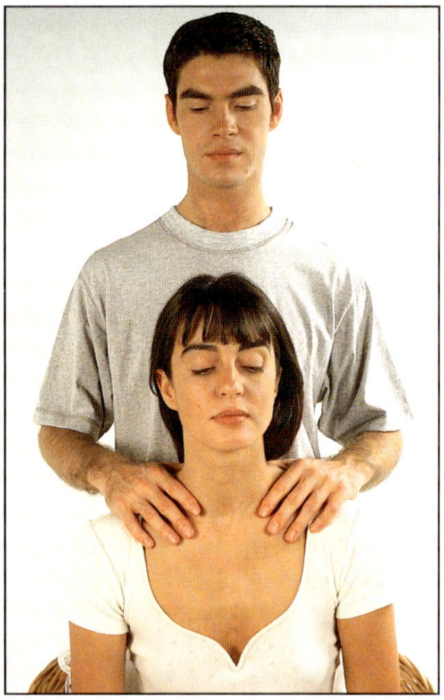

1 *Establish communication with your partner by placing both hands loosely on either side of the neck. Gently massage the shoulders; this helps to relax the breathing and creates a feeling of well-being.*

2 *Right: Tilt the head to the side and support with the palm of the hand so that the neck muscles can relax. Place the forearm across the shoulder and apply gentle downward pressure; hold for 5–10 seconds and then repeat with the other side. This movement is particularly good for opening the meridians running along the shoulders and neck.*

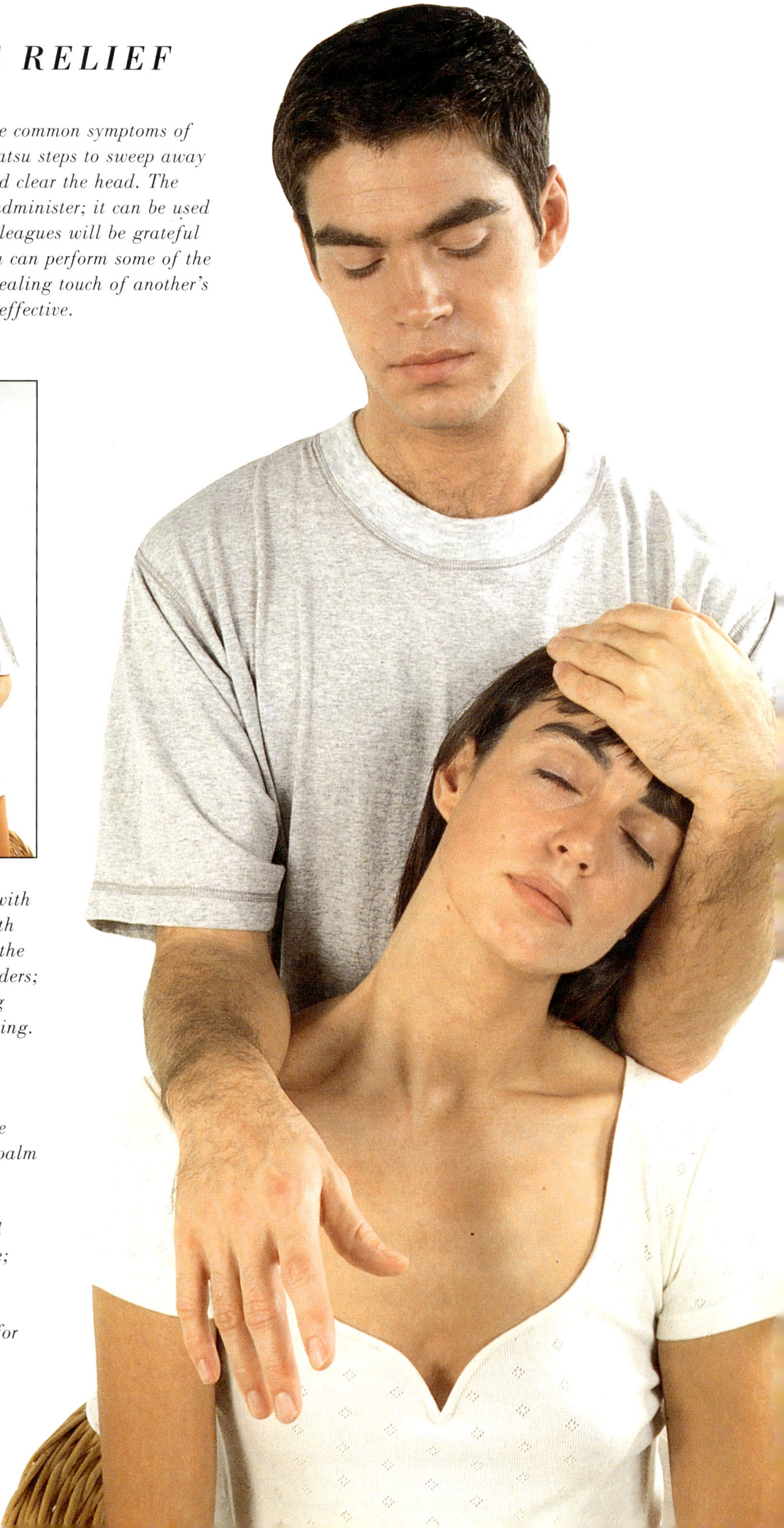

3 Supporting the head with the left hand, work with thumb and forefinger applying gentle pressure from the base of the neck to the nape. Hold at the nape of the neck for five seconds and then release the built-up tension.

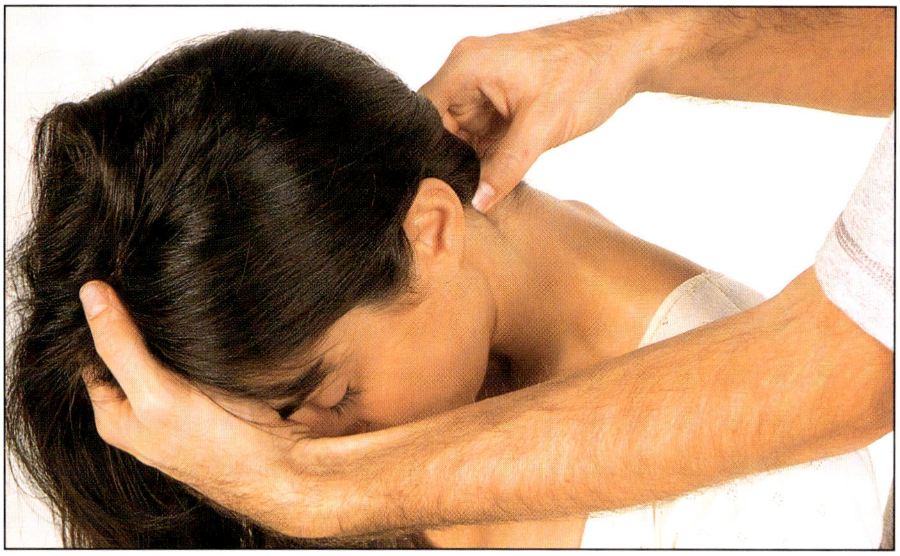

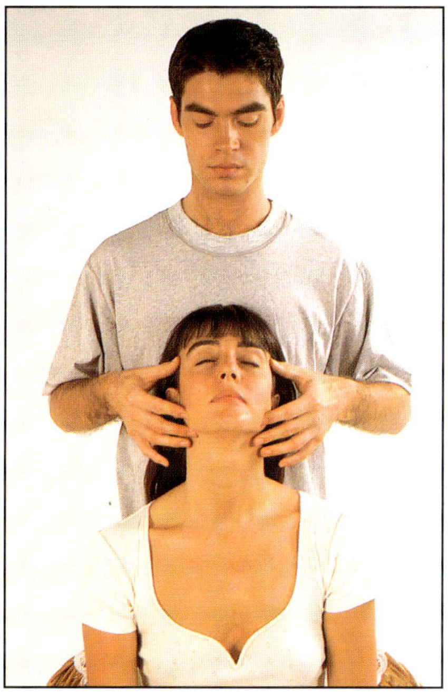

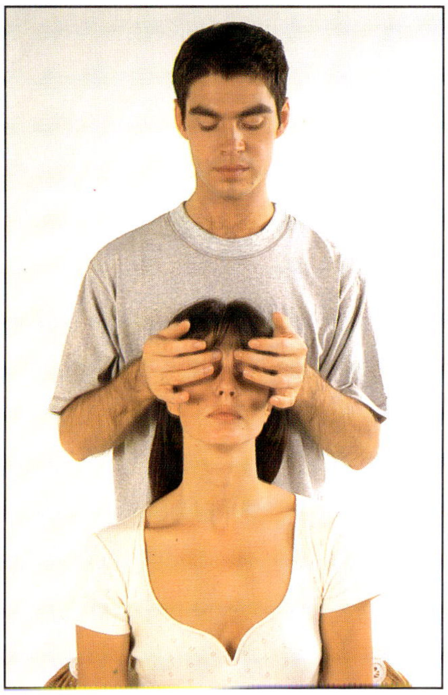

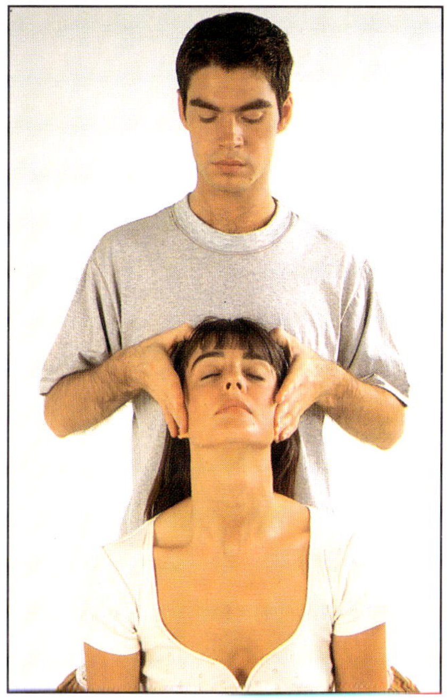

4 Tilt the head back slightly, supporting it on your chest. Place your thumbs on the temples with the fingers loosely resting on either side of face. Gently rotate the thumbs in small forward movements.

5 Find the pressure points just above the inner corner of each eye. Apply gentle pressure with the middle fingers to help disperse the pain. Hold the pressure points for five seconds.

6 Position your thumbs on either side of the head just above the hairline – approximately two inches (5 cm) apart – with palms pressed flat along the sides of the face. Press the thumbs evenly back along the top of the head. This is a sensitive but invigorating movement to end the treatment.

A shiatsu treatment is usually very effective for relieving stress and headaches but if your headache persists, consult a doctor. Avoid the treatment during pregnancy.

LEARNING TO RELAX

Relaxation is a prescription for health. Along with a well-balanced diet, an exercise programme, and a positive attitude towards recognizing and coping with stress, relaxation will help you balance the body and mind, even when you're worried and under pressure.

Exercise combats stress. The physically fitter you are, the better the body and mind can cope. Even burning off steam without losing self-control can be beneficial: a competitive racket sport, thumping the pillow, or going for a long walk can all release built-up tensions. Times of stress and emotional upset can make the body cry out for certain foods. Resist chocolate, cakes, ice cream or addictive stimulants like caffeine or nicotine. Feed the mind with a high intake of vitamin C from fresh fruit and vegetables, in particular citrus, berry and tropical fruits, and all of the B-complex vitamins.

WHOLE-BODY RELAXATION

Lie down straight with shoulders relaxed and even on the floor. Arms should be straight with elbows alongside the waist, palms turned upward. Relax your head and close the eyes. Breathe in deeply; allow your body to sink into the floor. Breathe out slowly; relax. Focus attention on your breathing; listen as you inhale and exhale and see how quiet the deep breathing can become.

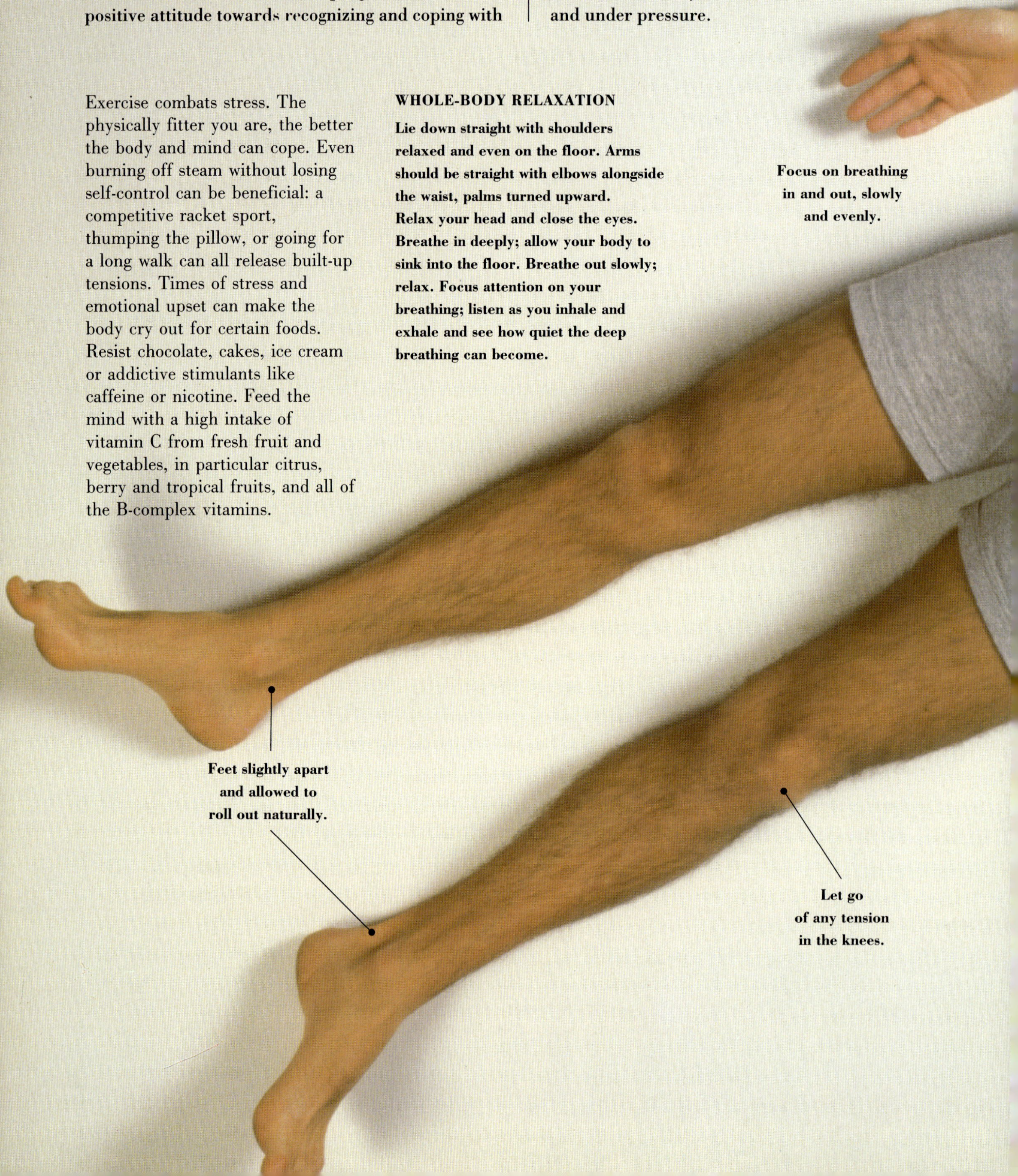

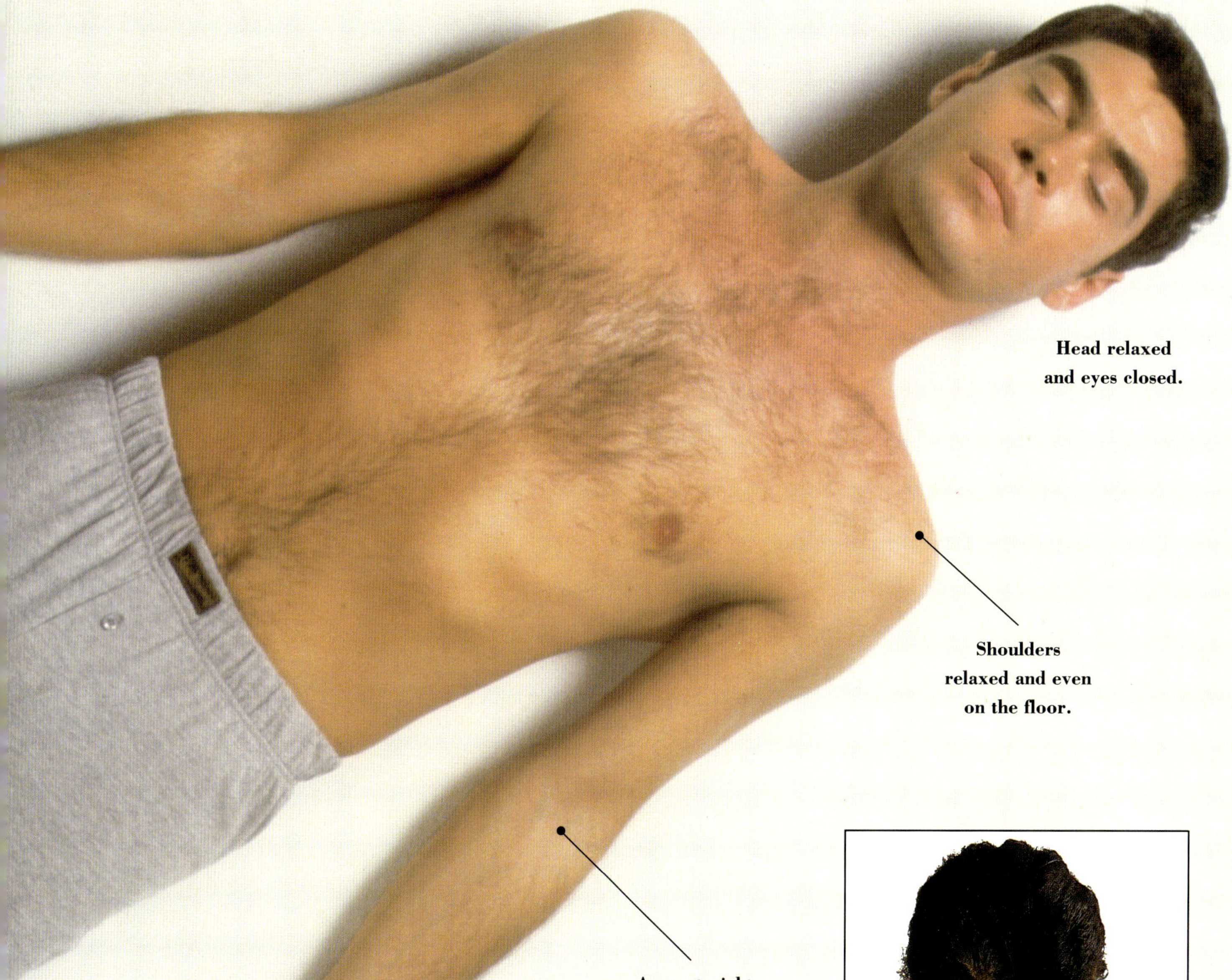

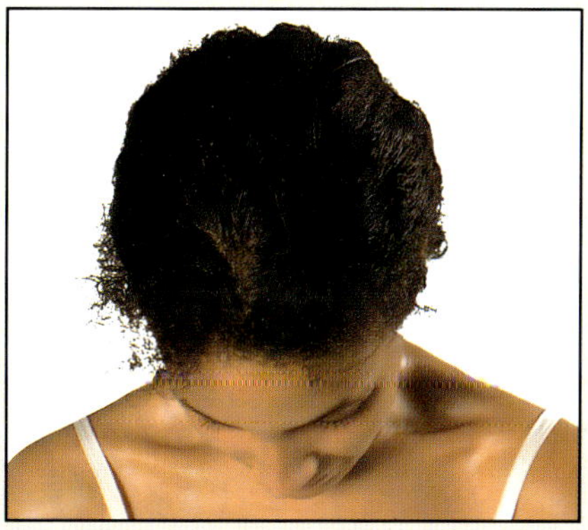

HEAD ROLL

To help ease tension around the head, neck and shoulders, try a simple head roll to start the relaxation process. Begin with head straight down toward the centre of the chest and roll the head slowly round to the right shoulder and then raise the chin. Lower the head and roll back to the centre and continue round to the left shoulder. Repeat the movement five times.

SHIATSU

The roots of shiatsu can be traced back over 5000 years to the ancient Chinese forms of medicine such as acupuncture and acupressure. However, it is a modern Japanese therapy, which fuses traditional Eastern practices with Western techniques of osteopathy. Literally translated the name means finger pressure – *Shi* (finger) and *Atsu* (pressure), although elbows, knees and feet are also used to press along the body's network of meridian lines and pressure points, releasing blocked channels of energy. It is an holistic method of alleviating pain and promoting health in the whole body.

SHIATSU MERIDIANS

Shiatsu is a manipulative therapy which uses static pressure applied to specific points and lines all over the body. The lines along which many of the points are situated are known as meridians. These meridian lines, which have been described as "channels of living magnetic energy", flow throughout the body and connect the main vital organs. It is this vital energy, known as "*Ki*", which keeps our bodies active, and the quality of our *Ki* depends upon our mental, emotional, physical and spiritual conditions.

An imbalance in a person's vital energy levels may manifest itself as a back problem, headache, or in many other ways. By working along the meridians, the therapist summons energy to the place most vulnerable and disperses the trapped energy from the areas where it is congested, thus restoring balance to the whole body.

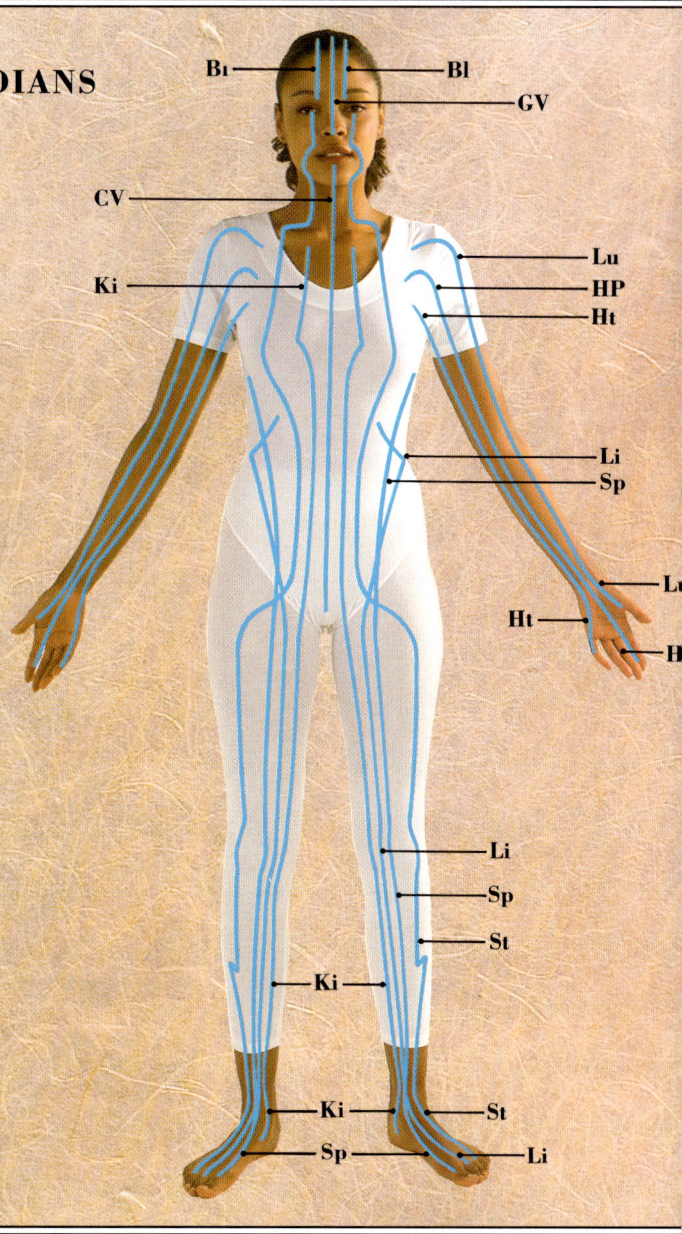

Giving a Shiatsu Session

If your partner closes their eyes, this can make the session a special time to relax and switch off the world. There is no need to talk during a treatment as the communication of touch can say so much more. One of the fundamental principles of shiatsu is to have simultaneous touch from both hands. With a two-hand connection a circuit is created, bonding the giver and receiver. To keep this link, one hand is stationary – the support hand – and plays the role of listening and comforting your partner, while the other hand – the messenger hand – moves and does all the work. The amount of pressure from both hands will vary with the area of the body you are working on. The messenger and support hands change roles many times throughout a session. What you are trying to achieve is two points of contact merging and feeling like one to both therapist and partner.

Even as a beginner use your senses of looking, asking, listening and touching. Listen to your partner's needs and ask about symptoms before giving a treatment. Your motivation to help can be felt by your partner through the hands, transforming the simplest techniques into a caring bond. Before giving a shiatsu treatment, calm the mind, as any tension will transmit itself to your partner.

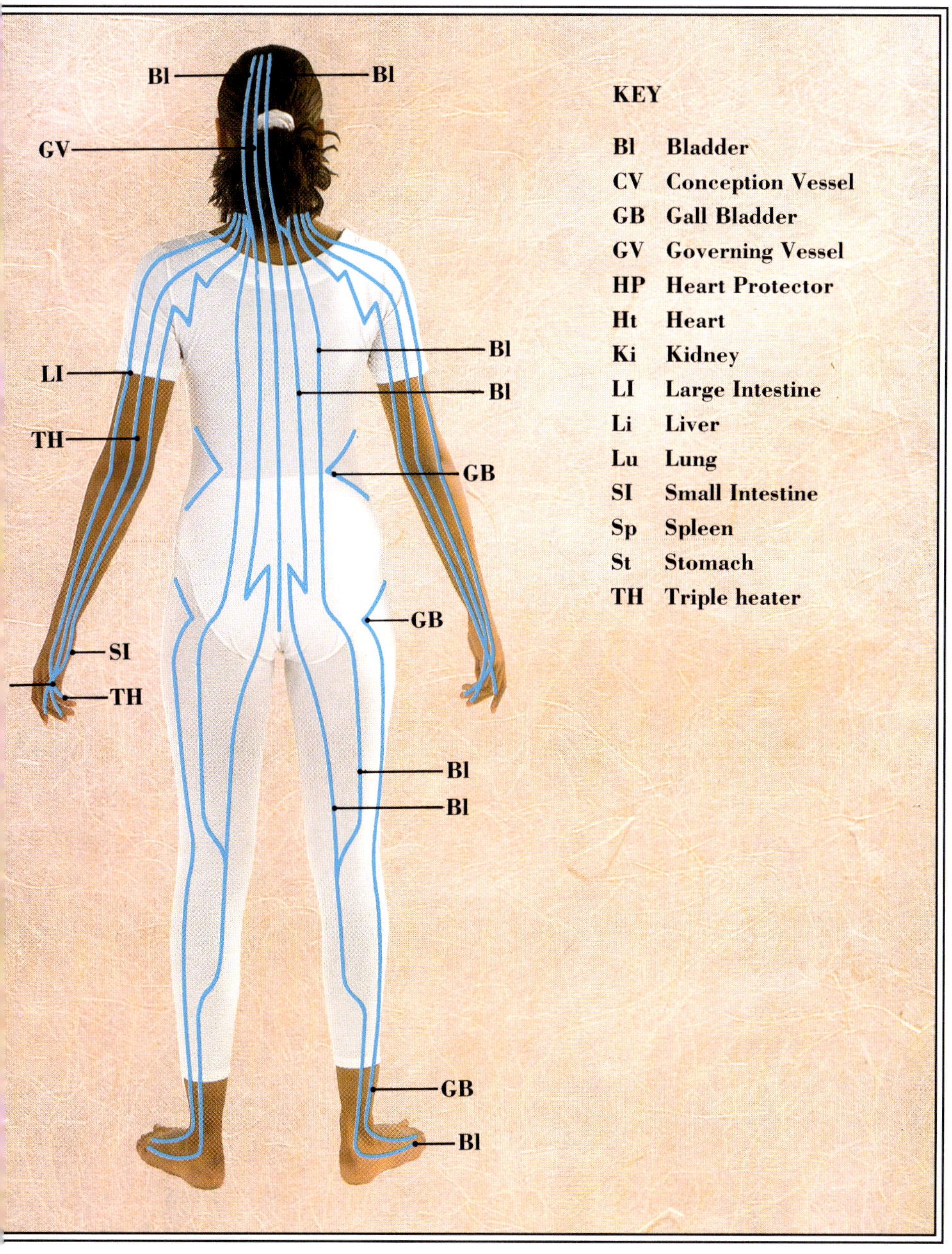

The Hara

The *Hara* is one of the most powerful energy centres of the body. In shiatsu terms it is known as the *Tanden*, and is located below the navel in the lower abdomen. It is the physical centre of the body and features prominently in all shiatsu treatments. The *Hara* incorporates the *Yin* (Earth) force flowing up the front of the body, and the *Yang* (Heaven) force flowing down the back merging into the lower abdomen. By focusing all movements from this centre, you can give harmonious and supportive treatments. Develop an open-posture principle in which your *Hara* is physically and energetically behind all your movements. This enables weight to be used instead of force. The simple rule is if you're not feeling comfortable and relaxed your partner will become aware of this.

Breathing is very important when stretching and applying pressure. Breathe in deeply and exhale as you move into a stretch, encouraging your partner to do the same.

Healing Energy

The aim of shiatsu is to balance the body's "*Ki*" energy levels. The rocking, kneading and stretching techniques are most effective in unblocking the congested areas. If your partner has a low energy level, and is generally fatigued, then slow, deep, static and perpendicular pressure will be more effective in strengthening the energy flow. Holding certain points from one to ten seconds is a general guideline but use your intuition as to how long you hold.

Practical Points

A shiatsu session normally lasts up to an hour. It is advisable to wear loose clothing so that your movements aren't hampered. The receiver is also clothed, but avoid bulky or constricting clothes that would impede contact with the body. Generally, the therapist works on the whole of the body and having discovered your problems may suggest simple practical exercises for home use to help the process of recovery. The effects of shiatsu may be felt immediately or later on in the same day, but if painful reactions are later experienced then your practitioner should be contacted. There are no two people with similar mental and physical complaints and the number of sessions will depend upon the individual's needs.

Shiatsu helps to keep open the communication between body, mind, emotion and spirit.

THE MAIN TECHNIQUES

PALMING

Palming is the simplest and most widely used technique in shiatsu. Palm pressure is gentle but firm, creating a supporting and soothing effect on any tense or vulnerable areas of the body.

Allow your hands to be relaxed so that your fingers can follow the contours of whatever part of the body you contact, then lean your body-weight through your palm, holding and waiting for the connection between your two palms. Lean back and without breaking contact, slide your hand along the body and lean forward again, creating stationary and perpendicular pressure.

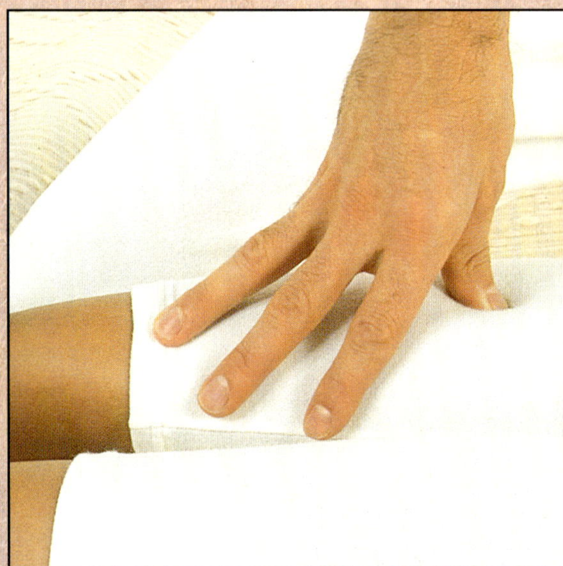

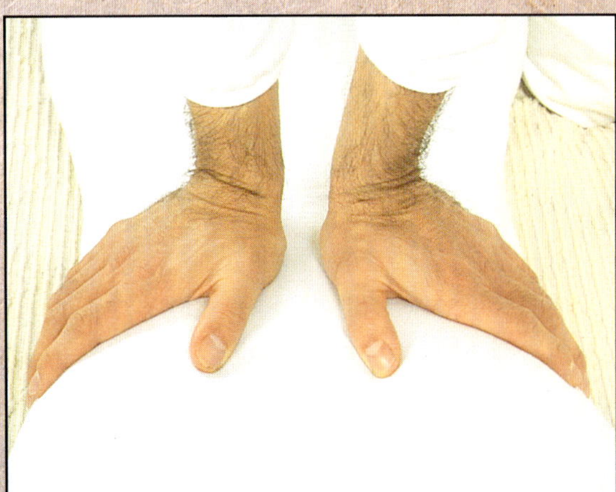

THUMBING

Thumb pressure is far more precise and penetrating than palming, and is used for working the points along the meridians. Place your thumbpads on the points. Use your extended fingers for support, so that the thumb remains straight. Lean your body forward so that most of the pressure is transferred through the thumbs. Make sure your nails are quite short to practise this technique or you may hurt your partner.

SIMPLE SHIATSU SESSION

The following sequences have been arranged so that each technique can flow smoothly into the next. Ideally the whole treatment should be experienced as a complete uninterrupted unit, not as a collection of separate movements. To achieve this, always maintain contact with your partner and make the transitions from one technique to the next with ease and fluency.

YANG

Position yourself at your partner's side. Take some time to centre yourself, clearing your mind so you can focus on your partner.

1 *Gently and firmly lay your hand on the small of your partner's back. This contact is an important time for both receiver and giver to attune to each other's energy. Use this time to assess the needs of your partner; feel the quality of the energy, physically, emotionally and spiritually. This can focus your intention in all the techniques to follow.*

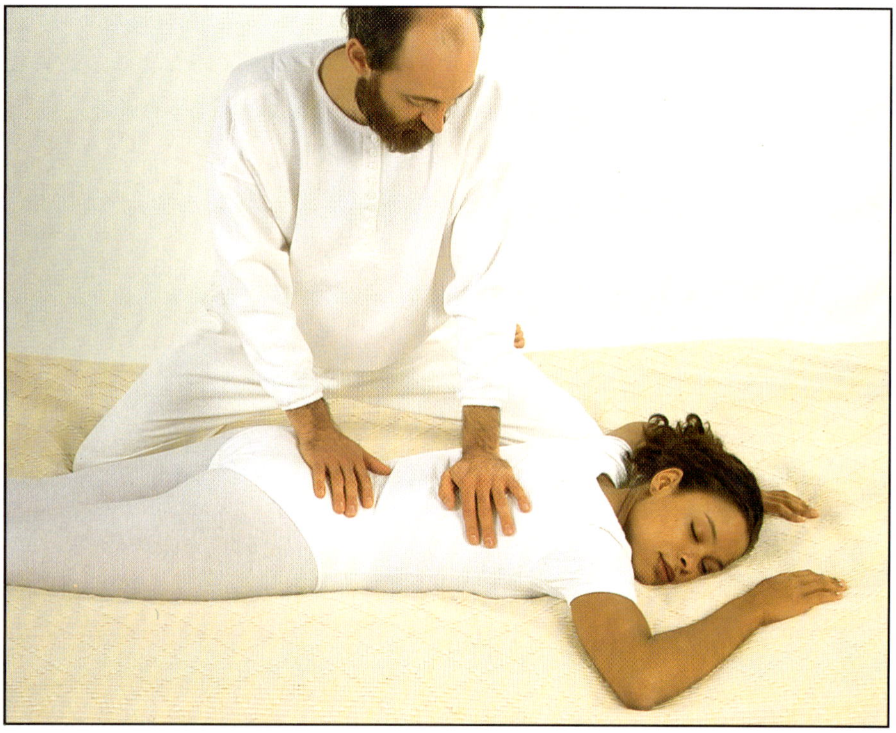

Left: This technique helps to disperse tension throughout, thus encouraging the energy to flow. It is useful to observe how your partner's body is moving. You will quickly be able to diagnose areas which may need more attention by simply observing which parts of the body are not moving as you rock.

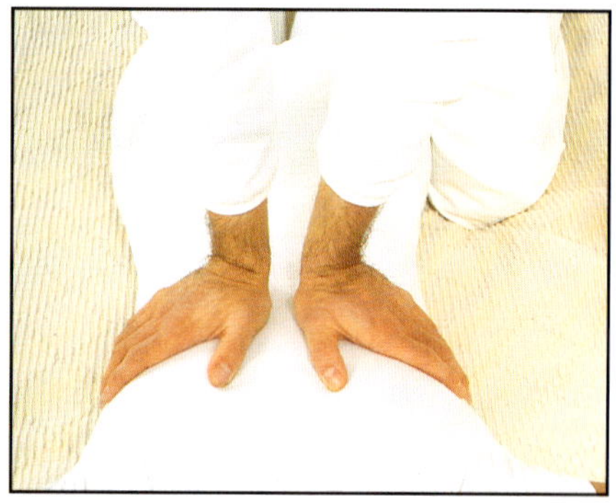

2 *Turn to face your partner and place the heel of the hands in the space between the shoulder blade and spine. With your knees apart begin to rock back and forth from your* Hara *(centre of the lower abdomen) and let the movement transfer through your hands so your partner's entire body moves in a wave-like motion. Continue to perform the rocking technique, working all the way down to the sacrum (lower back), moving the hands down the back in sequence.*

Repeat two or three times and then repeat the same movements on the other side of the spine.

3 *Come up on to one knee, keeping an open posture. Placing your palms no higher than shoulder-blade level, on your receiver's "out" breath, bring your body-weight forward applying perpendicular pressure.*

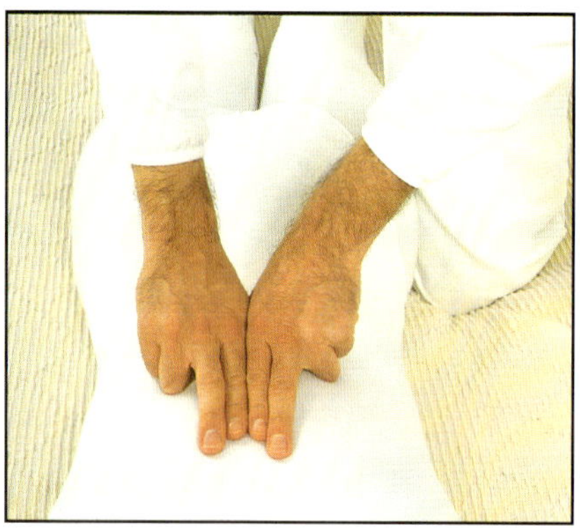

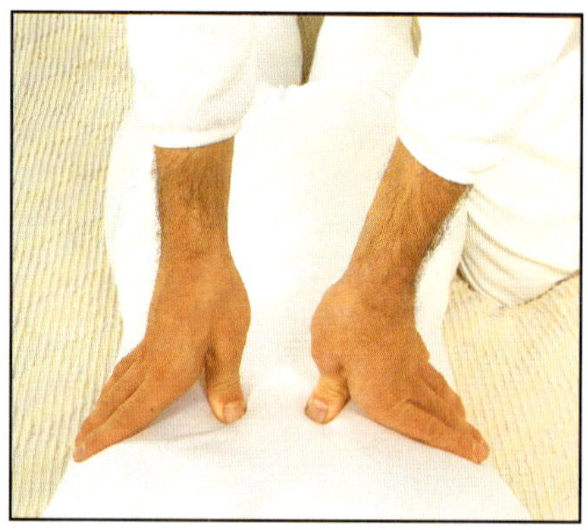

4 *Work down the back, moving a palm's width each time, and moving your body position to maintain perpendicular pressure. As you move below the ribs you may want to decrease the pressure slightly, as the internal organs are less protected here.*

5 *Having relaxed the back you can now locate the bladder meridian, which has a structural and energetic relationship with the nervous system. Measure two fingers' width from the centre of the spine and one hand's width down from the top of the shoulder.*

6 *Using the thumbs apply pressure at the points between the ribs. Thumb pressure is much more concentrated than palming. If you are unsure about how much pressure is appropriate, simply ask your partner how it feels.*

LEGS

1 *Move your body down level to and facing your partner's legs. With your support hand on the lower back (sacrum), your messenger hand rocks and kneads simultaneously down the near-side thigh and calf several times.*

2 *Next palm down the leg, avoiding pressure on the backs of the knees.*

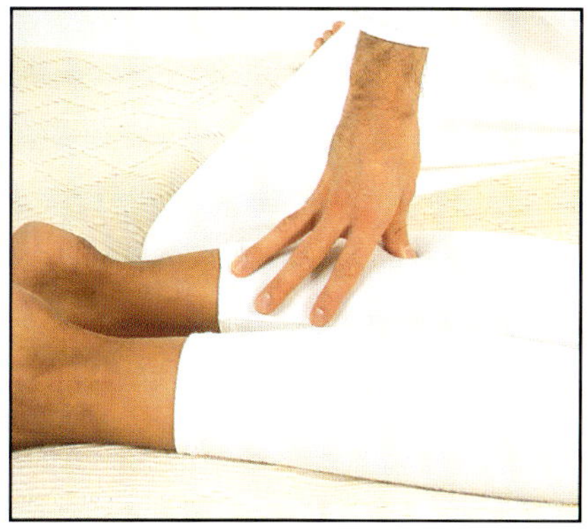

3 *Now thumb down the path of the bladder meridian. Depending on the length of the leg you may need to adjust your position. To avoid over-stretching, you can also move your support hand to just above the knee.*

4 *With one hand on the sacrum, use the other hand to bring the foot gently back toward the buttocks, taking into consideration the leg's stretching capacity. Hold for a few seconds and then release.*

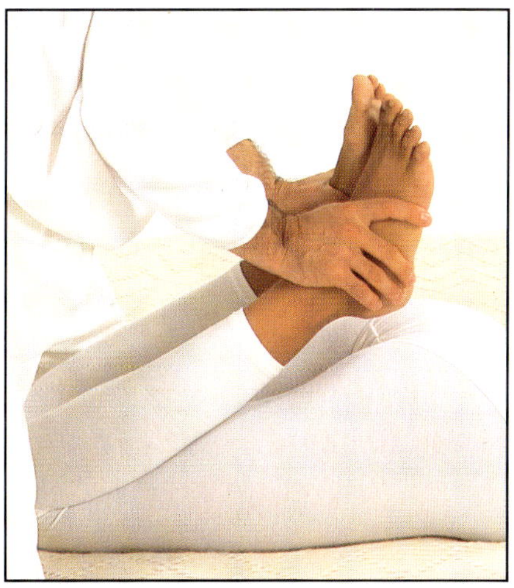

5 *Clasp both feet together and bend the legs, bringing the feet toward the buttocks. Hold this position for a few seconds and notice which foot goes closest to the buttocks to assess pelvic balance.*

6 *Cross this foot under the other foot and press them toward the buttocks on the "out" breath. Hold for several seconds then reverse the crossed legs and bend toward the buttocks once again.*

After these movements you will probably notice that the bending capacity of the legs has become more equal and the pelvis is more balanced.

Move round to the other side of the body and repeat the rocking, kneading, palming and thumbing on the other leg.

WORKING ON THE FEET

When "walking" on the feet make sure your position is well balanced as excess pressure or loss of balance may cause your partner pain.

Both the giving and receiving of pressure on the feet is very relaxing, and perfectly safe and easy to perform as long as you don't make any sudden or unexpected movements. Keep your body upright and relaxed as if you were going for a walk.

If there is too much of a gap between your partner's ankle and the floor, or the feet don't turn inward symmetrically, you may have to leave this technique out.

1 *Turn around so that your back is facing your partner and stand on both feet, shifting your weight from foot to foot. Control the movement from your hips.*

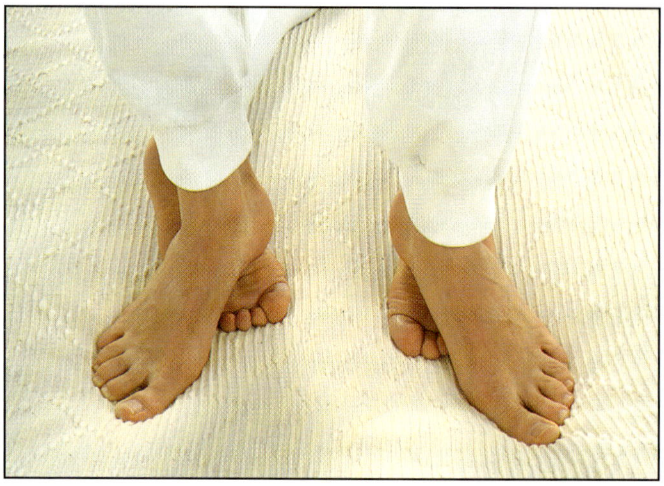

2 *Keep in one position and shift your weight back and forth from left to right several times and repeat on various areas of the feet.*

As with all the techniques, remember to observe your partner's facial expressions and breathing. These are obvious indications of how the receiver is feeling. Don't forget at any time that it's a human being you are working with, not just a body.

General pressure to the sole of the feet helps to stimulate the internal organs through the reflex areas and meridians. Walking on the feet is particularly good for grounding someone with too much mental activity.

YIN

Gently assist your partner to turn over into the supine position (on their back). Lying in this position we can be psychologically, emotionally and physically open, but we can also feel quite vulnerable. It is important to bear this in mind as you work to establish reassurance and trust.

Position yourself at your partner's side. Place one hand on your partner's waist, and the other hand on the abdomen with the heel of the hand just below the navel. Take a moment to listen with your hand to the rhythm of your partner's body. Feel the rise and fall of your partner's breath. Share the breath. This establishes a level of trust so

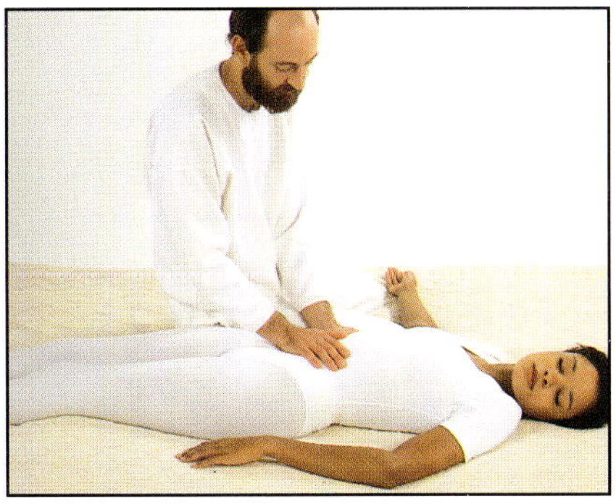

that you will be sensitive to any vulnerabilities or pains that might become manifest.

Gently palm around the abdomen in a clockwise direction. If you can coordinate your movements with your partner's "out" breath you should find that your partner gradually allows you to apply more pressure.

LEGS

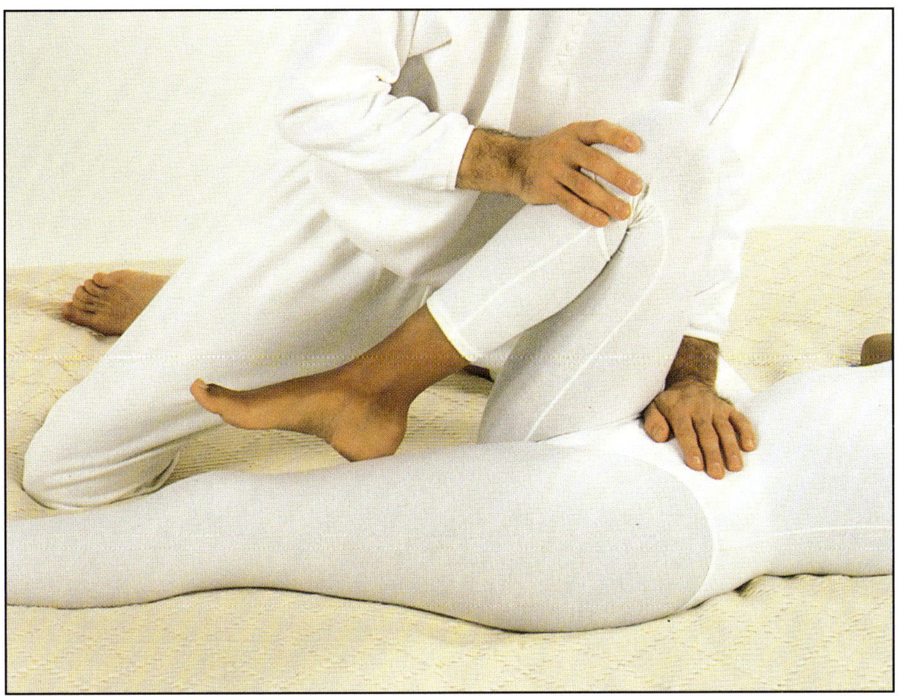

1 *Change your position to face across your partner, placing your uppermost hand on the* Hara *(lower abdomen). Place your other hand on the inside of the knee allowing your fingers to curl under the joint. Leaning back, simply allow your body weight to lift the leg. There should be very little effort involved in this. As the leg comes up, slide your hand from the inside of the knee to the upper shin.*

2,3 *Rotate the leg out from the body, focusing on the hip joint. Start with small circular movements and, releasing the leg as much as possible, gradually increase the rotation to the fullest range.*

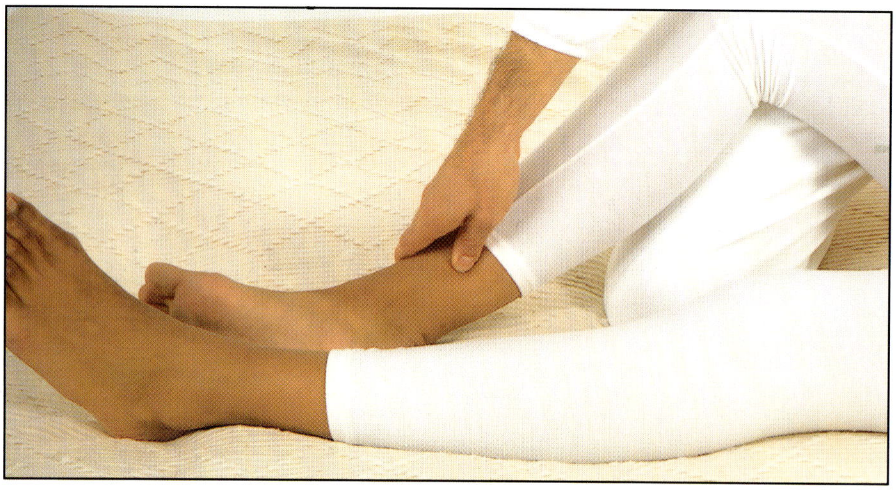

4 *Place the leg so that it rests comfortably with the toes at the level of the opposite ankle, with the spleen meridian uppermost. You may prop it up either with your leg underneath or a cushion. Palm up the inside of the calf along the* Yin *meridians to the knee. Thumb up the calf from the ankle to the knee.*

5 *Use your forearm to continue the pressure up the thigh. Rotate the leg once again then move down to your partner's feet.*

CAUTION

Do not give shiatsu on the spleen meridian during pregnancy if miscarriage is likely. Do not work below the knees in any pregnancy.

6 *Cup underneath the ankle in one hand. Place the other hand on top of the ankle. Bring your* Hara *into contact with the sole of the foot. Grasp it firmly and rotate your body from the hips. As you move your partner's body will move with yours.*

Repeat all the techniques on the opposite leg and complete this section of the sequence with your hand back on your receiver's Hara.

SHOULDERS, ARMS AND HANDS

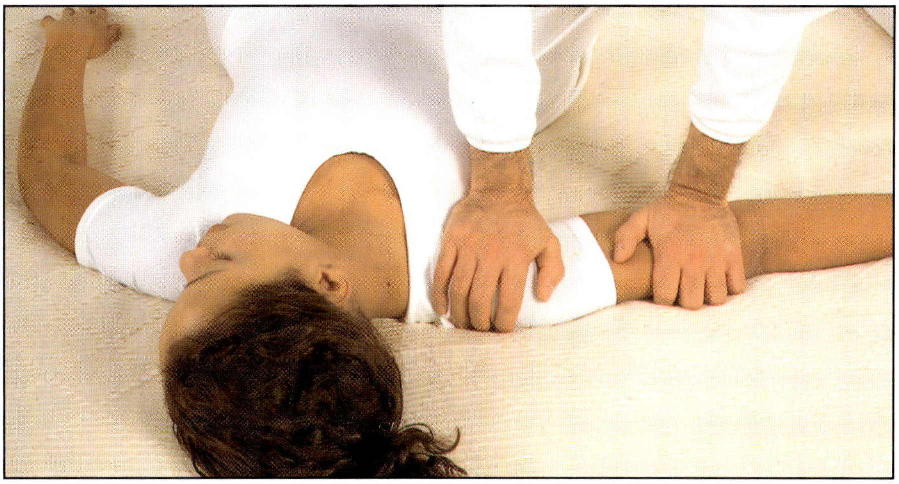

1 Kneeling up, bring your free hand to your partner's furthest shoulder. Place your other hand on the near shoulder. Your arms should now be crossed. With your receiver's "out" breath, lean forward on your hands, opening up the shoulder and chest area.

2 Maintain the support of the shoulder nearest you. With the other hand, as in the treatment of the legs, begin by gently rocking and kneading the arms from the shoulder to the hand. Position the arm at right angles to the body with the palms facing up. Then palm down the arm, avoiding pressure on the elbow joint. Follow by thumbing down the middle of the arm to the palm along the heart protector meridian.

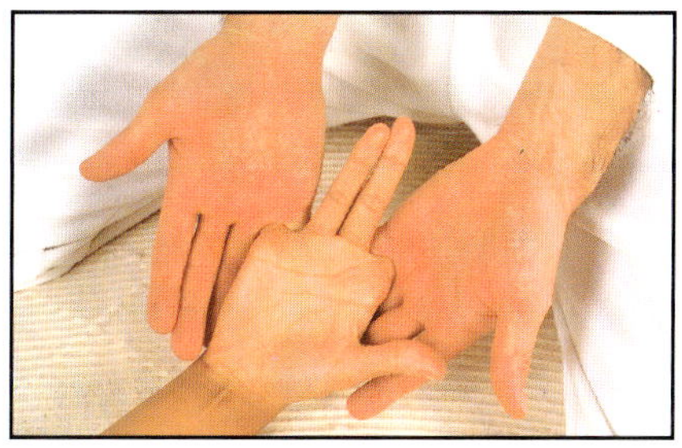

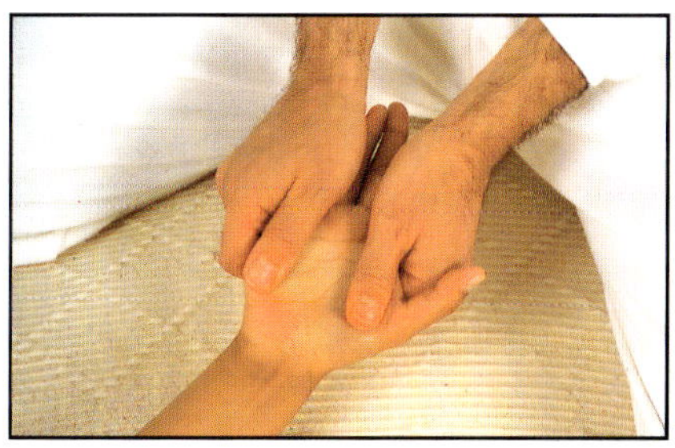

3 Grasp the wrist and move your body so that your outstretched leg is parallel to the arm, your foot resting comfortably against the upper torso. Gently lean back stretching the arm, giving counterpressure with your foot.

4,5 Link your little fingers inside your partner's index and little finger to stretch open the palm. Your thumbs are then naturally placed to work into the palm with circular movements.

6 *Place the support hand on the shoulder, tucking your thumb into the armpit. Hold the wrist, lift and loosen the shoulder joint.*

7 *Step forward with your outside leg, stretching your partner's arm to the floor above the head.*

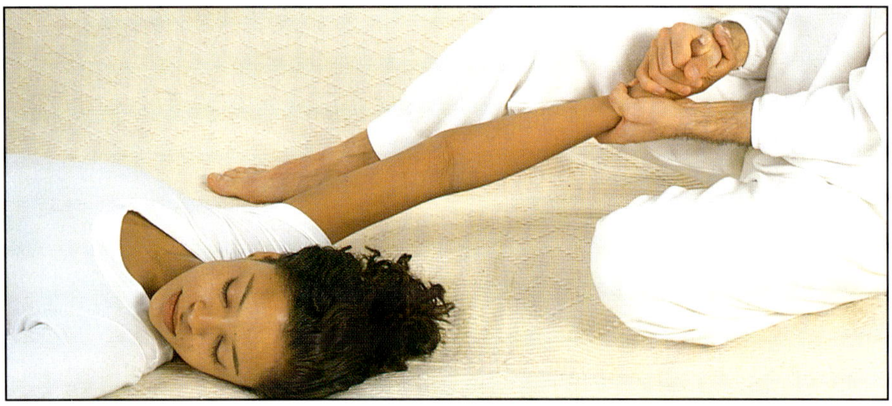

8 *Move your body so that by gently leaning back your partner's arm is stretched, using a two-handed grip to the wrist.*

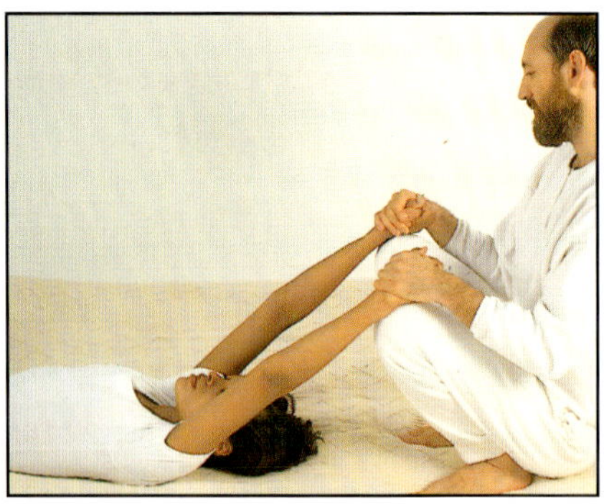

9 *Pick up your partner's other hand and rest the forearms on your knees.*

10 *Lean back, allowing your knees to slide up the forearms to the wrists. On the "out" breath, this makes a powerful stretch for the shoulders and chest.*

Repeat all the techniques on the opposite arm: stretching, rocking, kneading, palming, thumbing and massaging the hands.

To finish return again to the Hara *(lower abdomen area). Simply holding for a minute or two gives your partner time to feel the changes that have occurred.*

Break this final contact very slowly and if appropriate cover your partner with a blanket. Give your partner some time to experience how he or she feels.

One of the great benefits of shiatsu is that it encourages self-awareness. It is often in the still moments of a session, when we are just being with our partner, that both giver and receiver can have the most profound insights.

USEFUL ADDRESSES

AROMATHERAPY

ORGANIZATIONS

These organizations will provide information about accredited therapists and courses. Please always send a stamped, self-addressed envelope when writing.

Aromatherapy Organizations Council
3 Latymer Close
Braybrooke
Market Harborough
Leicester LE16 8LN
Tel: 0455 615466

Holistic Aromatherapy Foundation
16 Sunnyhill Road
London SW16 2VH
Tel: 081 664 6150

International Federation of Aromatherapists
Department of Continuing Education
The Royal Masonic Hospital
Ravenscourt Park
London W6 0TN
Tel: 081 846 8066

International Society of Professional Aromatherapists
41 Leicester Road
Hinckley
Leicestershire LE10 1LW
Tel: 0455 637987

National Holistic Aromatherapy Association
PO Box 18622
Boulder
CO 803-0622
USA
Tel: (303) 258 2791

International Federation of Aromatherapists
197 7th Street
Midland
Ontario L4R 3Z4
Canada

Australian Natural Therapists Association
PO Box 522
Sutherland
NSW 2232
Australia

Institute of Clinical Aromatherapy
PO Box 734
Skellenbosch 7599
South Africa

MAIL ORDER SUPPLIERS

Nina Ashby Aromatherapy
29 Arundel Road
Croydon CR0 2ER
Tel: 081 689 3949

Culpeper Ltd
Hadstock Road
Linton
Cambridge CB1 6NJ
Tel: 0223 894054

Kobashi
50 High Street
Ide
Devon EX2 9RW
Tel: 0392 217628

Eve Taylor
22 Bromley Road
London SE6 2TP
Tel: 081 690 2149

The Body Shop
Watersmead Business Park
Littlehampton
West Sussex BN17 6LS
Tel: 0903 731500

Neal's Yard Remedies
15 Neal's Yard
London WC2H 9DP
Tel: 071 379 0141

Rachel Stewart
Avalon Aromatics
20 Springfield Road
London SW19 7AL
Tel: 081 947 1567

The Body Shop (USA)
45 Holsehill Road
Cedar Knolls
NJ 07927
USA
Tel: 1 800 541 2535

Quintessence Aromatherapy
PO Box 4996
Boulder
CO 80306
USA

Just Good Scents
206 Collingwood Court
Edmurton
Alberta T5T 0H5
Canada

Essentially Yours
Factory 35
65-7 Canterbury Road
Montrose 3765
Victoria
Australia

RESIDENTIAL TREATMENTS

Henlow Grange
Henlow
Bedfordshire SG16 6DB
Tel: 0426 811111

Grayshott Hall
Headley Road
Grayshott
Nr. Hindhead
Surrey GU26 6JJ
Tel: 0428 604331

Champneys
Wiggington
Tring
Hertfordshire HP23 6HY
Tel: 0442 873155

HAIR AND BEAUTY THERAPY TREATMENTS

Michaeljohn/
The Ragdale Clinic
25 Albermarle Street
London W1X 3FA
Tel: 071 629 6969

Michaeljohn
14 North
414 North Camden Drive
Beverly Hills
CA 90210
USA
Tel: 310 278 8333

SHIATSU

The British School of Shiatsu-Do
188 Old Street
London EC1V 9FR
Tel: 071 251 0831

The Shiatsu Society
14 Oakdene Road
Redhill
Surrey RH1 6BT
Tel: 0737 767896

Clive Ives
45 Broderick Road
London SW17 7DX
Tel: 081 672 0477

The American Shiatsu Society
44 Pear Street
Cambridge
MA 02139
USA

FURTHER READING

AROMATHERAPY

Micheline Arcier, *Aromatherapy*, Hamlyn, 1990

Patricia Davies, *Aromatherapy: An A-Z*, C. W. Daniel, 1988

Judith Jackson, *Aromatherapy*, Henry Holt and Co, 1986

Marguerite Maury, *Guide to Aromatherapy: The Secret of Life and Youth*, C. W. Daniel, 1989

Shirley Price, *Practical Aromatherapy*, Thorsons, 1987
Aromatherapy for Common Ailments, Gaia Books, 1991

Maggie Tisserand, *Aromatherapy for Women*, Thorsons, 1989

Robert Tisserand, *The Art of Aromatherapy*, C. W. Daniel 1977
Aromatherapy for Everyone, Penguin, 1990

SHIATSU

Saul Goodman, *The Shiatsu Practitioner's Manual*, Infitech Publications, 1986

Shizuto Masunaga, *Zen Shiatsu*, Japan Publications, 1977

MASSAGE

Everyone enjoys massage. From babies to the elderly, from sportsmen and women to friends and lovers, all can benefit from this powerful form of communication. An effective aid to relaxation, massage helps to smoothe away stress, unknotting tense and aching muscles, relieving headaches and helping sleep problems. But massage is also invigorating: it improves the functioning of many of the body's systems, promotes healing and tones muscles, leaving you with a feeling of renewed energy. By mastering a few simple techniques and sequences, you will learn the language of touch – a valuable gift for yourself and others.

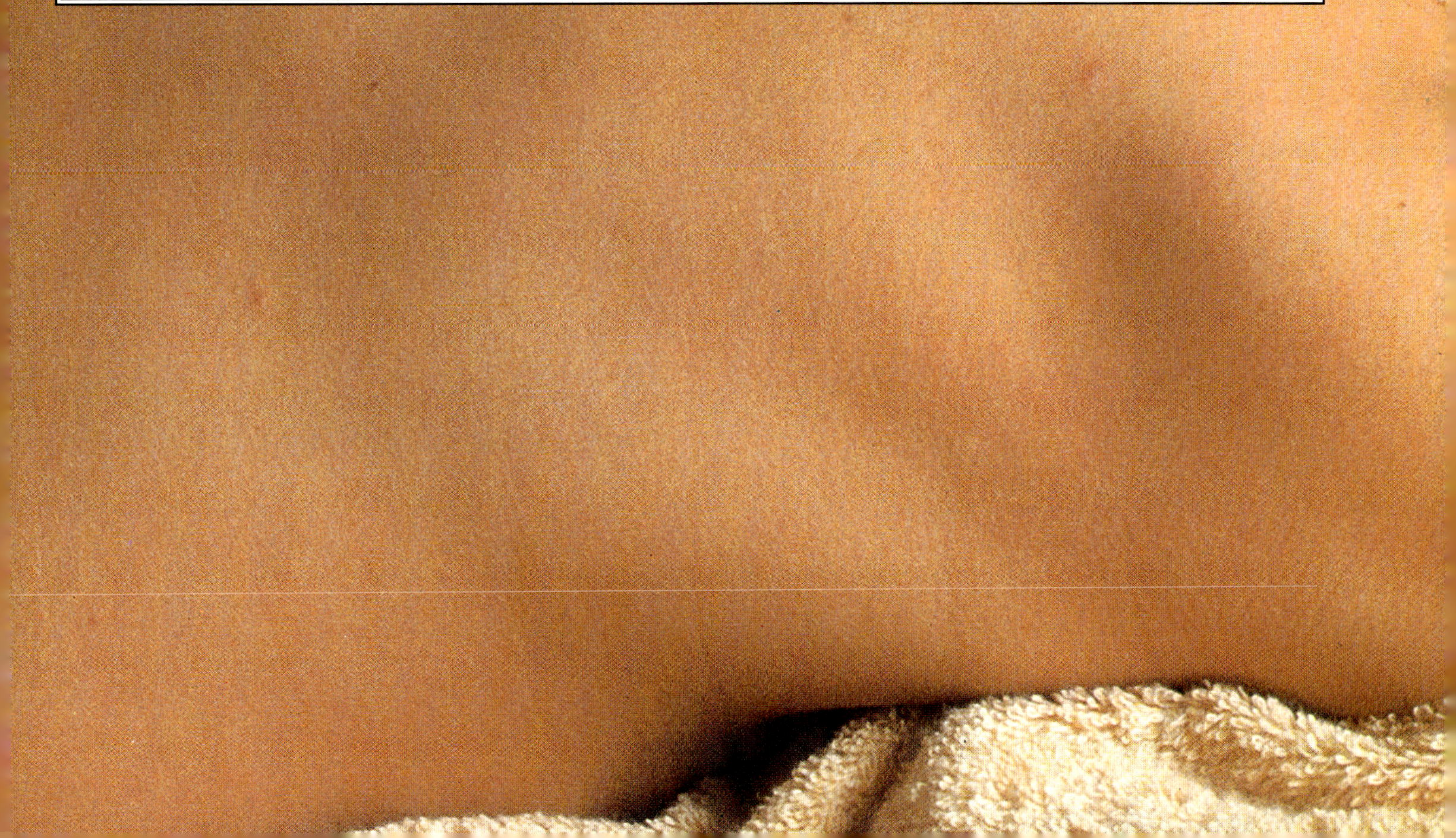

THE HUMAN TOUCH

The sense of touch is a powerful and highly sensitive form of communication. It is a natural reaction to reach out and touch, whether to feel the shape or texture of something, or to respond to another person, perhaps by comforting them. A mother cuddles her baby, family pets are stroked, sexual partners caress, and if we accidentally knock a limb we instinctively "rub it better".

To touch someone can mean various things in different cultures. There are many social restraints which inhibit touching in public. For us, a formal handshake, nod of the head, and even a peck on each cheek are all recognized forms of greeting, and yet you can carry them out without showing any real emotion. Indeed, our rather formal approach to physical contact is contrary to our most basic instincts and needs. Fortunately, we are now rediscovering the healing power of massage and other touch therapies which have been understood in other cultures for thousands of years.

THE DEVELOPMENT OF MASSAGE

History shows that although the early Egyptians made references to the benefits of massage, the Chinese were among the first to recognize its healing value at around 3000 BC. Roman and Greek philosophers and physicians prescribed it both for its restorative powers after battle and for general preservation of the body and mind. Although the Romans believed in its curative powers, the art of massage also became part of a daily ritual for relaxation. After bathing, oils would be used to anoint the body from head to toe, followed by a luxurious massage.

Herbalists throughout history have used massage to heal body and soul, both by applying balms and by laying their own hands on the afflicted to expel evil spirits and clear the mind. It wasn't until the eighteenth and nineteenth centuries, though, that massage became popular throughout Europe, thanks to the work of Per Henrik Ling (1776–1839). Ling was a Swede who travelled to China and returned with a detailed insight into their massage techniques. From these he developed his own system of massage based on a variety of movements, involving pressure, friction, vibration and rotation.

This wealth of practical knowledge soon spread, and medical and non-medical professions worldwide began exploring the benefits of massage. This eventually established the basis of massage today, which in many ways remains much the same now as those early Swedish techniques.

Along with basic massage we are now experiencing a revival of interest in many of the ancient arts which place such great importance on touch. These include aromatherapy, reflexology and shiatsu – all distinctive natural therapies which have a specific role to play in "alternative" health-care.

Below left: This Greek stone relief from the fourth century BC shows the physician Aesculapius treating a patient by "rubbing", as recommended by Hippocrates.

Right: As Europe emerged from the Middle Ages, massage once again became part of the bathing ritual, as shown in this sixteenth-century German woodcut of a public bath house.

EFFECTS OF MASSAGE

Massage can stimulate and relax the body and the mind. The skin, blood and lymphatic systems are stimulated, which boosts circulation, aids cellular renewal and removes toxic wastes. As tense muscles relax, stiff joints loosen and nerves are soothed, an all-over feeling of relaxation and well-being comes about.

The Nervous System

The nervous system is a highly complex network which relays messages from the brain to the rest of the body. The part of the nervous system which regulates many physiological functions leaves the brain at the base of the skull and runs down the spinal cord, protected by the spine's bony vertebrae. Millions of nerve endings run throughout the body, controlling much of the way it functions. Depending on the depth of the massage movements used, the nerve endings can be stimulated or soothed.

The Skin

With massage comes an increase in blood circulation. This helps the exfoliation of superficial dead skin cells, tones the skin and encourages its renewal process. Massage helps maintain the collagen fibres, which give skin its elasticity and strength, and keep wrinkles at bay. The activity of the sweat and sebaceous glands, which lubricate and moisturize the skin, is regulated.

Muscles

With the increase in blood flow, the blood's vital nutrients circulate more efficiently. Massage is popular with sportsmen and women because it can improve muscle tone, restore mobility, and ensure the elimination of waste products after exercise. With regular massage, strains and sprains heal more rapidly, while calf cramps and stiff muscles can become a thing of the past. Massage before an exercise session will help loosen and warm up the muscles, or afterwards it will ease sore, aching limbs.

Circulation and Lymphatic Systems

By dilating the blood vessels, massage increases the blood circulation. A good circulatory system means that an efficient supply of the blood's constituents, including oxygen and nutrients, reaches the billions of individual cells. This is vital for the healthy functioning of the whole body, from the muscles to internal organs such as the kidneys and liver.

At the same time the increase in blood circulation helps accelerate the lymphatic system, which absorbs and eliminates waste substances. Unlike the blood circulation, which has the heart to pump it round, the lymphatic system has no pump of its own and is dependent on muscular action for its efficiency. Massage is an important means of speeding up the flow of the lymph, encouraging a more effective filtering and elimination of waste throughout the body. An efficient lymphatic system provides the body with a strong immune system to fight against infections and disease.

Digestion

Massage mobilizes the digestive system so that the processes of assimilation and elimination are improved, helping problems like constipation and flatulence. The digestive system is quick to respond to stress, and the reduction in anxiety and tension which comes with regular massage has a regulating effect on the digestion.

THE BASIC TECHNIQUES

When many people think of massage they picture the vigorous pummelling and slapping often associated with puritanical health spas. In truth, firm massage can be highly beneficial without causing discomfort. Alternate firm and gentle flowing strokes to create a combination that will alleviate tension and muscular aches and pains whilst energizing and invigorating the body.

In Swedish massage there are four basic types of movement. Familiarize yourself with these different techniques before beginning the step-by-step, whole-body massage.

EFFLEURAGE

Effleurage describes long, soothing, stroking movements using the flat of the hand (or fingers if working on small areas). These are often used to apply oil evenly to the body. You can use one hand on its own or with the other providing support on top of it, both hands simultaneously, or one hand alternating with the other.

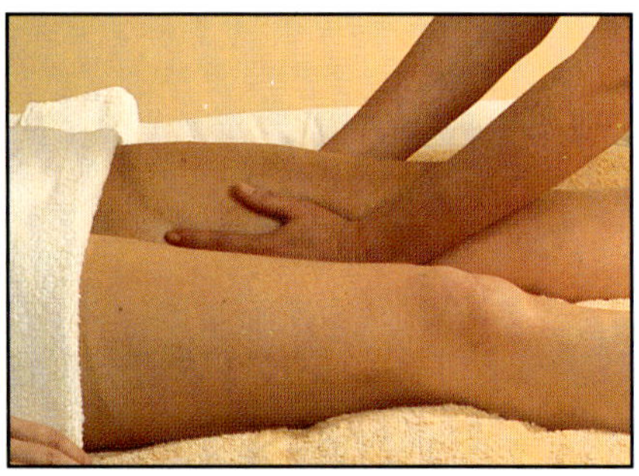

Relax the hands and mould them to the contours of the body. Apply slightly more pressure when you take the stroke in the direction of the heart to improve circulation and lymph flow. If you are working away from the heart, keep the pressure firmer on the return stroke. The movements should be fairly slow and continuous. Keep the hands in contact with your partner between strokes.

Effleurage is used to start off a massage, soothing the nerve endings and helping your partner get used to your touch. It is used again at the end of a massage for a relaxing finish. In between, *effleurage* movements provide an important link between other more stimulating strokes and are used to make first contact with a new area of the body. If you feel hesitant about what to do next, you can always insert some *effleurage*, so the continuity is not lost.

You repeat *effleurage* strokes several times. Each time try to start the first complete stroke with fairly light pressure, then apply slightly more pressure with the next complete stroke. Where there are larger muscle areas, such as the thighs and back, you can apply the most pressure for a more stimulating effect.

PETRISSAGE

Petrissage describes a number of movements which involve various ways of kneading, rolling and picking up the skin and muscles. These firm and strengthen the structures by stimulating the deep layers of tissue, and increasing the supply of blood to the area. They also improve the flow of lymph.

Generally a single group of muscles, or an individual muscle, is worked on at one time. The basic kneading action is very similar to kneading dough.

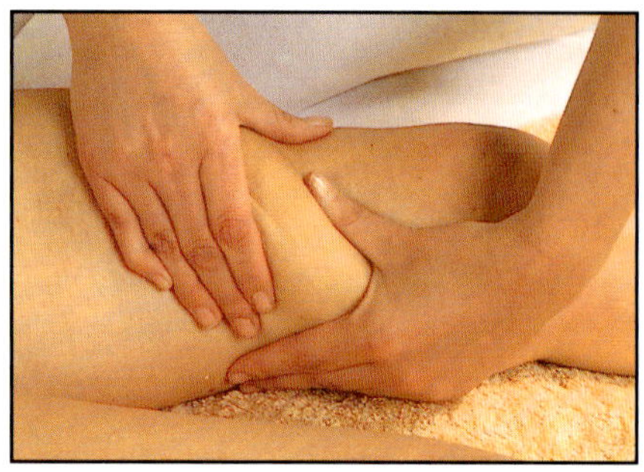

For *petrissage*, start with your fingers pointing away from you, press down with the palm, grasp the flesh between fingers and thumb and push it toward the other hand. As you release the first hand your second hand grasps the flesh and pushes it back toward the first hand. It is a continuous action, alternating the hands to squeeze and release.

With light kneading you are tackling the top muscle layers, whilst firmer kneading works on the deeper muscles, easing taut muscles and breaking down congested tissues to help the elimination of waste products.

FRICTION

Friction, or "connective tissue massage", is a penetrating circular movement which applies deep direct pressure to one particular site of muscular tension, using the thumb, fingertips or knuckles. It is a valuable technique for concentrating on specific areas of tightness and muscle spasm in the back.

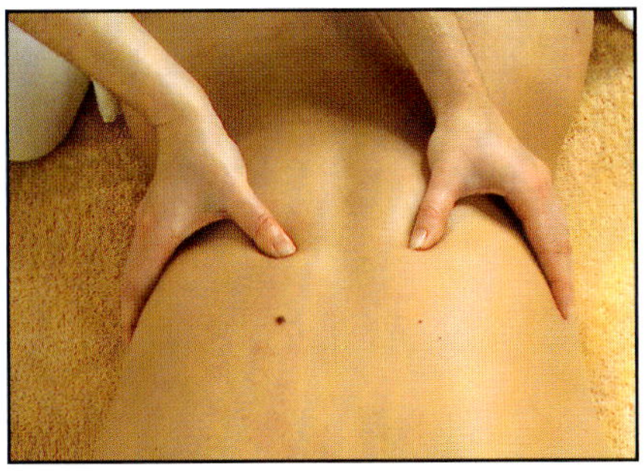

As you make the circular rotations you should actually feel the underlying tissues moving; you are not simply sliding over the skin's surface.

A variation on circular friction pressures is static pressure, where you lean gradually into the muscle, slowly deepening the pressure without the rotation action. Press for a few seconds, then gradually release.

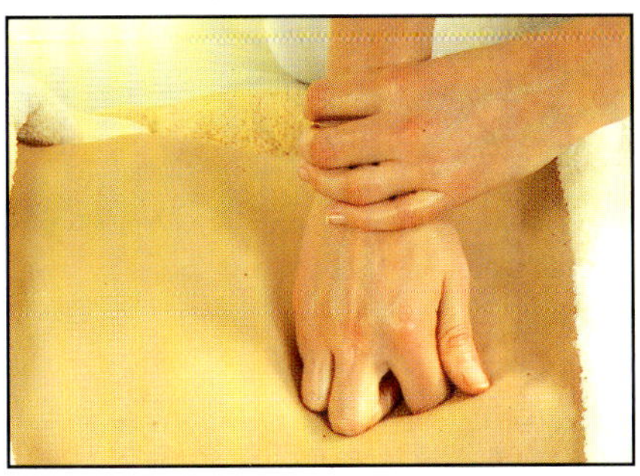

Another friction movement is knuckling: use the knuckles in a loosely clenched fist to produce rippling, circular motions. This is used to release tension up the sides of the spine and in other areas. Remember not to work right on top of the spine bone.

TAPOTEMENT

Tapotement, or percussion movements, are fast and stimulating. They include cupping, hacking, pounding (also called pummelling), which all sound like painful practices but when carried out properly should certainly not cause bruising or pain. (Don't use *tapotement* on particularly bony areas or on broken or varicose veins.) For all the movements, remember to keep the hands and wrists relaxed. All the percussion techniques are fast, precision actions, bringing one hand quickly after the other into contact with your partner. It is particularly important at the beginning to ask your partner whether you are applying the right degree of pressure.

These sequences stimulate the blood circulation, tone and help strengthen sagging skin and muscles. In particular *tapotement* can tighten up soft tissue areas, such as thighs and buttocks, which are prone to cellulite.

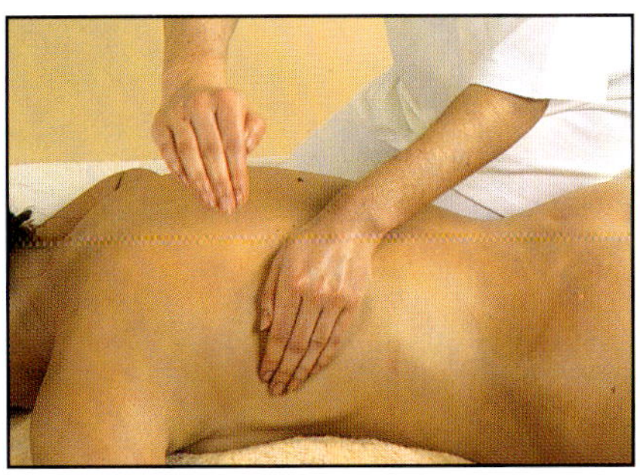

For cupping, gently curve the hands to make a loose cupped shape, bending at the knuckles while keeping the fingers straight and firm. Do not bend the fingers too far over. Using the cupped palm, make a bouncy, brisk, cupping action against a fleshy area, alternating the hands quickly. The fast, cupping action creates a suction against the skin. Try this movement on the back, buttocks and thighs.

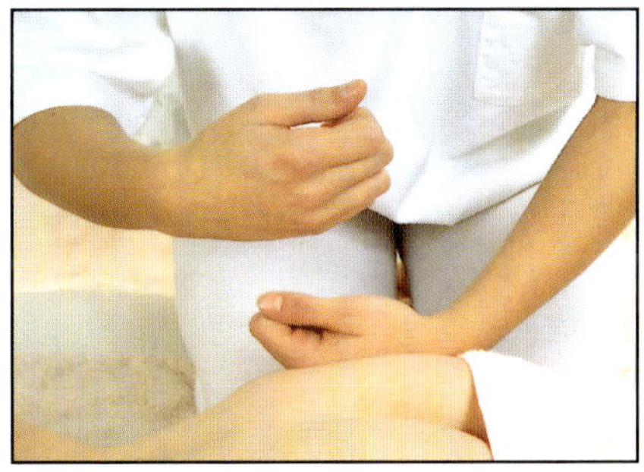

For pounding (or pummelling), loosely clench your fists, but keep the wrists relaxed. You can use the wrists in two ways: either striking your partner with the outer edges of the loose fist or with the front of the knuckles. Either way, the speed and rhythm of the movement is similar: brisk and firm, alternating the hands, without thumping your partner too enthusiastically. Once again, keep to the fleshier parts of the body, particularly cellulite zones such as hips, buttocks and thighs.

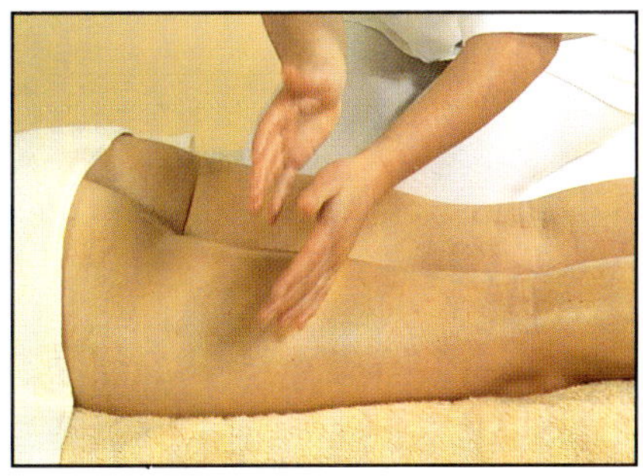

In hacking, the outer edge of the hand is used to stimulate the area by striking it quickly with alternate hands. You need to practise a brisk, bouncing movement, working rhythmically and rapidly over a fleshy area of the body. You need to have very relaxed wrists and fingers, and use the sides of the palm rather than the fingers. Used over the buttocks and thighs, hacking tones up muscles and disperses fluid.

Intersperse these brisk movements with the gentler, *effleurage* strokes, then go back to the pounding or pummelling for as long as you both feel comfortable.

WHOLE-BODY MASSAGE

Our whole-body massage is a comprehensive, top-to-toe sequence based on Swedish massage techniques, specially adapted for home practice. As a beginner you may find the full sequence too tiring at first. Until your hands and wrists build up their strength and you get used to positioning your own body comfortably to perform the massage, it is best to work on just a few parts of the body, such as the back of the legs, back and shoulders, or to perform fewer movements on each part of the body. Your partner will find it more relaxing if you perform one or two types of movement thoroughly rather than keep changing the strokes after a few seconds to cover all the steps. Always include *effleurage* strokes to begin and end a sequence, and never leave the body unbalanced – if you work on one leg or arm, you should repeat the same movements on the other side of the body.

COMFORT AND CLOTHING

If you are going to massage on the floor, put down a thick layer of blankets or towels, or a futon, to provide your partner with a firm, comfortable cushion. There is nothing more likely to reverse the relaxation process than a hard surface, a cold room and noise. Choose a quiet time, when you won't be disturbed. Your partner may need the room quite a lot warmer than you might expect. Being massaged on the floor might be extremely comfortable for your partner, but it can put a strain on the masseur's back and knees so, if you prefer, set up the same cushioning surface on a large table. It is not a good idea to massage on a bed – the give of a soft mattress can counteract much of your effort.

Have ready several towels, so that you can cover areas of the body which are not being worked on. Often a sense of modesty is crucial to relaxation, and the towels will also keep your partner warm. Move the towels around to cover most of the body, and especially an area you have just finished working on. You will need a cushion or towel to support the head, and it can be helpful to put a roll of towel under the knees when your partner is lying on their back. This relaxes the lower back. When your partner turns over on to the front, a towel under the chest can improve comfort.

Massage in loose-fitting clothes, with soft-soled, flat shoes, or work in bare feet. Take off rings and jewellery, so there is nothing to distract your partner, and make sure your nails are short! The more relaxed you are, as the masseur, the better. If you feel keyed up, try some deep, regular breathing exercises before you start. Take a few stretches, shake your hands to loosen any tension, and you're ready to start.

OILS

There are several oils which are appropriate for body massage. Stick to vegetable oils, rather than mineral oils such as baby oil. Grapeseed, sunflower or almond oil are good, basic vegetable oils, which are light and therefore not too sticky. Jojoba is a good oil for the face, especially if your partner has oily skin. Avoid oils with strong smells, such as olive oil. Also try experimenting by adding a little avocado, apricot or peach kernel oil if you wish, or buy ready-mixed massage oil.

Measure 3–4 tablespoons (45–60 ml) oil into a saucer or small container before starting your massage. You will quickly get used to how much oil to apply. The amount varies with the dryness of the skin, and how readily it absorbs the oil, but in general you need enough to facilitate the strokes without applying so much that your hands simply slide over the skin. If you need to apply more oil during a sequence, simply smooth a little oil into the palms of your hands and do some extra *effleurage* strokes.

CAUTIONS

Exchanging a regular basic massage is a luxury for both giver and receiver. However, specific problems should be tackled by a trained practitioner. Never massage right on top of the spine. Working down each side of the bony spinal column is fine, and produces many benefits, but you should avoid working directly on top of the spine.

There are occasions when it is not appropriate to massage. Avoid if there are any of the following conditions:

- heart condition
- high blood pressure
- bacterial or viral infection
- nausea or abdominal pain
- severe back pain which may be caused by the spine, especially if there are shooting pains in other limbs
- temperature or fever
- open wound or skin infection
- cancer
- post-operative recovery

If you are in any doubt, it is always best to check with your doctor first.

THE FULL MASSAGE SEQUENCE

Front of Body:
1 Legs 2 Feet and ankles
3 Arms and hands 4 Chest, shoulders and neck 5 Face
6 Abdomen and waist
Back of Body:
7 Legs and buttocks
8 Back and shoulders

FRONT OF BODY

The full massage begins with the front of the body, so your partner should lie face up with cushions or rolled towels wherever needed for support.

LEGS

Since legs carry the full body weight, the bones and muscles in the legs are the largest and strongest we have. A good leg massage can not only help to relieve strain and tension in the legs, but can benefit the well-being of the whole body. It's not unknown for backache to be traced to problems in the legs, and for a good leg massage to help alleviate the pain.

Leg massage stimulates both the blood circulation and the lymphatic system, and done regularly it helps to prevent varicose veins. Any congestion in the lower legs will be lessened with effleurage *movements taken up toward the lymph nodes at the back of the knee and in the groin. If legs feel puffy or swollen to the touch, make sure you use the gentlest of pressure. Firm massage on the larger muscles, such as those round the thighs, can dispel tiredness and stimulate a sluggish lymphatic system. Work more lightly over bony areas such as the shins and knees.*

VARICOSE VEINS

You need to take certain precautions if your partner has varicose veins. Never knead or put any pressure on varicose veins, and only massage the part of the leg which is higher than the area with veins (that is, only massage closer to the heart); never on or below the vein.

EFFLEURAGE

1 *Below: Kneel beside your partner's left ankle. With a little oil in the palm of your hands, start with your hands crossed over the ankle, in readiness to begin several long* effleurage *strokes. You will need more oil if the legs are particularly hairy or dry, but don't add too much in the first instance.*

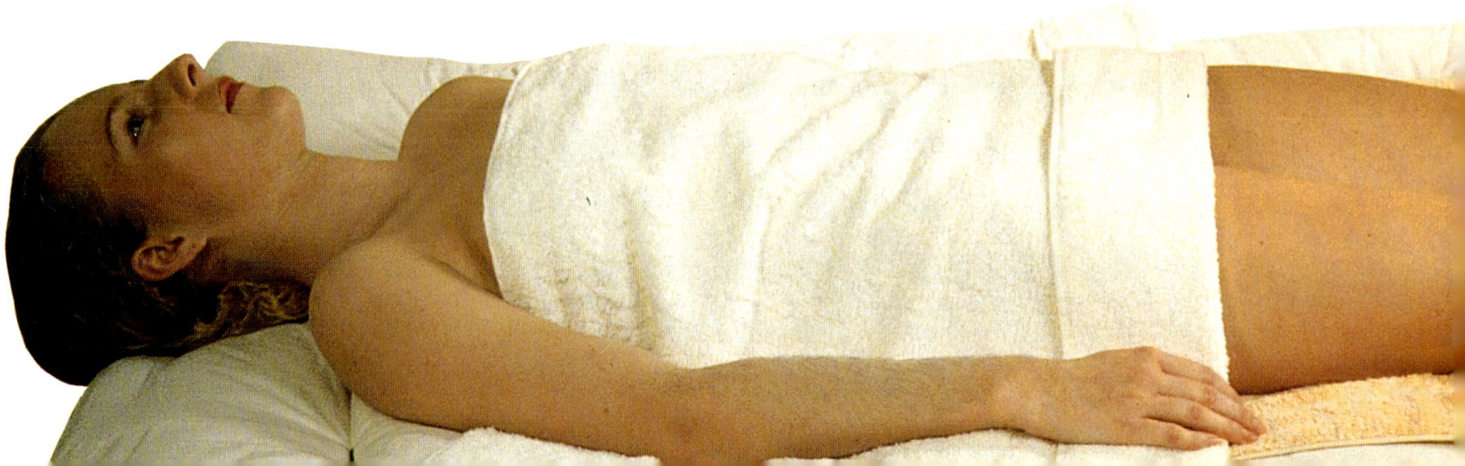

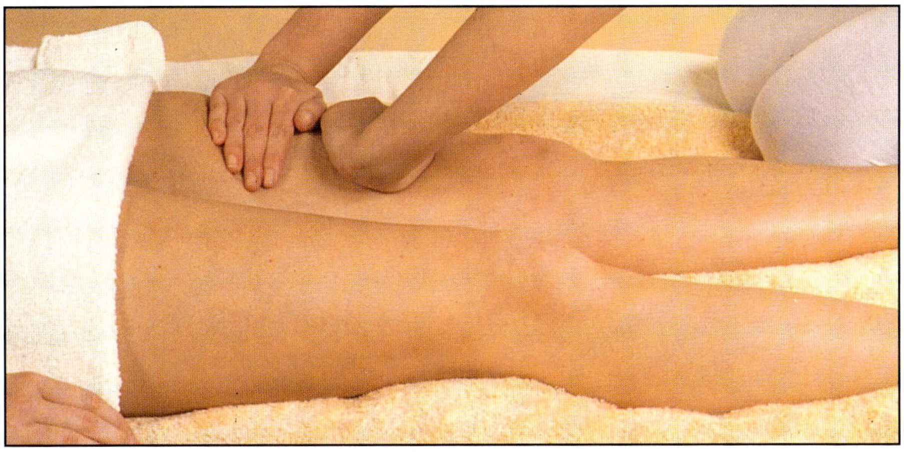

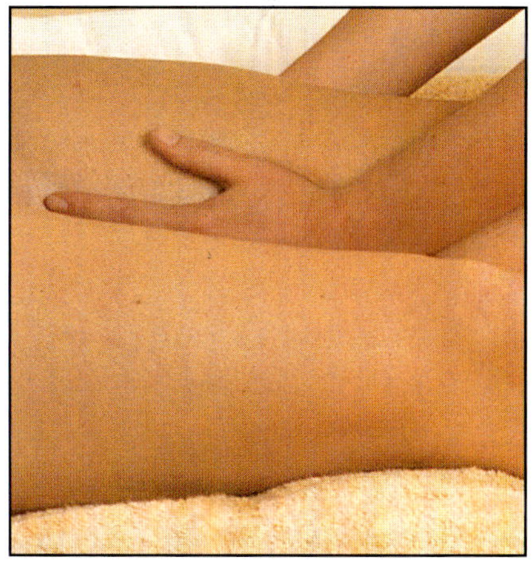

2 Keeping your hands crossed over the leg, slide the palms up the front of the leg, over the knee and up to the thigh, in one continuous, sweeping movement to oil the front of the leg evenly.

3 Turn the hands outward round the hip, separate them and bring the hands back down each side of the thigh.

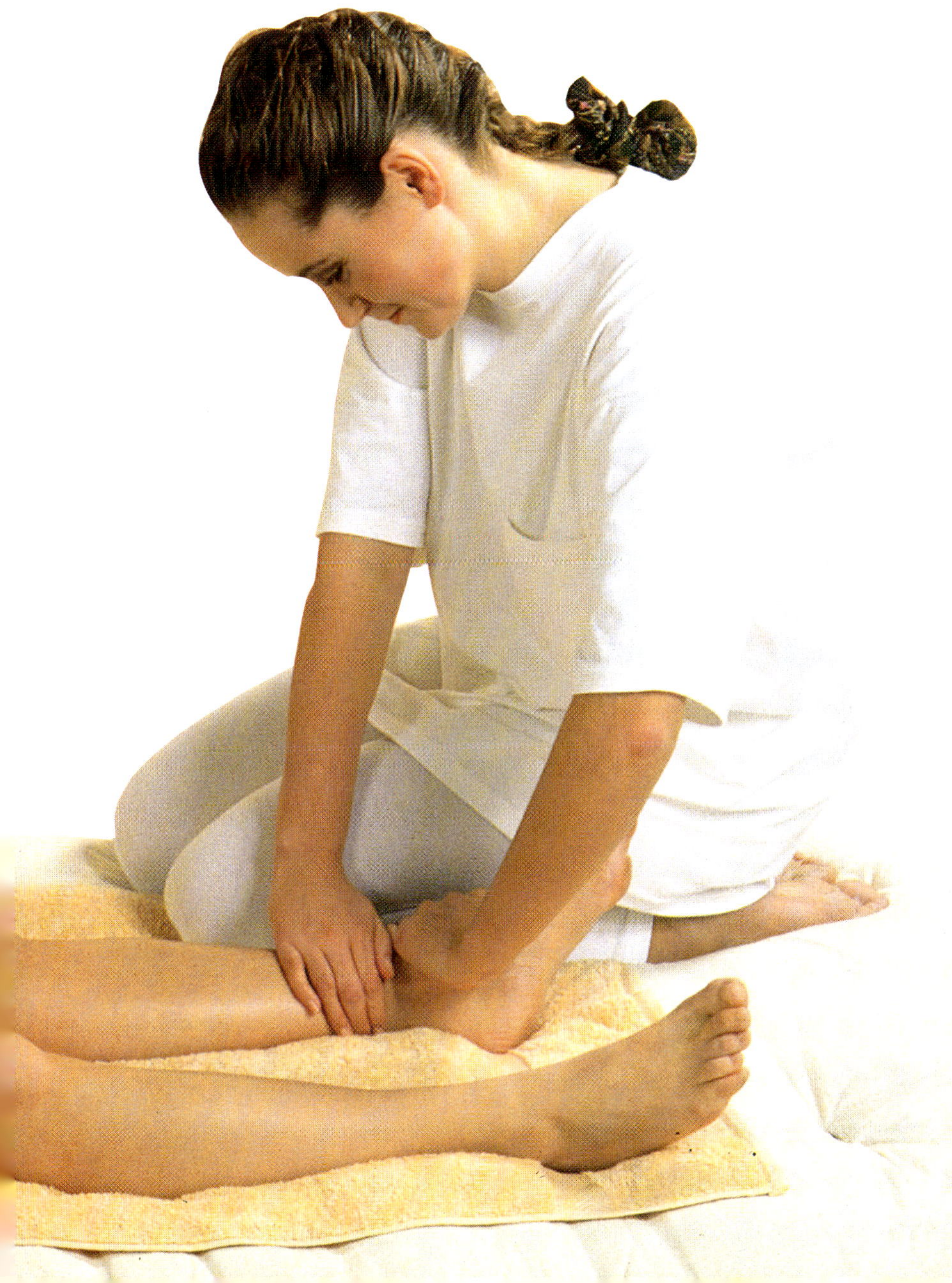

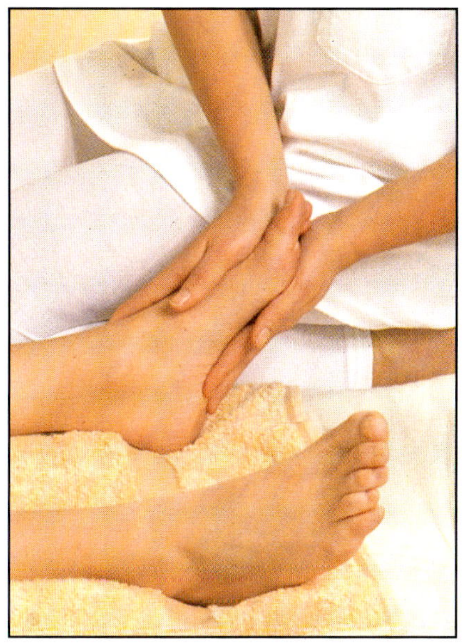

4 Continue to sweep the hands back to the ankle, and then over the foot to the toes. Then place your hands crossed over the ankle again, ready to repeat the entire movement.

Use some more oil if necessary, and this time use slightly firmer pressure on the upward stroke, then lighter again for the return. The stroke is smooth and continuous throughout.

Repeat the sequence over the whole leg once again.

THIGHS

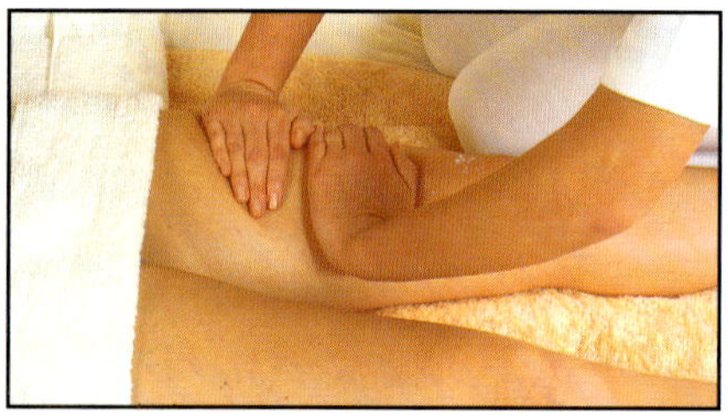

1 *Bring both hands up to just above the knee and move them up together, pressing the muscles firmly toward the upper thigh. You should be applying enough pressure to see movement in the muscles.*

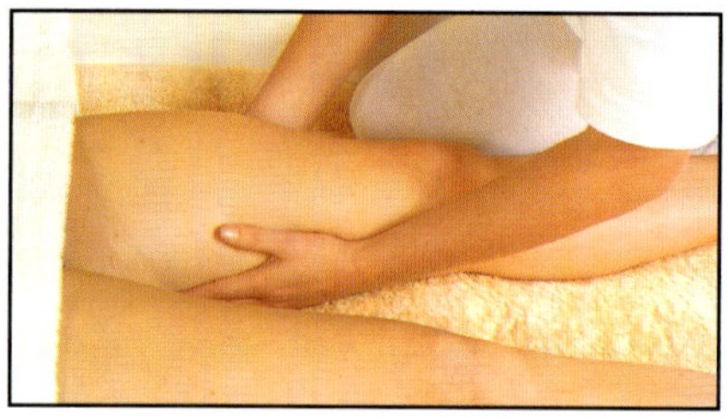

2 *At the top of the thigh separate the hands and using lighter pressure come down either side of the leg to the knee.*

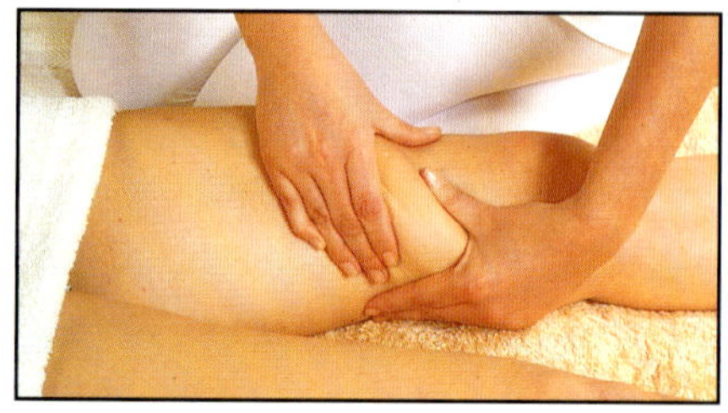

3 *Begin kneading the inner thigh with both hands. Squeeze, then release the muscles, picking up and rolling them as you do so. Continue the kneading action over the top and outside thigh.*

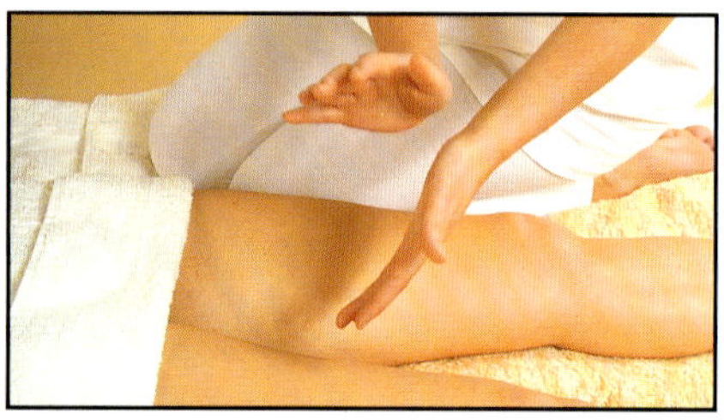

4 *Now use a hacking movement all over the thigh. Briskly strike the area with the outside edge of one hand after another, using short, sharp movements. Keep a fast repetition going.*

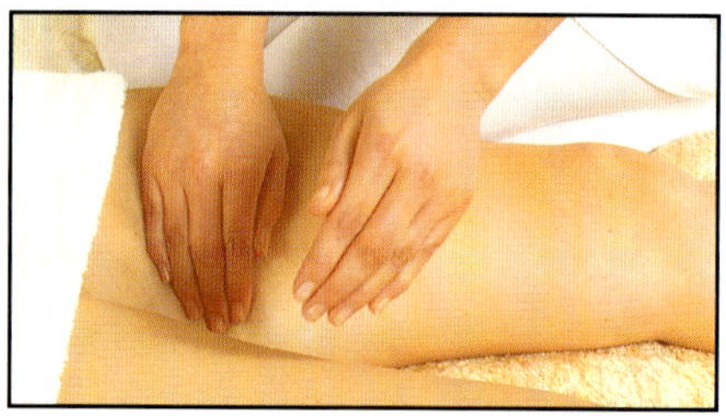

5 *Continue with cupping all over the thigh, working quickly. Expect quite a loud cupping sound, but check with your partner that the strokes are not too powerful.*

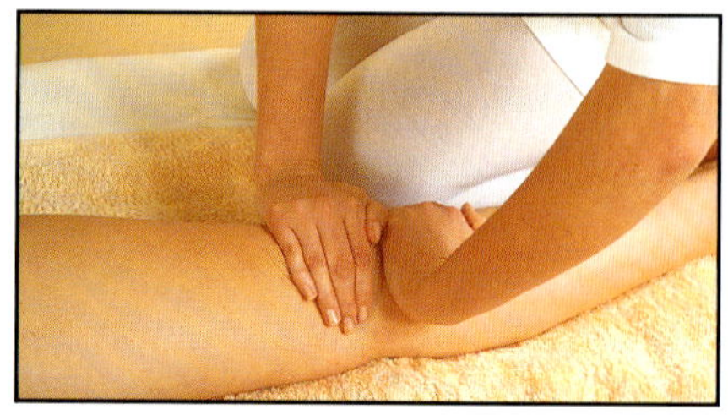

6 *Begin at the knee and do some* effleurage *strokes up to the top of the thigh, sweeping the hands outward and back down to the knee, to soothe the area after the series of stimulating movements.*

KNEES

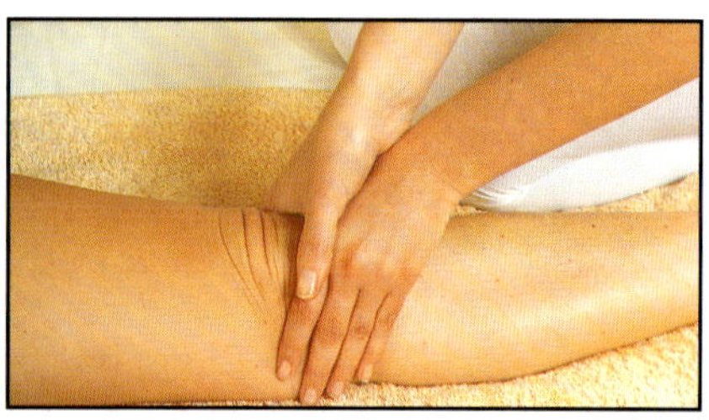

1 *Place both hands just below the knee. Lightly massage round the kneecap, using your fingertips to work gently into the muscles. Repeat three times.*

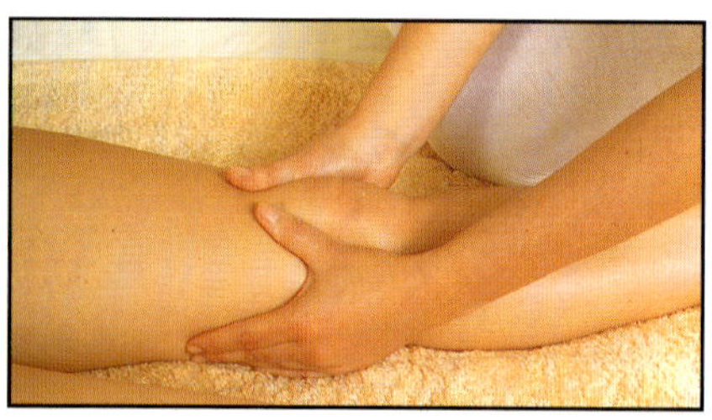

2 *Starting with your thumbs above the kneecap, with your hands under the knee for support, slowly draw them lightly round the outside of the kneecap and release. Repeat this movement three times.*

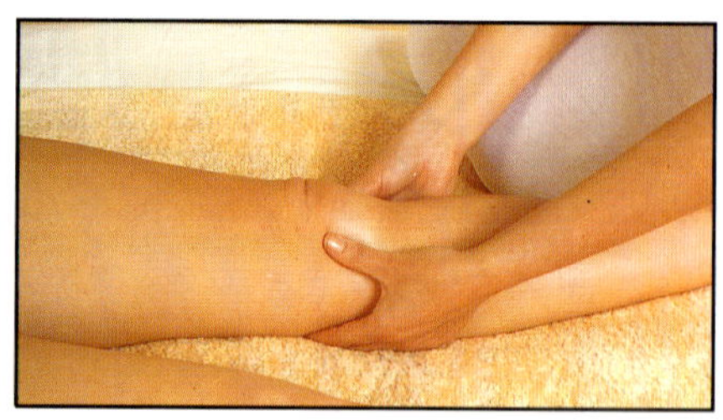

3 *Support the back of the knee with your hands and use your thumbs to circle gently round the kneecap, working downward. Return to the top of the knee and repeat three times.*

4 *Right: Raise the height of your hands above the knee. Work round the kneecap with one hand, loosening the muscles with your thumb and fingers. Use gentle, circular rotations to cover the area thoroughly.*

You may find it easier to support your wrist with the other hand.

Do some more effleurage *strokes, sweeping them up from the ankle to just below the kneecap and back down to the ankle. Repeat this several times.*

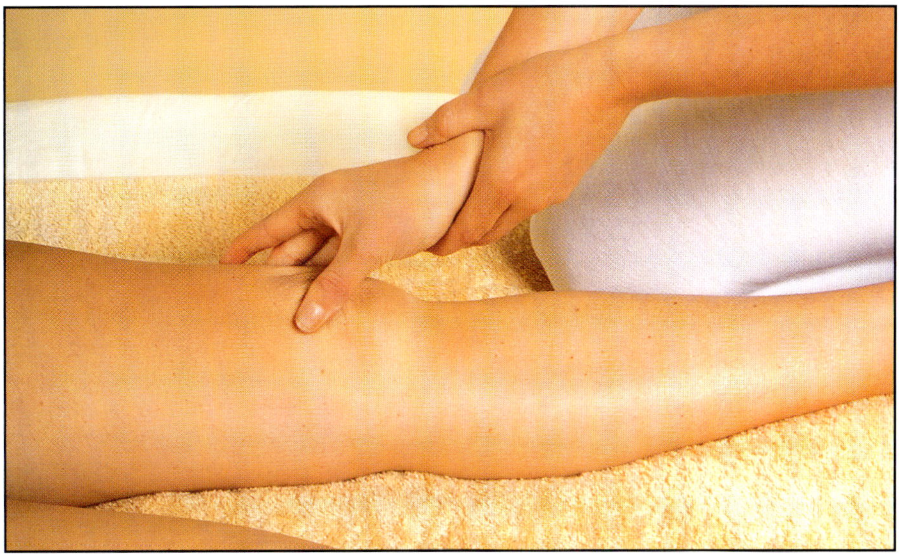

CALVES

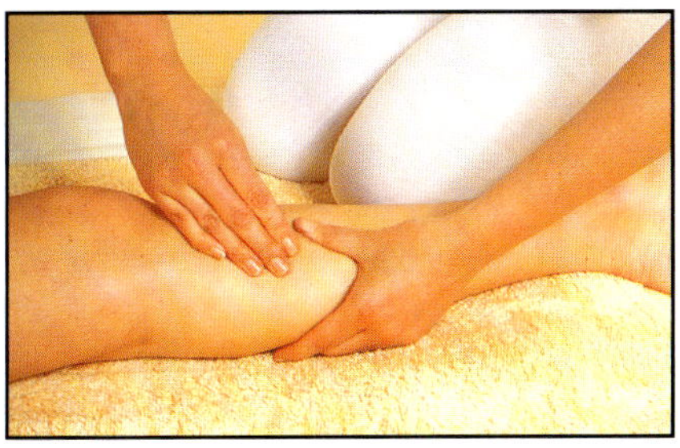

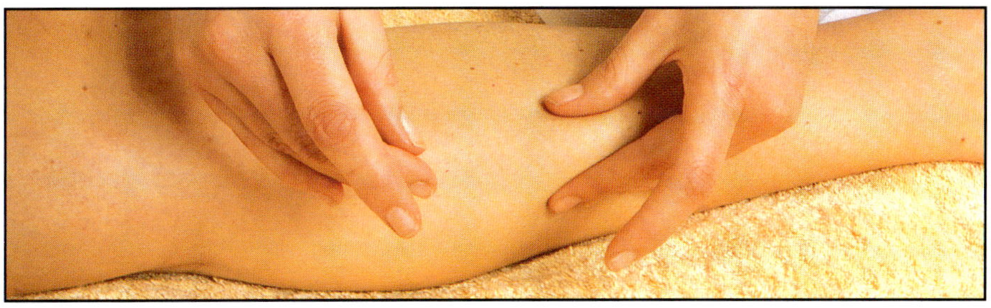

1 *Knead the calf muscles. Squeeze and release them, working from the ankle up to the knee.*

2 *Lightly and quickly pinch the fleshy part of the calf with the fingers and thumbs, one hand after the other. Check with your partner that you are not pinching too hard, although this needs to be felt to be effective.*

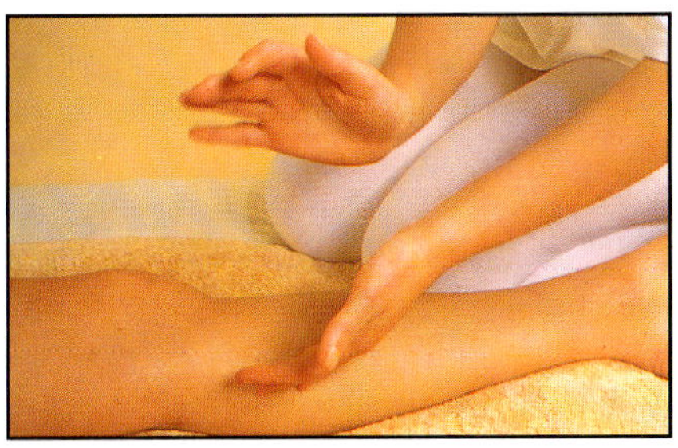

3 *Using the outside edge of both hands, alternately and rhythmically strike the calf muscles, working up and down the entire length, but keeping away from the bony shin area itself. Keep the hacking action short and brisk.*

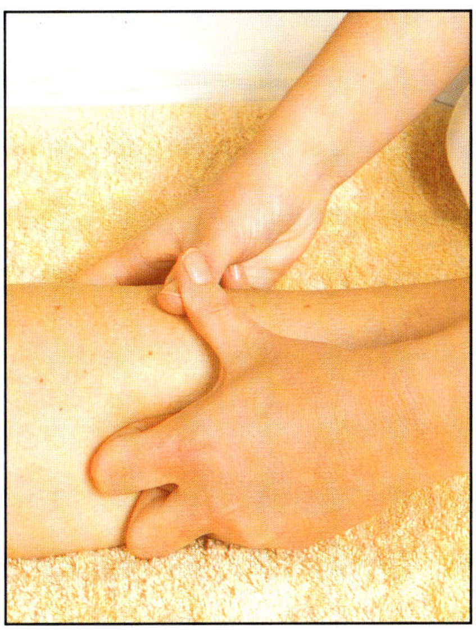

4 *Left: Starting at the ankle and crossing your thumbs on top of the shin for support, with loose knuckles make semi-circular kneading movements, working up and down the calf.*

Finish the leg with some effleurage *movements from ankle to thigh.*

FEET AND ANKLES

A foot massage is particularly relaxing after the legs have been worked on. It can alleviate anxiety and stress, stimulate the circulation and nervous system, help insomniacs to sleep, and energize anyone feeling tired and lethargic. There are thousands of nerve endings in the foot, particularly on the sole. Try to include the ankles too, to improve their flexibility.

Change the pressure of the strokes to suit your partner, remembering that deeper pressure tends to revitalize whereas gentle strokes increase relaxation throughout the entire person. When working on the feet it is best to use only a very little oil, otherwise your hands will slide around and tickle. If your partner's feet are hot and sticky, use a little talcum powder instead.

Before starting, you may wish to raise your partner's knee slightly with a rolled towel under them, to relax the muscles around the knee and in the lower back.

FEET AND ANKLES

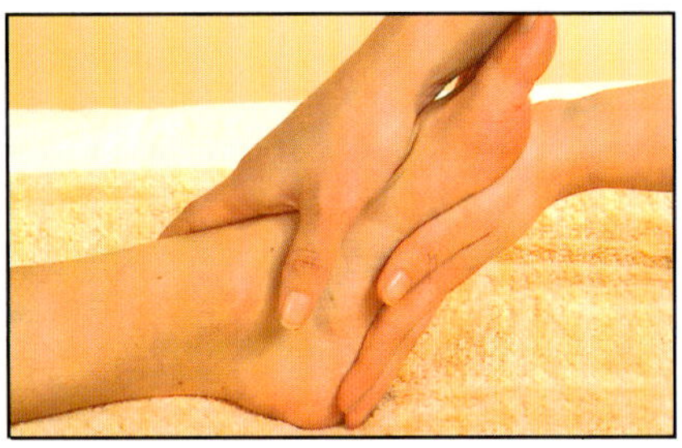

1 *Kneel at your partner's feet. Starting with the hands at the ankle, gently slide your hands toward the tips of the toes and then release them. Repeat several times. If you are using oil, apply it with this stroke.*

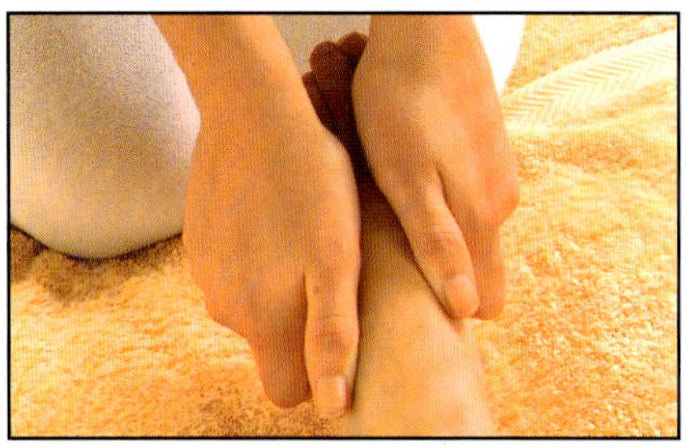

2 *With the heels of your hand, give a good stretch to the top of the foot. Draw the heel toward the sides of the foot to give the stretch. Repeat a few times, working slightly further down the foot too.*

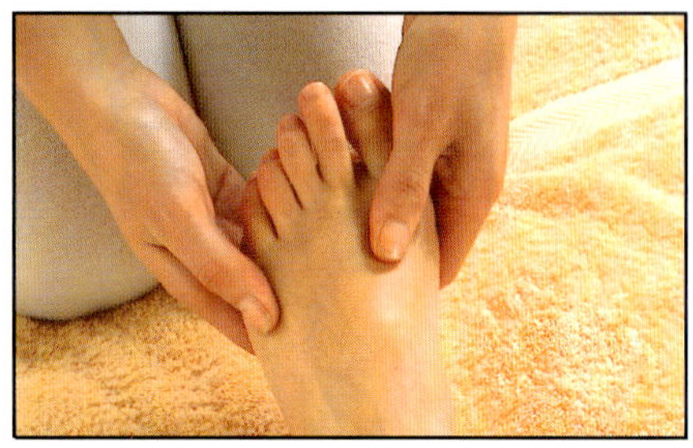

3 *Supporting the foot in both hands, find the furrow between each tendon and, using small, circular movements, work both thumbs up the tendons toward the ankle. Repeat three times on each tendon.*

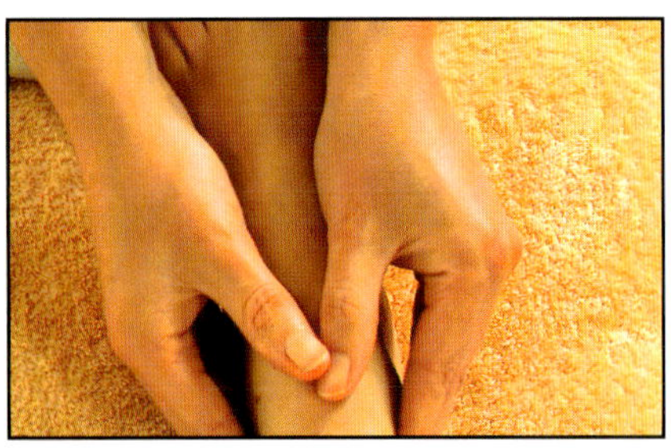

4 *Resting the thumbs across the top of the ankle, work the fingers right round the ankle bone using light, circular movements.*

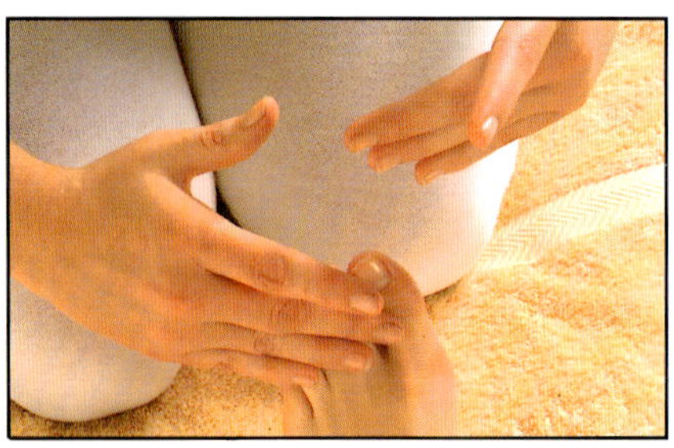

5 *Lightly tap the toes with your fingers to build up some gentle friction.*

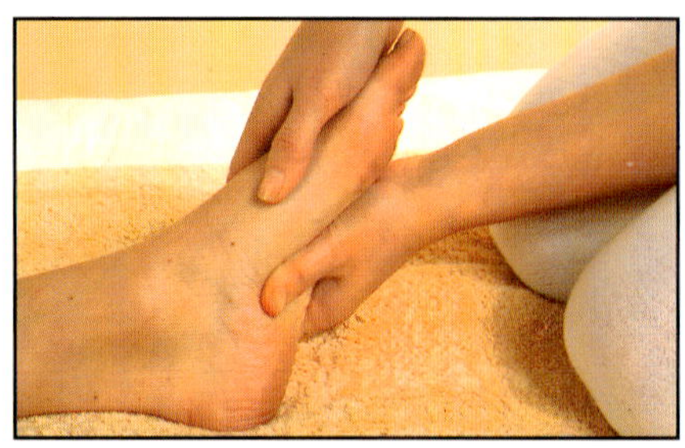

6 *Now knead the foot firmly, working particularly well into the arch. You will need to use different parts of the hand, such as the heel, knuckle and thumbs.*

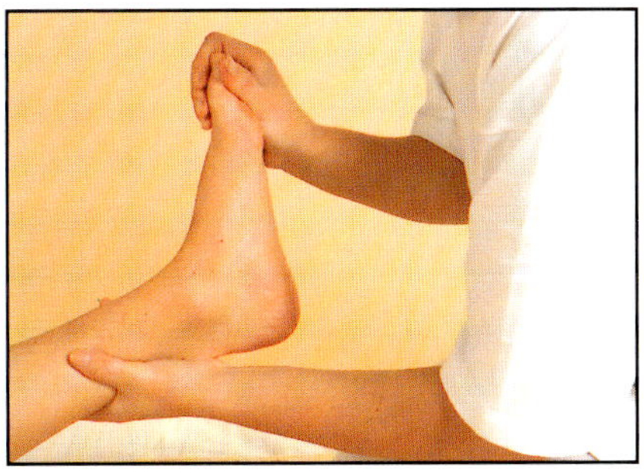

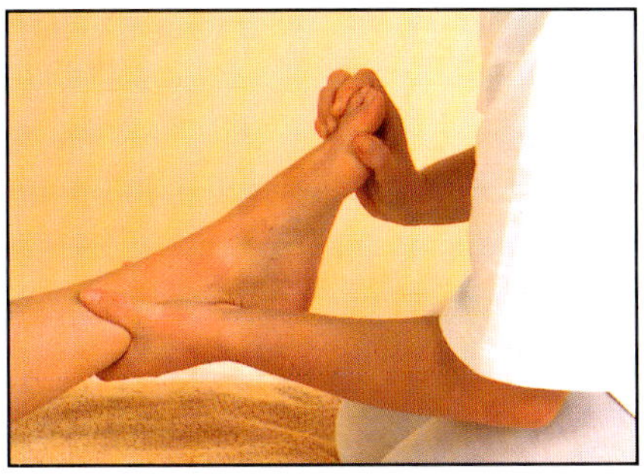

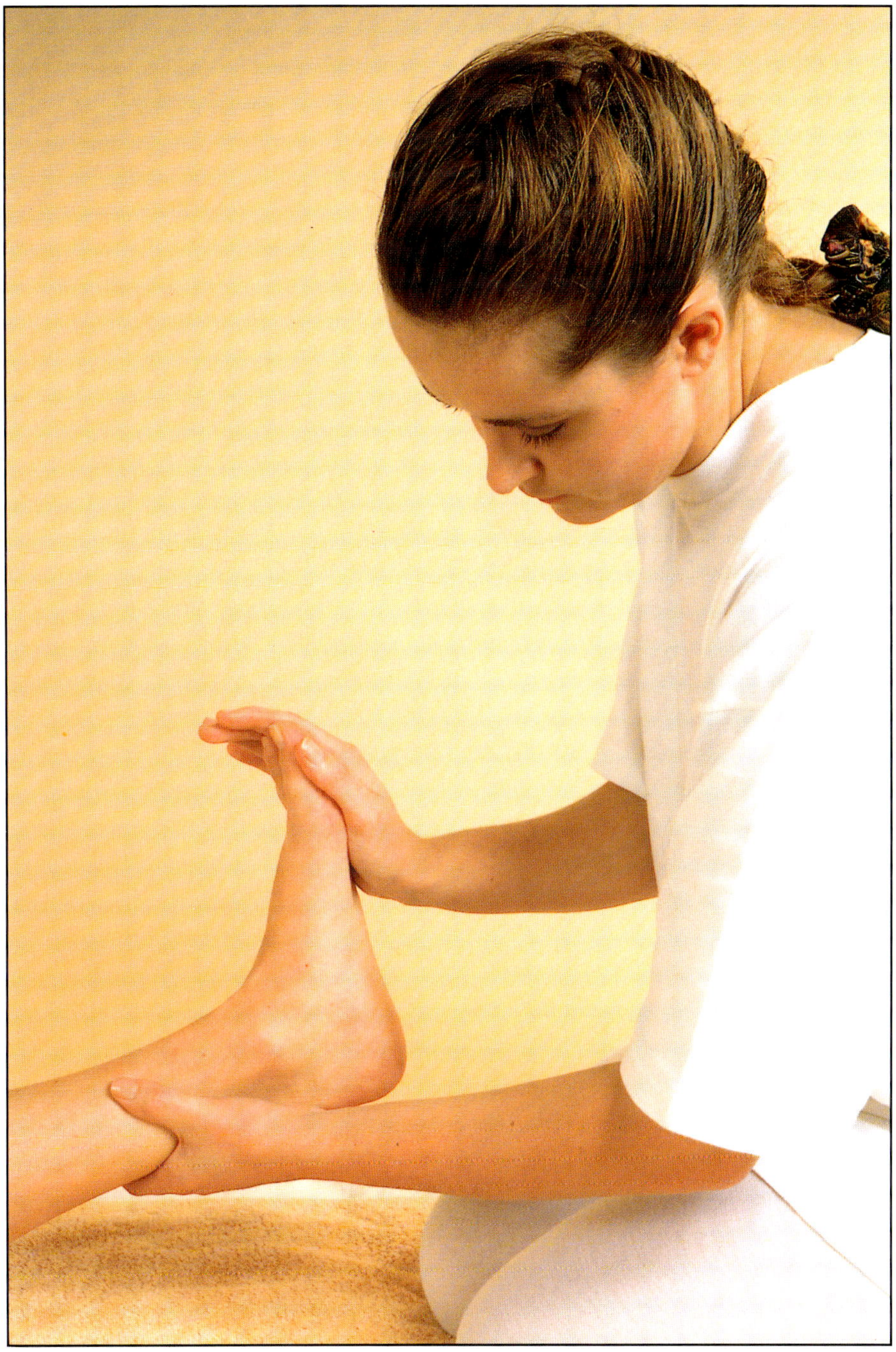

7,8 *Supporting the lower leg with your left hand, gently rotate the ankle three times in each direction, without forcing.*

9 *Right: Give the foot a gentle stretch backward and forward, to relax and flex the tendons. Supporting the back of the lower leg, use your other hand at the toes to push the foot gently away from you. To reverse the stretch take the hand over the top of the foot, and press the foot down, still supporting the lower leg with the other hand.*

10 *Finish the foot and ankle sequence with some long sweeping,* effleurage *strokes from the top of the foot up the lower leg and back down to the foot, to help reintegrate the foot and the leg. Repeat several times, varying the pressure.*

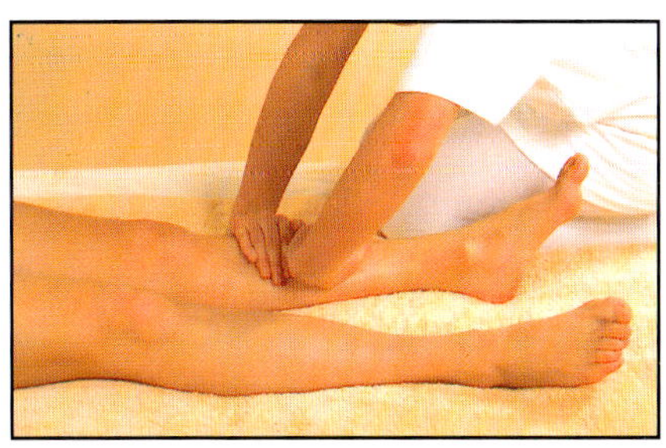

Move round your partner to kneel on the other side. Repeat the entire sequence on the front of the other leg and the other foot.

ARMS AND HANDS

Arms and hands can hide the most powerful emotions. Tight, clenched arms and hands often reflect insecurity, self-protection and unresolved anger. Whether the posture is intentional or sub-conscious, tension in the arms can cause headaches, neck pain, and aching shoulders. Don't be put off if your partner's arms are slim and bony, there are still important muscle areas there.

A hand massage feels surprisingly good, almost on a par with having the feet massaged. A lot of tension creeps into the hands: a massage is a reminder of how it feels to relax them. Massaging the arms and hands can liberate and relax not only the muscles but also the pent-up emotions, as your partner starts to feel the wonderful sensation of letting go.

ARMS

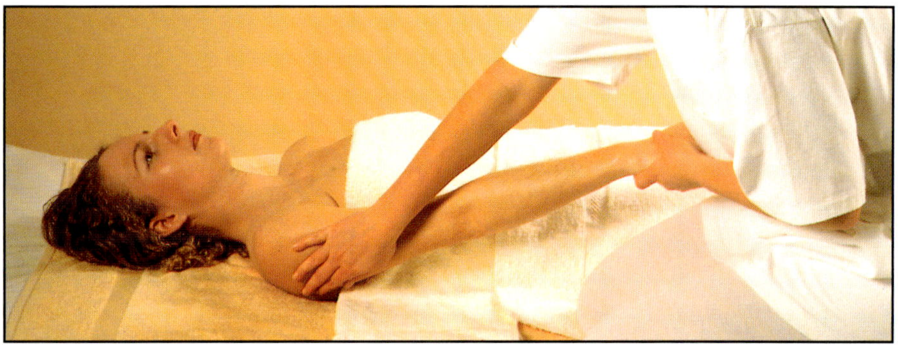

1 *Kneel halfway along your partner's right side. Holding the wrist with your left hand, lightly oil the arm using* effleurage *strokes, starting from the wrist and sweeping your hand up round the shoulder and down again. Repeat three times.*

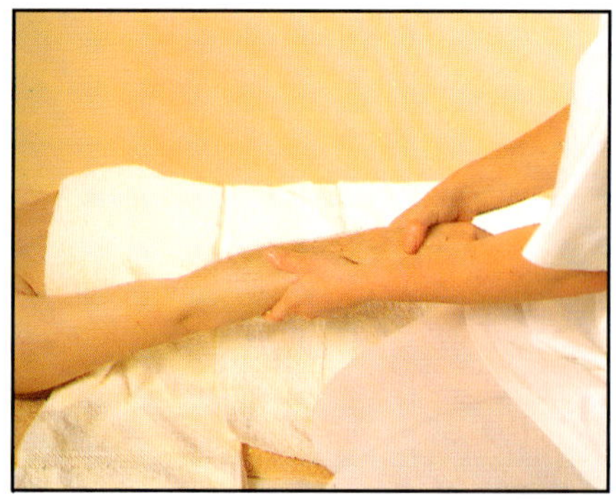

2 *Changing hands, so that your partner's wrist is supported in your right hand, use the left hand to stroke gently from the wrist to the shoulder, and back down again. Repeat several times.*

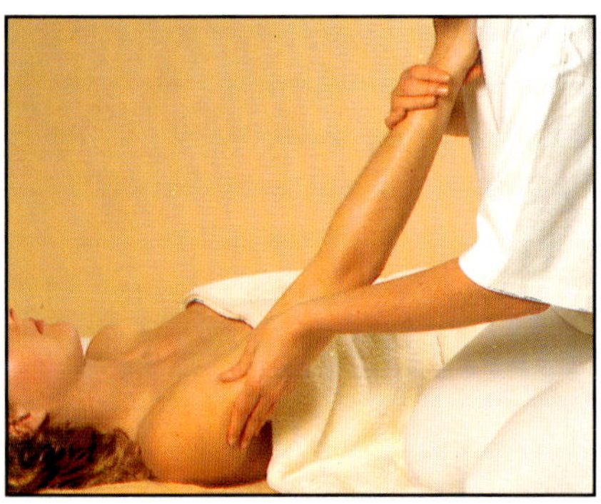

3 *Lift the arm and rest the hand on your right shoulder ready to start kneading. Support your partner's wrist with your left hand and use your right to knead lightly the muscles of the upper arm, working from elbow to shoulder.*

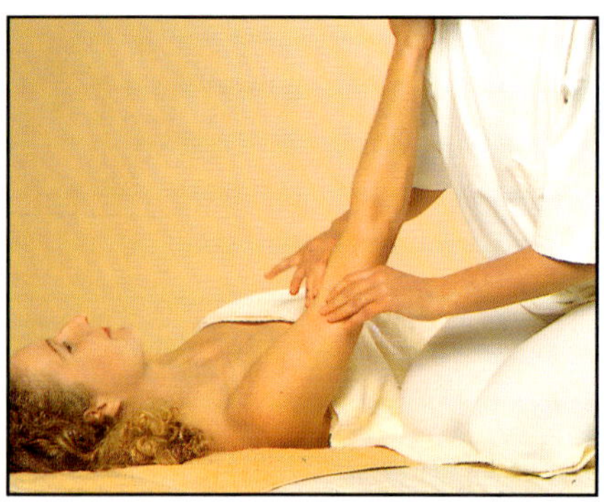

4 *Keeping your partner's hand supported by your shoulder, use the fingers of both hands to continue the kneading.*

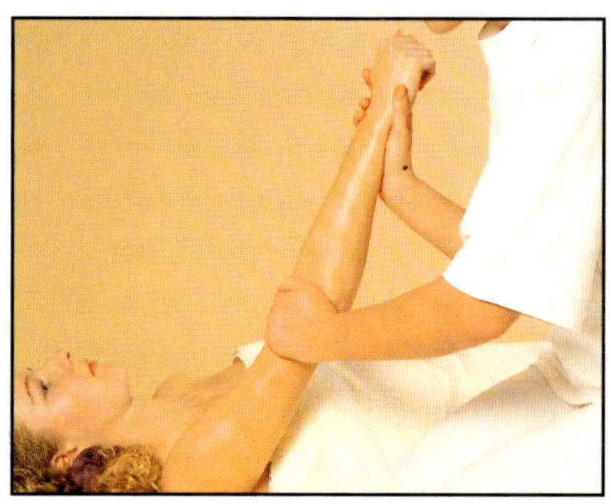

5 *Still holding the arm across the front of your chest with your right hand, do some* effleurage *strokes from the elbow up to the shoulder and back down again. Repeat three times.*

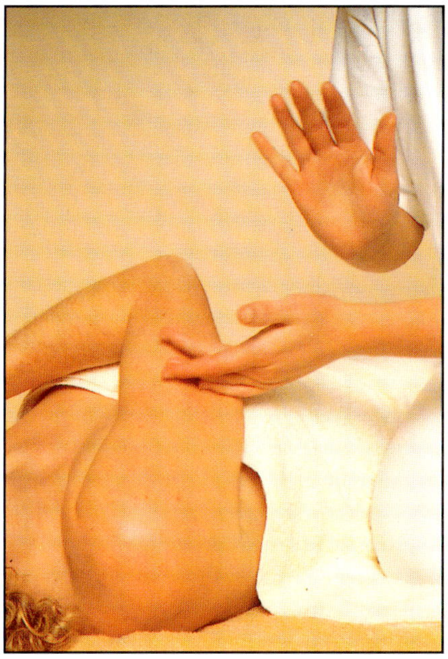

6 *Bend your partner's arm and rest the right hand on the left shoulder. Using the outside edge of your hands, do some short, brisk hacking on the outer and under sides of the arm.*

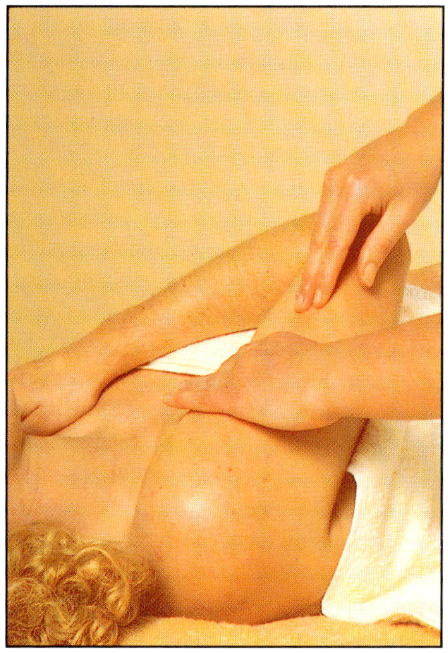

7 *With your partner's arm still bent, firmly knead the muscles of the upper arm with your right hand, using the left hand to keep your partner's arm stable.*

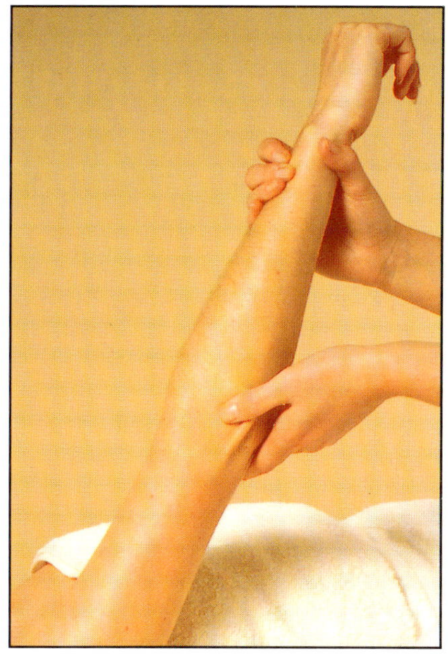

8 *Holding the wrist for support with your right hand, work round the outside of the elbow with your fingers and thumb, using smooth circular movements and covering the area thoroughly. As the elbows can get particularly dry you may need some more oil.*

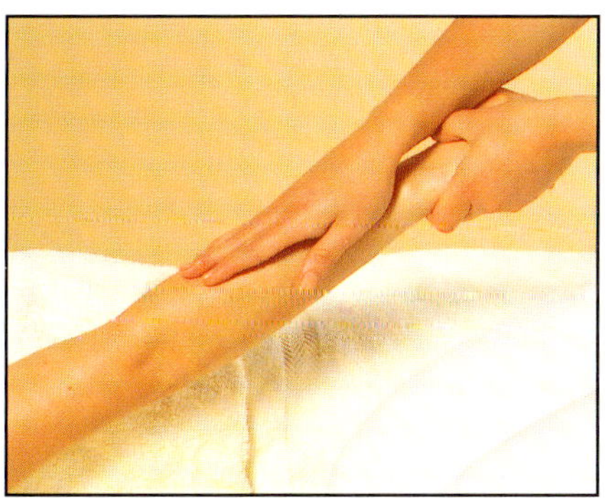

9 *To encourage further relaxation, hold the wrist with the left hand and do some* effleurage *strokes up and down the top of the forearm. Keep the pressure fairly firm.*

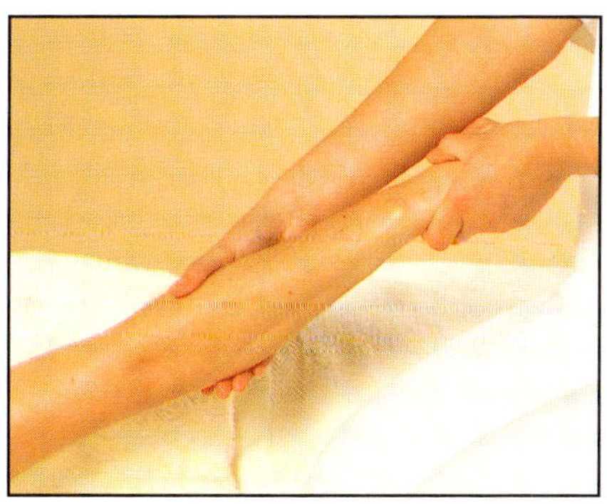

10 *Repeat these* effleurage *strokes on the inside of the forearm.*

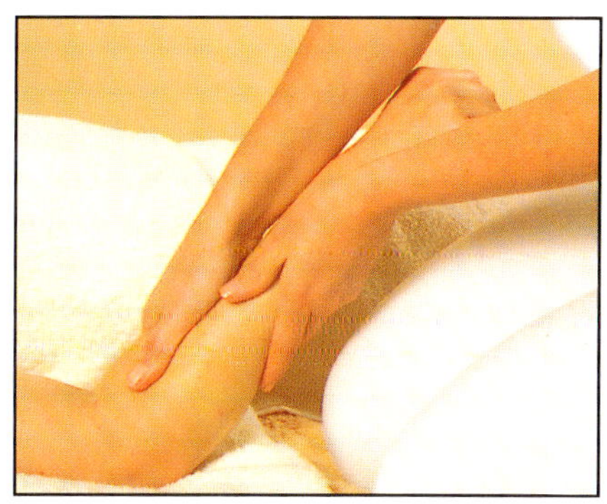

11 *Rest your partner's elbow back on the towel. Supporting the weight of the lower arm in your left hand, use your right hand to knead the inside of the forearm, starting from the wrist. When you reach the elbow glide gently back to the wrist to begin again. Repeat three times.*

Finish the arm with a few effleurage *strokes and then massage the hand and wrist (see the following pages) before moving on to the other arm.*

HANDS AND WRISTS

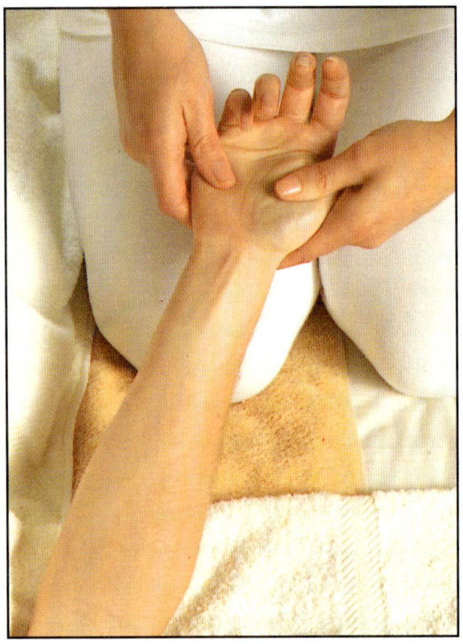

1 *Support your partner's hand in both hands and gently use the thumbs to knead the palm. This should be a continuous, circular action, with the thumbs alternately applying the pressure.*

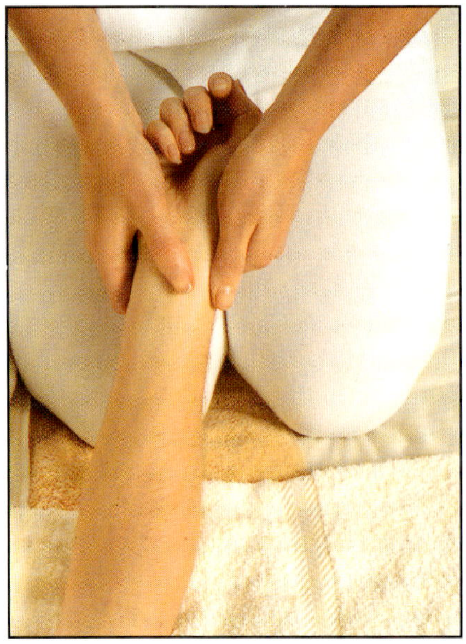

2 *Rest your hands under your partner's wrist and use the thumbs to stroke outward round the wrist. Then work with the thumbs up the inner forearm toward the elbow, using circular movements.*

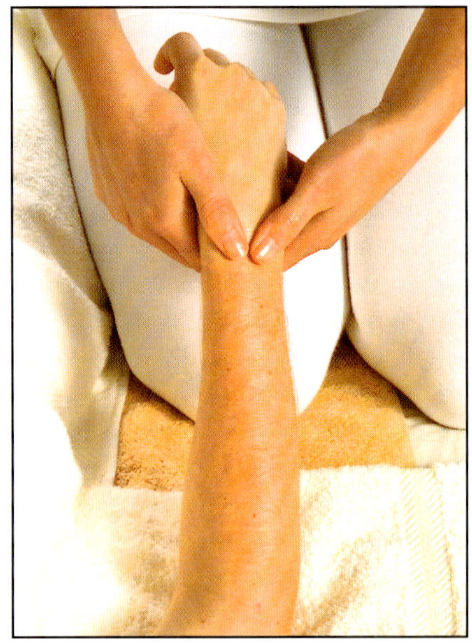

3 *Turn the hand over, supporting the wrist. Massage gently over the back of the wrist with your thumbs.*

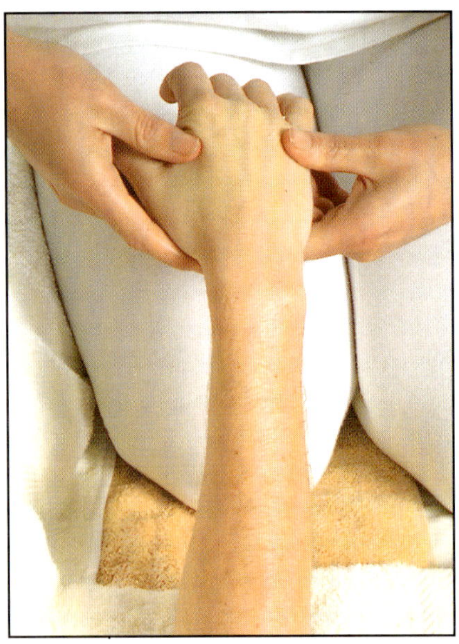

4 *Stroke up in between the tendons on the back of the hand with your thumbs, from knuckles to wrist, using light small circles. Repeat twice between each tendon.*

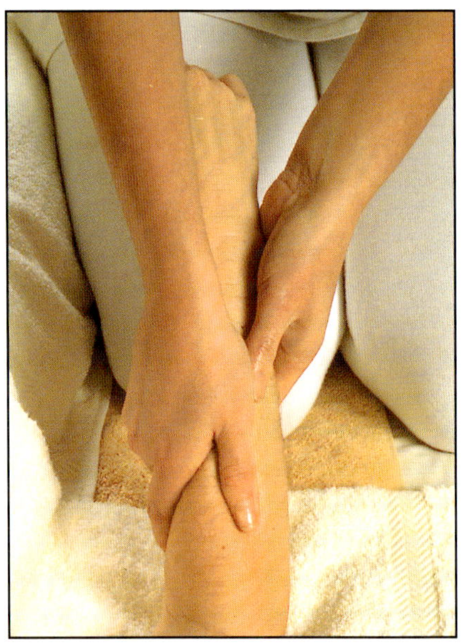

5 *Sweep the hands alternately up from the wrist toward the elbow, applying a fairly firm pressure with the inside edge of the hands. Repeat several times.*

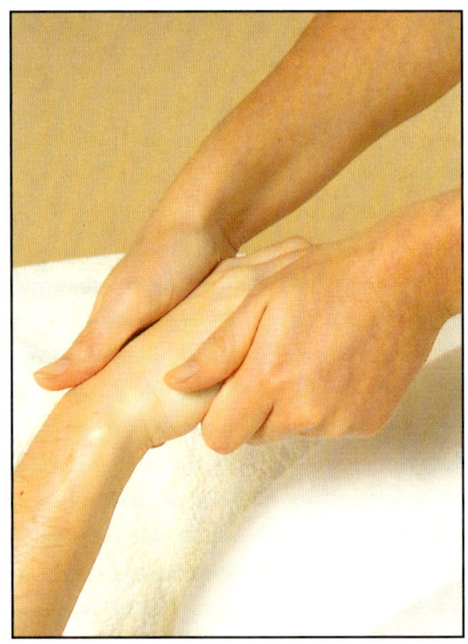

6 *Come back down to the hand and stretch the back of the hand, drawing your hands out toward the sides.*

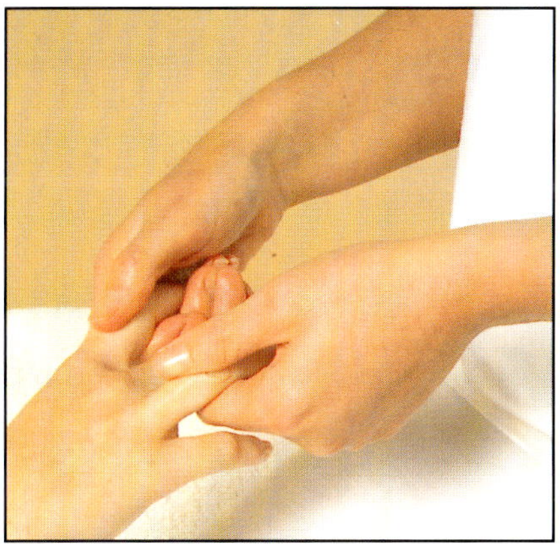

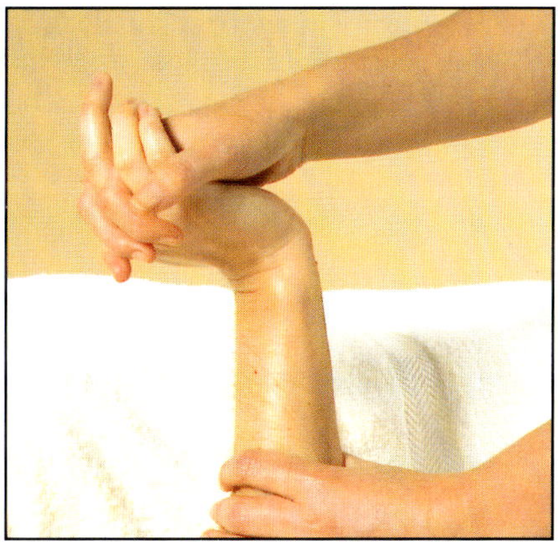

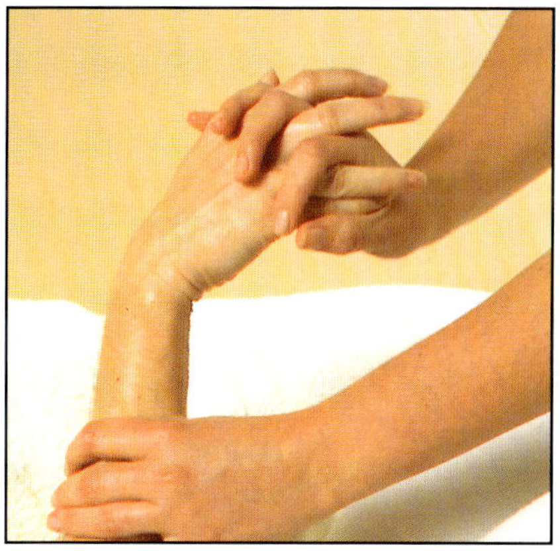

7 *With one hand make circular pressure movements round each of the three joints on each finger, starting at the tip. When you have worked round all three joints, gently rotate the finger twice. Then gently stretch each finger to release the joints.*

8 *Raising your partner's lower arm and supporting it with your left hand, clasp your partner's hand with your right hand, and gently rotate it in a half circle, three times in each direction.*

9 *Still supporting the lower arm, thread your fingers between your partner's and gently bend the wrist backward and forward three times, making sure that the wrist joint is not forced.*

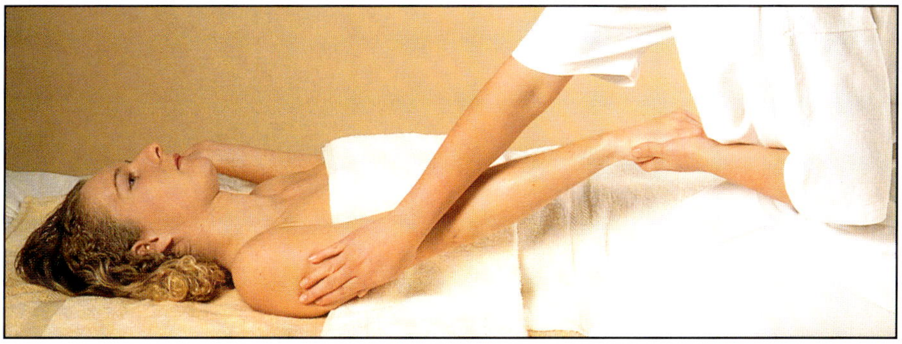

10 *Above: Finish the arm and hand sequence by stroking the entire length of the arm and hand with some soothing effleurage from palm to shoulder.*

11 *Below: Hold your partner's hand between both of your palms for several seconds then release, lowering the arm gently.*

Move round your partner to kneel on the other side. Repeat the arm and hand massage on the left side.

CHEST, SHOULDERS AND NECK

Ideally a chest massage should follow an arm massage and precede a facial massage. It's not only the hours spent sitting hunched over a desk that tighten and contract the chest muscles – clutching a car steering wheel, carrying heavy shopping, and poor posture all have a cumulative effect. Tension in the chest can also exacerbate inflexibility and stiffness in the neck and the shoulders. We tend to raise the shoulders toward our ears, until they become set rigid with tension. This sequence includes work to help these problems.

First check if your partner would be more comfortable with a small cushion or a folded towel under the head. They may or may not, but it is important that the neck should be comfortable. Kneel behind your partner's head to start the sequence.

CHEST

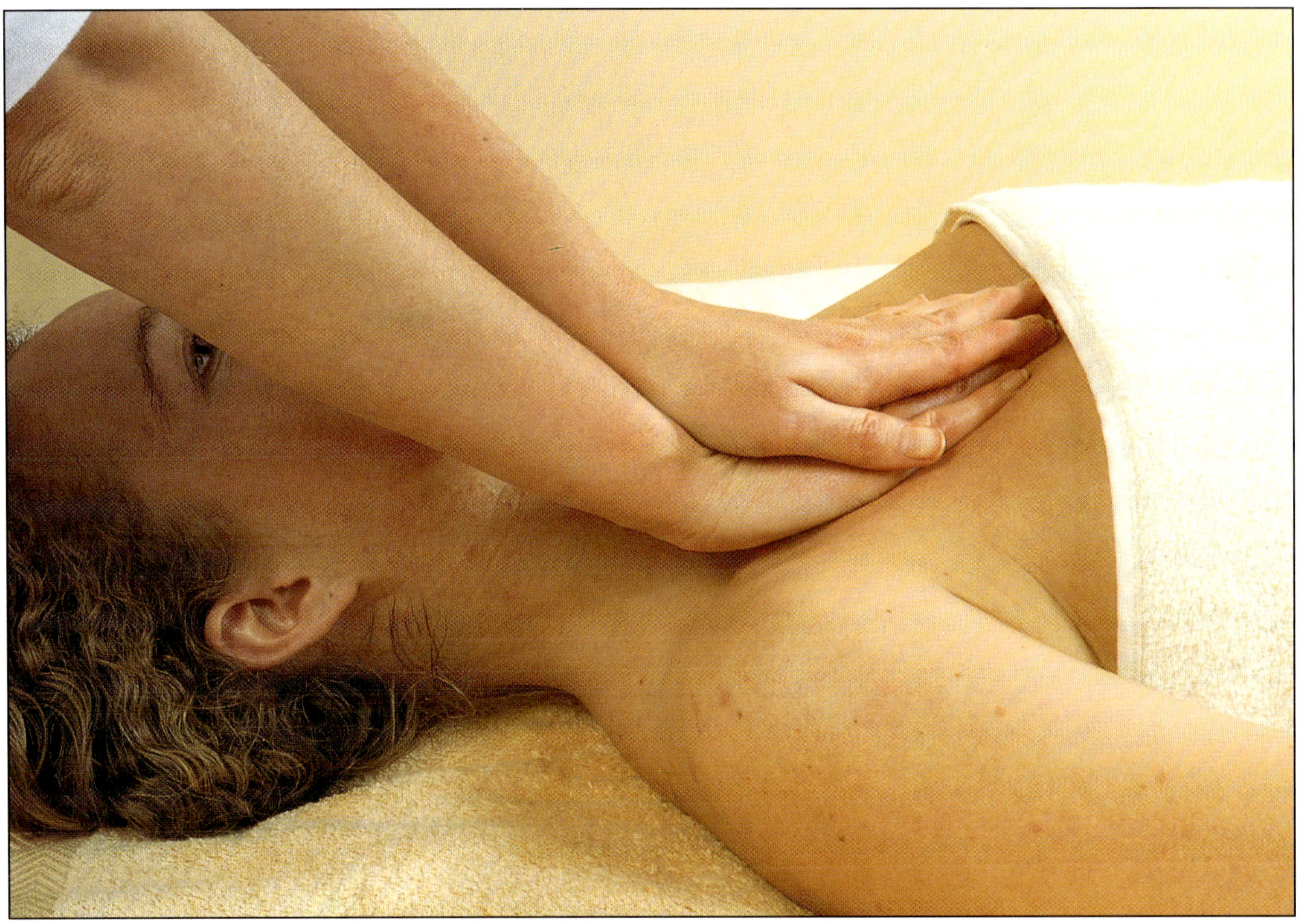

1 *Lightly oil the palm of your right hand, and with the flat of the hands placed on the chest, fingers pointing toward your partner's feet, place the left hand on top of the right. You will be doing reinforced* effleurage *on the right side of the chest first.*

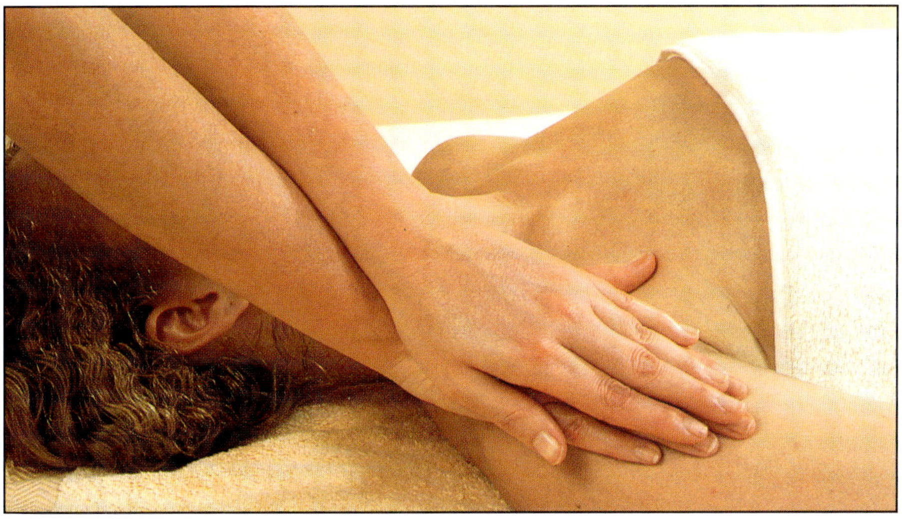

2 *Sweep your hands over the chest, toward and round the right shoulder, keeping the left hand over the right. The movement should be a continuous* effleurage *stroke. You should apply enough pressure to press the chest and shoulder toward the floor, so that they release as you lift off after the stroke. Repeat three times.*

3 *Continue the* effleurage *stroke, sweeping both hands round and up the right side of the neck.*

Repeat the sequence twice more, starting from the centre of the chest.

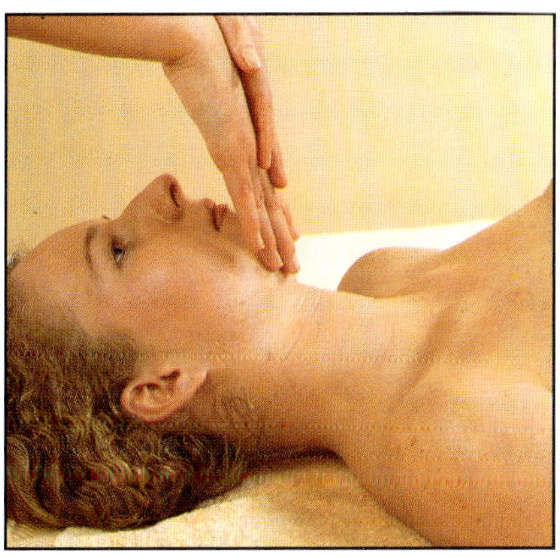

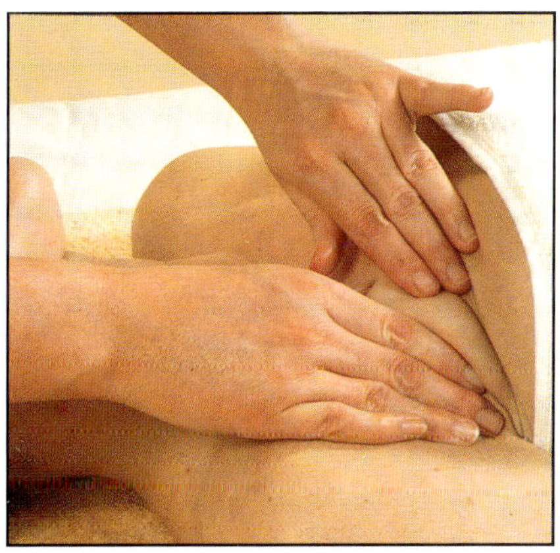

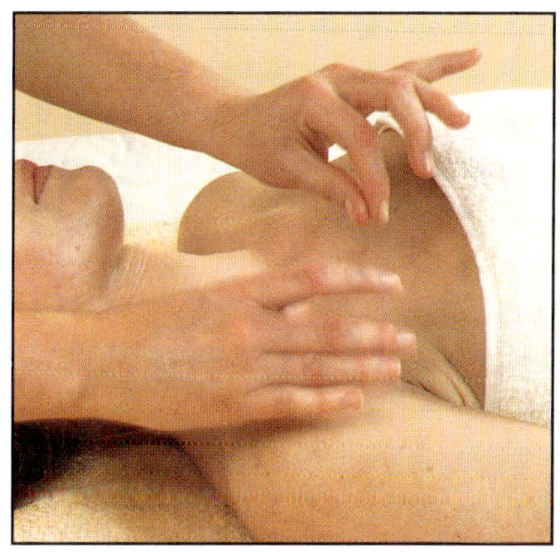

4 *Repeat the sequence once again, but this time finish by bringing both hands up to the jawline with the fingers resting lightly under the centre of the jaw.*

5 *With both hands, knead the fleshy area in front of the armpit. Pick up and release the muscles, squeezing them from one hand to the other.*

6 *On the same fleshy area, lightly pinch the surface muscles between the thumb and first finger. Alternate the hands swiftly in a rhythmical action, checking with your partner that there is no discomfort.*

Repeat the effleurage *strokes from the centre of the chest and over the right side of the neck in one continuous movement, to soothe the area you have worked on.*

Then repeat the entire sequence on the left side of the chest and neck, lightly oiling the palm of your left hand before you begin.

SHOULDERS AND NECK

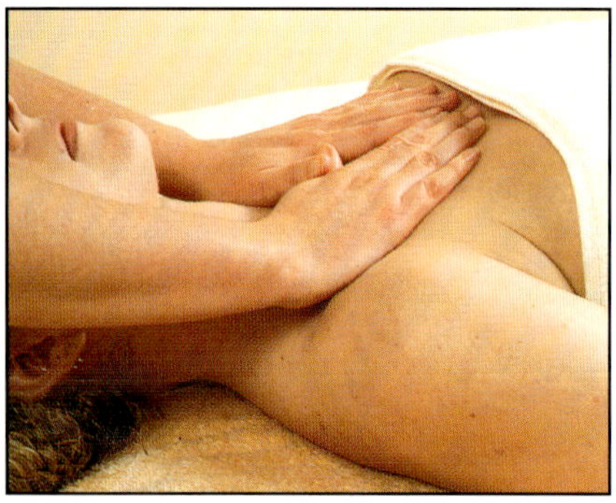

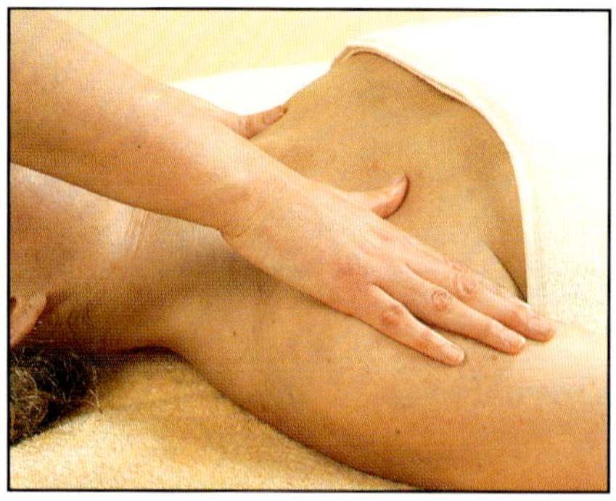

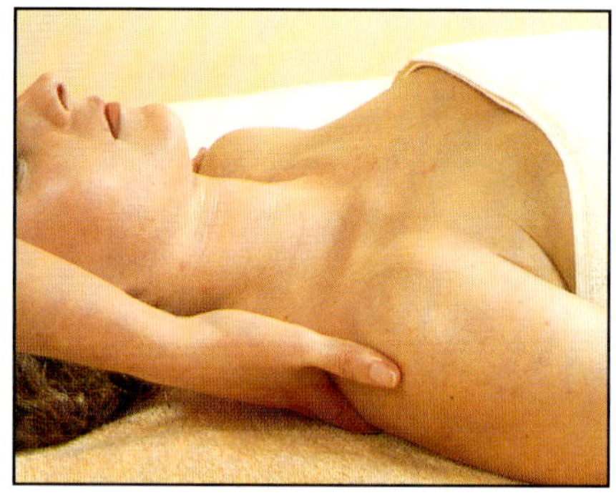

1 *Place both hands fairly firmly, side by side, over the front of the chest.*

2 *Sweep them out toward each shoulder with firm* effleurage *strokes, taking them over the shoulders, round under the upper back and up the back of the neck.*

3 *When you take the movement round the back and the neck gently lift the weight of your partner to give the muscles a gentle stretch.*

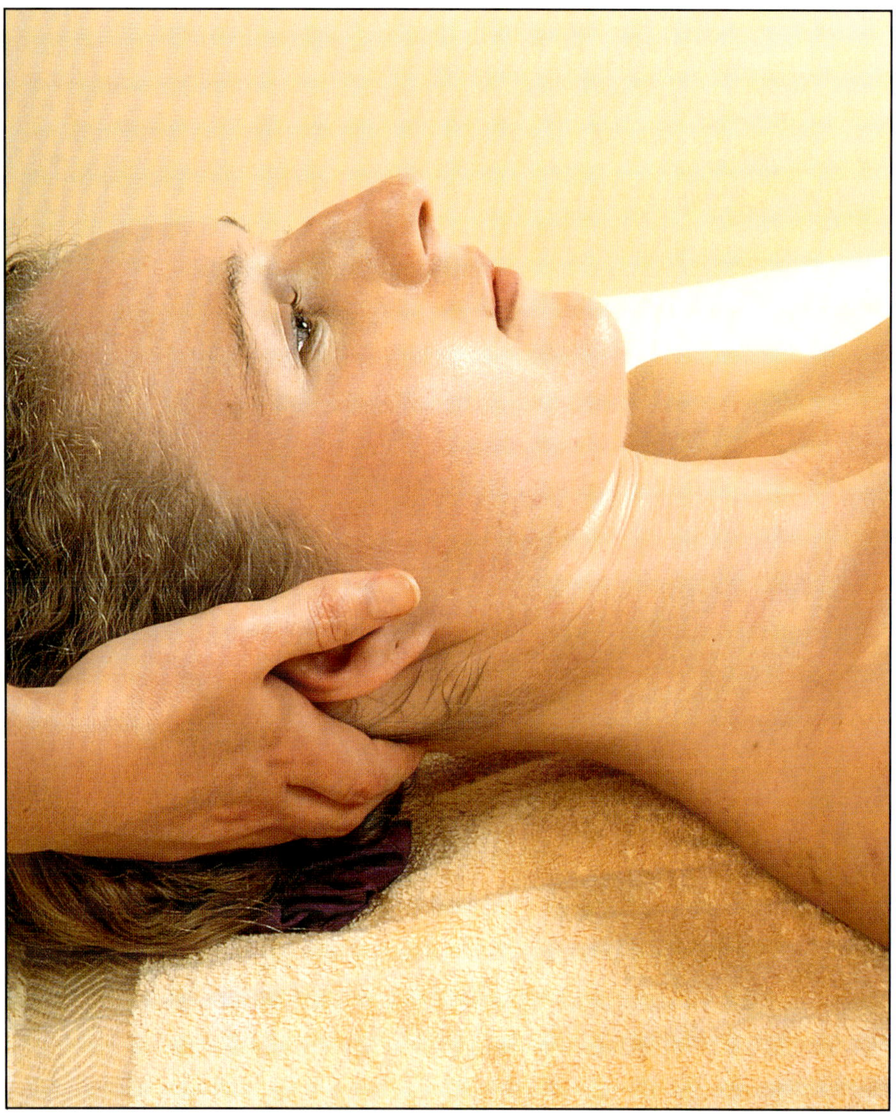

4 *Left: With the fingertips, work with circular pressures up the back of the neck to the base of the skull. These should be small, firm rotations, which you can feel easing taut muscles. You should spend some time on this area, which is often extremely tense.*

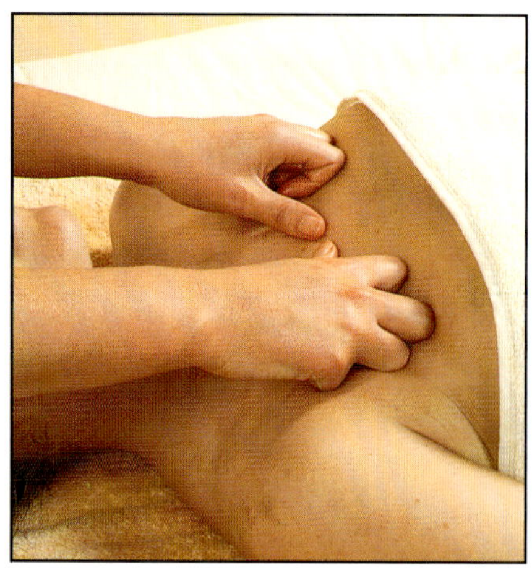

5 *With loose fists, use the knuckle area to ripple your fingers in semi-circular frictions all over the upper chest. Keep the half circles fairly small and apply quite firm pressure on the fleshier area, but avoid working directly on the collarbone.*

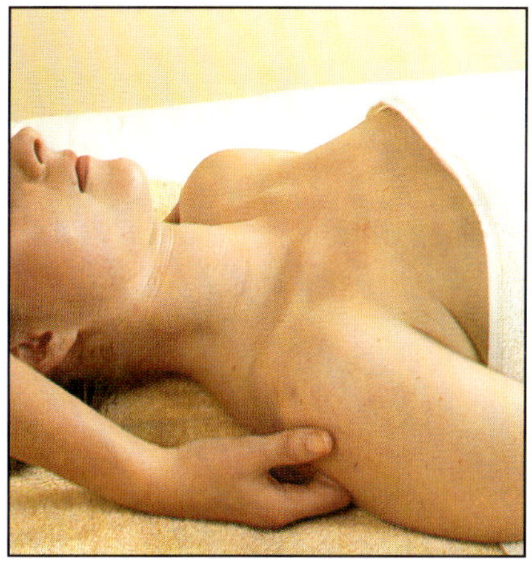

6 *Bring your loose fists under the upper back and continue to knead behind the shoulders and round the base of the neck.*

7 *Below: Finish with several* effleurage *strokes, starting at the front of the chest and stroking the hands over each shoulder, and up behind the neck.*

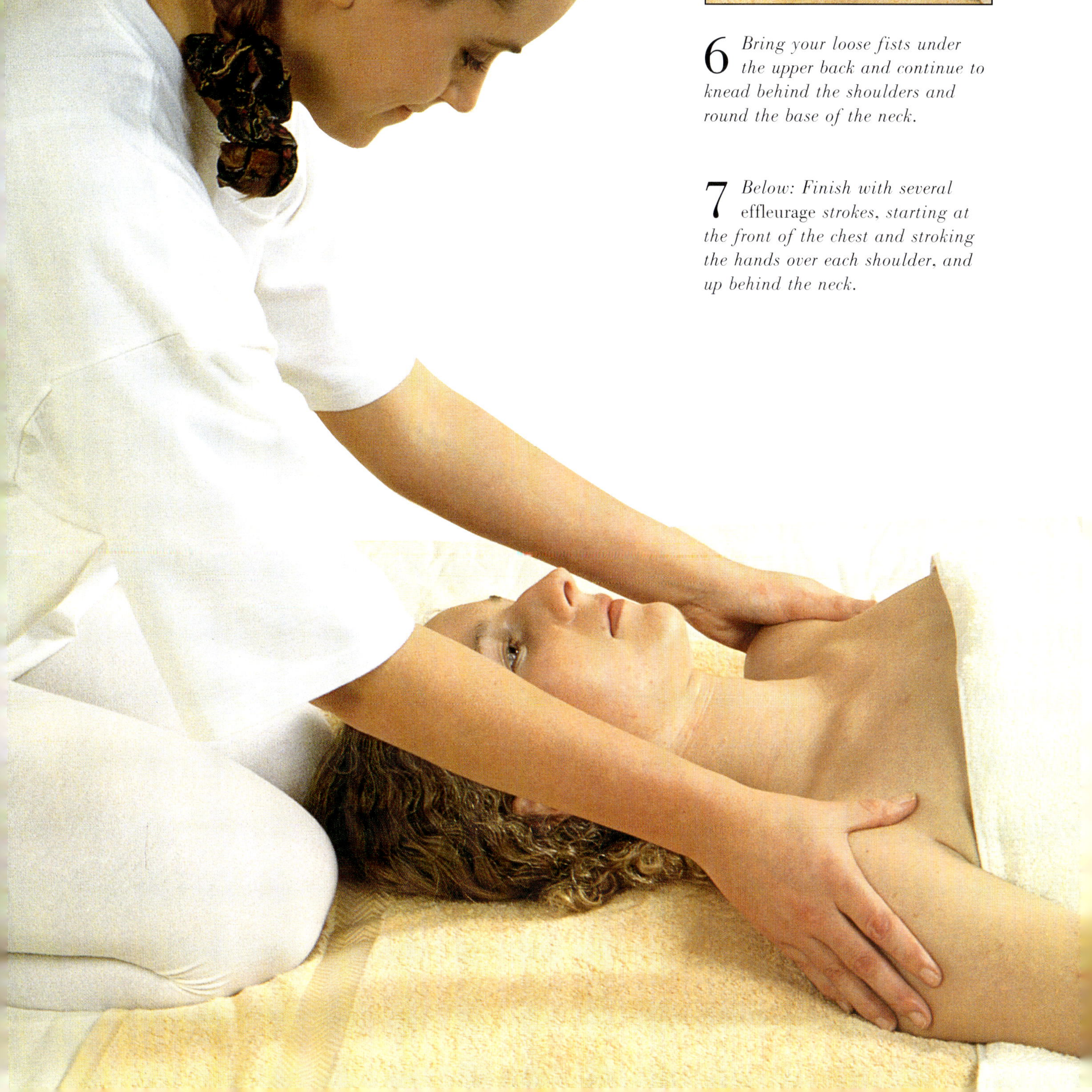

FACE

The face constantly mirrors our health and emotions. Stress and tension are reflected in a furrowed brow, and lines around the eyes, mouth and jawline. A face massage can soothe away headaches, anxiety and exhaustion and replace them with a feeling of serenity. It improves the circulation, giving the skin a healthy glow.

If your partner wears contact lenses make sure they are removed before you start a face massage. Use a little light facial oil, and don't let the oil get too near or in the eyes. Keep the hands relaxed. You may be surprised to find that the face is less fragile than it looks and you can apply quite deep pressure without discomfort.

Your partner will probably still prefer to have a small cushion or towel under the head. Use a towelling hairband to keep the hair off the face.

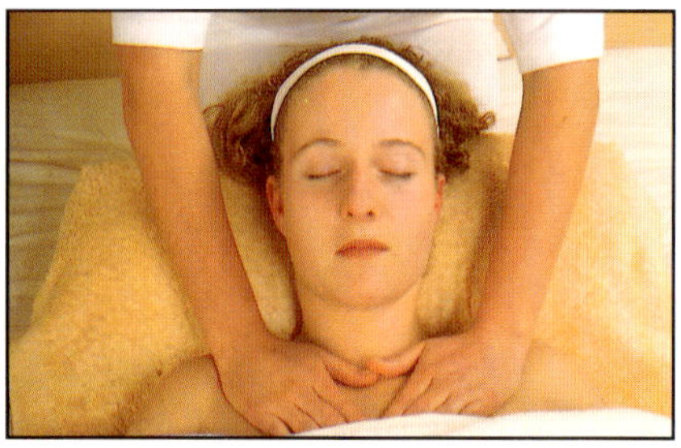

1 *Kneel at the top of your partner's head and lightly oil your palms. With your hands placed over the collarbone, pointing away from you, get ready to begin some gentle* effleurage *strokes.*

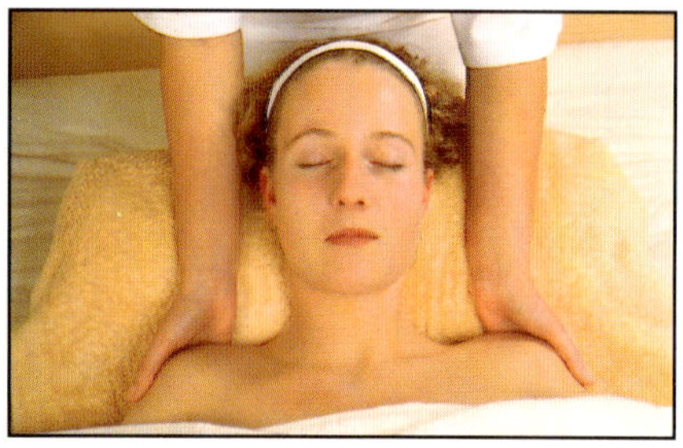

2 *Sweep your hands out across the shoulders, keeping the pressure light.*

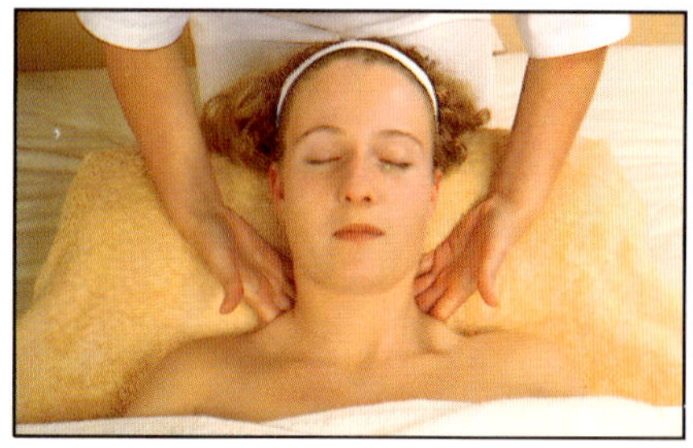

3 *In a continuous movement, bring your hands up round the back of the neck to the nape, pause for a moment, increasing the pressure slightly with the fingertips, then release and lift your hands away.*

Repeat the effleurage *sequence a minimum of three times.*

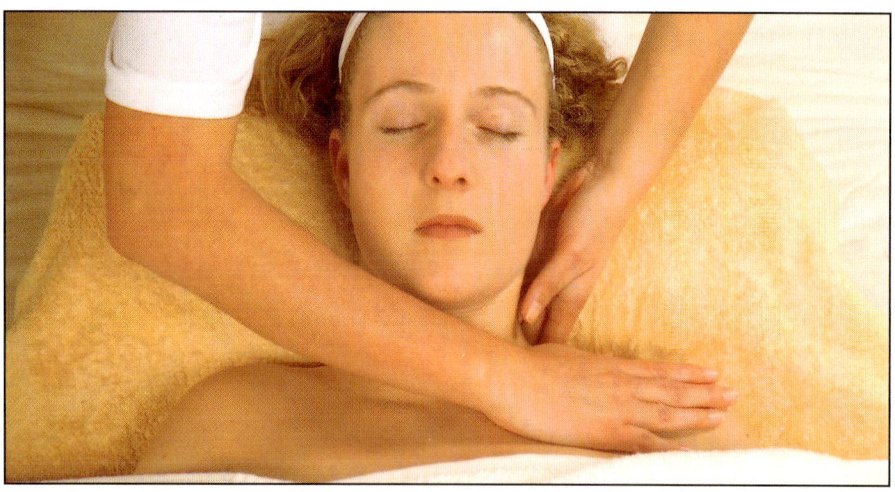

4 *Bring your right arm across the front of your partner so the hand supports the left shoulder. Using light upward strokes, sweep your left hand up from the top of the shoulder, up the side of the neck to the edge of the jaw. Repeat three times.*

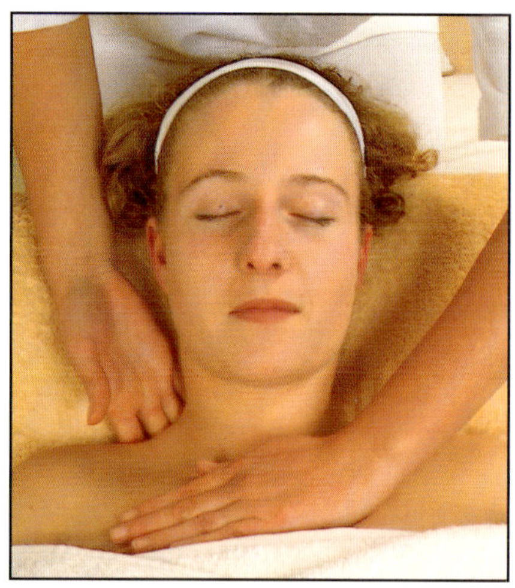

5 *Now repeat this movement on the other side of the neck.*

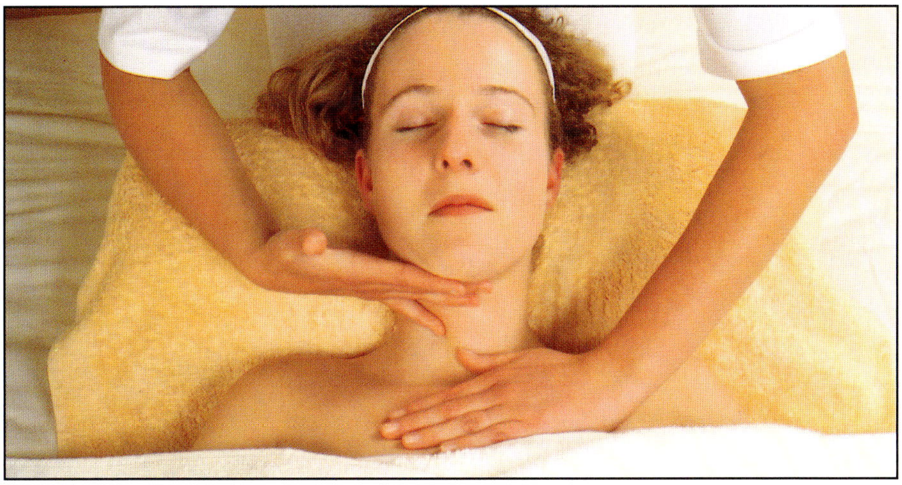

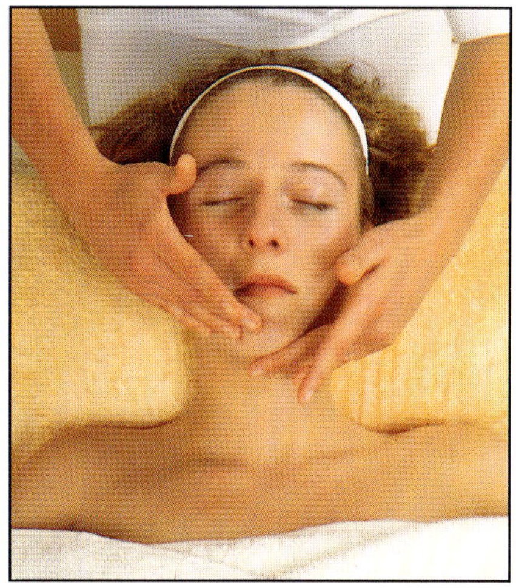

6 *Starting with both hands over the front of the chest, fingers pointing toward each other, lightly sweep the flat of one hand up the front of the neck to the jaw, flicking the hand away when you get there. As you flick the first hand away, bring the second up, so you stroke up with alternate hands. Repeat several times.*

7 *Bring both hands up to the front of the jaw. Alternately sweep one hand and then the other up along the jawline toward the ear. Repeat several times.*

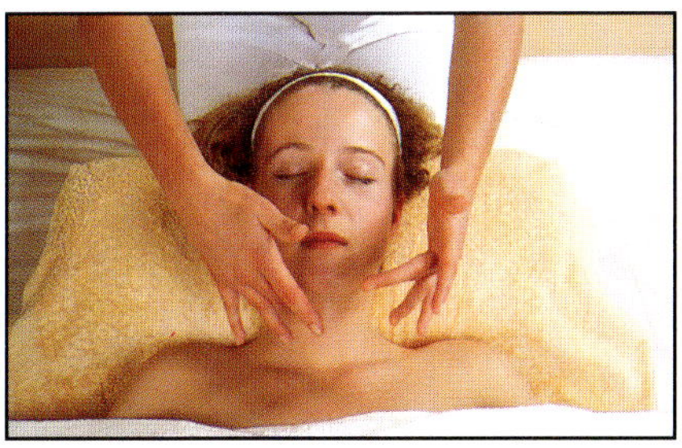

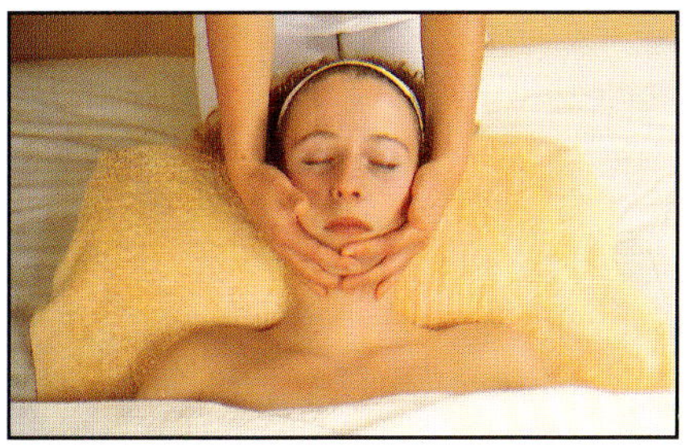

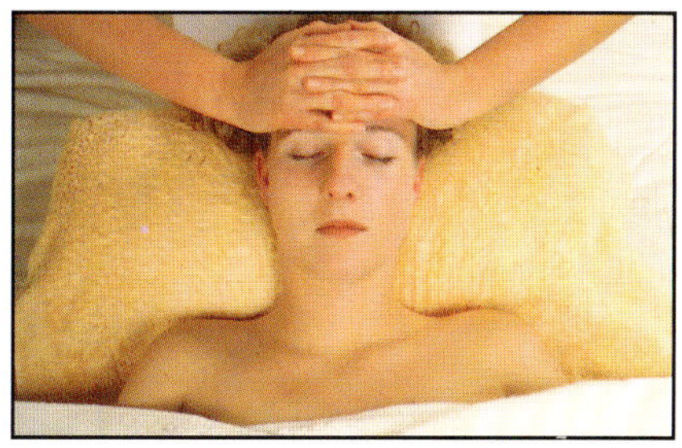

8 *Briskly tap the length of the jawline using the middle and ring fingers, starting from the centre front and working toward the ears. This should be a stimulating movement, so keep the patting quick and fairly firm.*

9 *Afterwards, soothe the area by cradling the face gently with both hands. Pause for several moments then release the hands.*

10 *Bring your hands up to the forehead. Loosely interlock your fingers, and using the palms apply gentle pressure over the forehead. Slowly unlock the fingers to release. Repeat three times.*

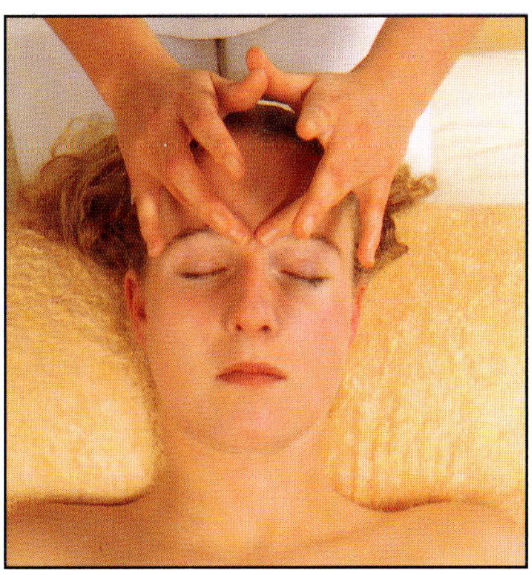

11 *Left: Starting with the third finger of each hand placed on the bridge of the nose, stroke out over the brows toward the temples at each side of the forehead. Come up the forehead a little and, starting again with both fingers at the centre front, repeat the strokes out toward the hairline.*

Repeat a couple of times more, bringing the fingers higher up the forehead each time, until the whole forehead is covered.

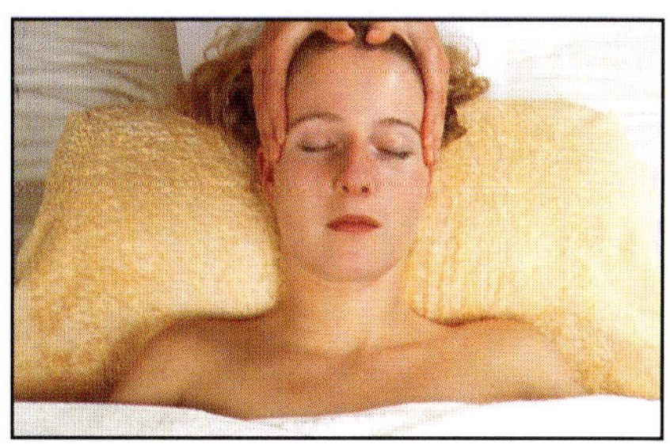

12 *To finish, place your hands on each side of your partner's head, and pause for a few seconds before lifting them away.*

ABDOMEN AND WAIST

Many people feel exposed and vulnerable when baring their abdomen so you will need to be particularly sensitive to your partner when it comes to this part of massage. Start with very gentle strokes, but try to be confident, as a gentle touch which is also tentative can feel unnerving for your partner.

Massage of the abdomen calms the nerves and can soothe stomach aches if they're caused by tension, poor digestion or period pains. It also stimulates the digestive organs so that elimination is improved. You should wait for at least an hour after your partner's meal before giving an abdominal massage.

Kneel beside your partner to do the massage. With a little practice you will find it is possible to tackle both sides from the same position. It helps to start and finish the massage by focusing on your partner's breathing so that your strokes coincide with the intake and expellation. To begin with, try slowly stroking your hands up from the lower abdomen to the chest on inhalation and down the sides on exhalation.

ABDOMEN

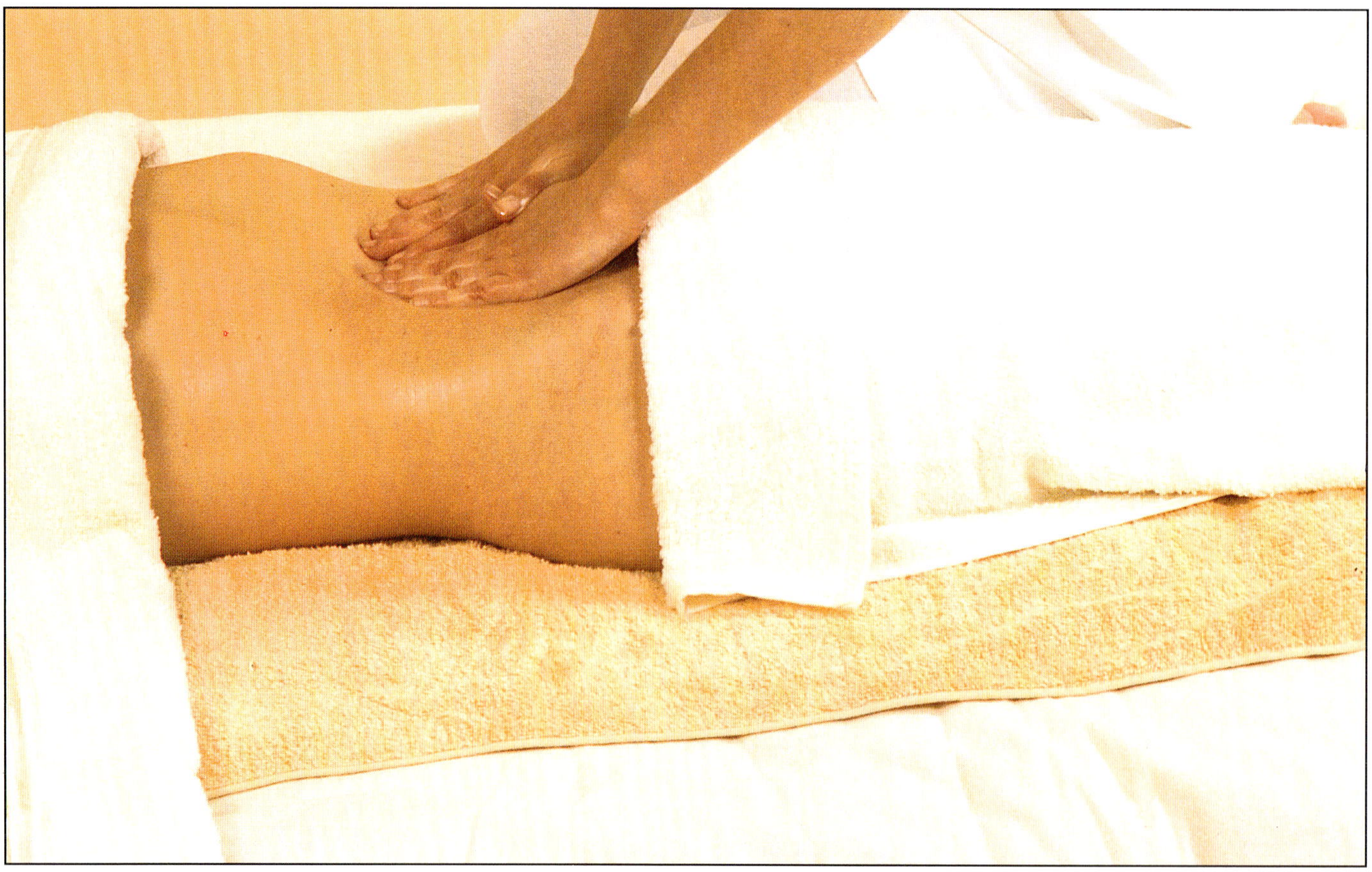

1 *Kneel beside your partner, level with the hips. Lightly oil the palms of the hands, and make contact by gently placing your hands together in a diamond shape over the lower abdomen, pointing toward the head. Keep the fingers together and the hands relaxed. Encourage your partner to breathe into the abdomen so you can feel it expand and contract. Work with the breath.*

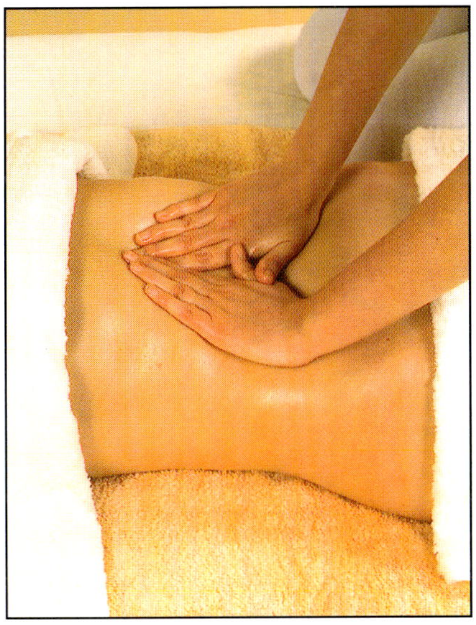

2 *Slowly slide your hands up the centre of the abdomen until you reach the ribs, making sure the pressure is even and not too firm.*

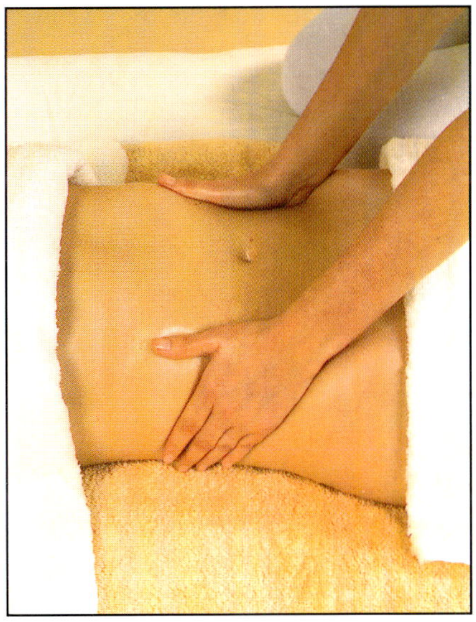

3 *Continue the movement by sweeping the hands out and round the sides of the waist. As you take them out from the ribs toward the sides you can apply a little more pressure, so that you feel the muscles being drawn outward.*

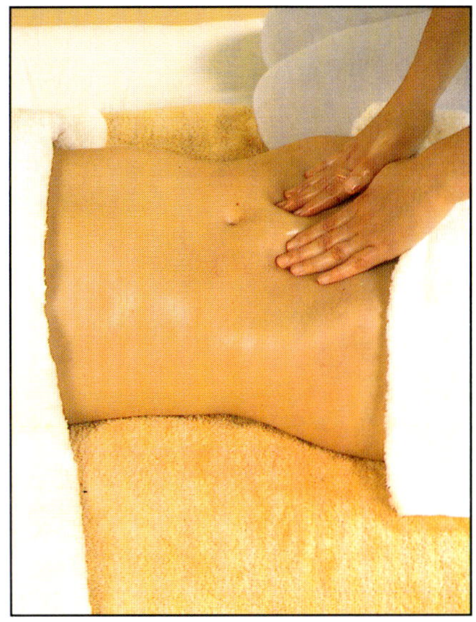

4 *Return to the starting position with both hands placed on the lower abdomen and repeat this continuous movement several times. Apply more oil as necessary.*

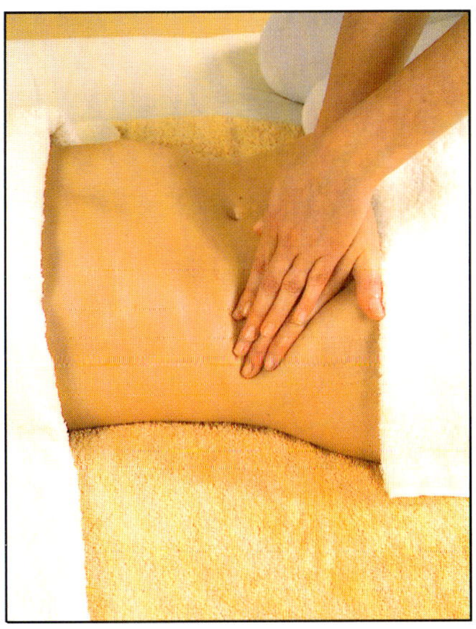

5 *Place both hands on your partner's lower abdomen at the right-hand side, ready to circle the navel. Your left hand rests over the right for support.*

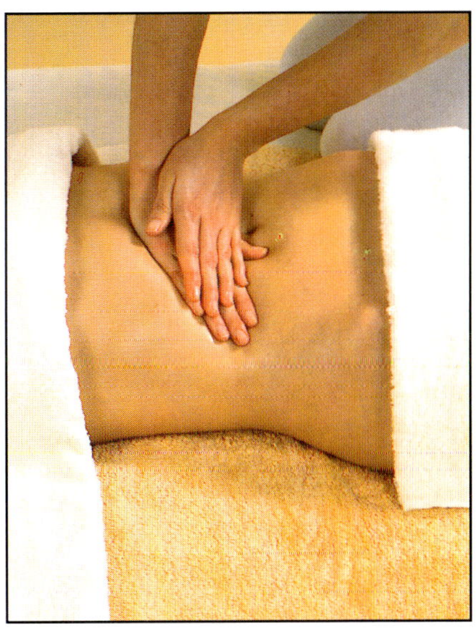

6 *Stroke upward, keeping the left hand over the right, until you reach the ribs. The pressure can be quite firm to stimulate the digestive system. Keep the stroke smooth and continuous.*

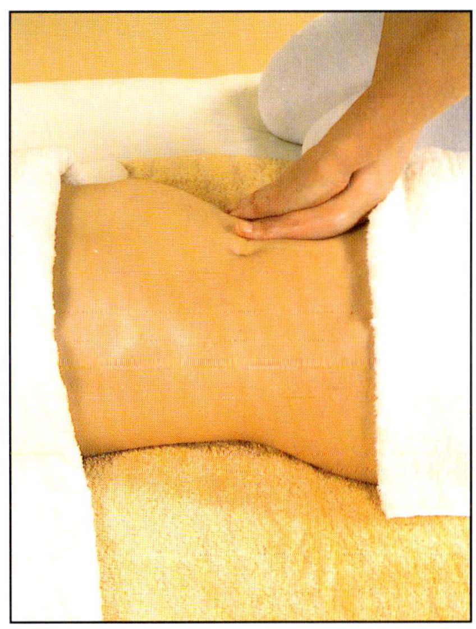

7 *Continue the stroke by bringing your hands across under the ribs, and down the left side of your partner's abdomen. It is important that the direction you work in is up your partner's right side, across and down the left side.*

Repeat the navel-circling movement three times, each time returning to the centre of the lower abdomen.

WAIST

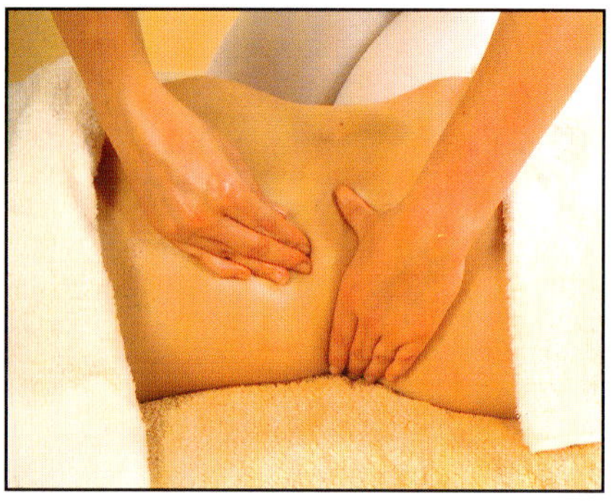

1 *Begin kneading round the waist area by squeezing and releasing the flesh from one hand to the other. These movements should be firm and stimulating.*

2, 3 *Right and below right: Cross your hands over your partner's waist so the palms are grasping the sides of the midriff. Briskly draw them up the side of the waist, uncrossing the hands over the top of the abdomen and turning the palms as they travel down the other side. Draw up again and recross the arms to the original starting position. Keep the speed of this fairly quick and apply firm pressure to draw the flesh up the sides, then lighten your touch across the top of the abdomen. Repeat four times.*

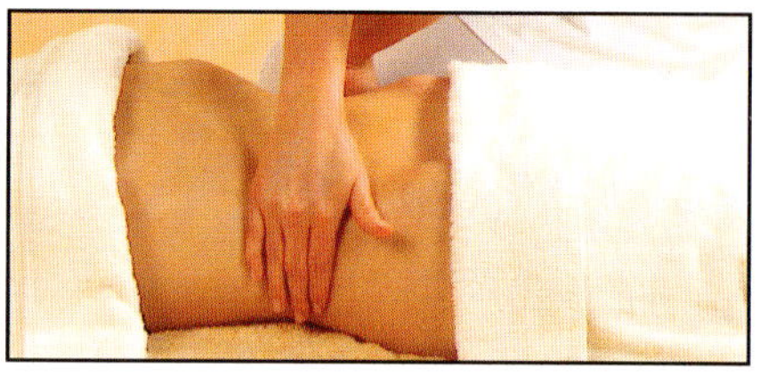

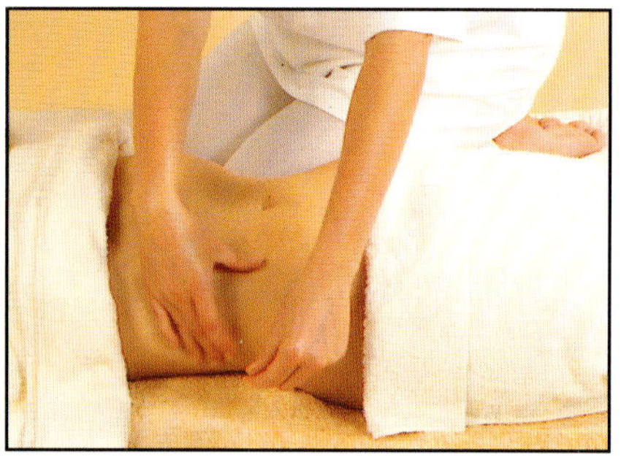

4 *Starting at the far side of the waist, lightly pinch the flesh between fingers and thumbs with brisk, short stimulating movements. Repeat on the other side of the waist.*

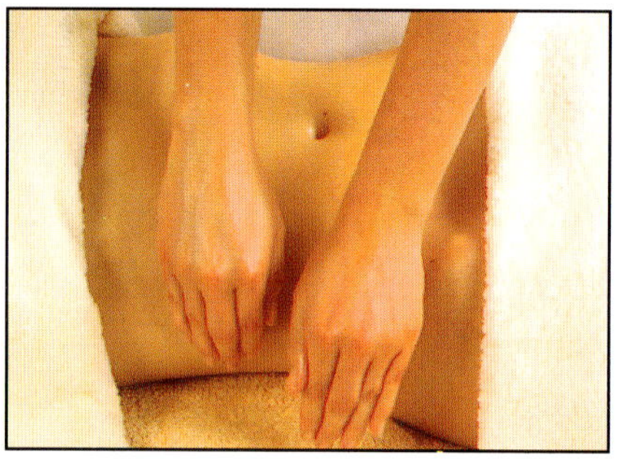

5 *With loosely cupped hands, lightly cup the side of the waist, keeping the pace fast and stimulating, but at the same time checking that it is not causing discomfort. The action should be enough to increase the flow of blood to the area without hurting.*

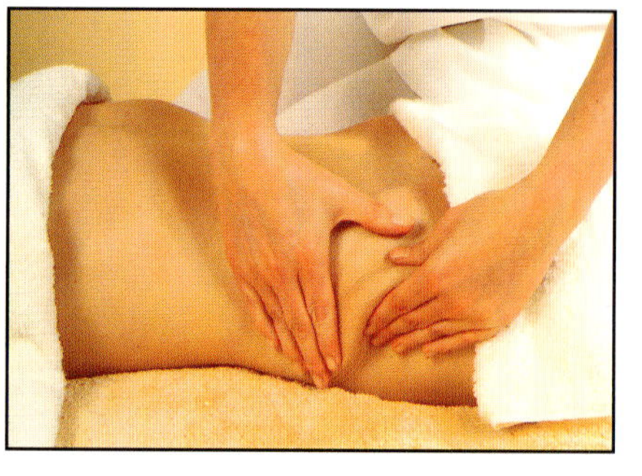

6 *Working on the top of the hip area, squeeze and release the flesh in a kneading movement, using deep and stimulating pressure.*

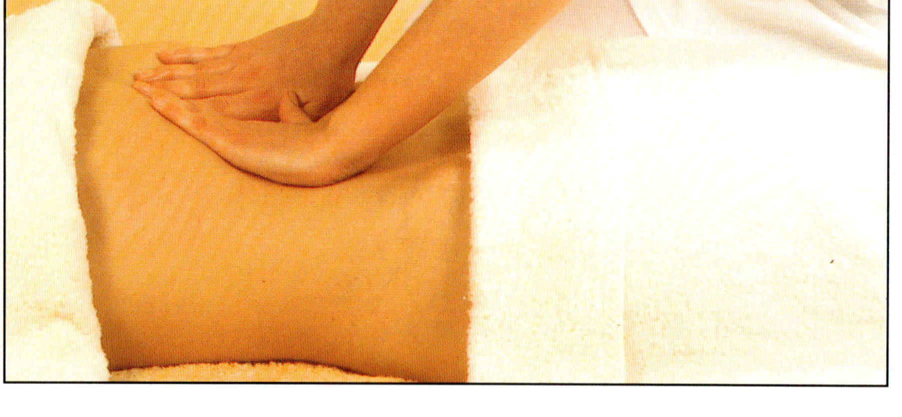

7 *Left: Finish the massage of the abdomen by repeating the soothing effleurage strokes from the beginning of the sequence. End with both hands placed over the centre of the abdomen, fingers pointing toward the head. Hold for a few seconds before lifting off.*

BACK OF BODY

Ask your partner to turn over on to their front, ready for you to start work on the back of the legs and buttocks. Rest their head to one side.

LEGS AND BUTTOCKS

The backs of the legs and buttocks offer plenty of scope for massage techniques. Most people can take plenty of firm massage on the larger muscles in the thighs and buttocks. The fleshy parts are ideal for kneading and squeezing and the firmer pressure can feel wonderfully satisfying. In contrast though, the most gentle effleurage *can still stimulate other body functions to improve their efficiency. Poor circulation and a sluggish lymphatic system can be considerably improved with a good leg massage. Tiredness and heaviness in the legs is alleviated and your partner should have a renewed feeling of energy afterwards.*

EFFLEURAGE

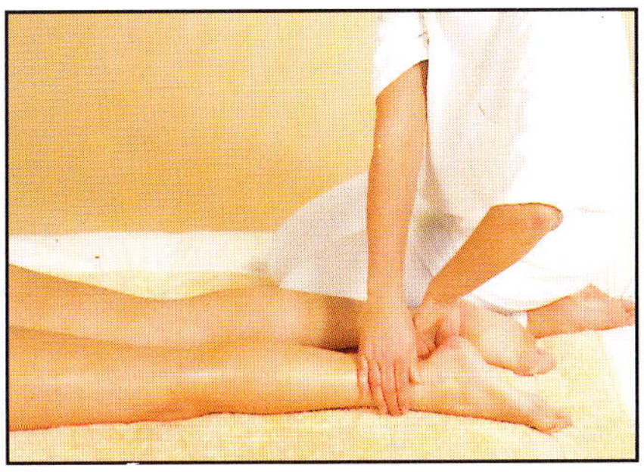

1 *Left: Start by kneeling on one side of your partner's ankles. You should be able to work on both legs from the same side. Begin by working on the leg furthest away from you.*

Lightly oil your hands and place them crossed over the back of the left ankle.

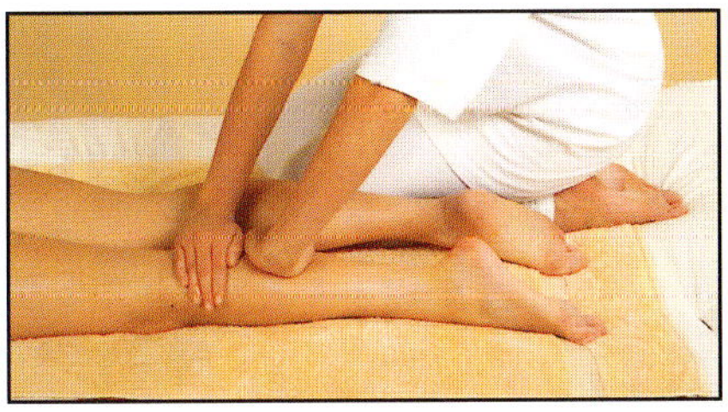

2 *In a smooth and continuous movement,* effleurage *up the leg, with right hand leading the left. When you get to the back of the knee pause for two seconds.*

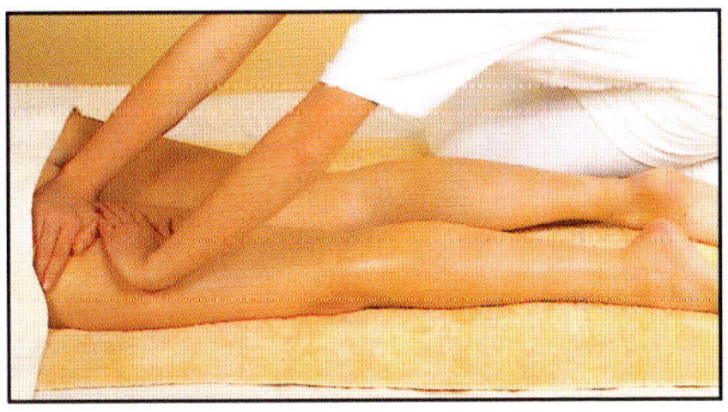

3 *Carry the stroke up the leg and at the top of the thigh cross the hands, keeping the pressure even and light.*

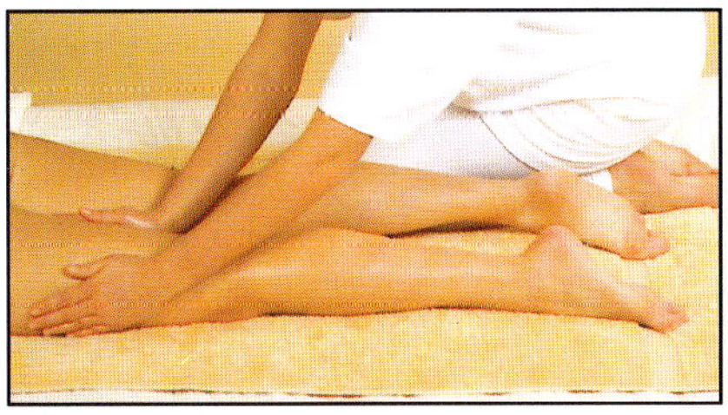

4 *Bring your hands back down the sides of the leg until you reach the back of the ankle again.*

Repeat the sequence three times, each time increasing the pressure slightly on the upward stroke toward the heart.

UPPER LEGS AND BUTTOCKS

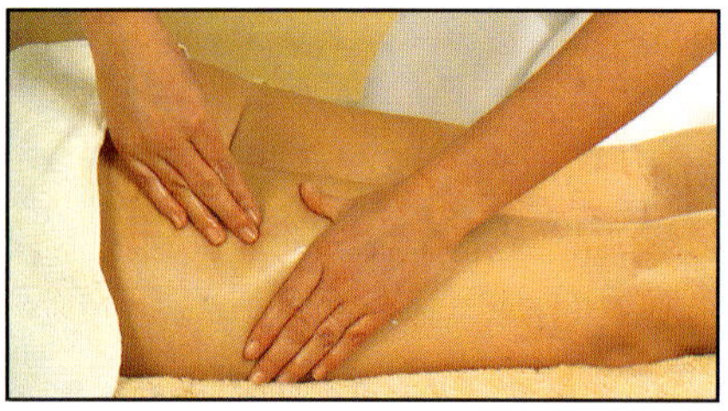

1 Move to a kneeling position beside your partner's upper leg. Using a firm kneading movement, squeeze and release the back of the thigh muscles, working up to the buttocks. You should be able to pick up quite a large area of muscle between the hands.

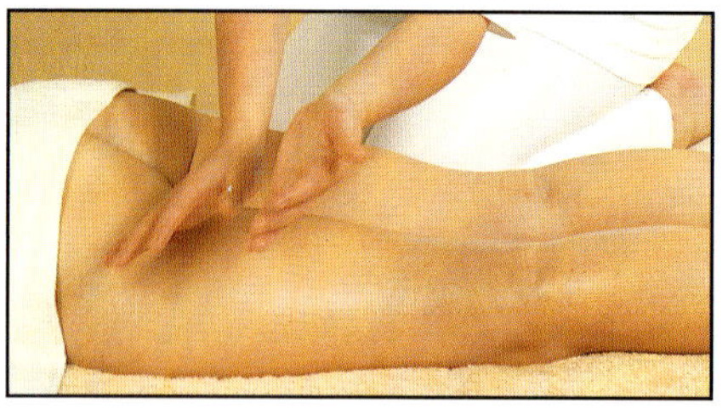

2 With the outside edge of the hands, do some short sharp hacking movements. Alternate the hands in a quick, repetitive action. Continue the hacking all over the back of the upper leg and the buttocks.

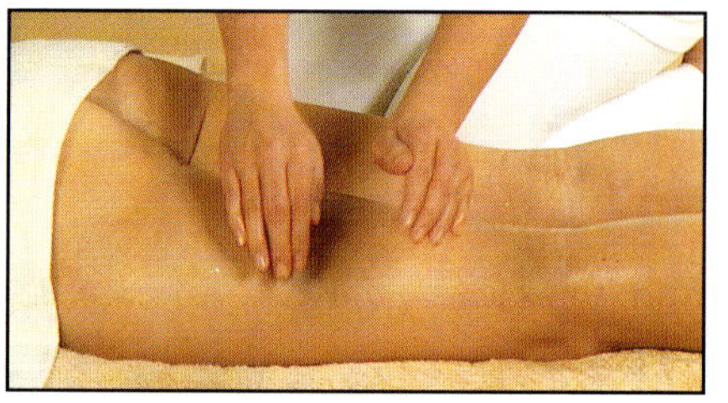

3 Continue working on the upper leg and buttocks, with some cupping. The cupping action should be short and fast to stimulate the whole area.

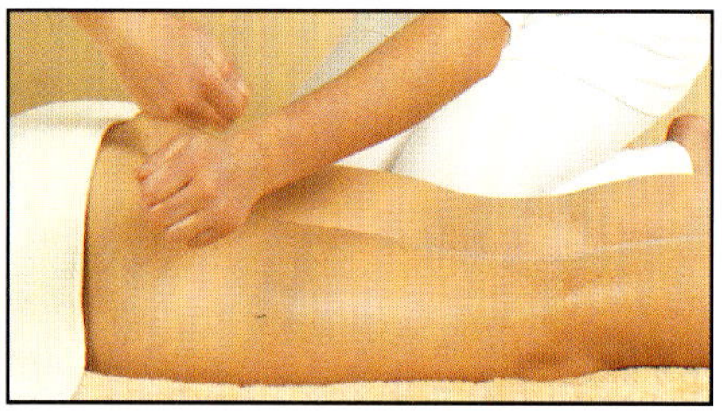

4 With loose fists, briskly pound the top and outside of the thigh. You can use the backs of your fingers or the outside edge of the fists. Use a firmer knuckling action over the buttock area.

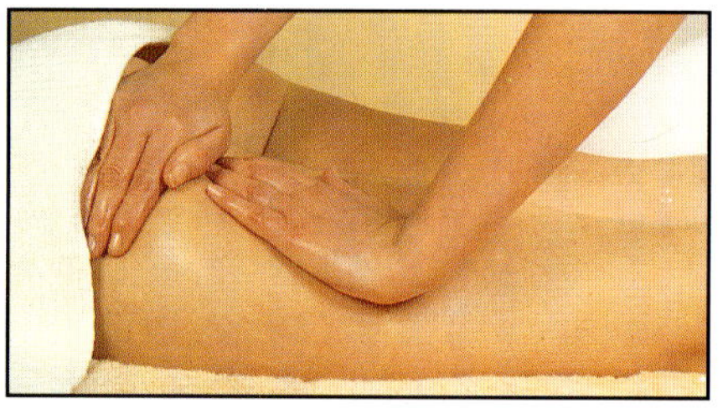

5 Follow this sequence of friction movements with soothing effleurage *strokes from the back of the knee to the top of the thigh, sweeping out and back down the leg to the knee.*

CALVES

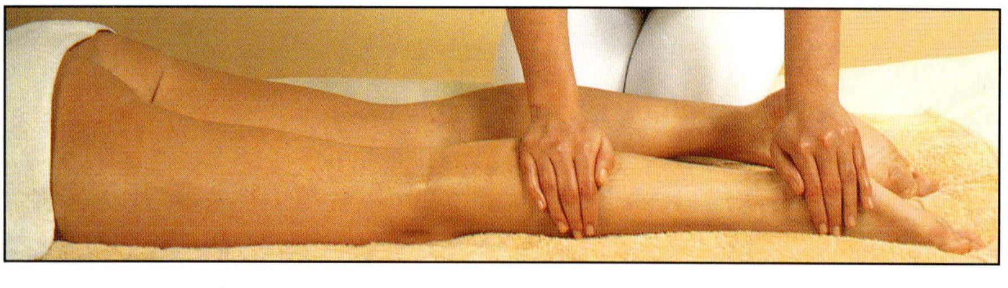

1 Move back down to kneel beside your partner's ankles. Lightly oil your hands again if necessary. Start with both hands on the back of your partner's ankle. Smooth your right hand up toward the knee, keeping your left hand on the ankle for support.

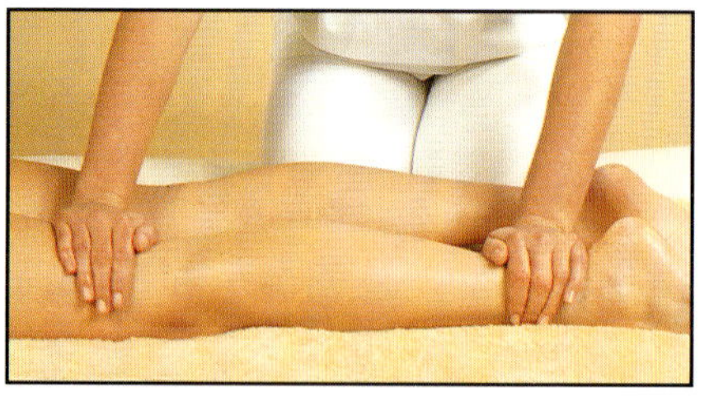

2 Continue to stroke the right hand toward the thigh, keeping the pressure light as you reach the back of the knee.

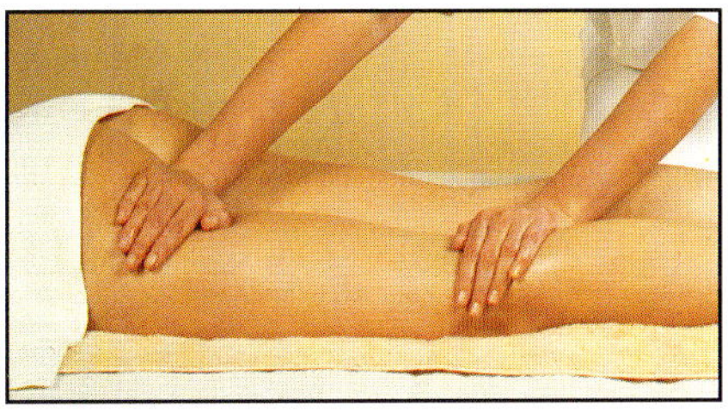

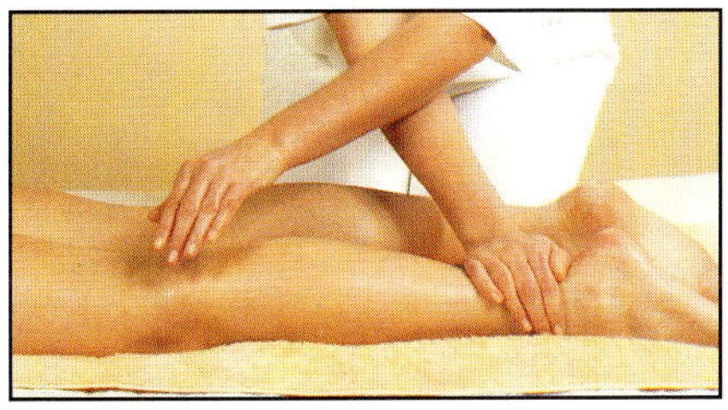

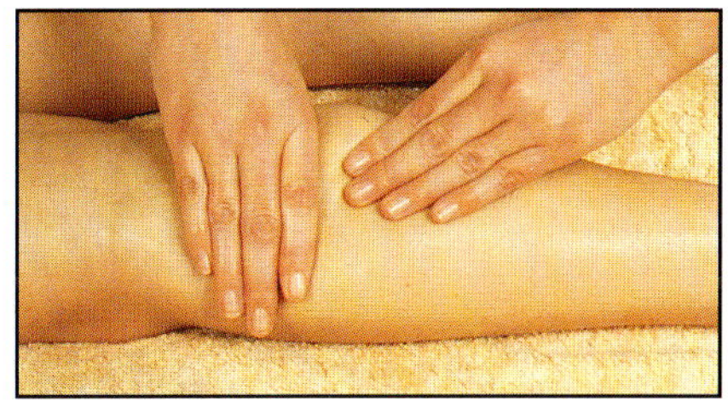

3 As you continue the stroke, taking your right hand up toward the top of the thigh, simultaneously slide your left hand up the lower leg to the back of the knee. Try to make this a flowing movement.

4 Without pausing, bring your right hand in a continuous stroke back down the leg. When you reach the knee you will need to slide the left hand off the knee, so the right hand can continue right down to the ankle again.

Repeat three times, or until you feel confident with the movement.

5 Start kneading the calf with both hands, working from the ankle up to the knee. Don't knead the back of the knee. Squeeze and release the calf muscle as you go. If your partner's calf muscles are particularly tight this kneading action may feel uncomfortable, so ask your partner if the pressure is right.

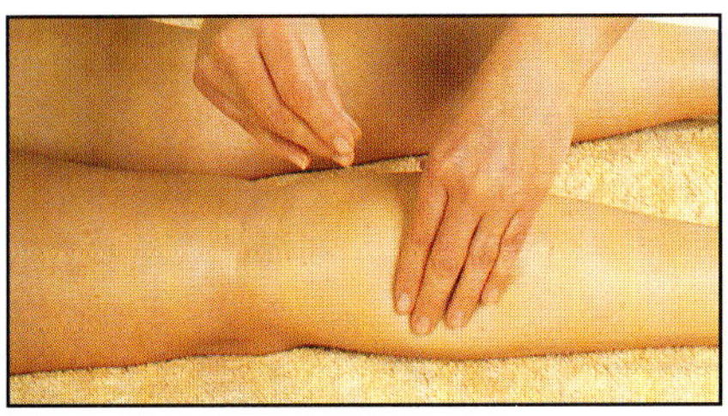

6 Do some short, sharp pinching movements all over the calf muscle, again checking that you are not hurting your partner.

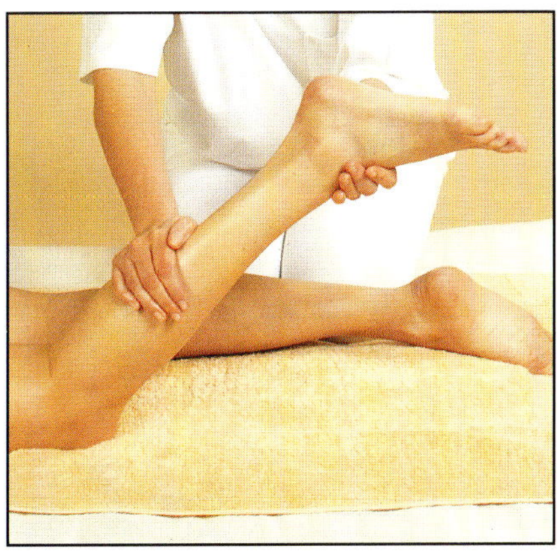

7 Left: Lifting and supporting your partner's leg in the left hand, slide your right hand up from the back of the ankle to the knee. Keep the pressure as firm as is comfortable. Repeat three times. Gently return the leg to rest on the floor.

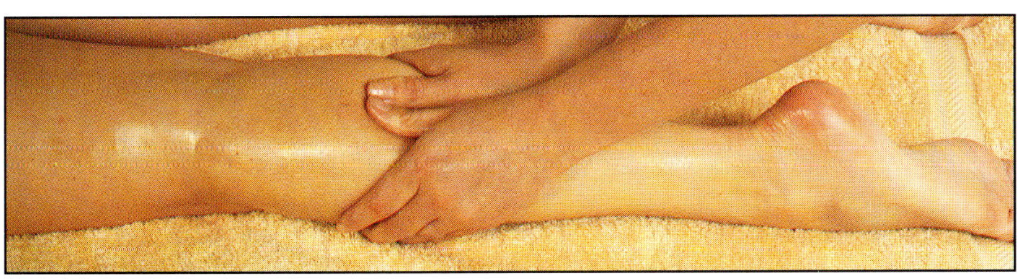

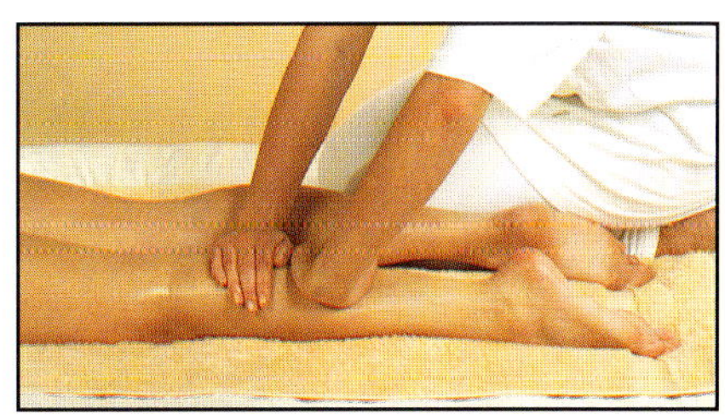

8 With your thumbs together start at the back of the ankle, and work up the back of the calf to the knee, applying pressure firm enough to release tightness in these muscles. When you reach the back of the knee, lighten the pressure and sweep your hands back down the sides of the leg to the ankle. Repeat three times.

9 To complete the back of the leg massage, repeat the effleurage *strokes from the beginning of the sequence, stroking the leg from ankle to thigh and back down to the ankle again. Repeat three times to soothe the leg.*

Repeat the entire back of leg massage on your partner's other leg, covering the leg you have worked on with a towel to keep the muscles warm.

BACK AND SHOULDERS

The back is an area of great strength and mobility, and it is the main supportive structure of the body. It therefore warrants more attention than most other areas. By working on the back you can reach nerves affecting every part of the body.

Full back massage, with emphasis on the spine and lower back, greatly alleviates effects of stress throughout the body, enhancing physical and psychological well-being. Smooth, flowing strokes stretch the muscles and tissues round contours of the back, and help restore flexibility for health and mobility, whilst stronger strokes along the spinal muscles and over the lower back bring deeper relief to aching or knotted muscles.

You should never massage directly on the spine itself, although working down each side is highly beneficial. Avoid using percussion strokes such as hacking and cupping on the kidneys, which are level with the waistline in the centre of the back.

First, make sure your partner is comfortable, lying face down with arms resting beside the face. Support the forehead with a rolled towel, and if helpful, use a pillow, cushion or rolled towel under the chest. It helps to have hair clear from the back of the neck.

EFFLEURAGE

Kneel beside your partner's right hip and oil your hands. With your first long effleurage *strokes try to concentrate on finding areas of particular tension and tightness.*

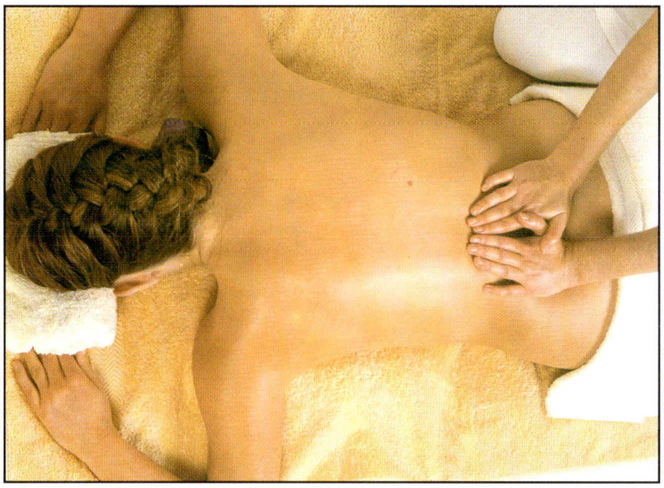

1 *Starting at the lower back begin the* effleurage *strokes. With thumbs crossed to connect the hands together, move slowly up the centre of the back, putting firm pressure on the fingertips.*

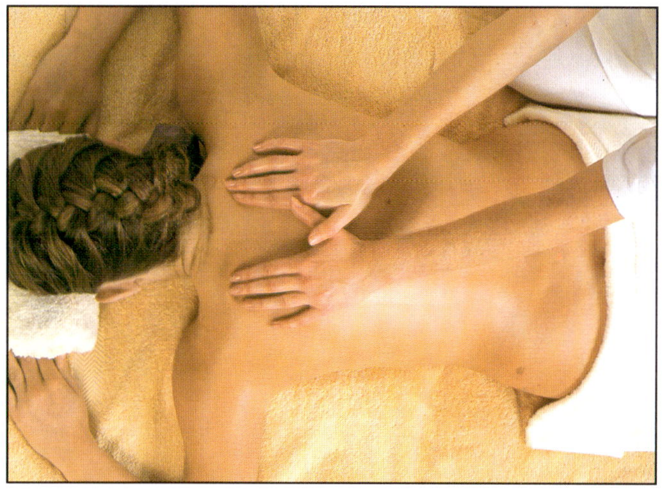

2 *Take the stroke up to the top of the back in a continuous movement.*

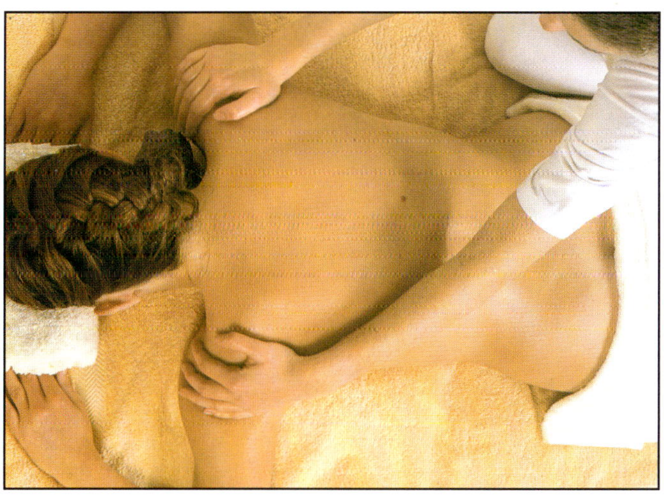

3 *Without a pause, separate the hands at the top of the back, sweeping them out and round the shoulders.*

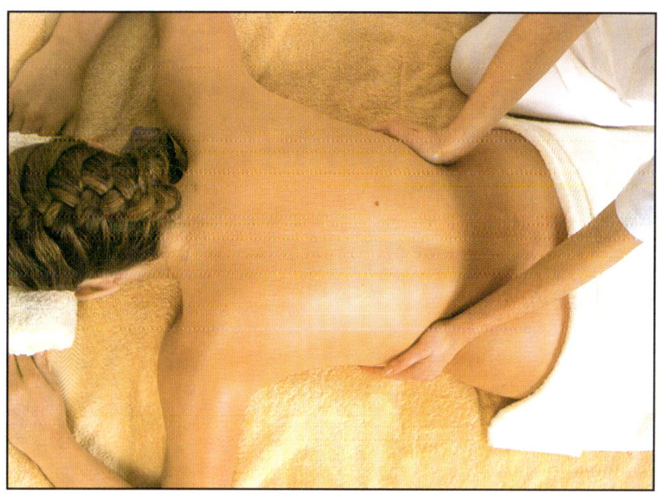

4 *Continue the stroke, bringing both hands down the sides of the back to the lower back, ready to begin again.*

Repeat this effleurage *sequence three times, oiling your hands each time.*

SHOULDERS

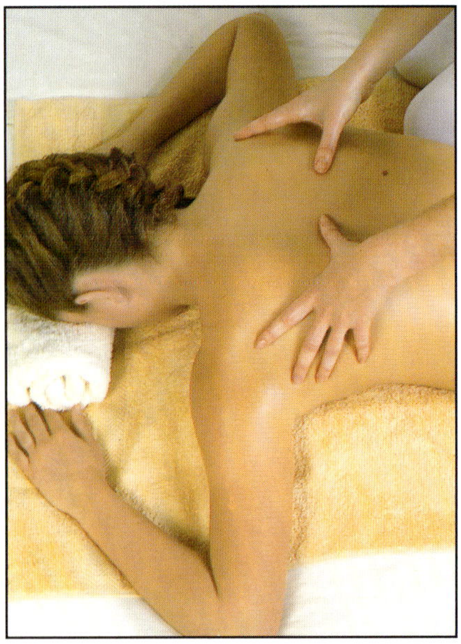

1 Using your thumbs each side of the spine, start level with the shoulder blades and make circling pressure movements, working quite firmly into the muscles.

2 Continue working up each side of the spine until you reach the nape of the neck.

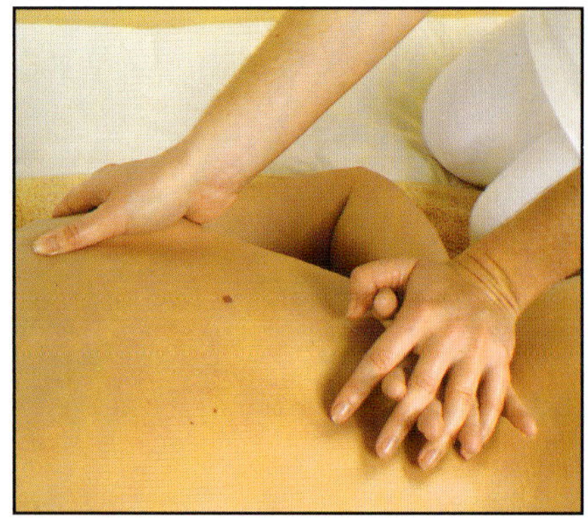

3 Carefully bring your partner's arm across the hollow of the back and clasp their right hand with your left to support the arm. The shoulder blade should now stick out slightly. With your right thumb make circular pressure movements over the shoulder area. Strong muscles support the shoulder blade and you can work firmly under the bone itself to release tightness in this area.

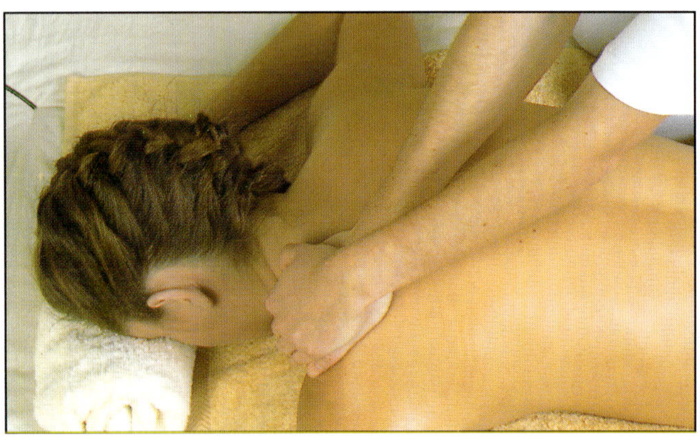

4 With your left hand resting over your right to increase the pressure, work in small, circular movements from the base of the neck out over the shoulder.

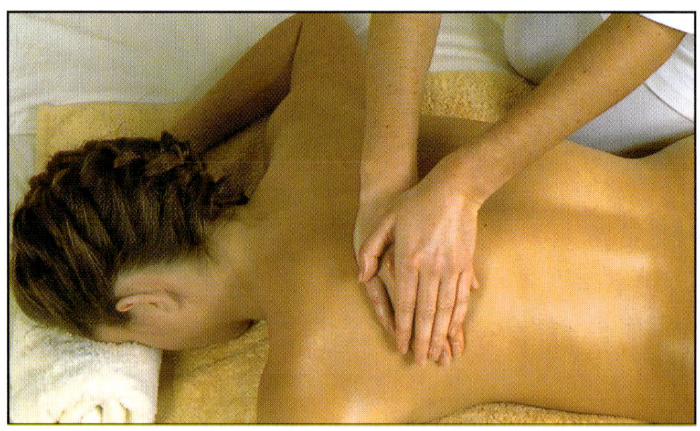

5 Continue round to the shoulder blade, using firm pressure to release tension in the muscle.

Move to the other side of your partner and repeat these steps on the other shoulder.

BACK

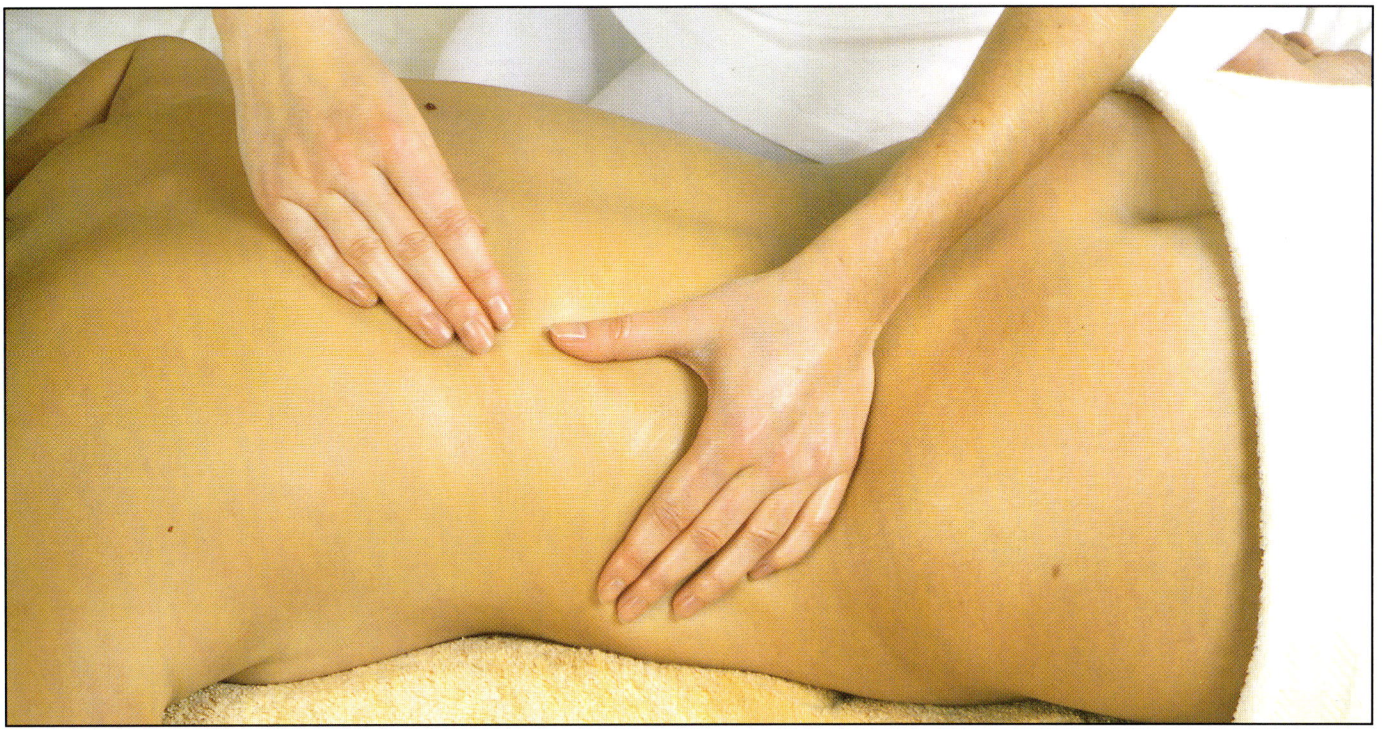

1 Kneeling to the right side of your partner, start to knead the far side of the back firmly with both hands, beginning at the outer sides of the waist. Pick up, roll and release the muscles, alternately pressing one hand toward another. Continue kneading up the back until you reach the shoulders. Start again at the waist but this time come closer to the spine and repeat the line of kneading up the back.

Repeat the kneading on the near side of the back. You should be able to do this without moving your kneeling position.

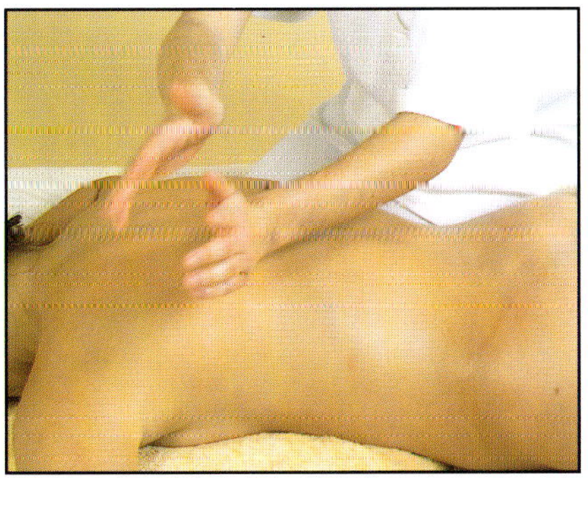

2 Using the outer edge of the hands, briskly and rhythmically hack from the lower back up to the shoulders, but avoid the bony shoulder blade. Try to visualize each side of the back divided into three sections, so you cover the whole back thoroughly.

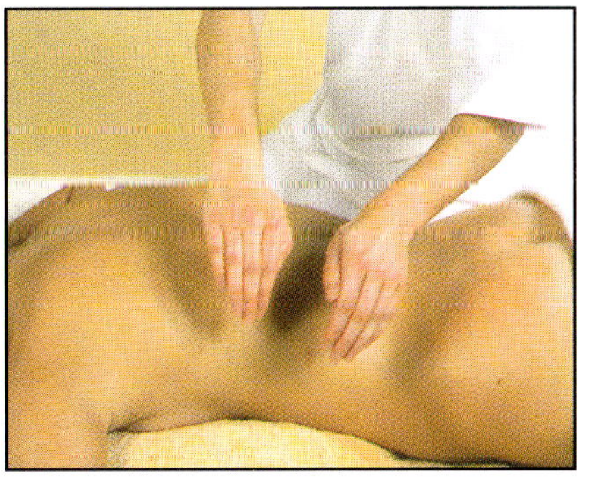

3 Start cupping from the lower back up the back and across the shoulders. The action should be quick, with alternate hands striking the back briskly.

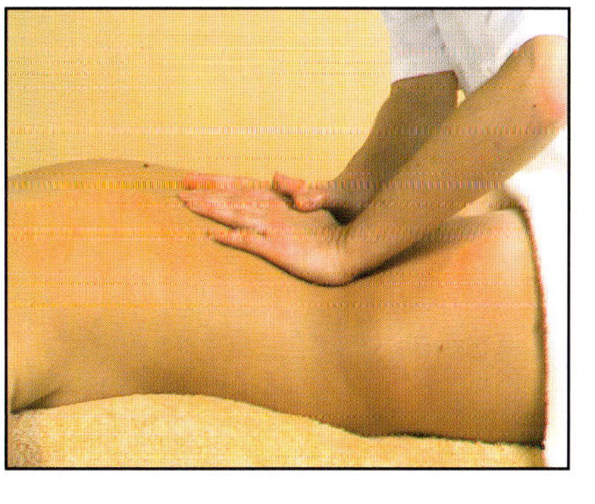

4 Repeat the effleurage strokes from the beginning of the sequence to soothe the back. Repeat a number of times.

SPINE

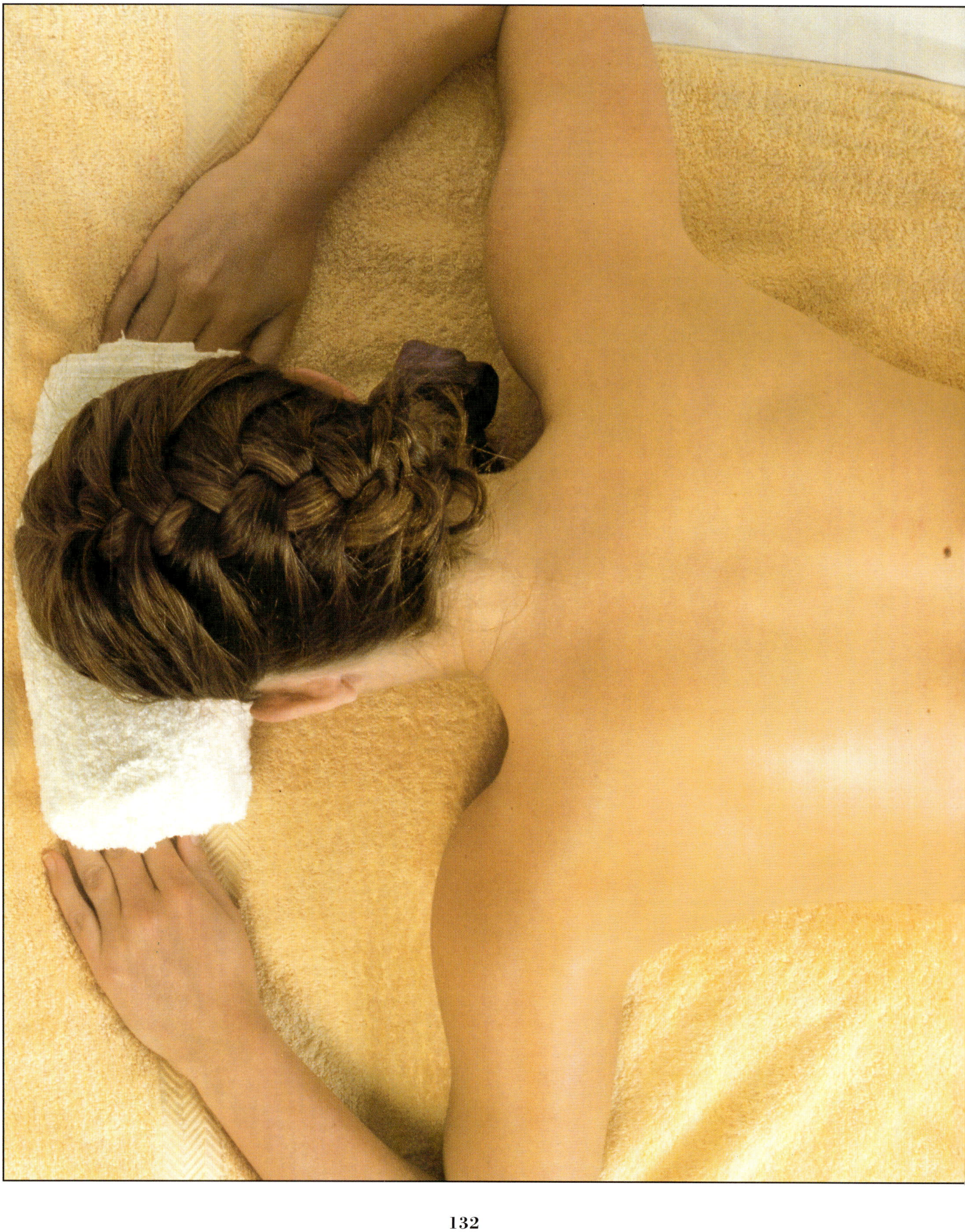

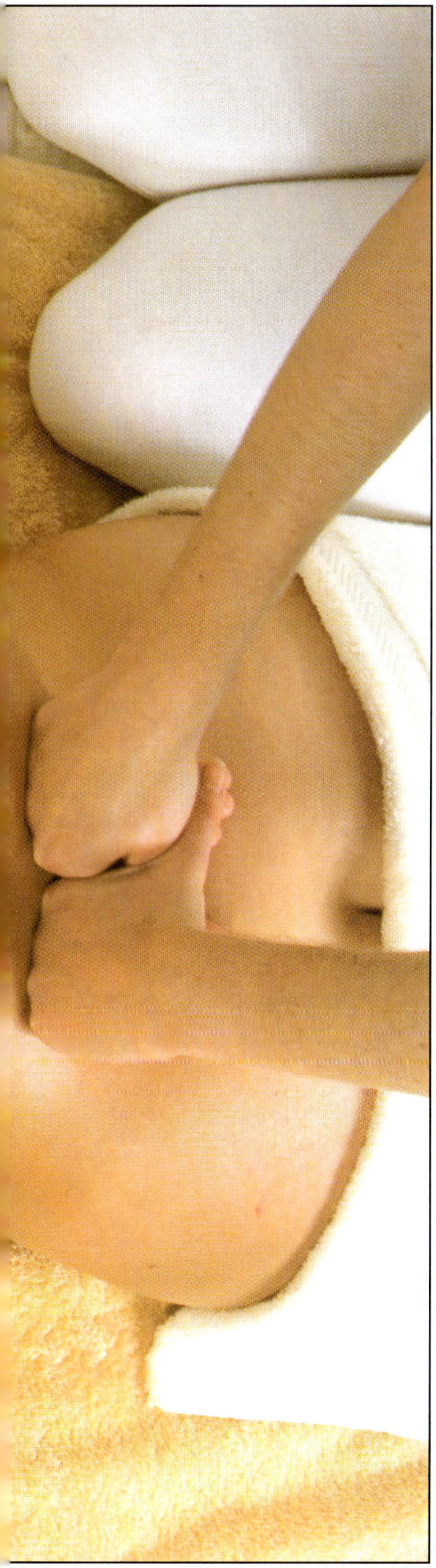

1 *Left: With loose fists, and thumbs crossed for support, push the top of the hands up each side of the spine to the nape of the neck.*

2 *Right: Uncurl the fingers when you get to the nape and sweep them back down the sides of the back. Repeat three times.*

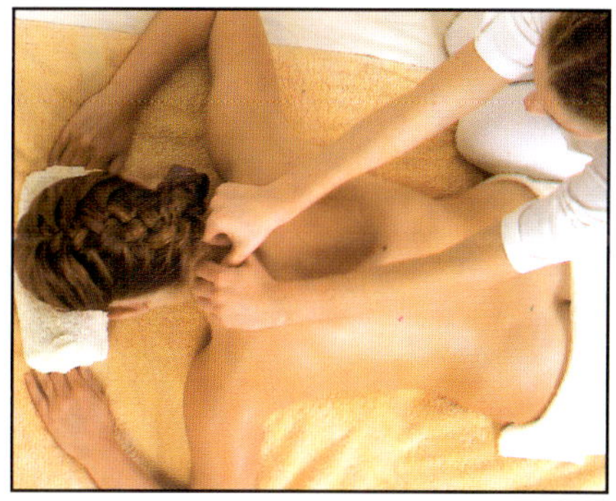

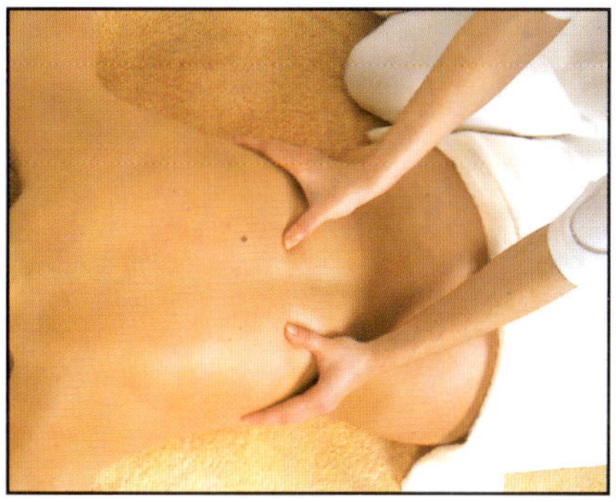

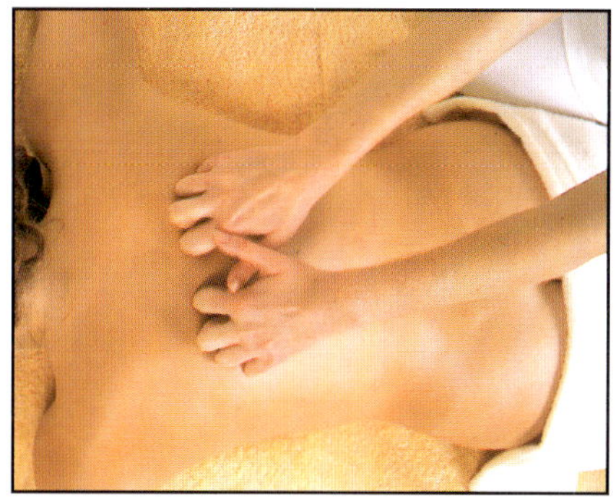

3 *Starting at the lower back, place the thumbs on either side of the spine, resting your hands either side of the back. Rotate the thumbs in small circles, travelling up the sides of the spine until you reach the hairline. Use firm pressure. Reverse the movement, circling your thumbs back down each side of the spine.*

4 *Starting at the lower back, use loose knuckles, crossing your thumbs over each other for support, to work up either side of the spine and back down again. Repeat twice.*

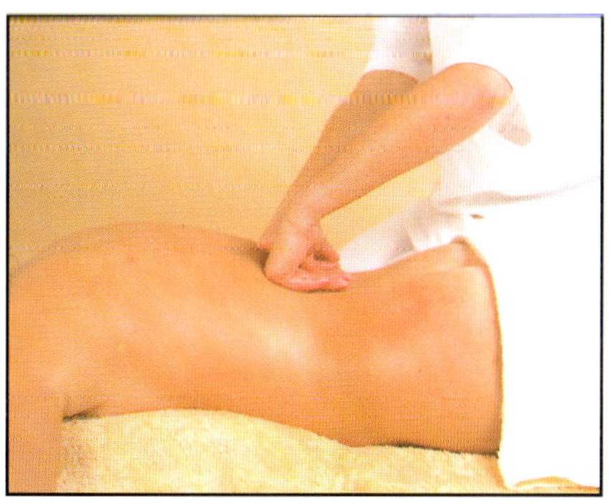

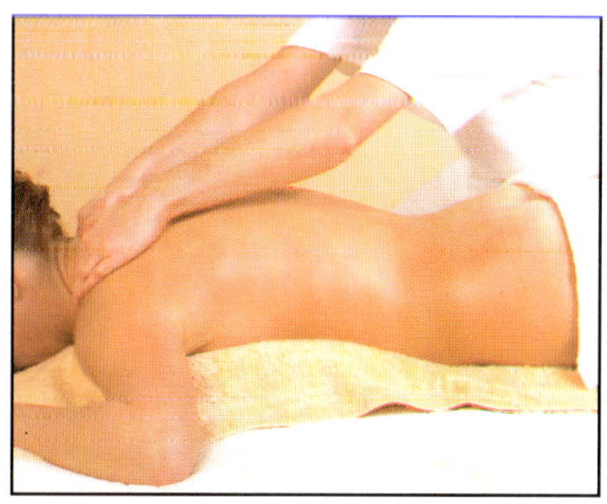

5 *Using the backs of your hands and starting at the lower back, push up either side of the spine to just above the waistline. Then sweep your hands outward and back down round the hips. Repeat three times.*

6 *To finish the massage, repeat the* effleurage *strokes from the beginning of the sequence, starting at the lower back, up the back, round the shoulders and down again to the lower back, in a continuous sweeping movement.*

SELF MASSAGE

A simple, effective self massage can do wonders to ease away tension and restore energy after a stressful, tiring day. After a shower or bath, massaging the body with lotions and oils is very relaxing and helps keep the skin in glowing condition.

You can use self massage to target particular aches and pains or areas of tension, for relief just where you need it. The beauty of self massage is you can do it to suit your needs and moods at any time – to unwind in the evening or to energize yourself in the morning.

SHOULDERS

1 *Sitting upright, start from the base of the neck and press down with your fingers along the top of the shoulders. As you reach the bony part of the shoulder, slide your hand back to the base of the neck, and repeat the pressing at least three times. Finish by stroking firmly from neck to shoulder and then repeat on the other side of the neck.*

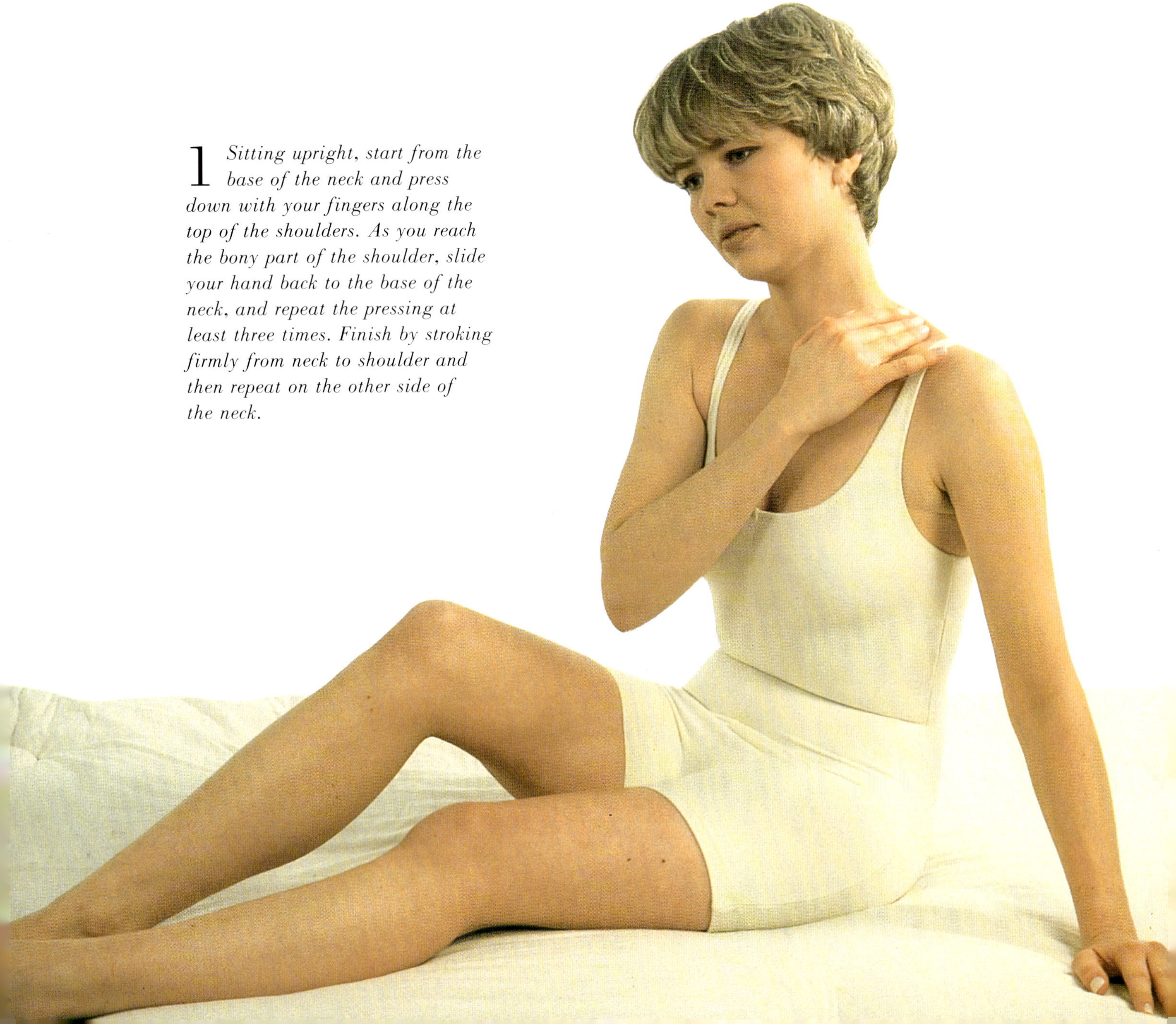

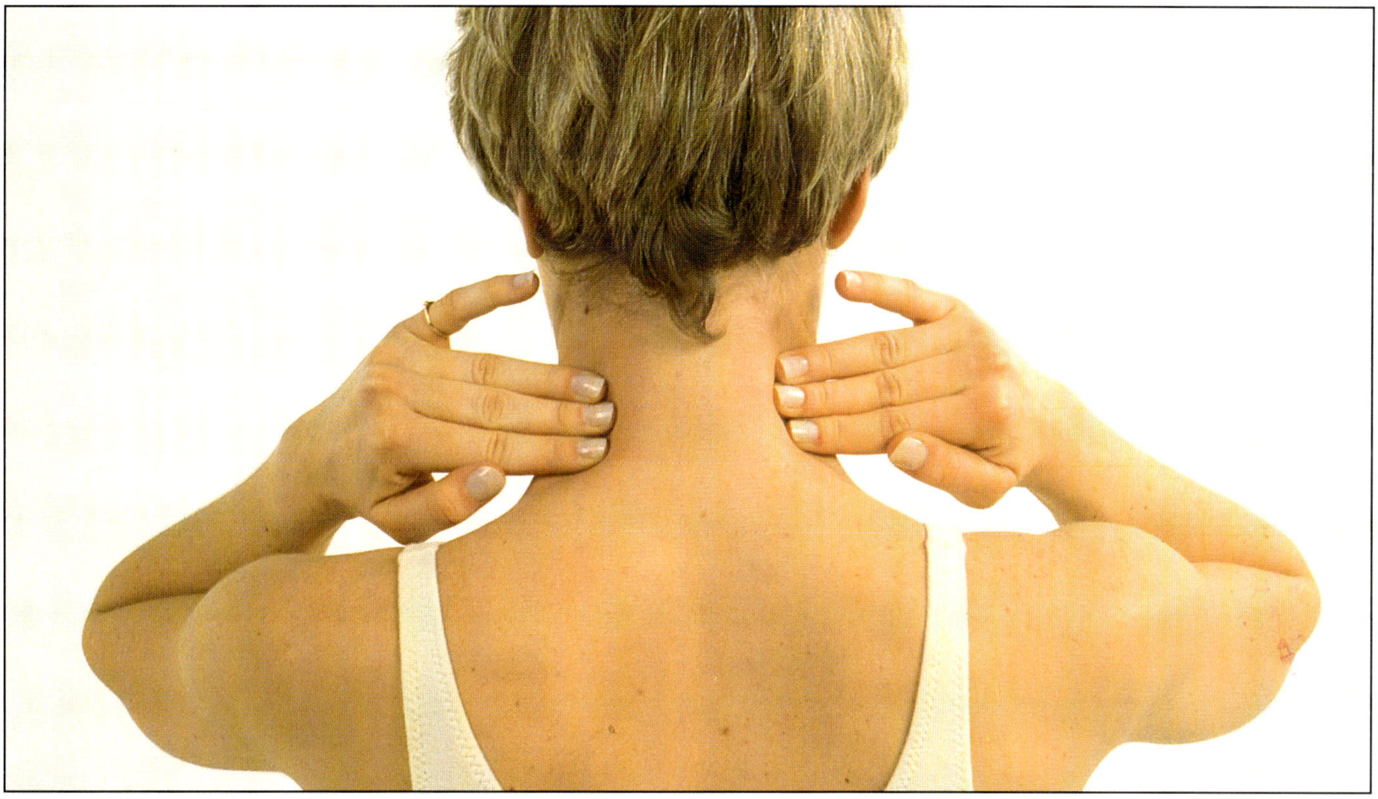

2 *Use the fingertips of both hands to make small circular movements, working up the back of the neck. Gentle circular movements, where you can feel yourself easing muscular tightness, are better than direct, static pressures on this area. Continue up and round the base of the skull.*

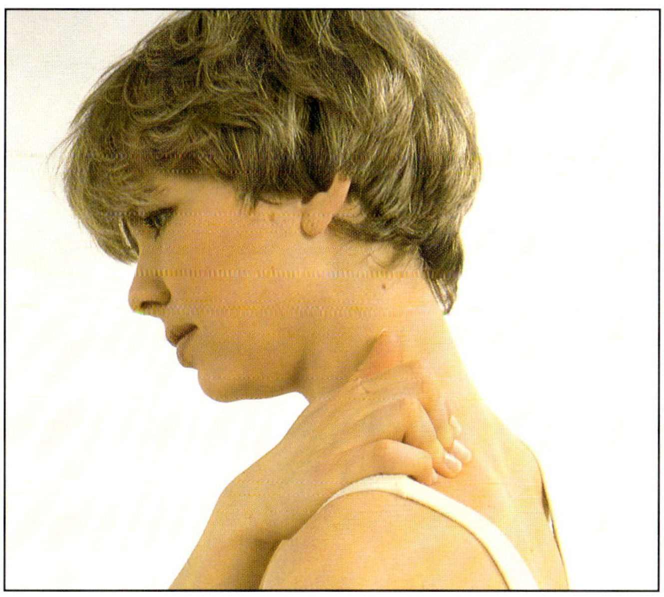

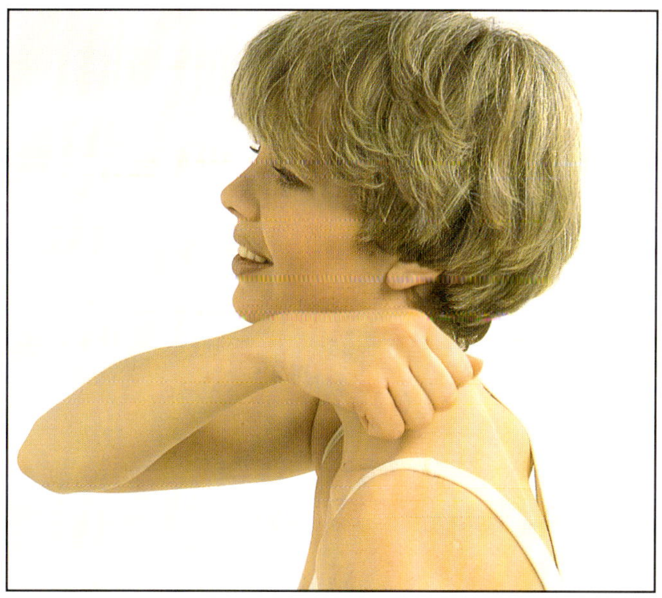

3 *Knead each shoulder with a firm squeezing action, rolling the flesh between your fingers and the ball of the hand. Repeat several times on each side.*

4 *With your hand in a loose fist, pummel your shoulder lightly, keeping the wrist and elbow relaxed. Use light, springy movements to stimulate the area. Repeat on the other shoulder.*

ARMS

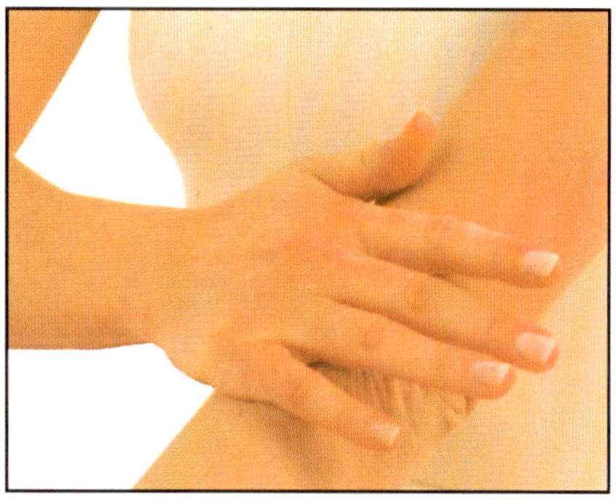

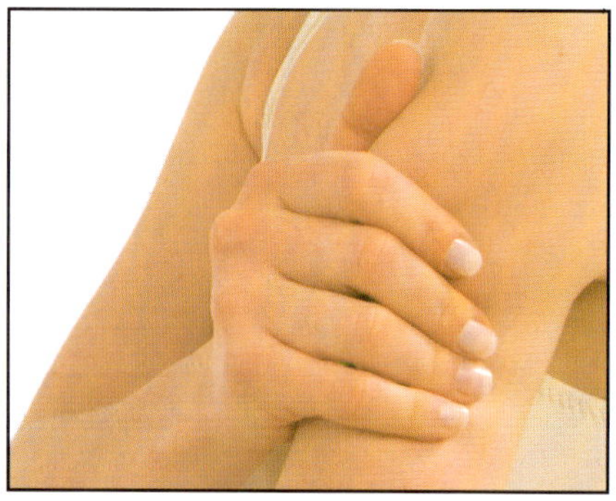

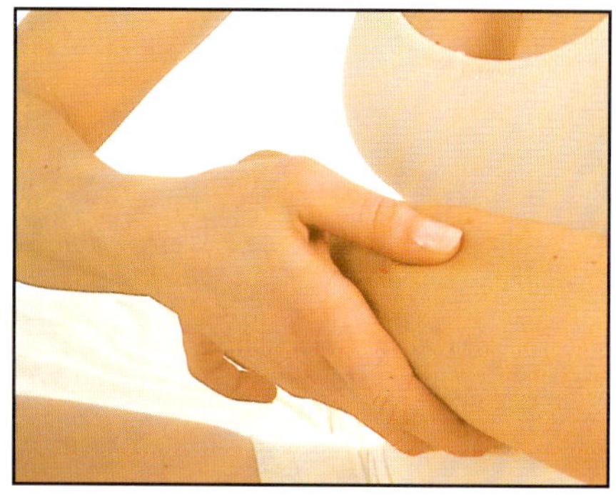

1 *Stroke firmly up the arm from the wrist to the shoulder, returning with a lighter touch. Repeat the stroke several times on different parts of the arm.*

2 *Pressing your fingers toward the palm of the hand, knead up the arm from the elbow to the shoulder. Cover the area thoroughly, working right round the arm.*

3 *Starting from the wrist, knead up the forearm toward the elbow, this time using your thumb to make circular movements.*

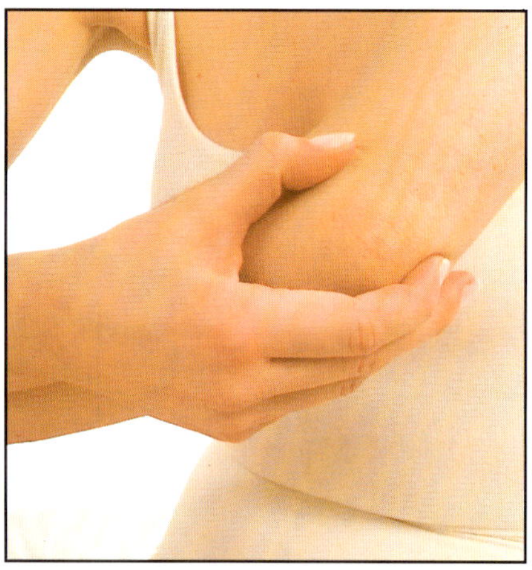

4 *With thumb and fingers make circular pressures round the elbow. First, work round the far side of the elbow with your working arm coming over the top of the arm you're massaging, then bend that arm up and work from the inside of your elbow. You may need more oil for dry elbows.*

5 *Right: Gently but briskly pat your upper arm, or use some gentle cupping. Follow with some* effleurage *stroking up and down the whole arm again to finish. Work on the hand before massaging the other arm.*

HANDS

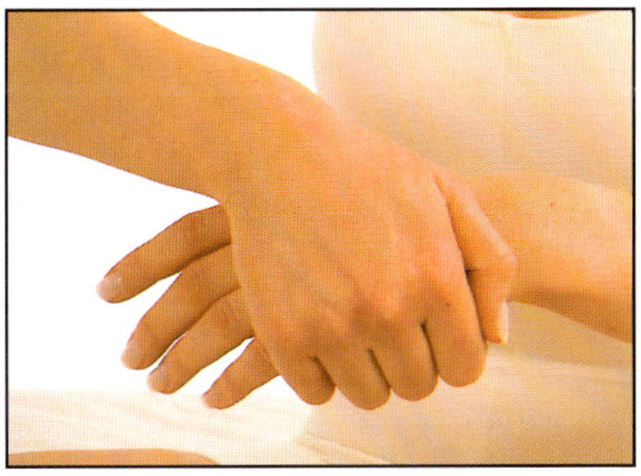

1 Squeeze the hand firmly, spreading the palm laterally. Cover the whole of the hand, fingers and wrist.

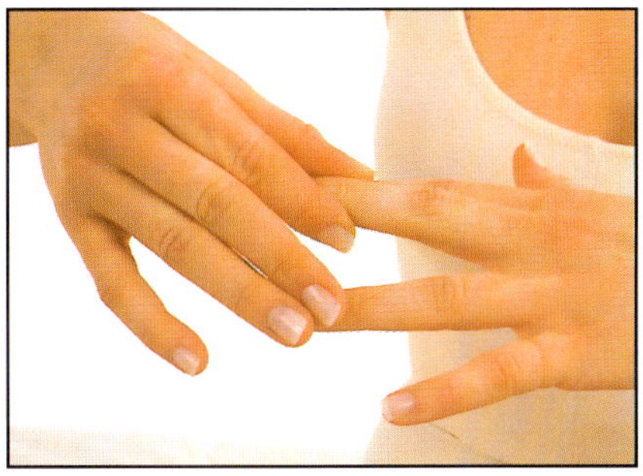

2 Using circular pressure, squeeze each finger joint between your finger and thumb. Then hold the base of each finger and pull the finger gently to stretch it, sliding your grip up to the top of the finger in a continuous movement.

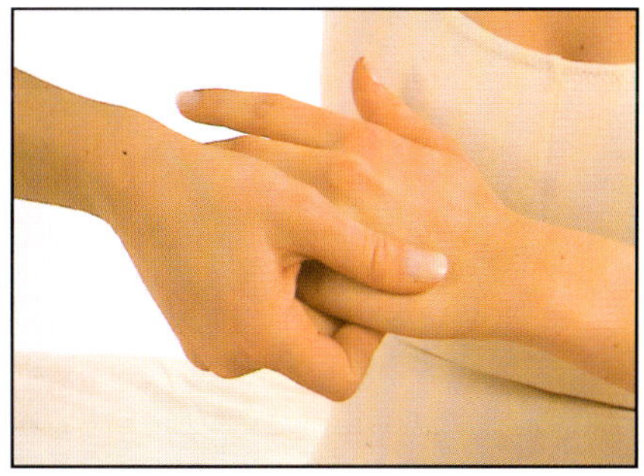

3 With circular thumb pressures, work up each of the furrows between the bones in the hand, from the knuckle to the wrist. When you have covered each furrow, smooth the hand by stroking.

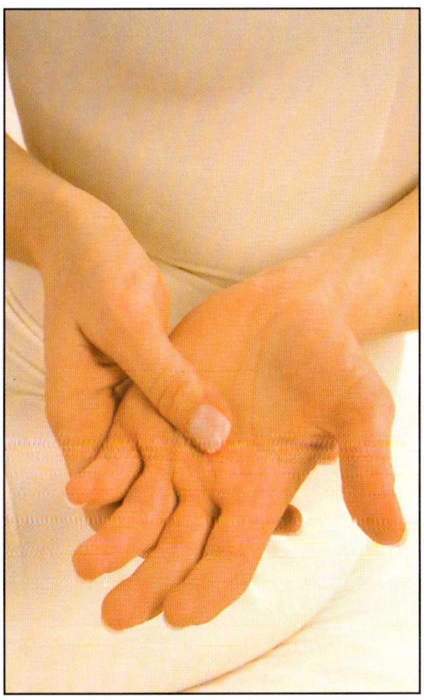

4 Turn the hand over to work on the palm. Cover the area with circular thumb pressures, paying particular attention to the heel of the hand and the wrist. Follow this with some deeper, static pressures all over the palm.

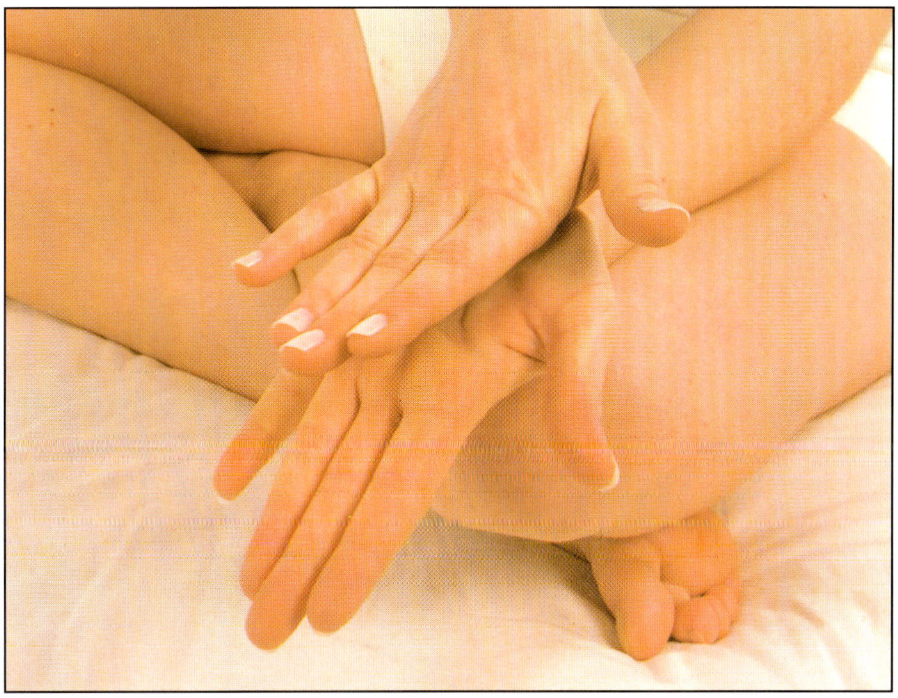

5 Finish by stroking the palm of one hand with the other. This can be quite a firm stroke, working from the tips of the fingers to the wrist, leading with the pressure from the heel of the hand. Stroke back to the fingers and repeat twice more, each time using slightly less pressure. Finally, stroke the inside of the wrist.

Repeat the whole of the arm and hand massage sequences on the other side.

BACK AND ABDOMEN

1 *Lie on your back, clasp your knees and gently rock backward and forward to massage the lower back, buttocks and hip joints and gently stretch out the vertebrae.*

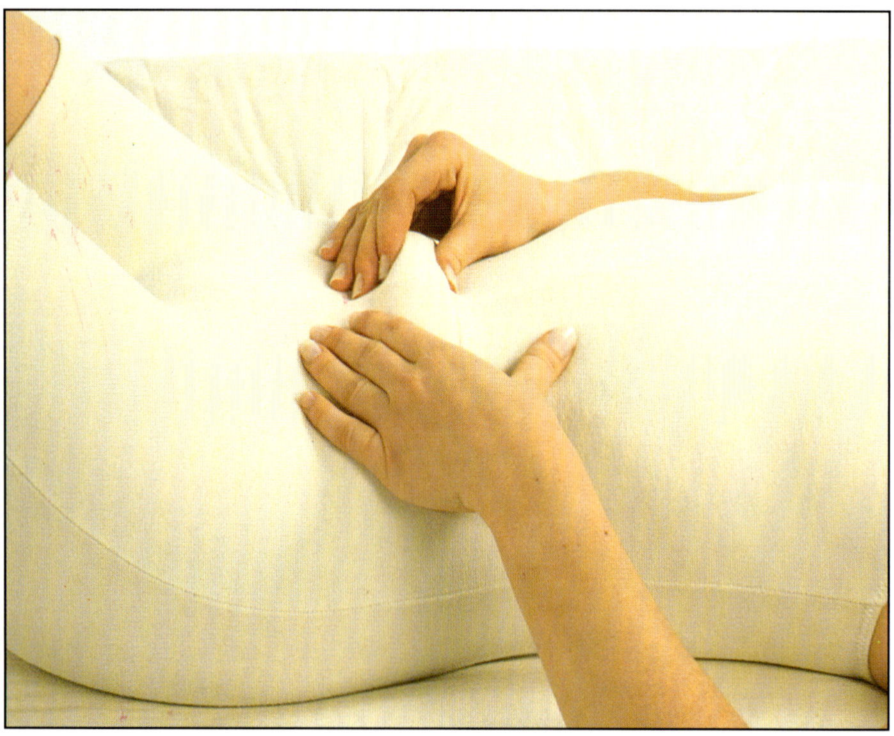

2 *Left: Bend your knees up and use some gentle* petrissage *to knead the whole of the abdominal area. When you have finished kneading, place both hands flat on the centre of the abdomen, fingers pointing slightly together, and pause for a few moments. Then smooth your hands outward over the hips and thighs in a long, slow, moulding movement.*

BUTTOCKS, HIPS AND THIGHS

1 Kneel up and pummel your hips and buttocks, using a clenched fist and keeping your wrists flexible.

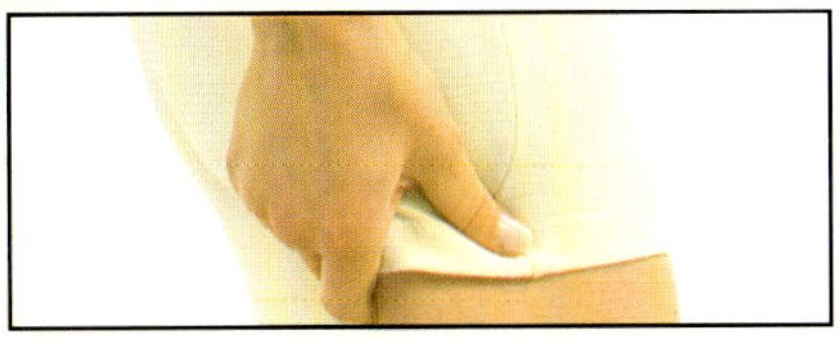

2 With the thumb and fingers, squeeze and release the muscles firmly and slowly, working from the top of the thigh over the buttock. Repeat on the left side.

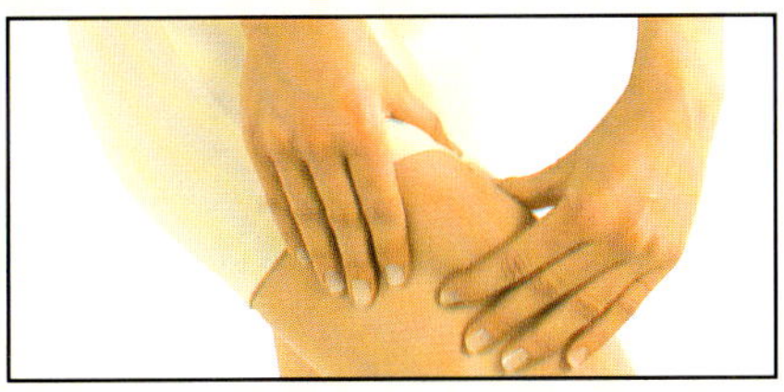

3 Use both hands to squeeze and release the muscles on the front and side of the thigh, kneading the entire upper leg. Repeat on the other side.

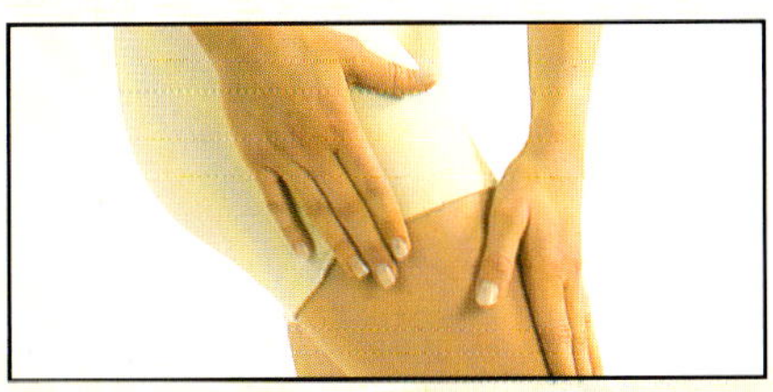

4 Starting at the knee, stroke up the thigh with both hands to soothe the leg.

LEGS

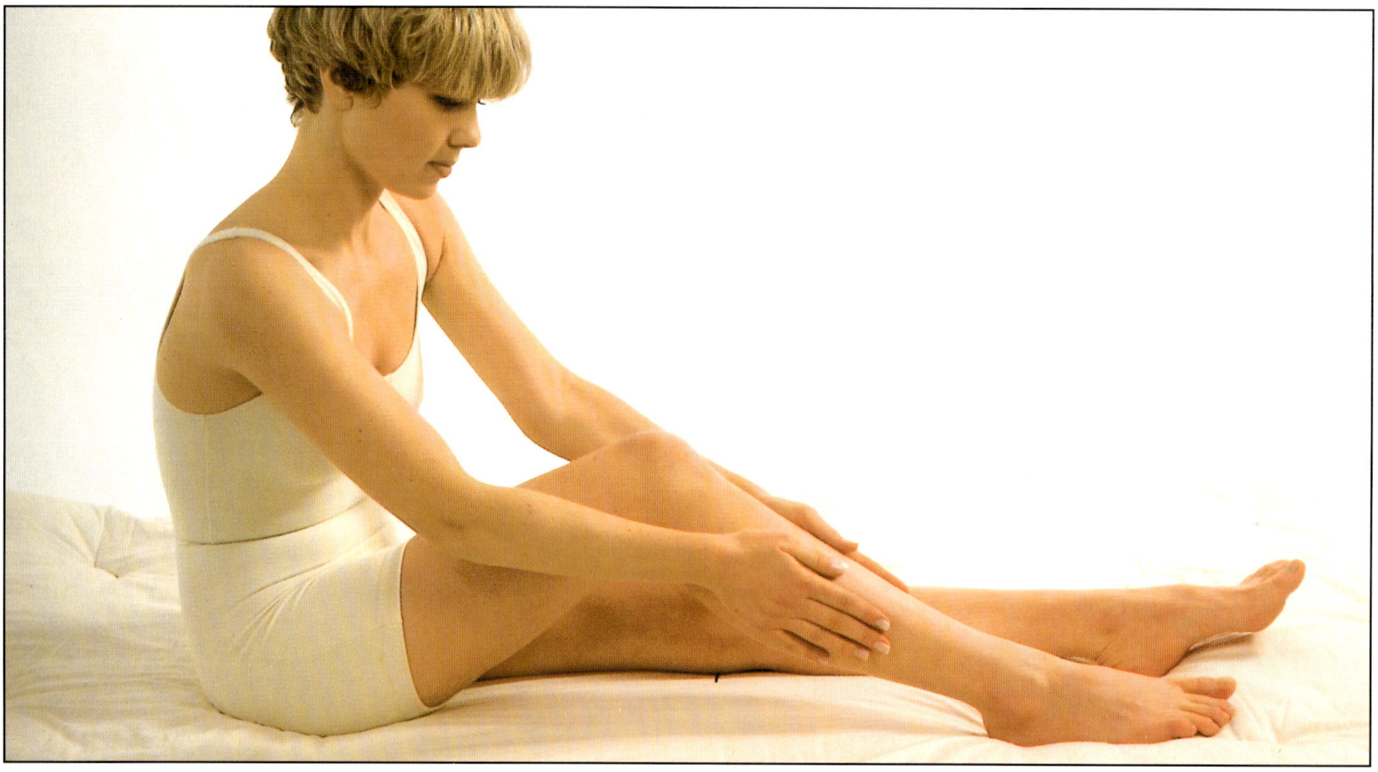

1 *Sitting down, with one leg raised slightly, stroke the leg with both hands from ankle to thigh. Begin the stroke as close to the ankle as you can reach. Repeat several times, moving round the leg slightly each time to stroke a different part.*

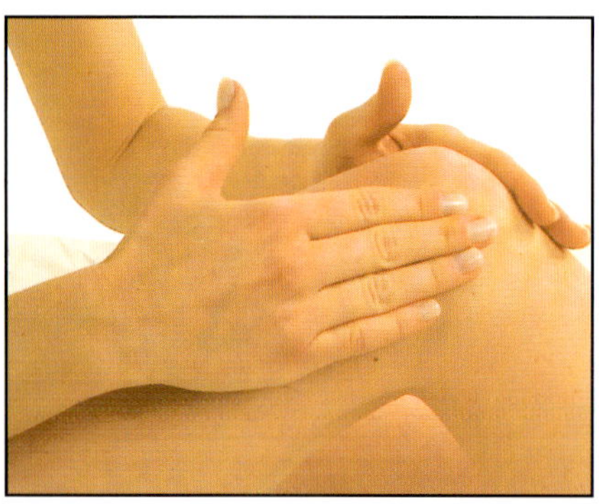

2 *Massage the knee, stroking round the outside of the kneecap to begin with, then using circular pressure with the fingertips to work round the kneecap more firmly.*

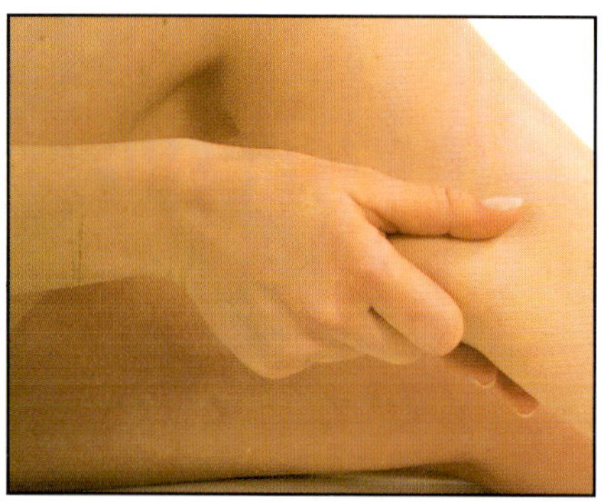

3 *Knead the calf muscle with both hands, using a firm* petrissage *to loosen any tension in the muscle.*

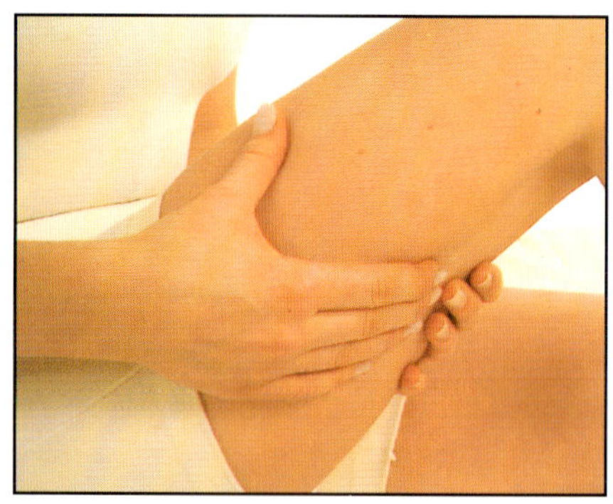

4 *Continue the kneading on the thigh, working over the top and outside areas with alternate hands. Whilst the leg is still raised, do some soothing* effleurage *strokes up the back of the leg from ankle to hip.*

Continue with the foot massage (opposite) before repeating all the steps on the other leg.

FEET

1 *Sitting down and leaning back, raise a leg, supporting the weight with your hands. Rotate the right ankle five times in each direction.*

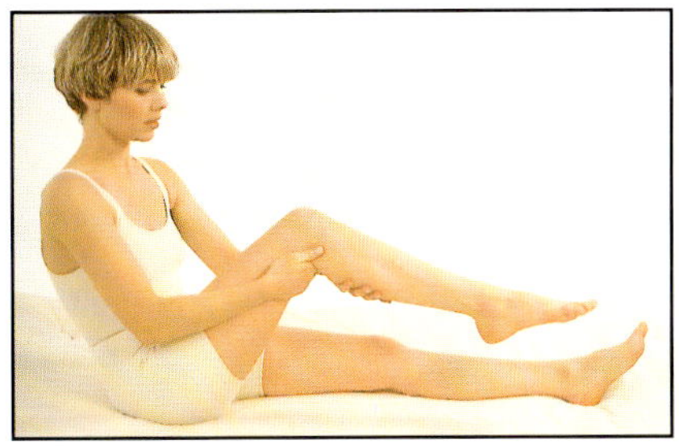

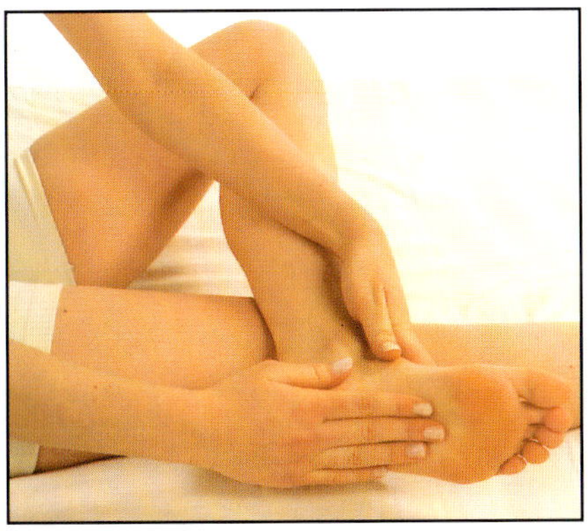

2 *Gently bring your foot over the other leg. With one hand on top of the foot and one underneath, stroke up the foot from toes to ankle. Repeat three times.*

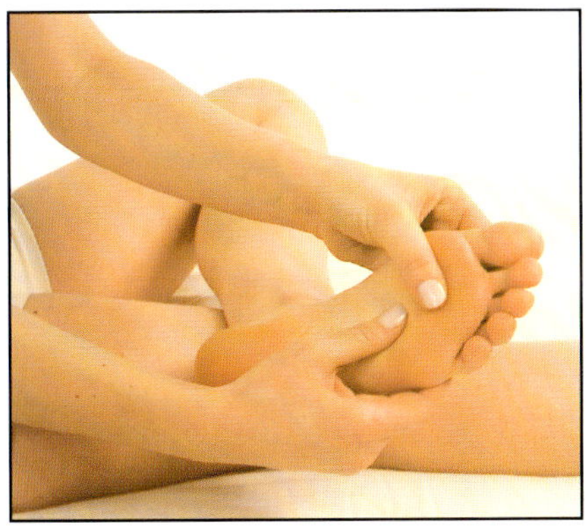

3 *With the thumbs, apply circular pressure over the ball of the foot. Work in lines from the inside of the foot to the outer edge. Repeat three times.*

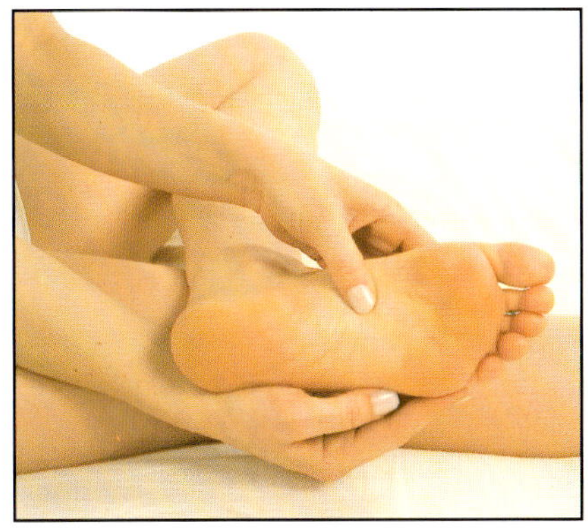

4 *Supporting the foot with one hand, continue the circular pressures over the raised instep, working from the inner to the outer edge. Repeat three times.*

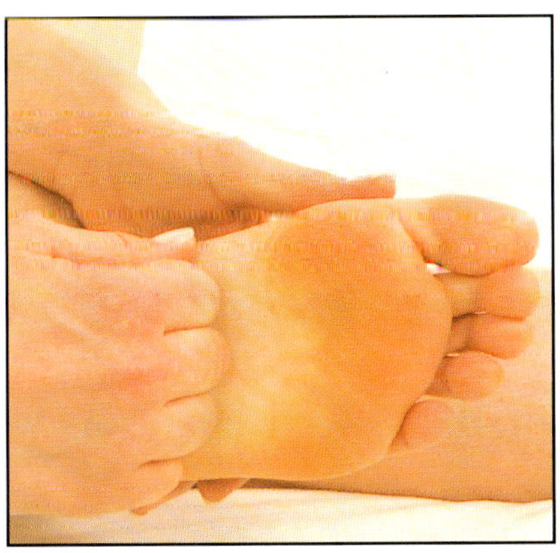

5 *Still holding the foot with one hand, make a loose fist with the other and firmly rotate your fist over the instep. Work thoroughly into the arch.*

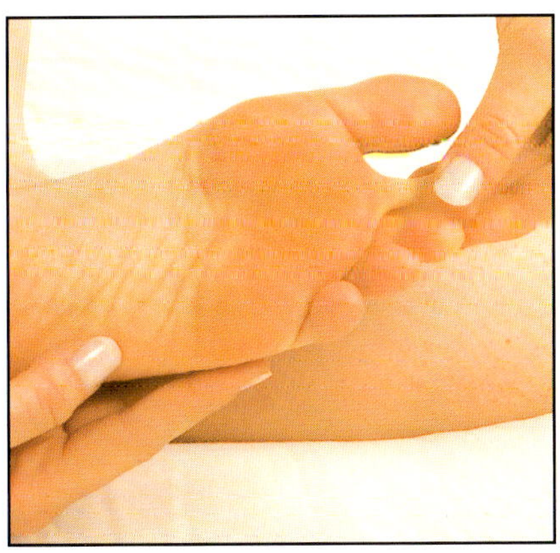

6 *Massage each toe individually. Slowly stretch the toe between the thumb and finger, pull gently, moving your fingers up the toe each time, until you reach the tip.*

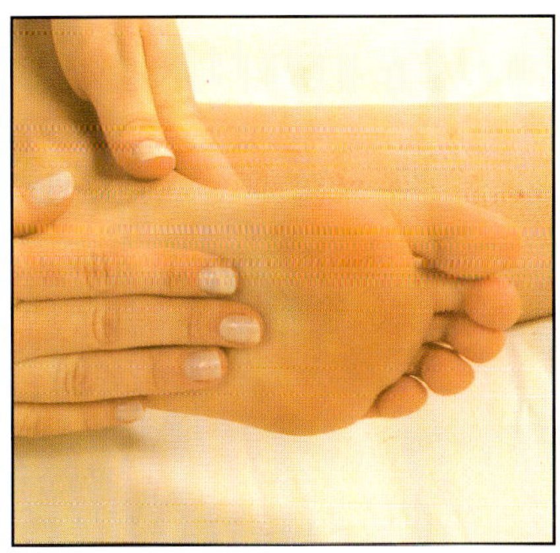

7 *Repeat the effleurage strokes of the foot, with one hand over and one under the foot, working from toes to ankle, several times.*

Repeat the leg and foot massage sequence on the other side.

MASSAGE AND EXERCISE

Professional sports people value massage very highly, not least because it works on several levels. Used before exercise it can prepare the body for the increase in activity not only by warming and loosening the muscles and joints (increasing their flexibility and helping to prevent cramp and injuries), but also by stimulating the system, both physically and mentally. This is the key to improved performance. After an exercise session, massage speeds up the elimination of waste products (in particular lactic acid) by stimulating the lymphatic system. The accumulation of these waste products during exercise is the cause of much of the stiffness and pain experienced afterwards.

STRAINS AND SPRAINS

A burning sensation under the skin is likely to indicate that muscles, fibres or ligaments have been strained – stretched beyond their natural limits. This is often the result of exercising without an adequate warm-up routine or over-exertion. A routine of pre-exercise massage and limbering will help to prevent strains. Gently massaging the affected area will also help to speed recovery.

Sprains are more serious and are caused by violent wrenching of a joint, most commonly the ankle, wrist or knee. The surrounding muscles, ligaments and tendons may also be damaged and the affected area may be extremely painful and swollen. Apply an ice-pack or cold compress for 15–20 minutes to reduce the swelling. When it is removed you can start to massage the area gently (as shown opposite), taking care not to work directly on the swelling. Rest the ankle as much as possible and use a support bandage.

A serious sprain should always be checked by a doctor in case a bone has been fractured, and a sprained knee always requires medical attention.

CRAMP

You don't have to be a fitness fanatic to suffer from cramp. On the contrary, it is usually underused or ill-prepared muscles which go into cramp. It doesn't even take movement to set it off: the searing pain of cramp can occur in the middle of the night, when the reduced circulation has caused muscles to contract. Frequent cramps may indicate generally poor circulation or a deficiency of calcium or salt. Massage will increase the blood circulation to alleviate the pain. You should also try to stretch out the affected muscle.

BACKACHE

Back strain is the most common source of debilitating pain. Most sports put increased strain on the legs, buttocks and back. Previous injuries can make the back prone to recurrent pain. Awkward, inappropriate or excessive exercise can also cause trouble. You should never subject the back to unnecessary strain. With regular and thorough back massage (particularly before exercise) the likelihood of injury is reduced. If, however, you want a quick warm-up for the back, or an after-exercise sequence, follow the instant back and shoulder massage. Always consult a doctor, osteopath or chiropractor if in any doubt about the seriousness of a back problem.

WITH OR WITHOUT OILS

You don't always have oil at hand, and it certainly isn't crucial for massaging unexpected strains, sprains and cramps. If you do have some light vegetable oil nearby, all the better, but don't worry if you don't.

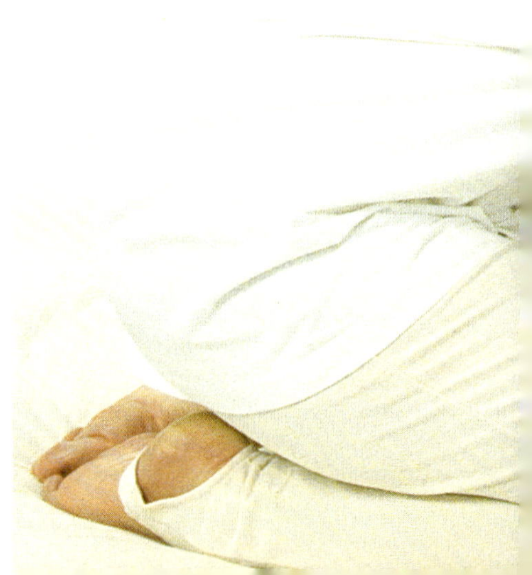

ANKLE STRAIN OR SPRAIN

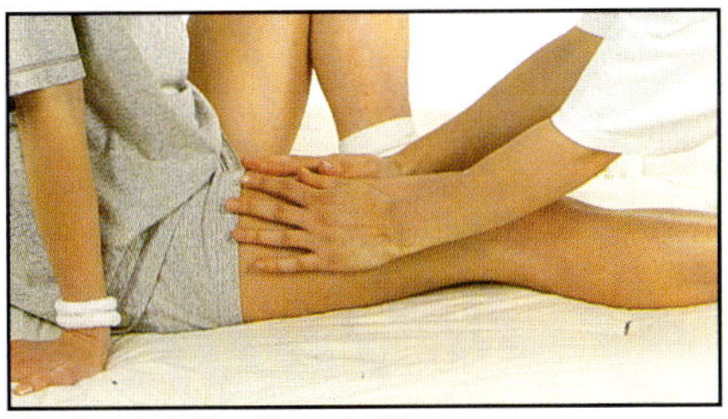

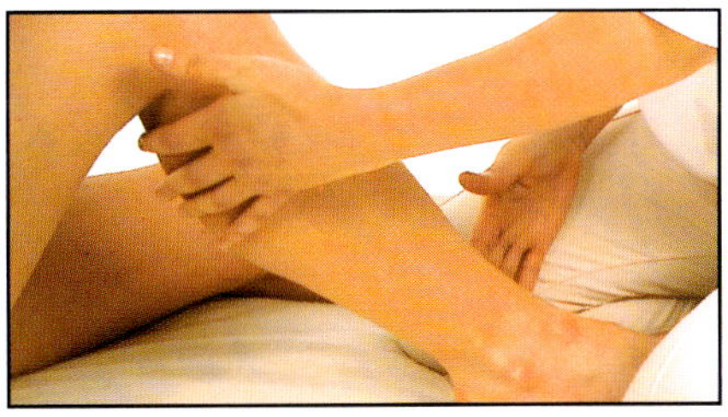

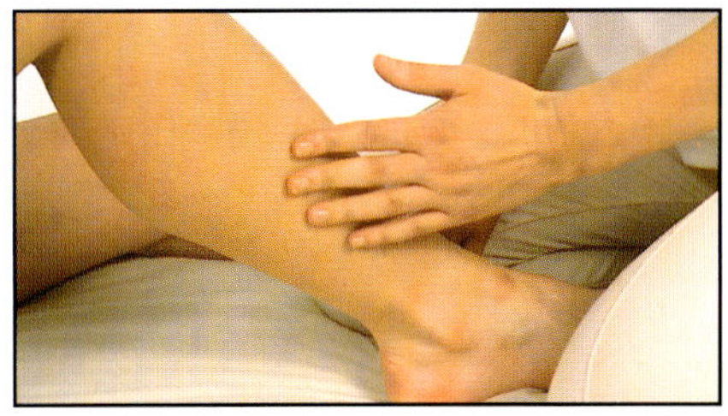

1 *Above and below: Avoid working directly on the swollen area. Start with gentle* effleurage *strokes working from the knee toward the thigh. Massaging in the direction of the lymph nodes in the groin will help drain away the fluids that have accumulated round the joint. Lightly stroke back to the knee. Repeat several times.*

2 *Help your partner to bend the affected leg. Continue the* effleurage *strokes on the lower leg, this time working from the ankle to the knee, alternating your hands. Repeat several times, then gently squeeze the calves with one hand, with the other supporting the foot.*

3 *Concentrating on the ankle area, stroke extremely gently all round the ankle with short upward movements. Check that this is not causing discomfort.*

CALF CRAMP

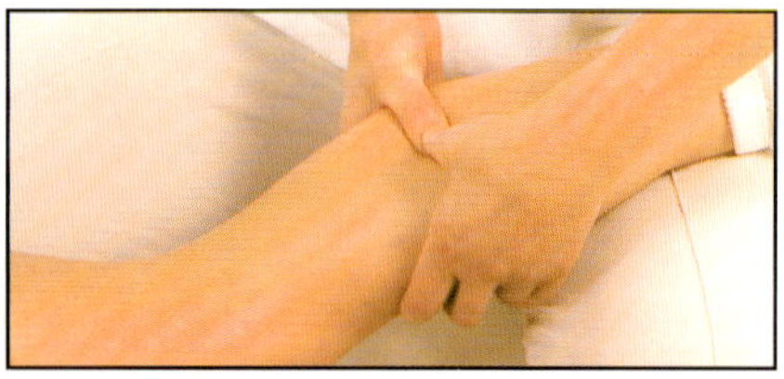

1 *With your partner lying face down and the foot supported across your leg or a small pillow, gradually apply direct thumb pressure into the belly of the cramped calf muscle for eight to ten seconds.*

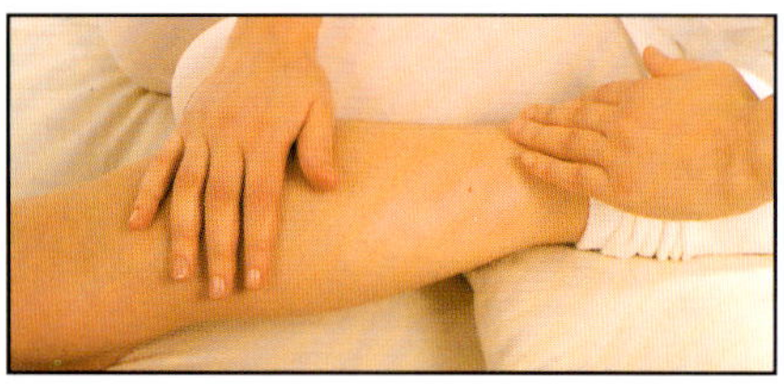

2 *Do some* effleurage *strokes, working from ankle to thigh and back down again.*

SELF-HELP STRETCH

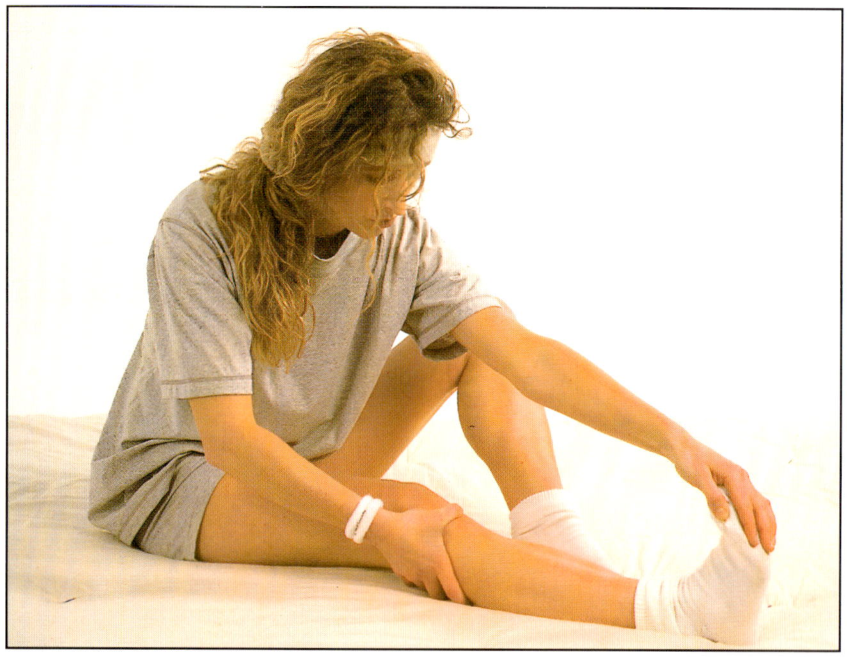

A good way of dealing with calf cramp is to sit down with the affected leg straight and stretch the toes toward you. Hold this position for eight seconds and then release. Repeat a few times, until the spasm seems to be lessening. Then knead your calf muscle using firm pressure. When the muscle feels more relaxed switch to effleurage *strokes, working up the leg.*

HAMSTRING CRAMP

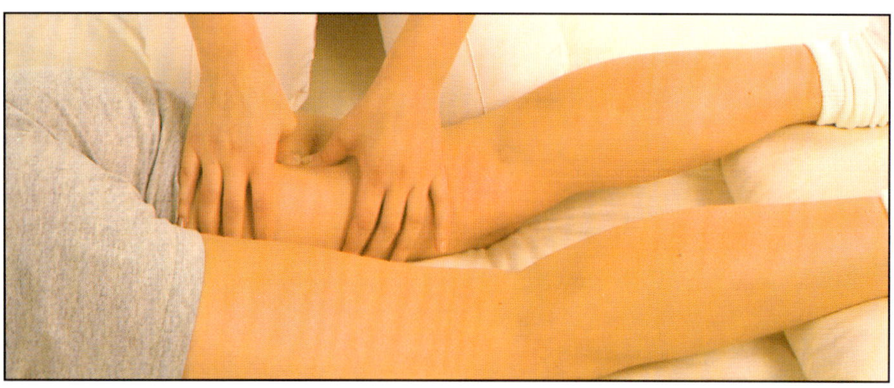

1 *With your partner lying face down and the ankles raised on a small pillow or cushion, begin massaging up the back of the thigh using alternate hands in slow, rhythmical stroking movements. Then apply static pressure to the middle of the thigh with the thumbs, holding for eight to ten seconds.*

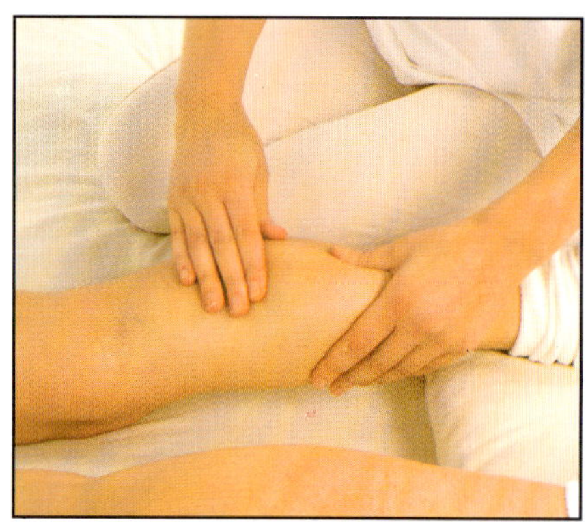

2 *Firmly knead the calf muscle. Squeeze, press and release the muscle using one hand after the other. Finally, do some soothing* effleurage *strokes up from ankle to thigh and back down again.*

HAMSTRING SELF-HELP STRETCH

Lie down flat, with the affected leg raised and the other knee bent. Stretch the muscle by pulling the thigh gently toward the chest.

Then firmly stroke up the back of your thigh for eight to ten seconds. Start to knead the back of the thigh until you feel the muscles begin to relax. Finally stroke over the area to soothe it.

TENNIS OR GOLFER'S ELBOW

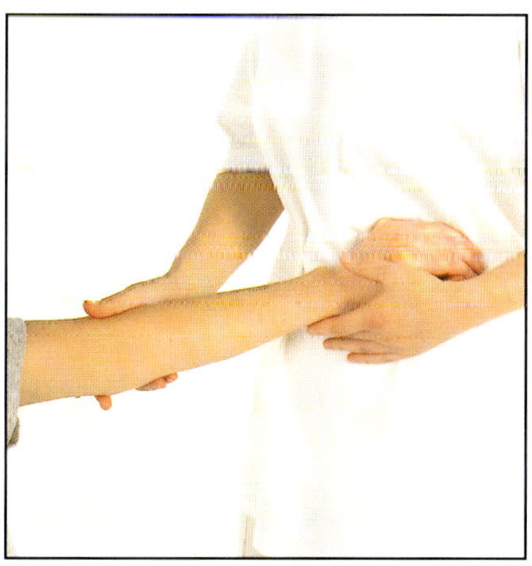

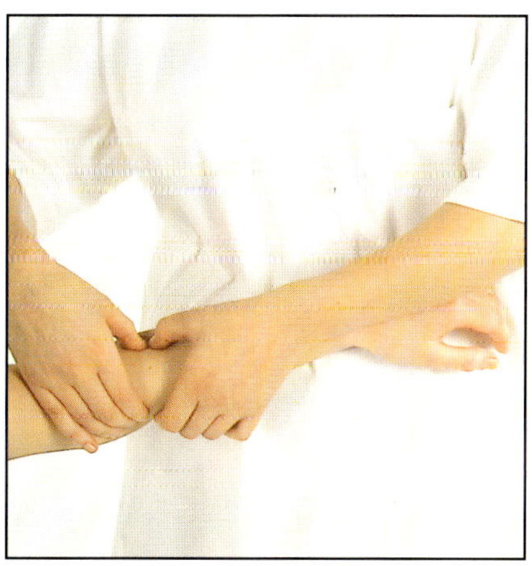

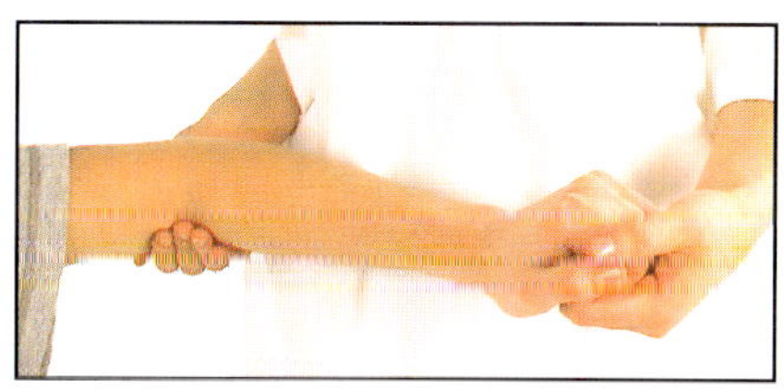

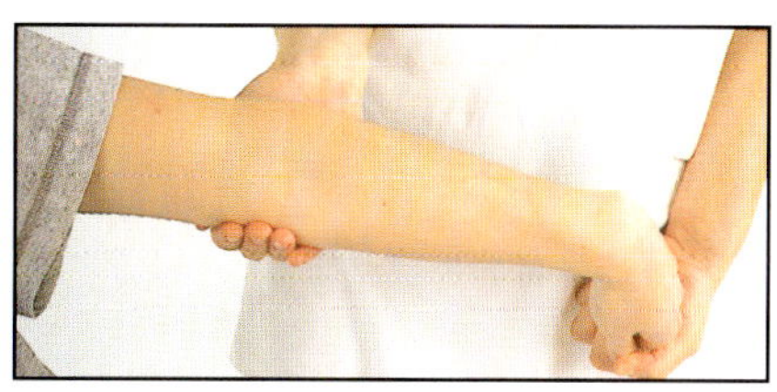

1 *Support your partner's wrist in one hand and use soothing* effleurage *strokes along both sides of the arm, stroking from the wrist to the elbow and back again. Repeat several times.*

2 *Rest your partner's hand against your side. Continue working up from the wrist to the elbow and back, making small circular movements with both thumbs, paying particular attention to the muscles in the forearm.*

3, 4 *Secure your partner's hand in yours, and with the other hand supporting the elbow, flex the elbow forward, bringing the hand back to give the tendons that attach to the bones a good stretch.*

BABY MASSAGE

A newborn baby instinctively responds to touch, and massage between mother and baby is a marvellous way of enhancing the natural bonding. All babies have this powerful sensitivity to being caressed and cuddled. Watch how a baby tightly curls its hands or toes as soon as something touches them.

There is no fixed sequence for massaging a baby. Keep the movements gentle and flowing. The simple action of gently stroking a baby will strengthen the natural bonding, and soothe and reassure the baby too. Massage has been shown to help calm difficult or colicky babies, and alleviate wind and other digestive problems. It may also build resistence to coughs and colds. Use a little light vegetable oil which is easily absorbed, such as sweet almond or sunflower, taking care to avoid the eyes.

GETTING COMFORTABLE

Lay the baby gently on the back on a warm, soft towel between your legs, or on your lap, whichever is most comfortable. Pour about 1 teaspoon (5 ml) of sweet almond oil into a small dish. Make sure your hands are warm and that the room is quiet, very warm and there are no draughts. After a baby's bathtime is ideal.

WORKING ON BABY'S FRONT

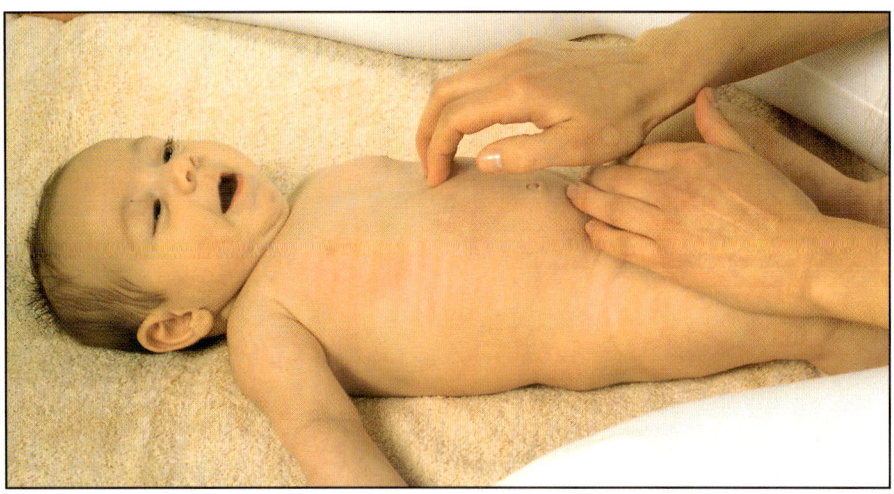

1 *Slowly and gently, smooth a little of the oil all over the front of the baby's body, shoulders to feet, avoiding the face. Lightly stroke down the chest and abdomen, with the tips of your fingers. This is a delightful stroke which can be used to calm a baby anytime.*

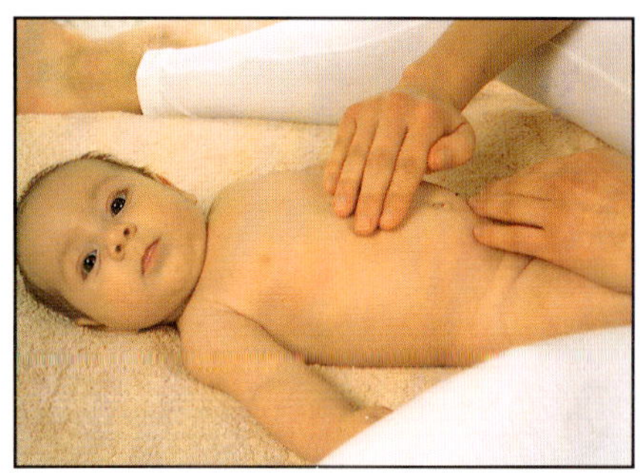

2 *Keeping the pressure very light, smooth both hands over the abdomen in continuous circular strokes, working up the baby's right side, across and down the baby's left side. Keep the movement continuous by lifting your left hand when your arms cross. Repeat these circular strokes several times.*

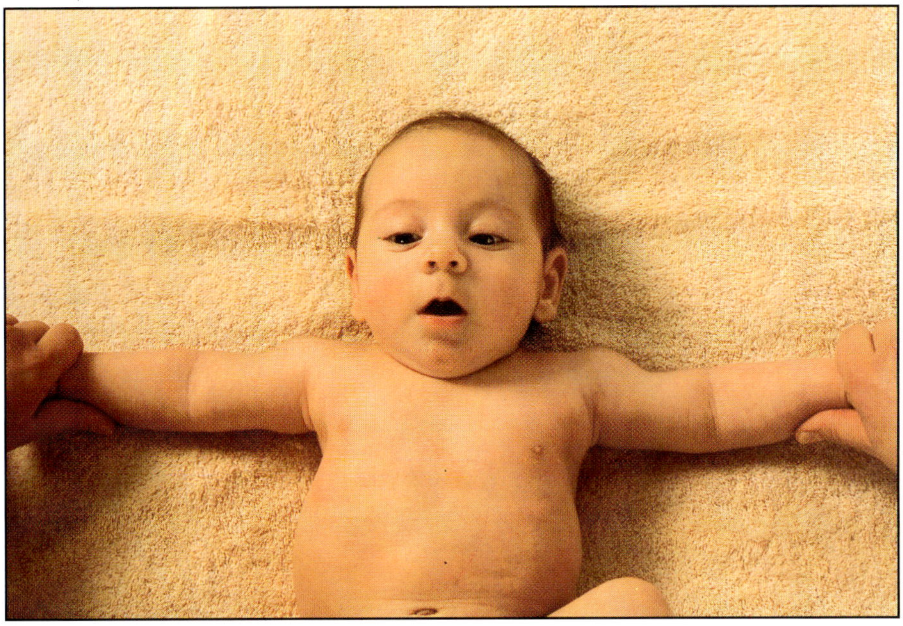

3 *Left: Gently stretch out both arms to the side, spreading the hands and fingers if the baby will let you. Gently squeeze out along the arms, then massage the wrist and palms with light, circular thumb movements. Finish by stretching out each finger with a slight pull.*

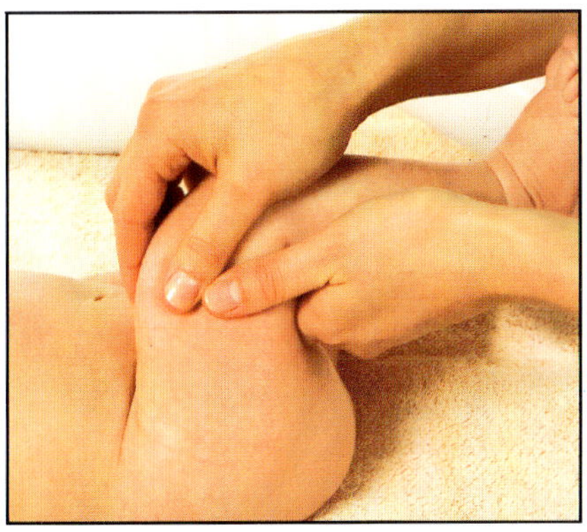

4 *Move on to the legs and feet, working on one leg at a time. Support the leg with both hands and gently squeeze and release the fleshy part of the thigh. Then, supporting the leg with one hand, stroke the leg from the knee to the thigh and back down again.*

5 *Right: Move your supporting hand down to behind the ankle. Gently smooth the palm of your other hand over the top of the foot from toe to ankle and back again. When you get to the toes, very gently stretch each one in turn.*

Repeat steps 4 and 5 on the baby's other leg.

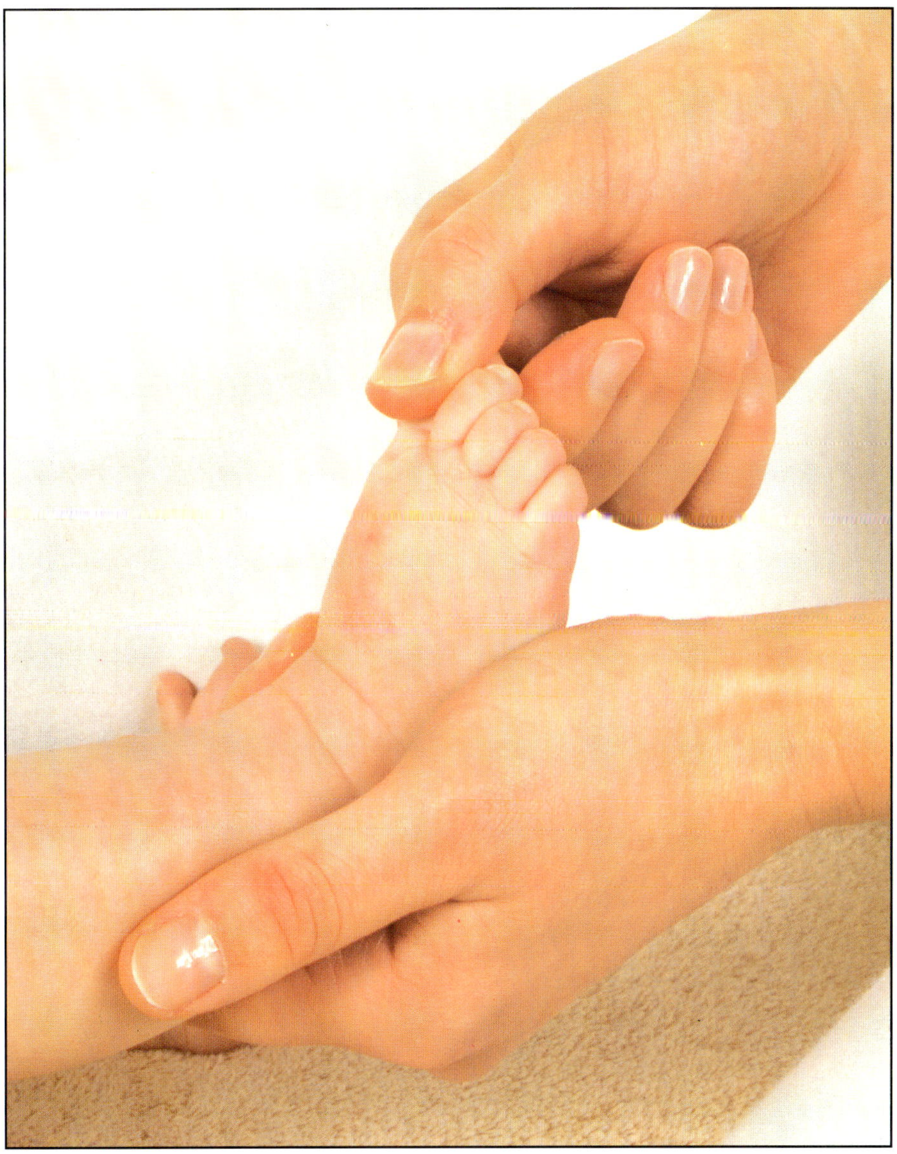

WORKING ON BABY'S BACK

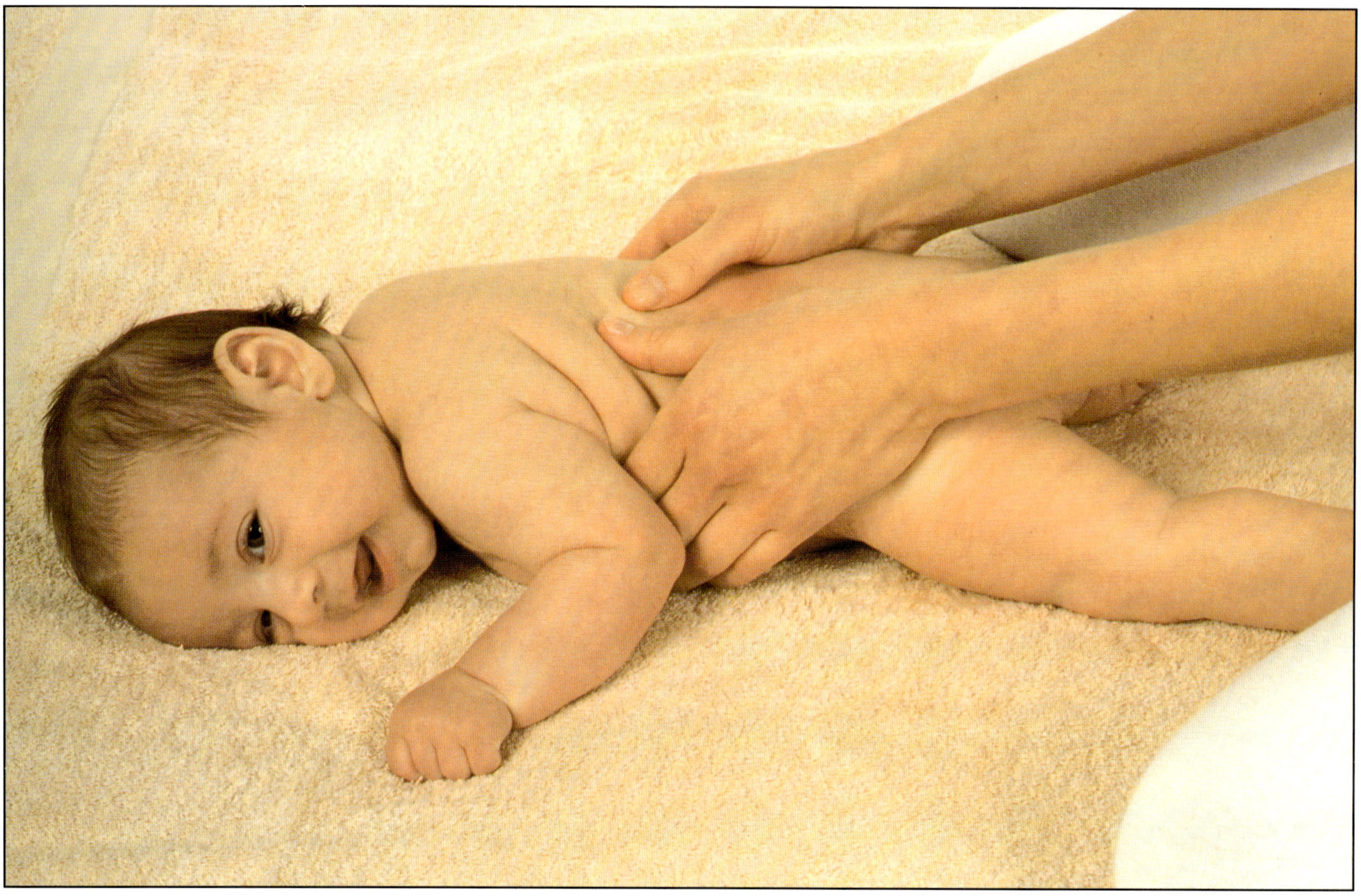

1 *Turn the baby over on to the front. Begin by stroking up the whole back to distribute a little oil. Take your strokes round the sides as well and then up the legs, back and out over the arms. Gentle massage on the back like this is particularly soothing because of its calming effect on the spinal nerves.*

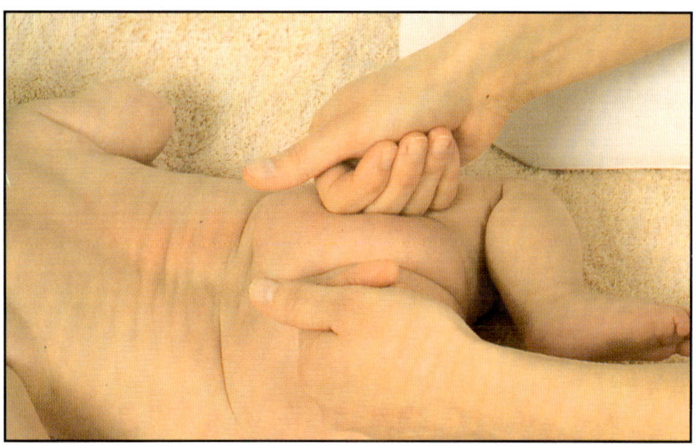

2 *Gently knead and squeeze the buttocks to stimulate the circulation. Make a loose fist and rotate over the buttocks, in circular movements.*

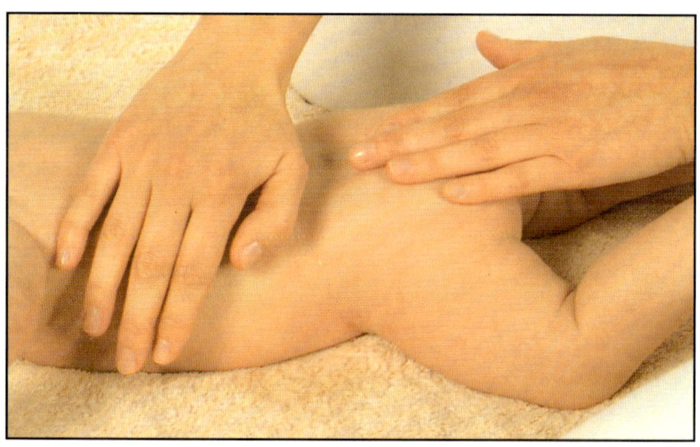

3 *Alternating your hands, one over the other, gently stroke up one side of the back to the shoulders and down again. Repeat on the other side of the back.*

4 *Bring both hands round the sides of the upper body, and use your thumbs to massage gently up the back to the base of the neck, and down again. Include some gentle massage with the thumbs on the shoulders.*

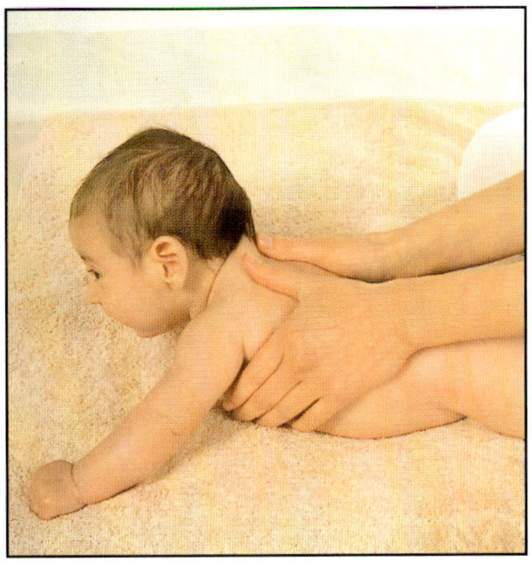

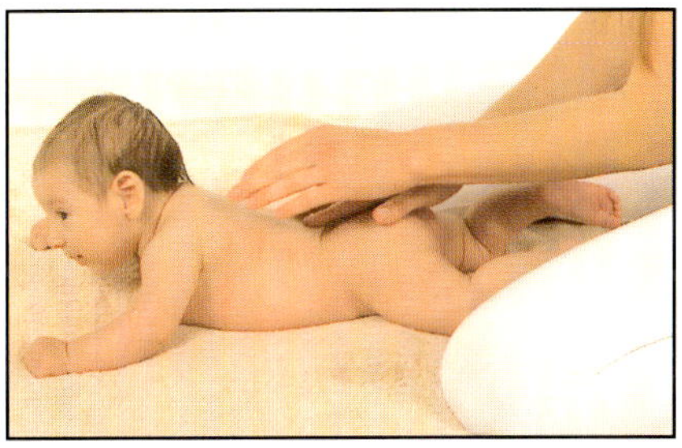

5 *To finish, repeat the feather strokes used at the beginning of the massage, working all over the back from neck to buttocks.*

MASSAGE FOR OLDER PEOPLE

As we get older, painful, stiff joints, rheumatism and other signs of wear and tear become all too common. There are many ways to minimize the discomfort that the aging process brings. Good nutrition and remaining as active as possible are as crucial as ever, and massage can help in reducing pain, alleviating stiffness and retaining mobility. Increasing the blood circulation and gently releasing stiffness and inflexibility, it is a good way to help keep active. It isn't necessary to lie down – sitting on a chair is fine for massage of the neck and shoulders, and you can raise the leg on a stool for a leg, foot and ankle massage.

Research suggests that stroking pets can help to lower blood pressure, relieve depression, speed recovery and may reduce the chances of a heart attack. Your pets will enjoy it too!

Many older people suffer from aches and pains brought on by cold damp weather. A warm bath using aromatic essential oils such as lavender or sandalwood can comfort, soothe and relax you. Follow the bath with a gentle massage, and you will make headway in practising self-help. Massage stiff joints such as at wrists, knees, ankles and the hip. If the joint is affected by rheumatoid arthritis, massaging above and below the swollen area can relieve pain by relaxing the surrounding muscles. Avoid any swollen or inflamed areas.

The general wear and tear of joints which comes with aging is called osteoarthritis, and usually affects hips and knees in particular. Because the pain is often caused by the surrounding muscles, rather than the joint itself, massage can help to soothe the spasm and relieve pain. So long as the area is not swollen or inflamed you can massage the joint itself, working gently into the area which hurts most.

Massage can help to fulfil the deep-seated need for touch and communication, bringing psychological as well as physiological benefits, and contributing to a well-balanced lifestyle.

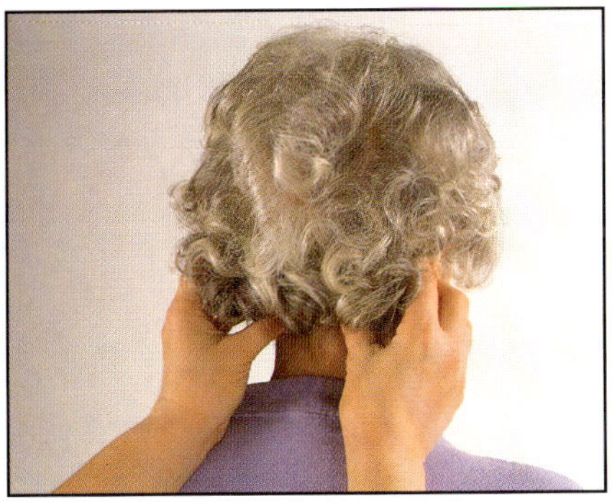

1 *Start by gently resting your thumbs on the base of your partner's skull, just under the bony part. Relax your hands round each side of the head. Slowly and without too much pressure, slide your thumbs up through the hair, until you get halfway up the back of the head. Repeat three times, from the base of the skull to halfway up the head, to stimulate the nervous system.*

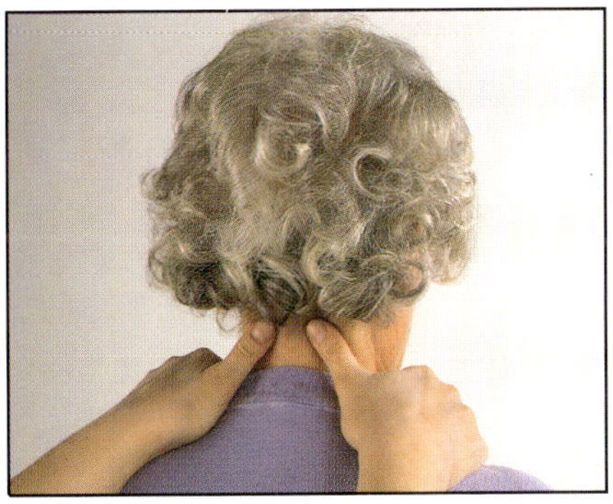

2 *Place the thumbs on the back of the neck and press gently, starting at the base of the skull and working down in a straight line toward the shoulders. This will loosen stiffness and relieve tension in the area. Repeat three times down the centre each time.*

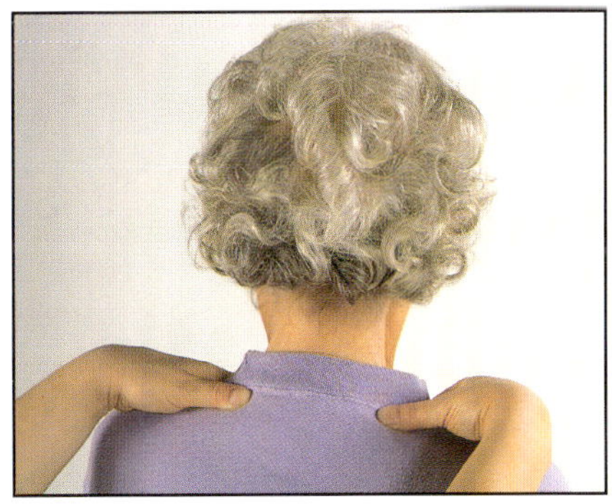

3 *With your hand on either side of the neck, gently knead the tops of the shoulders, squeezing and releasing the muscles between your thumbs and fingers. Repeat three times the full length of the shoulder.*

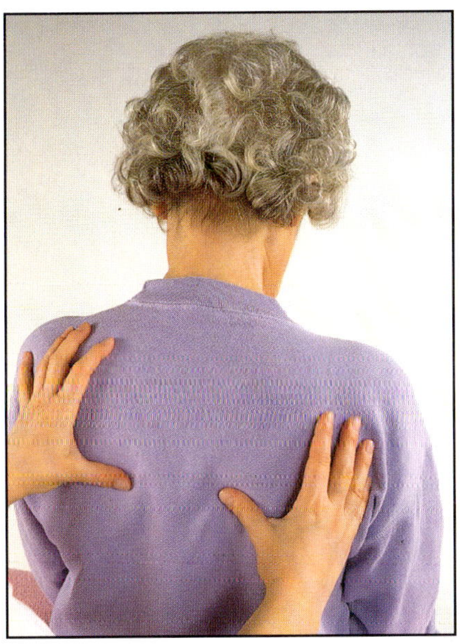

4 *Bring your hands lower down the back near each shoulder blade, and use thumbs and fingers to massage upward over the shoulder blades, right up to the top of the shoulders. Slightly push into the back and release. Repeat from start to finish three times. You can vary the movement slightly by rotating the fingers as you work up.*

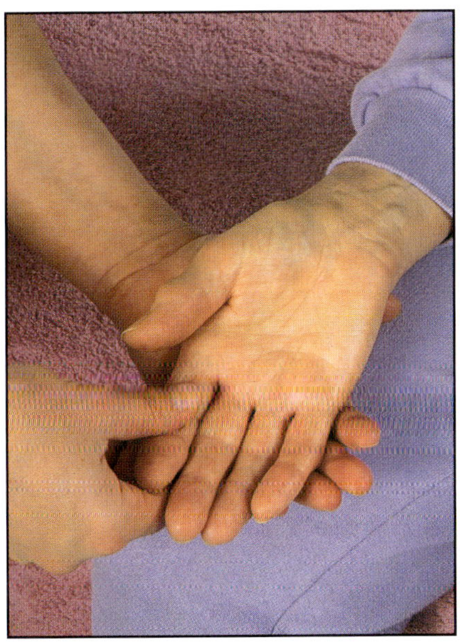

5 *Use any of the massage or self-massage techniques for the hands or feet, but avoid working directly on any joints inflamed with arthritis. Work above and below a swelling and then stroke up the limb toward the nearest lymph node. This stimulates the elimination of waste products and reduces inflammation.*

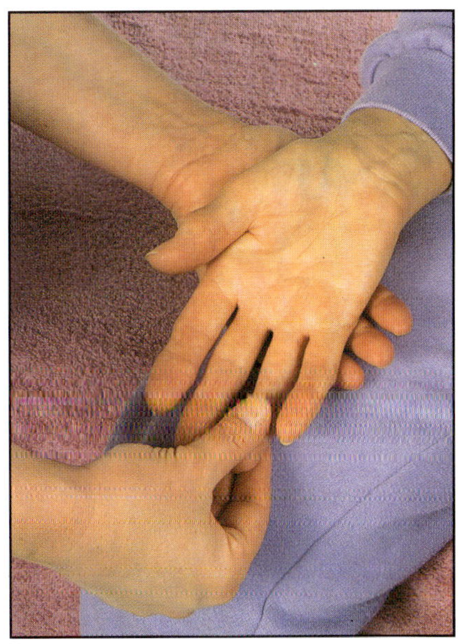

6 *If there are no signs of inflammation, you can use circular thumb movements all over the palm, then turn the hand over and work along each finger to the tip. Gently stretch each joint as far as it will go without causing pain, and then soothe the whole hand with firm strokes toward the wrist.*

THE SENSUAL TOUCH

In the right circumstances, with a softly lit room, relaxing music, and using some of the more aphrodisiac essential oils such as rose, patchouli, neroli or sandalwood, a massage can be a highly pleasurable and sensual experience, relaxing the body and arousing the senses. Intuition will play a larger part in a sensual massage, as you discover which areas have the strongest impact on your partner's senses. It certainly isn't just the most obvious erogenous zones that bring pleasure – the back of the neck, scalp, solar plexus, inside of the elbows, hands and feet are just a few others.

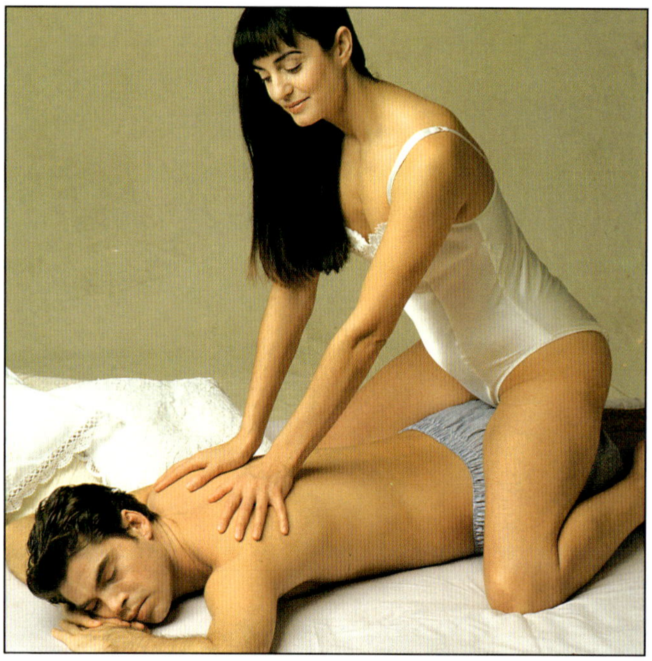

1 *With your partner lying on their front, start by resting your hands gently on the back of their shoulder blades. Fan the palms out across the back, sweeping your hands out and around over the shoulders.*

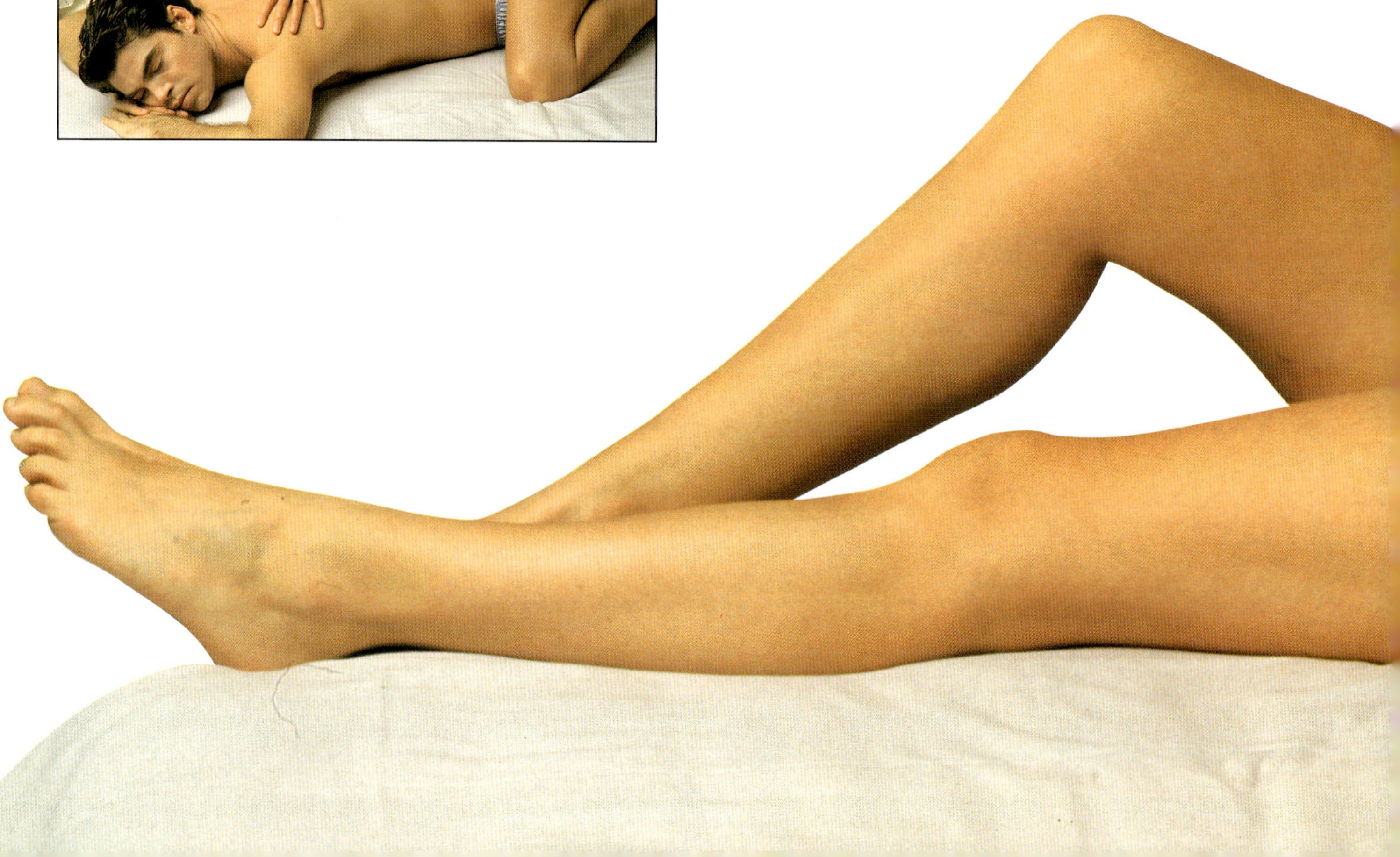

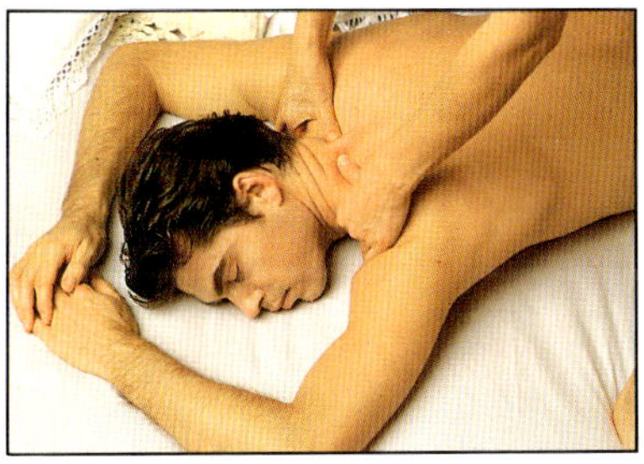

2 *Knead firmly along the top of the shoulders, squeezing and releasing the muscles each side of the neck and shoulders. As the shoulders start to relax, work more deeply into the muscles.*

Below: The back can be extremely sensitive to touch of many different kinds. Try sitting back to back and moving gently together, feeling the contours of your partner's back against yours. Press against each other so that you can feel the pelvis, the spine and the shoulders. Rest your head back on your partner's shoulder, and enjoy the feeling of your backs exchanging warmth and energy. Hold for a count of ten and repeat on the other side.

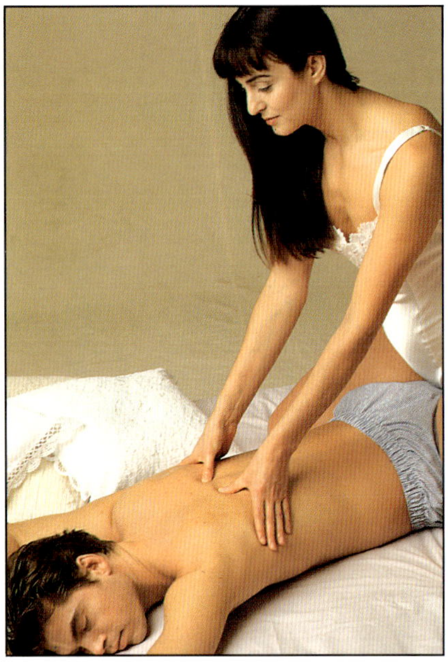

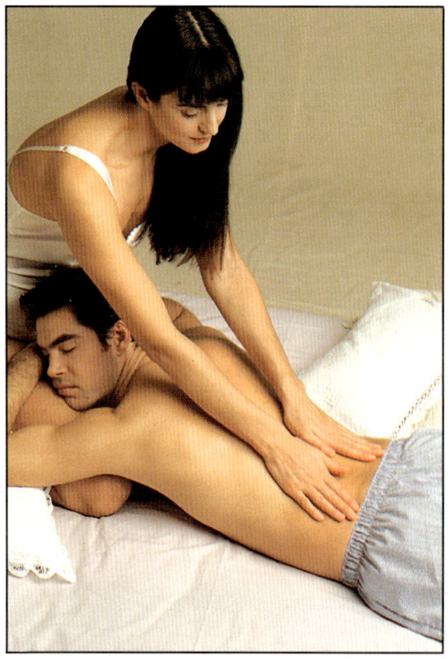

3 *Check that your partner's head is still comfortable, then beginning at the nape of the neck let your thumbs gently stroke down each side of the spine. When you get to the lower back return up each side of the spine, this time working with slightly more pressure and rotating the thumbs to release muscular tension. Work up and down the spine two or three times.*

4 *Move round so your partner can rest their head on your thighs, and with long,* effleurage *strokes, massage the length of the back from the neck right down to the buttocks and back up the sides of the trunk. Repeat three times.*

5 *Starting at the lower back, gently stroke up either side of the spine, making light feathery strokes with your fingertips. Repeat three times, making the strokes lighter each time, until they can barely be felt.*

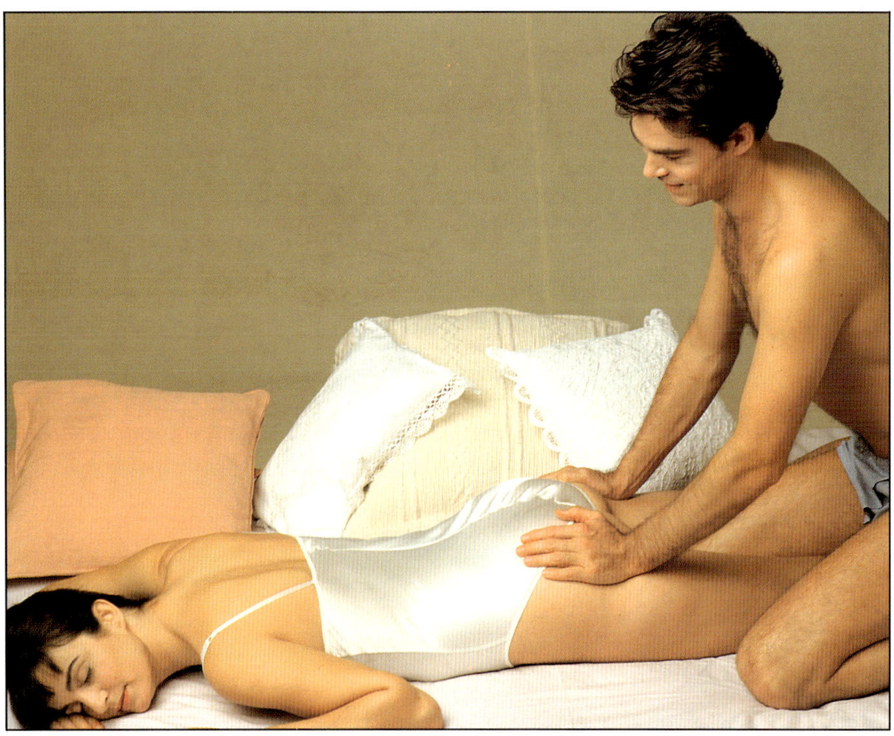

6 *Left: Massage the lower back with some kneading. Using the flat, and in particular the heel, of the hand, knead the buttocks, then come back to the start and work over a different area. The nerves that cross this area relate to the man's groin, and the woman's uterus. The buttocks themselves are highly erogenous areas.*

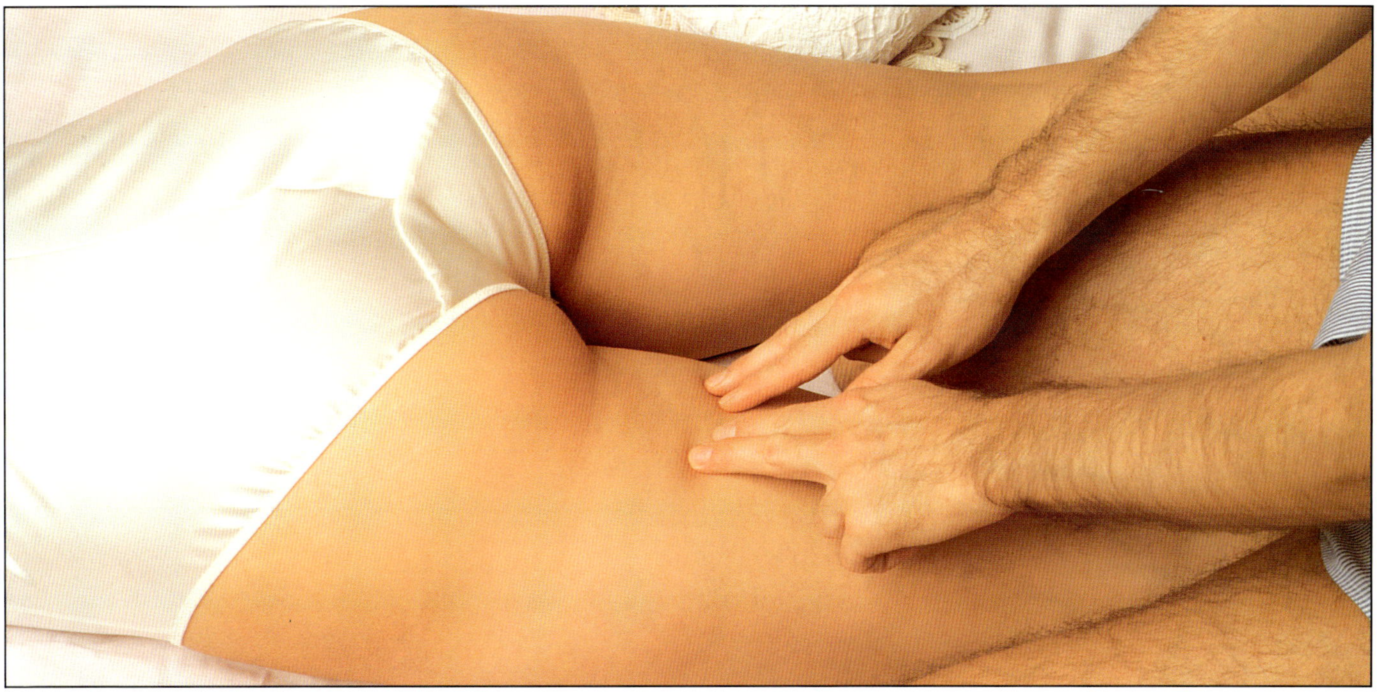

7 *Curling your third and fourth fingers under, place your hands toward the top of the upper legs and circle your first and second fingers outward, one hand alternating with the other. This should be a slow, leisurely stroke with varying pressure.*

8 *Support your partner's leg across your thigh and circle your thumbs over the calf, alternating the thumbs and applying firm pressure.*

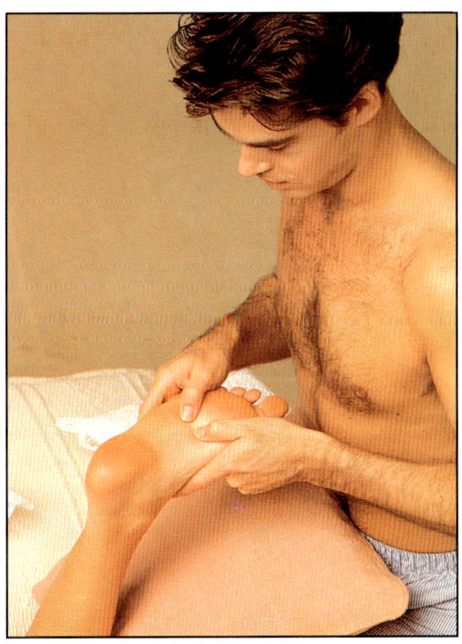

9 *Raise your partner's foot, supporting its weight in your hands. Knead the instep firmly, using the thumbs to apply the pressure. Work all over the ball of the foot up toward the big toe.*

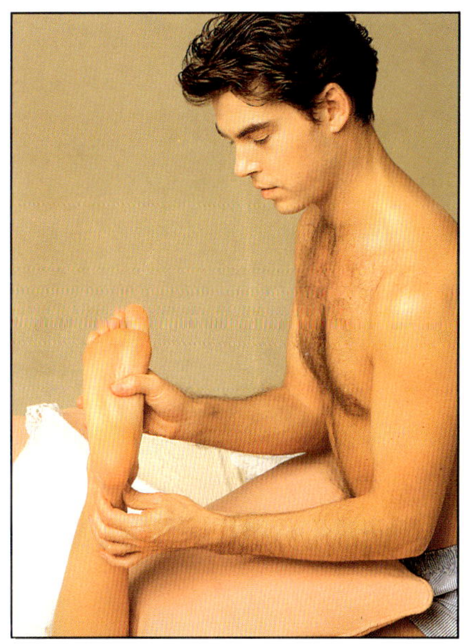

10 *Support your partner's foot in one hand, and place the thumb of that hand firmly over the centre of the instep. This has a wonderful, calming effect. With the thumb and first finger of the other hand, stroke round the ankle using circular movements.*

11 *At this stage, lie down facing each other, making sure you are both comfortable and well supported with plenty of cushions. Gently caress your partner's hands.*

12 *Gently stretch and release your partner's wrists, by flexing the hand backward and forwards. Softly stroke the inside of the palm with your fingers. Repeat on the other hand.*

13 *Gently massage each finger, beginning with the thumb or little finger and working from the base joint to the tip. Try squeezing, rubbing and circular movements, and gentle pulling.*

14 *Supporting your partner's elbow in one hand, use the other to caress and stroke the inside of the wrist just below the thumb, which is a particularly sensitive area. Continue working over the whole of the wrist area, using gentle circular thumb movements. Repeat on the other wrist.*

15 *Left: With feather strokes, use your fingers to stroke up the soft inner arm. This is a highly sensitive area when lightly touched and the effect is both stimulating and relaxing. Repeat on the other arm.*

16 *Left: Use long* effleurage *strokes up and down the inner thigh area. Then massage closer to the highly erogenous region of the groin.*

17 *With a feathery touch, stroke across the shoulders and up the neck, covering the sides, front and back. You can run your fingers up through the hair as well. Spend more time caressing the base of the neck, which arouses strong, sexual responses.*

18 *Right: Finally, trace round the ear with your fingers, starting at the outside and circling toward the centre. Continue with soft pinching movements round the outside edge and on the lobe, where you will be triggering sexual responses from the adrenal gland and sexual organs.*

INSTANT MASSAGE

Sometimes, the idea of having tension in your shoulders and neck massaged away, without stopping to find the right place and the time to undress, is a particularly tempting one. There is increasing interest in learning how to do a shoulder massage with the minimum of disruption, especially in offices. Even at home, there are times when nothing is better than someone giving you a ten-minute shoulder and neck massage, in the comfort of an upright chair. There is no need to use oil if you prefer not to, and you can work through light clothing if simpler.

1 *Ask your partner to sit astride a chair facing the back. You can offer a folded towel or cushion for comfort. Standing behind your partner, begin by leaning on your forearms so that your weight presses down gently on to the fleshy part of the shoulders.*

2 *With your partner leaning forward, use effleurage strokes from the bottom of the shoulder blades, up the back and out over the top of the shoulders to finish at the top of the arms. Repeat four times.*

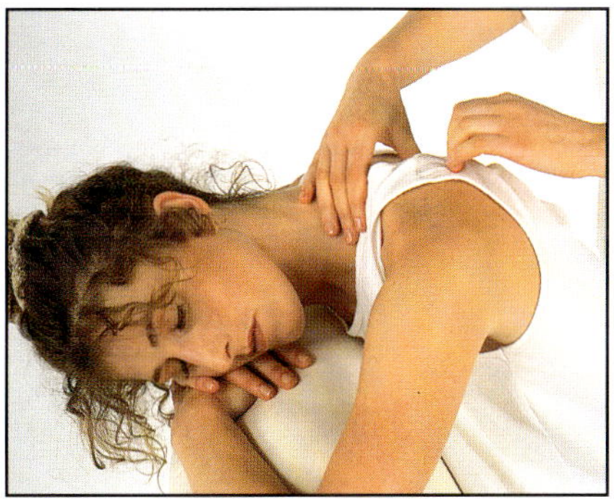

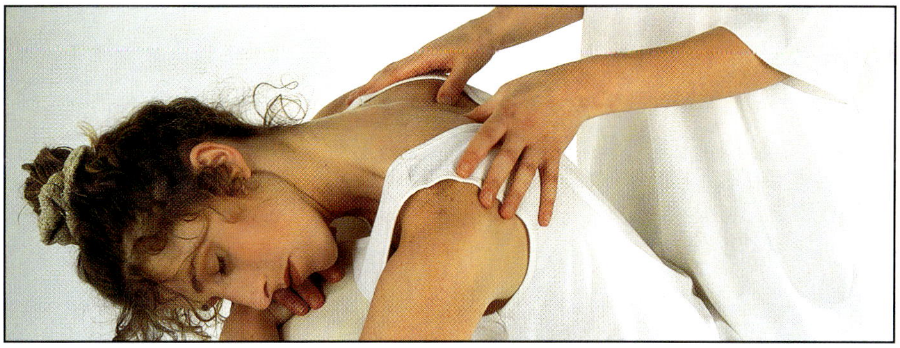

3 *With a firm* petrissage, *use both hands to knead out along the shoulders from the sides of the neck to the upper arms.*

4 *Starting as far down the lower back as you can, work up the spine with small circular frictions. Continue up the sides of the neck to the base of the skull, then glide back down and work up again, this time moving out over the shoulders as you reach the top.*

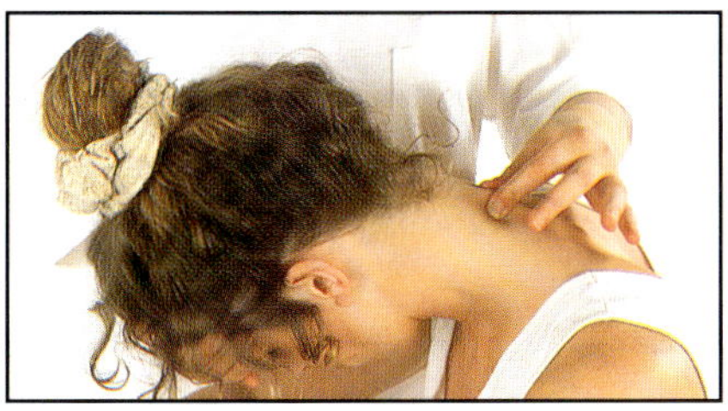

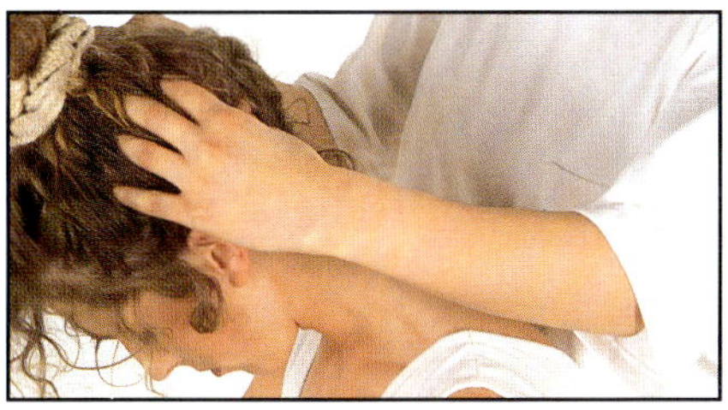

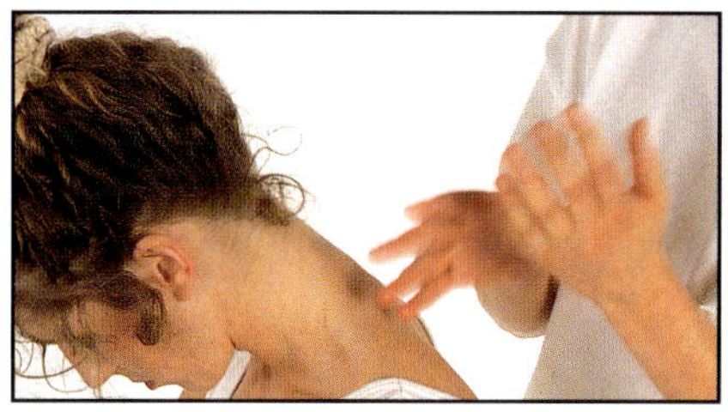

5 *Moving round to the side of the chair, tilt your partner's head forward and support it with one hand. With the thumb and finger of the bther hand, grasp the neck firmly and massage with circular movements, working up the neck and into the base of the skull.*

6 *Working from behind your partner again, massage the back of the head with both hands coming over the forehead and down to the temples with small circular pressures, moving the scalp against the skull. Lighten your touch at the temples.*

7 *First on one side and then the other, do some hacking across the fleshy parts of the shoulders and upper back, using the outer side of your hands to make short, brisk movements. Keep the wrists and hands very relaxed.*

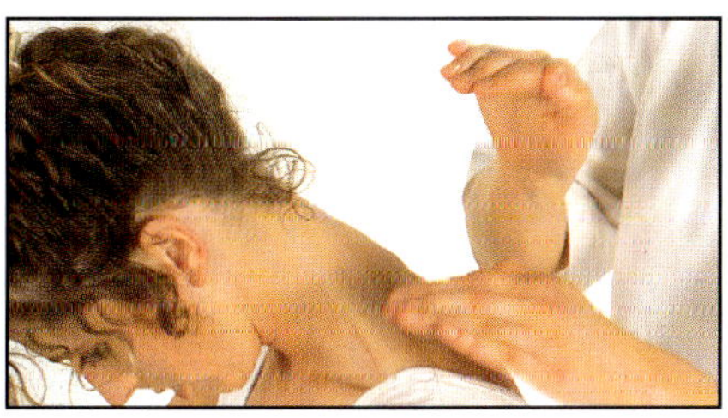

8 *Continue with a brisk cupping action across each shoulder, working on one side at a time.*

9 *Right: Finish the sequence by gently stroking down the entire back with one hand following the other. Repeat five times with each stroke getting lighter.*

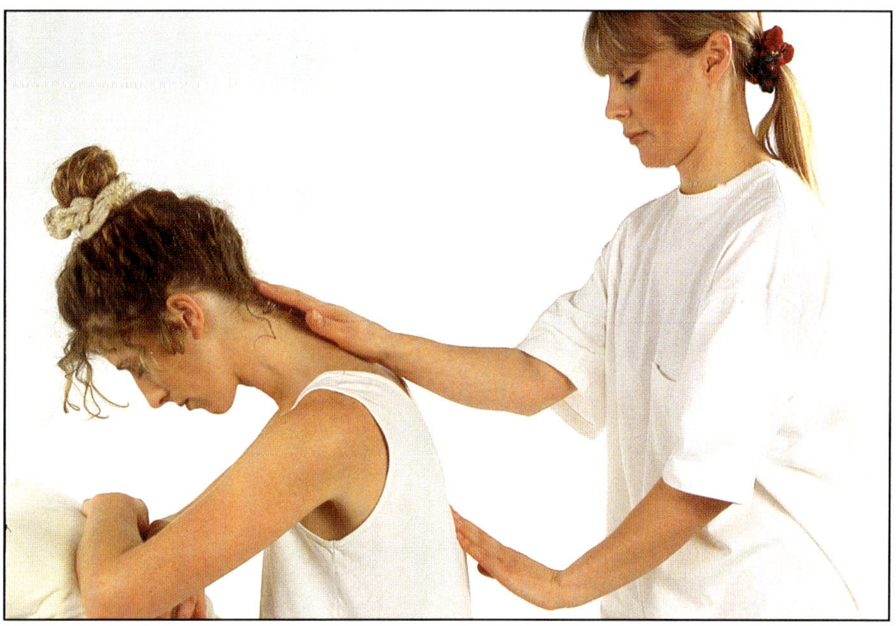

REFLEXOLOGY

Most people enjoy massage to the feet – one of the most sensitive parts of the body. All foot massage is beneficial and relaxing, but reflexology provides a more specific method of working to diagnose problems and stimulate health in the whole body. It is based on the principle that the body can be divided into ten vertical zones, each corresponding to an area of the foot, so that the feet are in effect a map of the body. A sensitive area of the foot indicates a problem in the corresponding organ of the body and by working on the appropriate trouble-spot, the larger problem can be helped. Reflexology can be an effective way of relieving pain and helping to restore the body's natural balance and well-being.

FOOT CHARTS

The foot charts are only guidelines for interpretation. When you find a tender or congested part of the foot you may look for that part on the charts and see approximately which reflex the tenderness lies on. This is only a rough guide because every pair of feet are different and will not be the same shape as your chart. Also, the charts are two-dimensional and your body is three-dimensional and therefore the reflexes on your feet reflect this. In reality your organs overlap each other, whereas the charts are much simplified for clarity, to give an idea of where things are.

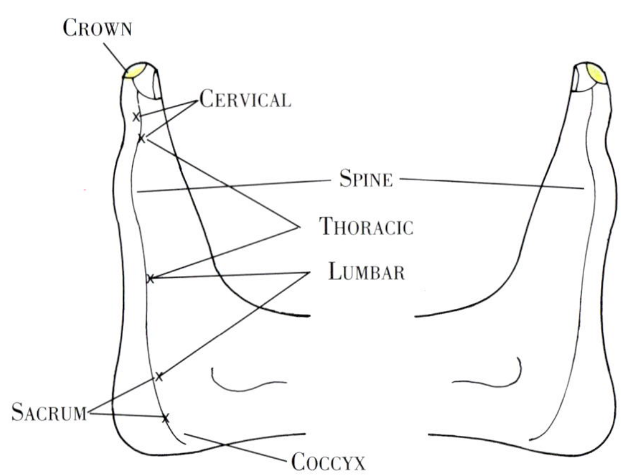

SPINAL REFLEX

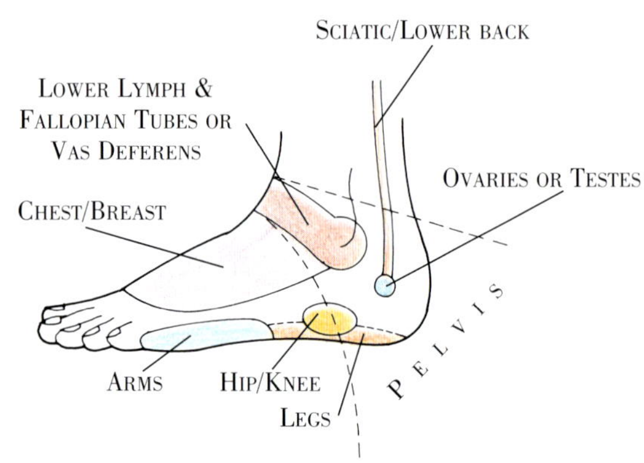

OUTER FOOT

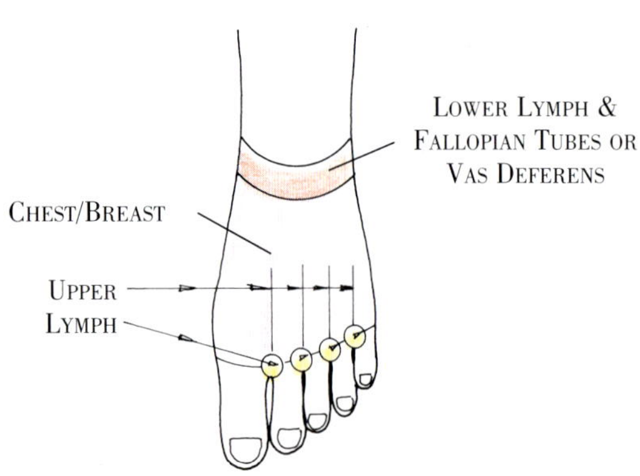

TOP OF FOOT

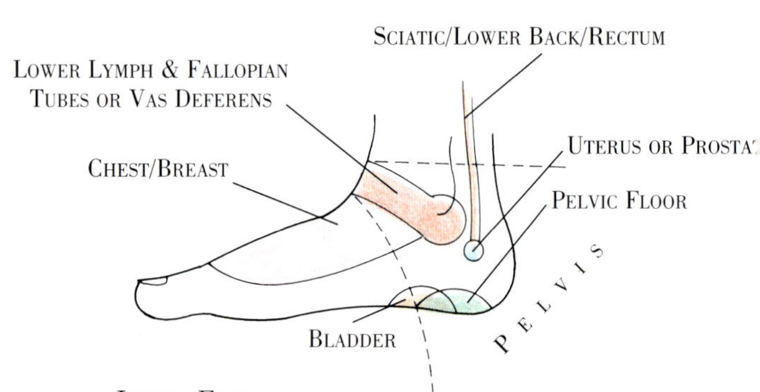

INNER FOOT

THE BACKGROUND

The concept of using the body's reflexes for therapeutic purposes is not new – the early Chinese developed the technique of acupressure thousands of years ago. This provided the basis of knowledge about reflex zones and points and connections between different parts of the body. We know that the early Chinese, Japanese, Indians and Egyptians worked on the feet to promote good health, and many of the long-established principles developed by these civilizations are used in modern-day practice.

Reflexology as it is known today is based largely on the work of Dr William Fitzgerald and Eunice Ingham. Dr Fitzgerald devised his own system of acupressure points which produced an analgesic effect when stimulated. He found that the body could be divided into ten zones running from the top of the head to the tips of the toes, and that everything occuring in a specific zone of the body could affect the organs and other parts of the body in that zone. The theory was refined in the 1930s by a young physiotherapist called Eunice Ingham, who introduced a special grip technique and the action of the thumb on the foot and developed a more intricate zone system. Since then, the system has been further refined into the internationally recognized method that is practiced today.

Modern reflexology offers tremendous health benefits: it reduces stress, improves circulation, cleanses the body of impurities and toxins, and can revitalize energy levels.

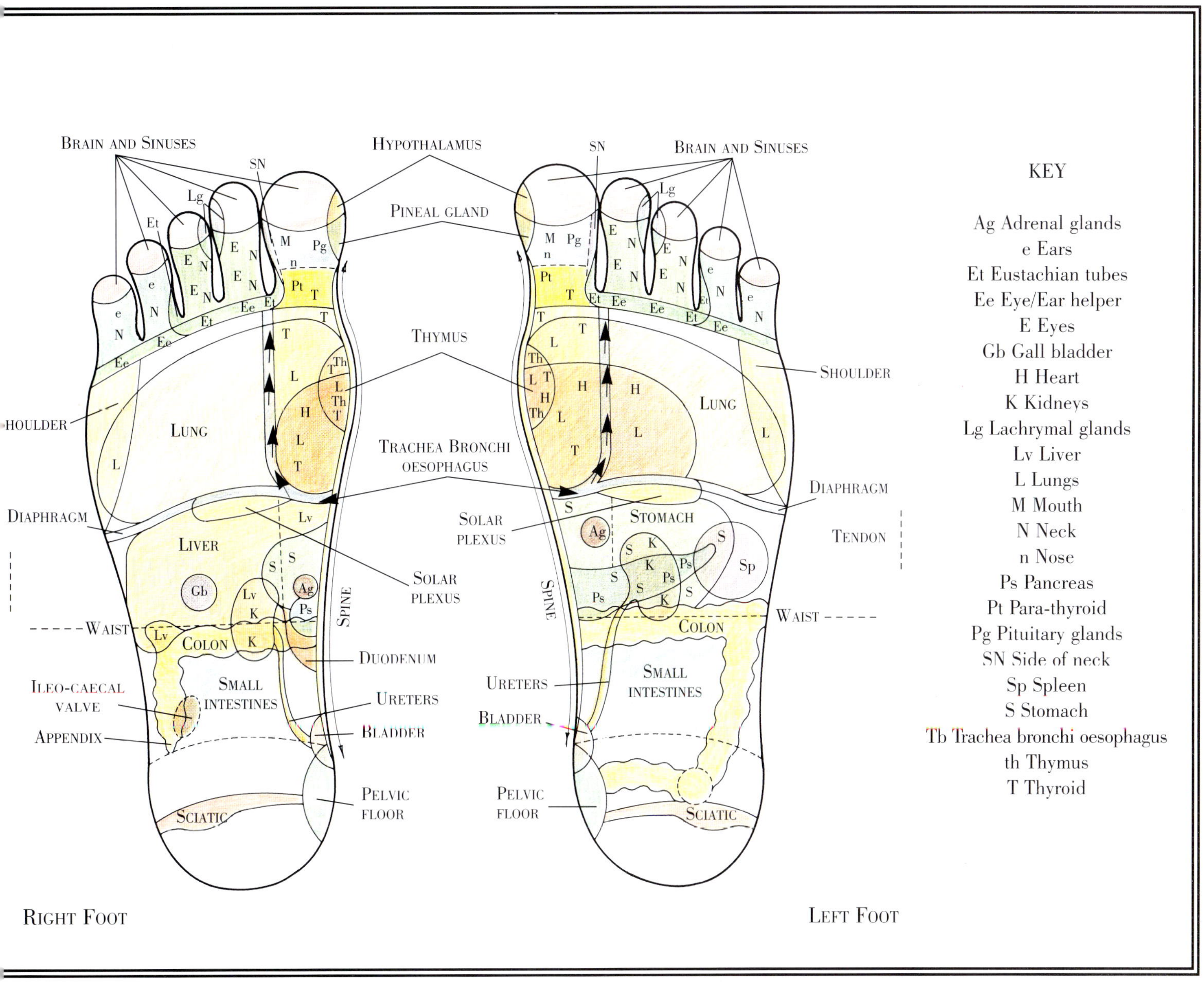

BASIC REFLEXOLOGY TECHNIQUES

THE TREATMENT

Advanced diagnosis is a trained professional skill but some basic techniques can easily be used in a foot massage. You can also use them to work on your own feet, sitting with one ankle supported on the opposite thigh.

The following points will ensure a relaxing session:

- Work with your partner's foot in your lap or supported at the right height with cushions or bolsters.
- Your partner can sit in a comfortable chair with a footstool or small table to raise the feet.
- Ensure the back, neck and knees are properly supported, so your partner can relax completely.
- The massage is given without oil. You can dust the feet with talcum powder or work directly on the skin, if you prefer.
- Make sure your nails are short and well filed.

The following sequence of movements offers an introduction to reflexology. It is necessary to hold the foot correctly so that all points can be reached and stimulated with ease. The hands will swap their holding and working roles according to the part of the foot to be reached, so practice with both hands.

Apart from proper holding, the main principle to observe is leverage. Use the rest of the fingers in opposition to the working thumb to obtain more effective contact with the foot, or the thumb in opposition to the working finger in finger walking.

GREETING THE FEET

Below: The initial contact with the feet sets the tone for the whole treatment. Gently holding both feet relaxes them, allows you to learn about your partner and establishes a relationship.

ANKLE ROTATION

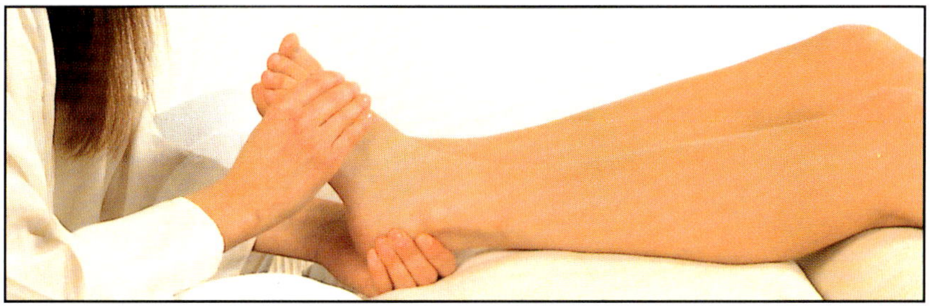

Begin with some relaxing movements. Stabilize the ankle by holding the right foot in the left hand, supporting the heel.

Gently wrap the fingers of the working hand below the base of the toes. Rotate the foot several times in each direction.

ANKLE STRETCH

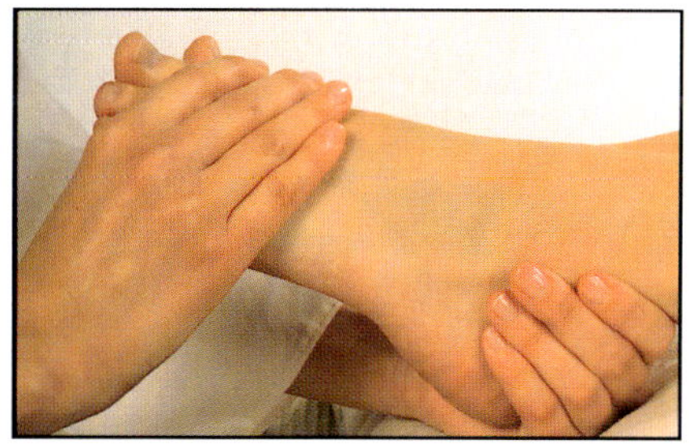

Using the same hold as for the ankle rotation, stretch the foot back and forth slowly to release tension in the Achilles tendon, taking care not to force the ankle joint. Then work all round the ankle, applying pressure. This area corresponds to the reproductive organs, legs and lower back.

SOLAR PLEXUS RELAXATION

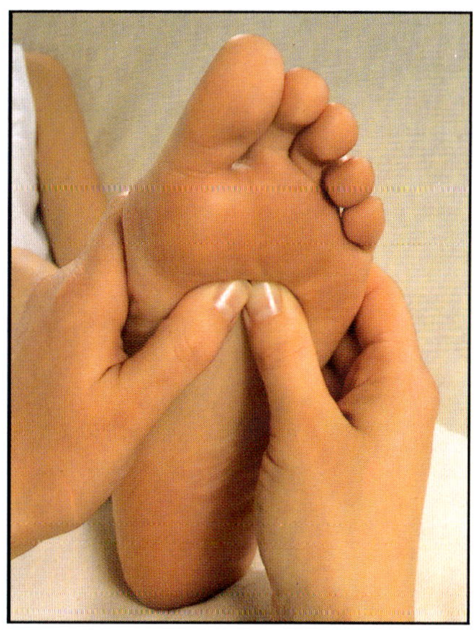

Place both thumbs on the solar plexus point located in the centre of the ball of the foot where there is a little indentation. This is a good relaxation exercise, particularly if your partner is very tense or nervous. You can also work on both feet simultaneously.

THUMB HOOKING

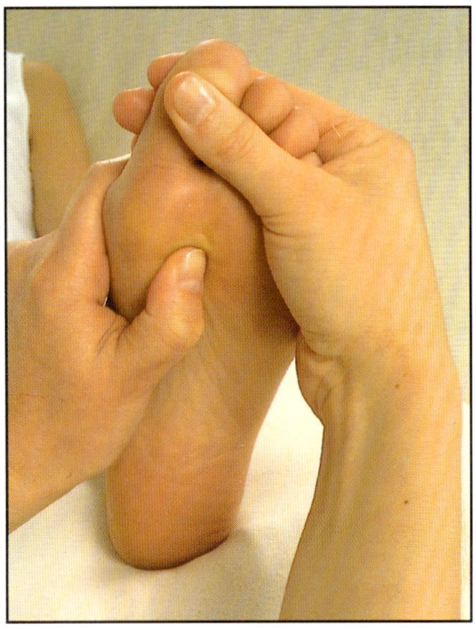

Place the outer corner of the thumb on a reflex point, with the thumb flat. Bend the thumb at the first joint to apply pressure, and pull back across the point. Use the other fingers for counter-pressure and raise the wrist to increase the pressure. Hooking is used to stimulate points that are too small for the walking technique (see right), such as the pituitary point, the solar plexus and lymph drainage points, and any point of soreness.

THUMB WALKING

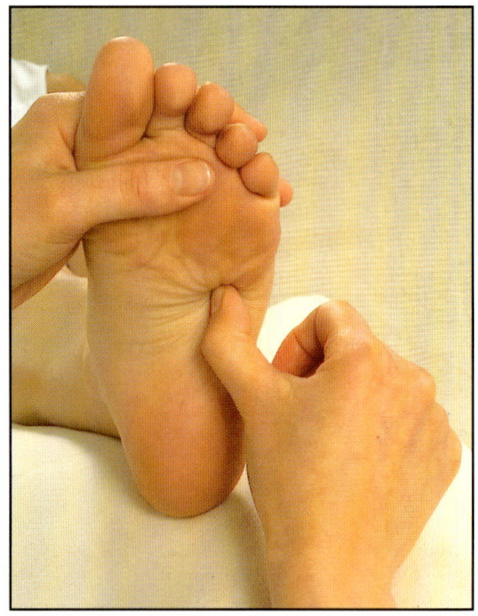

This is the principal technique for covering large areas. Thumb walking starts in the same way as the thumb hook and then the outside corner of the flexed thumb is rocked slightly forward. Maintain steady pressure as the thumb walks, avoiding an "on-off" movement. Press along the diaphragm line under the ball of the foot, then stimulate the spinal area along the main arch of foot from the heel to the big toe.

FINGER WALKING

1,2 *This technique is used to work on the top of the feet. The principle is the same as for thumb walking: flexing the first finger joint and rocking forward. With the holding hand, support and spread the toes, and push on the ball of the foot with the thumb of the working hand to provide leverage. Finger walk from the base of the little toe up to the ankle. Begin again, walking between the troughs of the next toes, toward the inside of the foot.*

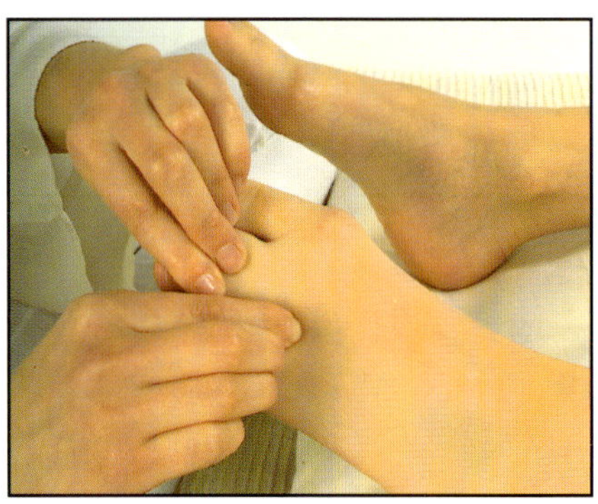

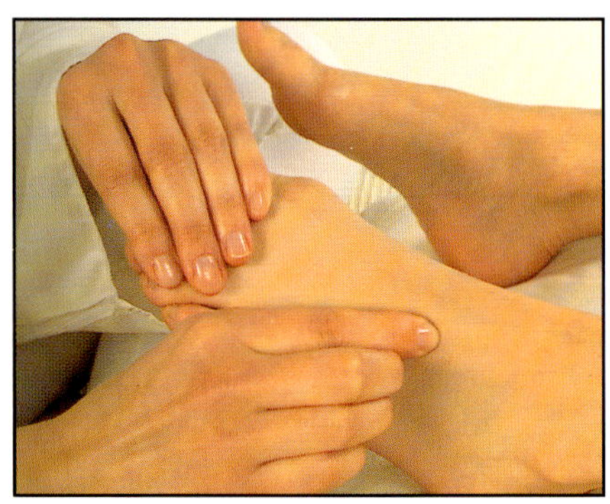

This helps to relieve tension in the chest and lung area, and the areas for lymph drainage and vocal chords which are located between the big toe and second toe at the top of the foot.

STROKING THE FEET

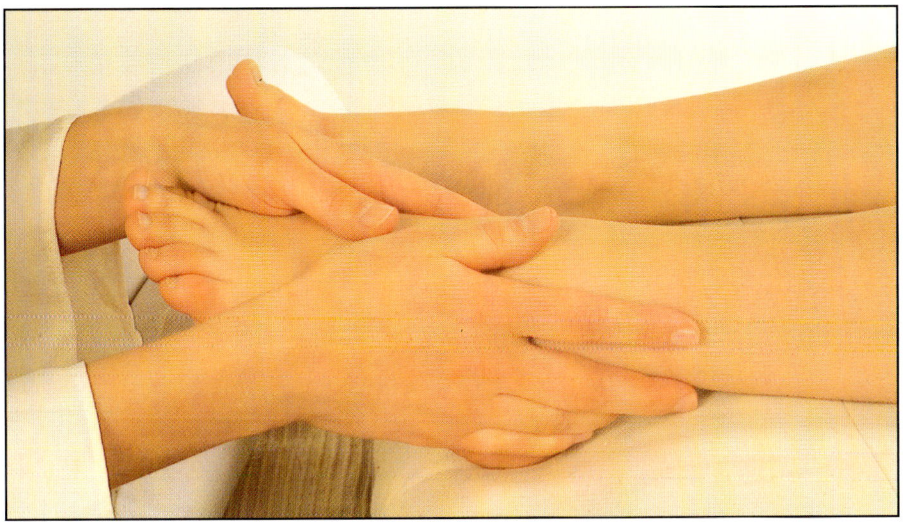

Left: Using alternate hands, stroke the foot softly from the ankles to the toes to smooth and relax the whole area of each foot.

DESSERT STROKE

Right: Take the foot in both hands and slide the hands gently up and down. Dessert strokes are enjoyable and can be used throughout the treatment to soothe and relax your partner after a sensitive reflex has been worked on. Always end the session with dessert strokes to rebalance the whole foot.

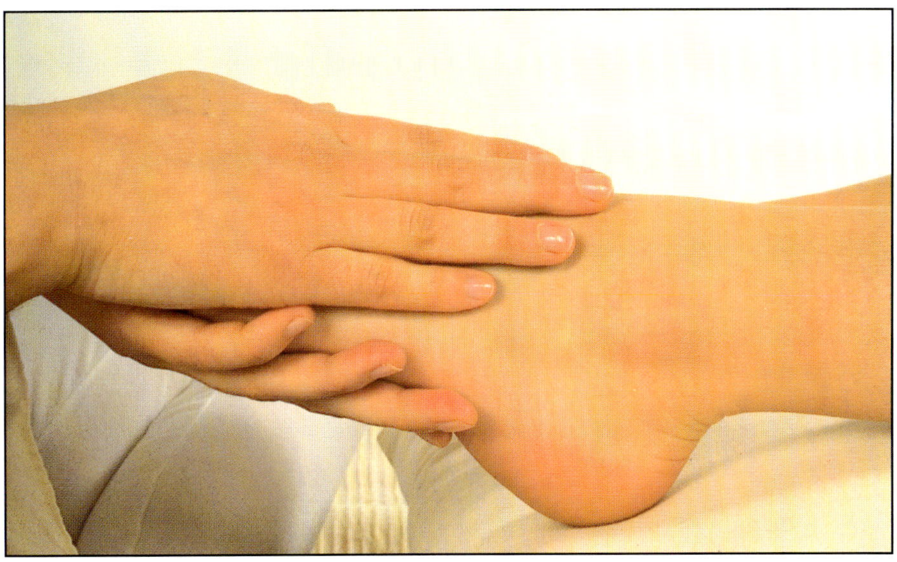

For an effective treatment:

- Explore the foot with the outside edge of the thumb, by the nail, but be careful not to dig with your nail.
- Make regular eye contact with your partner to check responses to specific pressures and to detect painful or sensitive areas.
- Pay extra attention to sensitive areas, which may feel granular, as these are usually due to calcification or deposits of lymph fluid. Work on them thoroughly to disperse the blockages and release energy in the zone.
- Work on each area of the foot several times and make sure that no area is left out.
- Work through each foot once to find sensitive areas and then a second time to reintegrate the foot and body.
- Join the movements and areas of the foot with dessert strokes.
- Always keep contact with at least one hand.
- Knuckling can be used to cover large areas of the foot.

USEFUL ADDRESSES

MASSAGE

ORGANIZATIONS

Association of Physical and Natural Therapists
93 Parkhurst Road
Horley
Surrey RH6 8EX
Tel: 0293 775467

British Massage Therapy Council
9 Elm Road
Worthing
Sussex BN11 1PG

Institute for Complementary Medicine
Unit 4
Tavern Quay
London SE16
Tel: 071-237 5165

PRACTITIONERS AND COURSES

The Bluestone Clinic
34 Devonshire Place
London W1N 1PE
Tel: 071-935 7933

Champneys
Chesham Road
Wiggington
Tring
Herts HP23 6HY
Tel: 0442 863351

Henlow Grange
Henlow
Bedfordshire SG16 6BD
Tel: 0462 811111

Grayshott Hall
Headley Road
Grayshott
Nr Hindhead
Surrey GU26 6JJ
Tel: 0428 604331

London College of Massage
5 Newman Passage
London W1P 3PF
Tel: 071-323 3574

London School of Sports Massage
88 Cambridge Street
London SW1V 4QG
Tel: 071-233 5962

Massage Training Institute
24 Highbury Grove
London N5 2EA
Tel: 071-226 5313

Northern Institute of Massage
100 Waterloo Road
Blackpool FY4 1AW

American Massage Therapy Association
820 Davies Street
Evanston
IL 60201
USA

Boulder School of Massage Therapy
PO Box 4573
Boulder
CO 80306
USA

The Connecticut Center for Massage Therapy
75 Kitts Lane
Newington
CT 06111
USA

Australian Natural Therapists Association
PO Box 522
Sutherland
NSW 2232
Australia

South African Institute of Health and Beauty Therapists
PO Box 56318
Pinegowrie
22123
Johannesburg
South Africa

REFLEXOLOGY

The British School of Reflexology
92 Sheering Road
Old Harlow
Essex CN17 0JW
Tel: 0279 429060

British School of Reflex Zone Therapy
87 Oakington Avenue
Wembley Park
London HA9 8HY
Tel: 081-908 2201

International Institute of Reflexology
15 Hartfield Close
Tonbridge
Kent TN10 4JP

Reflexologists' Society
39 Presbury Road
Cheltenham
Glos GL52 2PT
Tel: 0242 512601

International Institute of Reflexology
PO Box 12642
5650 First Avenue North
St Petersburg
FLA 33733-2642
USA

FURTHER READING

MASSAGE

Nigel Dawes and Fiona Harrold, *Massage Cures*, Thorsons 1990

George Downing, *The Massage Book*, Wildwood House, 1973

Fiona Harrold, *The Massage Manual*, Headline, 1992

Tina Heinl, *Baby Massage*, Prentice Hall, 1983

Nitya Lacroix, *Massage for Total Relaxation*, Dorling Kindersley, 1991

Sensual Massage, Dorling Kindersley, 1989

Lucinda Lidell, *The Massage Book*, Ebury Press, 1984

Clare Maxwell-Hudson, *The Complete Book of Massage*, Dorling Kindersley, 1988

Sara Thomas, *Massage for Common Ailments*, Sidgwick & Jackson, 1989

Jacqueline Young, *Self Massage*, Thorsons, 1992

REFLEXOLOGY

Dwight C. Byers, *Better Health with Foot Reflexology*, Ingham Publishing Inc., 1983

Kevin and Barbara Kunz, *The Complete Guide to Foot Reflexology*, Prentice Hall, 1982

Laura Norman with Thomas Cowan, *The Reflexology Handbook*, Judy Piatkus, 1988

a l e x a n d e r t e c h n i q u e
a l e x a n d e r t e c h n

alexander technique

People tend to associate the Alexander technique with relaxation, alternative medicine, body massage and with "posture". Yet it is actually much more than that.

One way towards a clearer understanding of the technique is to begin by stating what it is not. The Alexander technique does not train its teachers to make a medical diagnosis of their students, nor does it focus on any division between the mind and body. The technique believes in the indivisibility of the two and in their psycho-physical unity. Above all, the technique's main objective is to encourage people to use themselves, their bodies and minds more effectively in their day-to-day lives.

The technique's preventive role is an efficient tool which maintains tone and general well-being. It also helps to improve posture and relieve related pain. In fact it can assist people with stress-related illnesses such as respiratory and gastro-intestinal problems, as well as psychosomatic conditions. It can help those who suffer from psychological distress, such as depression, as well as facilitating recovery from accidents and injuries. The technique can even assist people with mechanical problems, such as frozen shoulder, tennis elbow and arthritis. Above all, it helps promote muscle tone and general well-being while encouraging poise and flexibility. The technique aids the well in addition to those with ailments.

the alexander technique principles

Once you start studying the technique, it quickly becomes clear that it helps you in all kinds of ways that other alternative remedies do not. That is not because it is superior, but because of its key agenda. As shown here, it helps us focus on our minds and bodies in new ways, and on aspects of our being that we might take for granted. The technique gets us back to basics.

Primary Control

"Misuse" occurs by contracting the muscles of the neck and pulling the head back and down into the shoulders. This has the twin effect of actually compressing the spine and narrowing and shortening the stature, creating tensions throughout the body. It is definitely something to be avoided.

Frederick Matthias Alexander discovered that the relationship between the head, the neck and the back, or "primary control", mechanically controlled movement and co-ordination in the whole body. To make ourselves aware of this consciously in our daily activities is the basis of good use.

See how this model is misusing himself. He is leaning over to the right, shortening and creating an imbalance in his body.

Inhibition

In its psychological-physiological sense, inhibition means a fast-moving yet natural control of your reactions, suppressing and smothering any possible spontaneity.

However, Alexander discovered that if he managed to stop himself from behaving in his habitual way, he could choose how he wished to respond to a stimulus. If someone rings the doorbell, your immediate response may be to go straight to the door. In doing so, you will be responding habitually. If you stop yourself from responding automatically, you then choose exactly how you will approach the door with the minimum effort.

Concepts

The concept of end-gaining is extremely important in the work of Alexander technique teachers. Alexander realized that the habits he was encountering were far more deep-rooted and powerful than he had at first thought. The most serious of these was the tendency to try to react impulsively – end-gaining. End-gaining means reacting immediately and too quickly to a stimulus, without thinking. You respond by wanting something to happen, and become interested in the end result instead of being in the present. A typical example is if you are going to be late for an appointment and start to worry about the consequences. You get worked up during this process, forgetting that you might be sitting on a train, and that things are happening around you. In effect you are letting your thoughts take the situation into the future, instead of being in the "here and now", in the present.

Cutting yourself off from your environment has inevitable consequences for body positioning. It tends to lead to a pulling back of the head, a rounding of the back, a tightening of the legs and a loss of connection between the arms and the back. The gaze becomes fixed, the breath held. Essentially, the whole person is affected, both in mind and in body.

Alexander suggests you should use your "means-whereby". To put Alexander's conclusion into context, if we accept that we cannot change circumstances, we can change our approach to our bodies and allow ourselves to experience the new. It is then possible to learn to be in the moment rather than the past or the future, and to maintain a sense of inner balance and unity.

Direction

Directions are signals given by the brain to parts of the body prior to or during physical action. It is possible to alter these signals to promote a positive change. You will find that the combination of direction and inhibition enables one to transform habitual ways of moving and eliminate old patterns of misuse.

Note how this model is walking. Her head, neck and back are all correctly aligned. Her arms are free to move in a relaxed way.

Natural Poise

Nothing is more elegant and enviable than someone with perfect poise. It is something most of us have when young, but sadly it can be quickly lost to laziness and bad postural habits. In fact, it is quite easy to be totally unaware just how bad our posture is. At various times during the day it is worth freezing your movements, and taking a good look at yourself. You will be surprised at how often you fall well short of the ideal. Sitting at work is probably the one situation when your back is almost always wrongly positioned, becoming increasingly hunched, tense and stiff. Once you have ascertained exactly when and how you are going wrong, you can start putting matters right. If in any doubt, just look at young children. They instinctively know how to move gracefully and effortlessly without strain. That is something we should all try to emulate.

This child carries his toy close to his body., allowing it to lengthen and relax. This ensures good nervous energy and blood flow and allows full expansion of the lungs for breathing.

The Human Skeleton

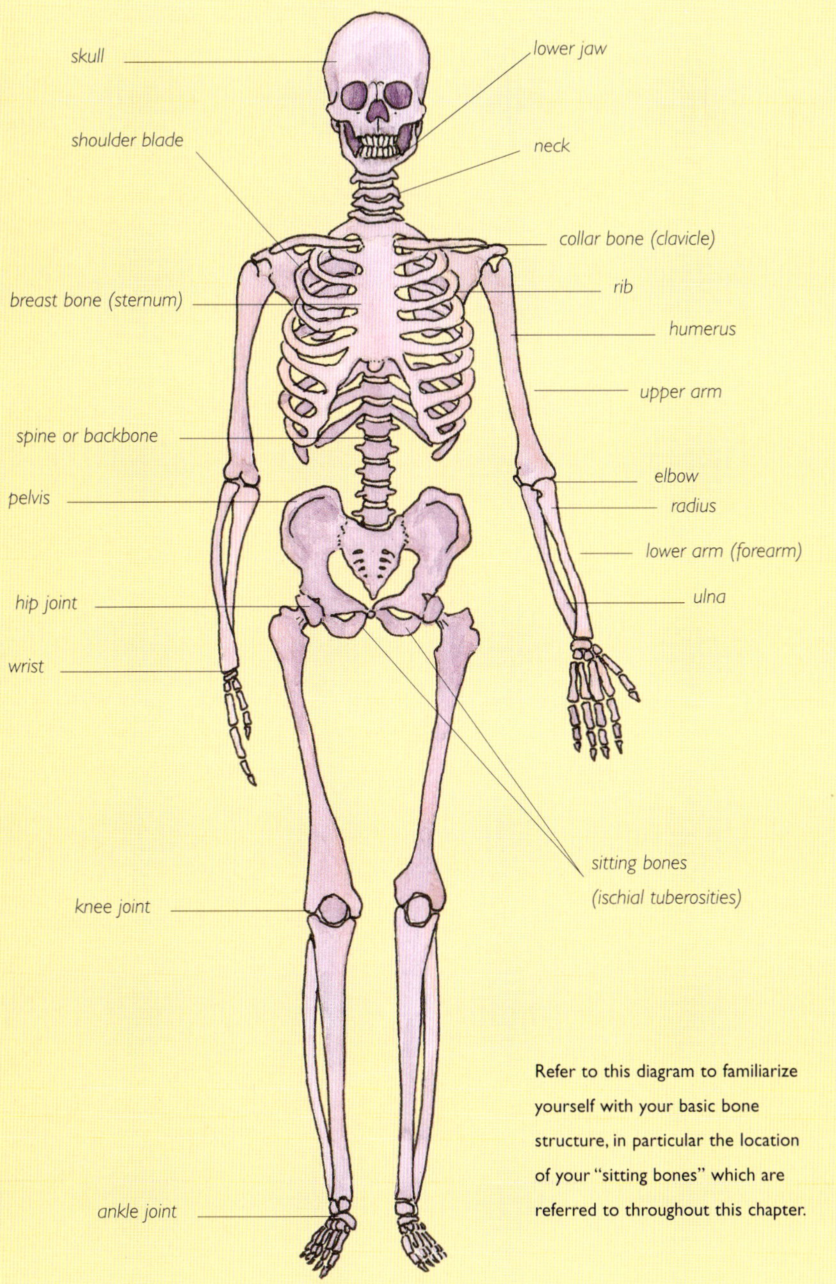

Refer to this diagram to familiarize yourself with your basic bone structure, in particular the location of your "sitting bones" which are referred to throughout this chapter.

Primary Directions

- Think of freeing the neck.
- Let the head go forward and up.
- Let the back lengthen and widen.

Note how this child is using his joints to squat, and how he simultaneously holds the plastic bag quite effortlessly.

"Possession of property … a means to happiness not an end."
Thomas Jefferson

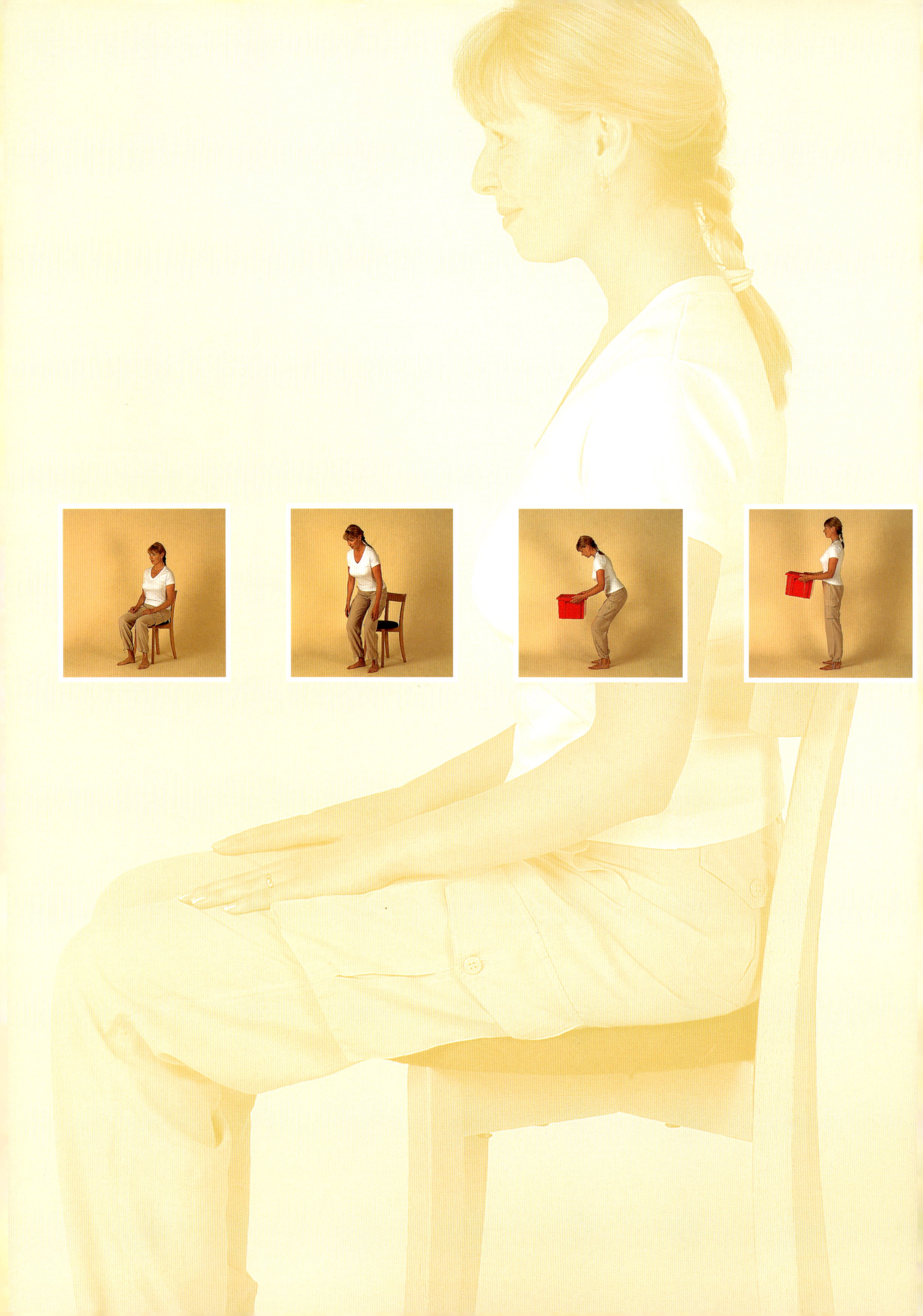

putting the alexander technique into practice

putting the alexander technique into practice
putting the alexander technique
into practice

A certain, rightful degree of commitment is paramount during a course of lessons because the older and more set in your ways you are, the longer it can take to change, to release unnecessary muscular tension, and to re-educate the system. Success, however, is not hard to achieve but note that it will not happen overnight, and that some slight pitfalls are always going to be inevitable, so do not be put off.

For example, you may well find yourself trying to do the directions as a routine mechanical exercise when in reality success lies in the power of the body and mind uniting as one, and in the power to think about what you are doing. Do not imagine there are any short cuts, there are not. There is also the distinct possibility that you might be tempted to give up out of sheer frustration because your time scale is too unrealistically short and limiting, and you have not allowed sufficient time for a significant, quantifiable improvement. Do not be hard on yourself, and do not imagine that you can become an expert in a ridiculously short space of time. The technique deserves more respect.

What therefore follows is the identification of the main procedures that we use most often in daily life, the areas that most concern us. In fact, the use of the word "procedure" is quite deliberate because it totally avoids the suggestion of a mind-body split and maintains a sense of psycho-physical unity. The emphasis throughout is on the means of achieving these procedures, but with the minimum of muscular tension and effort. Many students have said that a course of lessons in the technique could be compared to learning to drive or learning a new language. Dedication and determination are a sure basis for total success.

use of the eyes

If you want to know something about someone, just look straight into their eyes. They reveal an amazing amount about their current frame of mind. You can easily spot the depressed, dull and lifeless by their deadpan, almost one-dimensional eyes; the totally alert looking for a lively reply; the sad; the plaintive; the cheeky; and the happy. The technique reminds you how to stay lively and alert, and in touch with the rest of the world.

STAYING ALERT

If you observe people when they are either standing or walking, they often seem to be completely locked in a private world of their own, totally unaware of their own surroundings. They have stopped communicating with that is out there. When the gaze is fixed, the breathing also tends to suffer. It becomes rather restricted and there is less freedom in the body. The gaze should therefore be directed towards the outside world, taking in information so that you are not exclusively concentrating on what is happening within.

One of the strongest habits that a teacher perceives is the tendency of certain pupils to look down, not with their eyes, but by a general collapsing motion from the neck. This is the result of a fundamental misunderstanding of the alignment of the head, the neck and the back, and the position of the joints in the body.

Note how the models in this sequence of photographs (*below*) are using their eyes. Which do you think is the correct position? Can there be any doubt?.

> "It's no good shutting your eyes if you're crossing a busy road."
> *F. M. Alexander*

Here children are using their eyes to look at their toys. They have not disturbed the alignment between their heads, their necks and their backs, thus maintaining their good use.

In this position, the model is breaking the alignment between her head, her neck and her back as she looks down, thus using her neck inappropriately.

Note how the model is correctly aligned. She is maintaining her length and her width. Her eyes are alert and taking in her surroundings.

Here the model is breaking at the neckline and pulling her head back to look up, disturbing the alignment between her head, neck and back.

the semi-supine position

Standing for long periods easily compresses the spine. Lying down in a semi-supine position is a way of alleviating unnecessary tensions in the muscles and joints, and should be practised every day for at least 20 minutes. It encourages a better awareness of the head-neck-back relationship. This position does not necessarily need monitoring by a teacher, and it also gives you much needed time for yourself.

THE POSITION

Try to keep your eyes alert and open. It is preferable to avoid closing them because you will probably find it quite difficult not to fall asleep, which is definitely not the point of the exercise!

During your daily 20-minute session try and give yourself the time to practise some sharp, well directed thoughts to avoid your mind from wandering and spreading out, covering other possible important issues. This session can also encourage you to put into practice your excellent skills of observation. A good practice is to go over the primary directions, and to notice if you are aware of any tension in your body and to address it without trying to correct it. That is the secret of success.

Books are used to support the head. If you have too many, however, your chin will drop and you will feel pressure on your throat.

Correspondingly, if you do not have enough books your head will tilt back and will not be properly supported.

MOVING INTO THE SEMI-SUPINE

It is preferable to lie down on a hard, carpeted surface or alternatively on a rug on the floor. Avoid beds as they will not offer you adequate support. The number of books you need will depend on their thickness, and will also vary from person to person.

To lie down on the floor, place the books far enough behind you to give enough space for the whole of your torso and your bottom. When sitting, you can place your hands palms down on the floor behind you to help you lower your back. Take care not to stiffen the arms or to hold your breath in the process. To get up, it is preferable to roll over to one side, leading with your eyes rather than your head, and following with your torso and legs. Then place the free hand flat on the floor and go on to all fours. Be careful to maintain the alignment between your head, your neck and your back and not to hold your breath. Walk your hands back so that you move your bottom back towards your heels.

Make sure that your legs are about hip-width apart and that your knees are directed towards the ceiling.

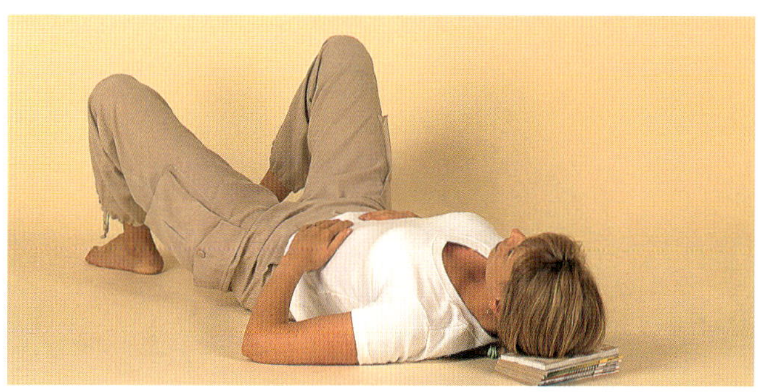

If your knees are falling out, you will probably lose the contact between the inner side of your foot and the floor.

sitting and standing

Correct posture is as much about what is right as what is wrong. It is vital that you know what to do, and what not to do. It is easy to start out with correct posture, but fall into bad habits. You must know when to correct yourself. Remember to keep a straight alignment between head, neck and back, and to keep your legs hip-width apart with knees pointing forward, in the same direction as your feet.

SITTING

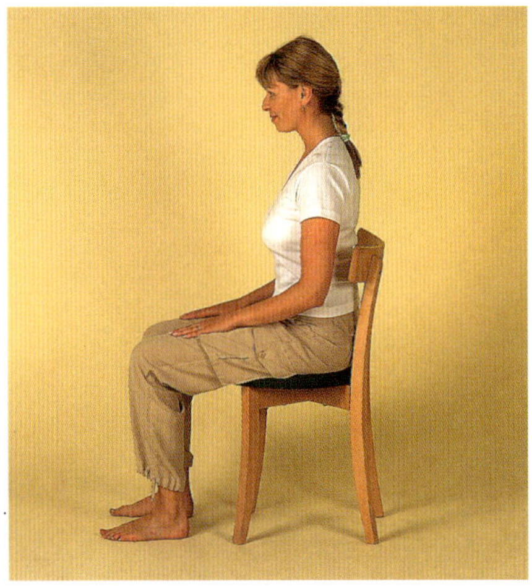

Correct: think of the shoulders going away from each other.

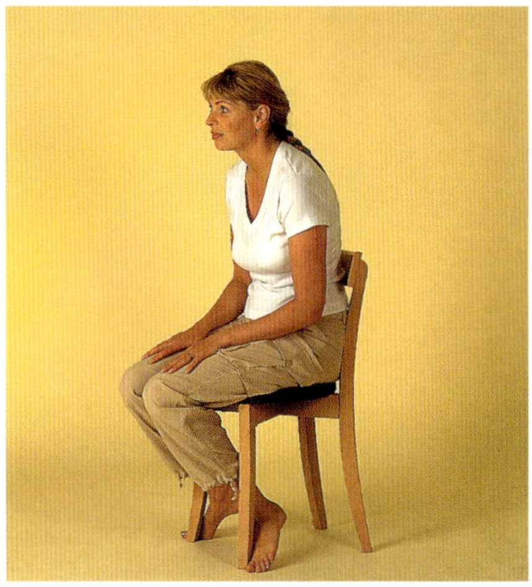

Incorrect: rounded shoulders and feet wrapped around chair legs.

Incorrect: arching the back, folding legs and leaning to one side.

FROM SITTING TO STANDING

It is well worth practising this basic technique several times to perfect it. You will be surprised how ingrained bad habits are. Start by placing your legs about hip-width apart. Avoid pushing firmly up with them; that is not the object. Also, make sure that your feet are flat and are not placed so far forwards that coming up to stand is in any way difficult. Finally, remember to lead with the head; that is the key to getting this technique right.

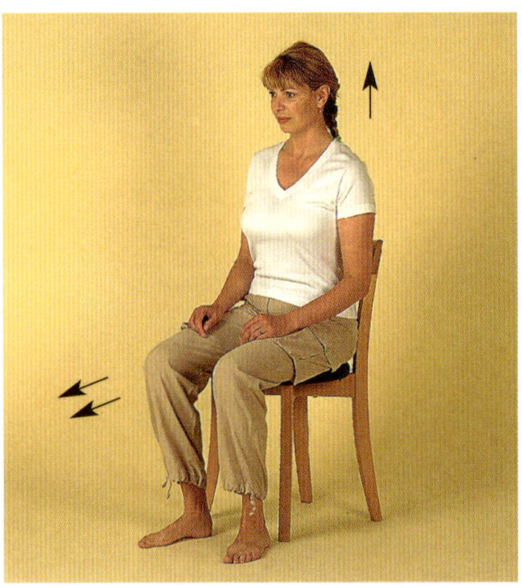

1 Here the model is relaxed, feet apart, hands resting comfortably, ready to go into the standing position.

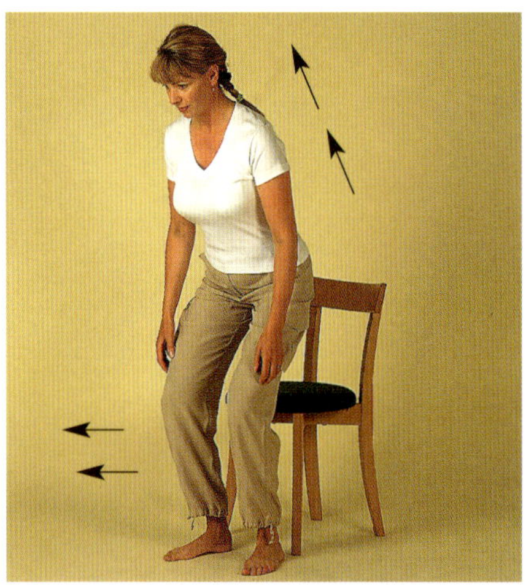

2 As she stands she has managed to keep the correct alignment between her head, neck and back.

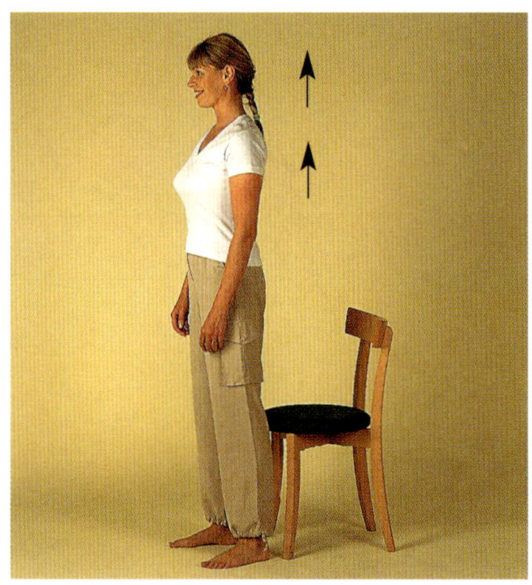

3 Having hinged from the hip, sending her knees forwards and away over her feet, she is now properly upright.

reaching and handling

It is impossible to avoid two basic movements, reaching and handling. Yet how many of us know how to do them properly, according to the Alexander technique? Reaching means keeping the alignment between the head, neck and back, whether you are low down or standing up. If you are indeed squatting, it is important that you allow your hand to lead your movement. Let everything else follow behind.

HANDLING

See how the model's weight is balanced over the feet, and how she is allowing her hand to lead her wrist and arm.

Here, the legs are straight and the head is pulled back, causing a lot of strain on the neck, and the shoulders are tense.

See how the arms remain well connected to the shoulder blades and back. Also, there is no tension in the arms and wrists.

GOING UP ON TIPTOES

When going on tiptoes correctly, the weight that is placed on the middle of the feet when standing is placed on the balls of the feet, as the head leads the body forwards and upwards. It is important to maintain the alignment between the head, the neck and the back. The breath is not held, and the eyes are alert.

Look at how this model is going on tiptoes to enable her hand to lead her arm to close the window.

Note how the model is well poised and correctly aligned. There is no undue stress on the body.

Here the head contraction is severe. The model is holding his breath, causing unnecessary tension in the body.

"monkey" or bending

The position known as the "monkey" enables us to move with more flexibility in our daily activities. It is a useful means of moving from standing to sitting or squatting, as well as helping with lifting, picking things up, working at a desk, washing, ironing, and participating in sports such as skiing and golf. The "monkey" respects the relationship between the head, neck and back.

THE POSITION

The "monkey" position might sound tricky, but it really is not. Try it slowly, see how it works, then try it again at a more natural speed. It basically involves the head moving forwards and up, and then the knees moving forwards and away over the feet to counterbalance the bottom going back over the heels, enabling the arms to move freely. It is also important to remember that when you go into "monkey" you must review your primary directions. What is more, stay alert at all times, and avoid fixing your gaze or holding your breath. Such moves will quickly undermine the marvellous effects of the "monkey".

To be more precise then, stand with your legs hip-width apart, with the feet slightly turned outwards. Your weight should be evenly distributed, neither too far forwards nor too far back on your feet. To start going into the "monkey", allow the knees to bend slightly over your feet as you tilt forwards from your hip joints, making sure your head, your neck and your back are aligned. Avoid collapsing over yourself!

One final point is to make sure you think of widening and lengthening your back as you widen across the shoulder girdle, to allow free movement and your arms to hang freely. This extra tip will ensure you enjoy the full effect of "the monkey".

This model is in the correct "monkey" position. Her head, her neck and her back are aligned. Her knees are bent forward and away from her hips.

When going into the "monkey" avoid retracting the head back and down into the spine. Note how the model has rounded her shoulders and pulled in her knees.

Here the model is not bending her knees as she bends forwards. Her back is collapsed over her body, and her legs are straight and braced.

everyday situations

In everyday situations it is important to pause before reacting, to make sure you are so positioned that you do not misuse yourself. The more aware you are, the more likely you will encourage muscular release through your whole system. Equally, the more at peace you are, the easier it is to apply the principles of the Alexander technique. The following excellent examples show how the "monkey" can keep you healthy.

Note how the model's back is correctly aligned, keeping to the head-neck-back principle. See how she is using her joints and allowing her widening arms to handle the dish.

How things can go wrong. Here the model has started pulling her head back. Also, her back is rounded, her legs are braced and her arms have become much too tense.

In this highly incorrect stance, the man is collapsing from his waist down as he begins works in the garden. His shoulders are far too rounded, and his head is being pulled back.

In this correct procedure, the model is neatly poised and balanced, and she is well aligned to begin her ironing. Her hand, wrist and arm are also free as she holds the iron. The other crucial point to note is how she is widening across her upper arms. It is clear that she looks balanced and feels alert.

See how the model is using the whole of his back quite correctly. He is sensibly allowing his weight to come back on to his heels, and his knees go forwards and away over his feet.

An example of how not to do it. Here he is completely out of alignment. You can sense it is not right, but why? He is actually pulling his head back, rounding the back, and holding in the arms. This position is entirely the result of bad habits. Without the Alexander technique, he would never know how to right this.

"lunge monkey"

The "lunge monkey" is similar to the "monkey" because the knees go forwards and away, and the torso tilts slightly forwards from the hip joints. Also, one foot is placed behind the other, and the legs are placed hip-width apart, enabling you to balance the upper part of your body on to the forward or the back leg whenever the need arises. In this way, your weight is placed forwards or backwards according to your activity.

BENDING

The "lunge monkey" is extremely useful when you need to lift something heavy from the floor; when you need to move an object from one side of a surface to another, for example during cooking; or when you need to push or pull something rather heavy into place.

When you adapt the "lunge monkey" it is important to remember to keep your head, your neck and your back correctly aligned. The legs must be hip-width apart, with the arms hanging freely on either side of your torso.

Also, allow your weight to move to the right on to the right foot (or to the left, as the situation demands). If moving to the left, reverse the instructions.

See how the model has collapsed badly from the waist down. Her shoulders are rounded, the legs are straight and the knees are braced, causing tension.

Observe how the model has gone into the "lunge monkey". Her head, neck and back are neatly aligned, and her knees are going forward away from her hips.

Note how the model has completely lost the correct alignment with her back as she squats. Her head has dropped, and her shoulders are hunched and rounded. Furthermore, she looks ill at ease and uncomfortable. There is no poise or grace. This position is definitely one to avoid.

In this correct procedure, observe how the model's head, neck and back are correctly aligned. Her shoulders are widening across her upper arms. She looks well balanced, and fully in control of her movements. Also note how her heels are tucked in under the bottom. The position is also easy to get into.

SQUATTING

In Western societies most people find it difficult to squat in their everyday lives. Young children have very little difficulty in doing so, but as we grow older we lose the necessary flexibility to squat as our joints become less mobile.

A low "monkey" or semi-squat is the best way that an Alexander teacher can re-introduce a student to squatting over a series of lessons. To squat, follow the same guidelines as for the "monkey", but with a wider stance. Remember to maintain the alignment between the head, the neck and the back, and to allow the joints in the hips, the knees and the ankles to be free. As you go into a deeper squat you might find that your heels come off the ground. This does not present a problem as far as the technique is concerned, so long as you keep your balance. As a general rule, go only as far as you feel comfortable.

the technique in the home

The key point to note about the Alexander technique is that it is not an abstract theory that you can apply when the mood takes you. It is a specific, practical everyday guide that will help you enormously whether you are bending, squatting, lifting or carrying. It gives you terrific control whatever you are doing, injecting extra confidence that will keep you alert and relaxed.

BENDING

Note how the model is tilted forwards to get a greater range of movement. His arms are free, supported by his back.

Now he is incorrectly bending forwards from the waist. His legs are braced, and his head is pulled back.

Here the model has aligned herself nicely to make the bed. Her legs are bent, creating a greater range of movement.

SQUATTING

This model is lunge squatting to brush up dirt from the floor. She has maintained her good use, giving herself a maximum range of movement. She looks good and feels good.

Here, in an incorrect example of how you should sweep the floor, the model is badly restricting his range of movement. He is quite clearly unbalanced, and feels totally uncomfortable.

Note how this man is squatting sensibly to plant a rose bush in his garden. By placing himself at the same level as the rose, he is allowing himself a greater range of movement.

lifting and carrying

A lot of back pain is the result of lifting heavy weights. To avoid back strain, stand near to the load by placing your feet either side of it, and maintain the alignment between head, neck and back. Go into the "monkey" or "lunge monkey" and squat. Then bend your arms so that your elbows are close to your body. Make sure that you widen out across the upper arms, and avoid tension in the arms and wrists.

LIFTING

1 Once you are holding the load as closely to your body as you can, come out of a squat or lunge squat into a "monkey" before standing.

2 Lift the weight in a flowing action, that does not jar or suddenly pull against the back. If the weight proves too heavy, it is easy to bend and put it down.

3 To place the load back on the ground, reverse the process and apply the same principles, making sure that your head, neck and back are aligned.

CARRYING

Here the model is carrying all her shopping bags in one hand, creating an imbalance as she is pulled down to the left. She is raising her right shoulder in an attempt to support her handbag.

This model is carrying her shopping bags sensibly and correctly so that they are evenly distributed on both sides. She is well balanced and able to walk freely. She looks content.

Look at the excellent way this mother is carrying her child. Her weight is evenly distributed and she is holding the child close to her body, firmly supporting his upper and lower body.

daily routines

The most surprising point about the Alexander technique is that it is not just for big, set piece movements such as lifting heavy weights, when doing it incorrectly can obviously lead to back problems. The technique even extends to the minutiae of life, routines that we completely take for granted, such as eating, drinking, and driving. If you had always wondered how they should be done, read on. These tips will make all the difference.

EATING AND DRINKING

If you are standing upright while you are drinking remember that you still need to be fully alert at all times. Therefore, make sure that you do not fix your gaze rigidly and thereby lose all communication and contact with the outside world. You also need to ensure that your head leads you away from your heels (see the section on Standing for further guidance). You will find that your shoulder girdle brings mobility to your arms, and that the pelvis provides stability which simultaneously facilitates mobility in your legs.

The very same principles also apply to eating. Whether you are going to eat something from your hand or use a fork, it is all too easy to forget your posture completely. Remember that you should not totally focus on the matter in hand, but that you must also consider your stance, alertness and poise.

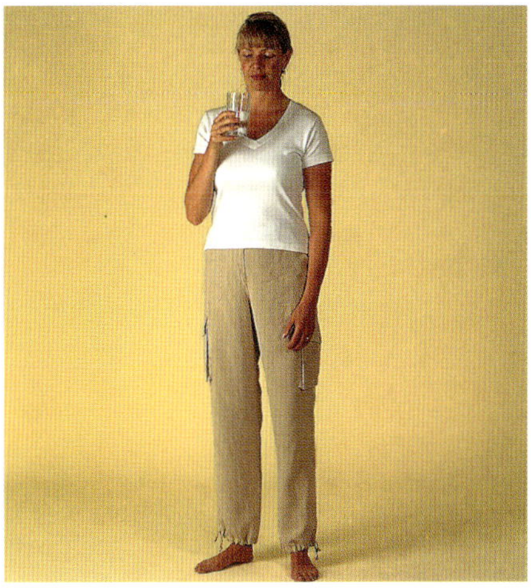

Avoid gripping or clutching your glass. Be aware of the connection with your arm, which links to your back and then into your heels. As you raise the cup to your lips, bring your weight back on to the heels, so as not to pull in your lower back. Also, bring the glass to the lips, rather than leaning down into it.

Take some time to consider how you are seated at the table and then bring the food up to your mouth, rather than the reverse. Your feet should be correctly positioned on the floor. You should also be aware of both your sitting bones, and how your back should be lengthening and widening. This position also aids digestion.

DRIVING

Most of the problems experienced by drivers are due to fixed postures, long journeys and poor seating support.

Too many people who spend huge amounts of time driving find themselves constricted by the position of the steering wheel and the pedals. Such a cramped environment is bound to lead to stress and strain on the back, and equally on the arms and legs.

When choosing a car take time to see whether the seat is firm and supportive. If you already own a car and it does not have a lumbar support adjustment, you can use a wedge-shaped cushion to give you adequate support in the lumbar area and the pelvis. It makes a vital difference.

You should be able to reach the pedals quite easily. A wedge-shaped cushion is extremely useful to avoid a poor, slumping position.

See how the model is badly collapsing forward, how the neck is being strained and the arms are rigidly tense. Such a position will cause lots of discomfort.

office work

Before reading it is important to spend some time considering exactly how you are going to sit in order to avoid badly slumping, which is very easy to do, especially in a big old comfortable armchair. Once you get drawn into what you are reading it is virtually certain that you will completely forget about your posture. It is vitally important that you do not end up creating all kinds of stresses and strains in your body.

READING AND WRITING

When you are sitting at your desk or at a table, it is important that you adjust your chair in such a way that your lower arms and hands can be placed on the surface of your table or desk at a right angle. If your chair is too close you are likely to end up lifting your shoulders to adjust your arms. If your chair is too high, you will probably find that you start slumping. You must also avoid crossing your legs, and do make sure that your feet remain comfortably flat on the floor.

A useful trick when reading is to use a sloping board to avoid slumping over your desk or table.

Note how the model is holding her body badly with her arm, and how her legs are folded, offering no support.

Keep the alignment between your head, your neck and your back.

This model is firmly gripping the pen, causing tension in her wrist and hand.

Here the model is tensing her wrist, hand and arm, restricting her movement.

DESKWORK

An increasing number of people are complaining of neck and shoulder tension, wrist problems and back pain resulting from their working environment. Some cases are directly linked to badly designed furniture, awkward or unfavourable sitting positions and immobility. In other instances, although chairs and work surfaces are good, the posture is poor. You must therefore remember your primary directions: the head, neck and back should be aligned, and the head should be lengthening away from the sitting bones.

How not to do it. See how the model is slumping badly, causing unnecessary tension in the spine, so weakening the muscles surrounding the torso.

Here the spine is correctly aligned, and the head is poised gracefully above the neck. The feet are well placed on the floor, nicely apart.

office equipment

The office is not what it used to be. It now offers amazing improvements in high-tech equipment, but also plenty of opportunities for repetitive strain injury, aching backs and tense necks. The temptation is to spend far too long in one awkward position. So always be aware of what you are doing, how long it will take, and the best position you need to adopt. Such awareness makes all the difference between a good and bad day.

MOBILE PHONE USE

Here the model is pulling her head down wrongly towards her mobile phone to talk, and slouching.

In this example the model has maintained her balance throughout her body. She looks poised and relaxed.

Observe Yourself When the Telephone Rings

Do you snatch and grab it? Or do you try to give yourself some time before you pick up the receiver? Next time the telephone rings, stop and go over your primary directions. Make sure that you bring the receiver up to your ear rather than suddenly leaning down towards it, thus compromising your position.

WORKING AT A COMPUTER

If you are working at a computer or portable computer, use your eyes to look down towards it. Avoid lurching at the neck as you will lose the correct alignment with your back.

Here the model badly collapses over her computer. She has lost the correct alignment between her hands, her wrists and her lower arms. Her shoulders are far too hunched.

Here the model is incorrectly holding in her wrist, arms and shoulders, causing unnecessary strain and discomfort. She will soon feel very uncomfortable, and have to adopt a new position.

t'ai chi

T'ai chi ch'uan is an ancient form of slow, graceful and rhythmic exercise which originated in China, where it is still extremely popular, often being performed in public parks in the fresh morning air. It has its roots in Taoist philosophy. The movements of the t'ai chi form gently tone and strengthen the organs and muscles, improve circulation and posture, and relax both mind and body. Its name translates as "supreme ultimate fist", but this is not its true meaning. "Strength within softness", "poetry in motion" and "moving harmony" all come closer to expressing the spirit of t'ai chi.

T'ai chi has been variously described as a system of health, medicine, physical co-ordination, relaxation, self-defence and consciousness raising, as well as a means of exercise and self-development. It is all these things. The style shown here is the Yang-style short form, as developed by Professor Cheng Man-Ch'ing, which is the one most practised in the West.

Unlike the "hard" martial arts which rely on force and speed, t'ai chi is "soft" or "internal". Its emphasis lies in the yielding aspect of nature when overcoming the hard – like the waterfall which eventually wears away the rock beneath. It teaches patience and relaxation, and fosters an understanding of the co-ordination of mind, body and spirit. It is the perfect antidote to the stresses and strains of today's modern lifestyles.

t'ai chi for health or self defence

If you simply want to go out and strike a pose, jumping about like Bruce Lee, t'ai chi is not for you. It is a very serious, highly regarded ancient technique that has two major qualities. It improves your health, and teaches you how to overcome stronger hostile forces when you are under attack. The most amazing part of t'ai chi is the way its movements are almost balletic.

The Benefits of T'ai Chi

Although t'ai chi can eventually be used in self-defence, and most classes do incorporate some of its practical applications, it is initially practised mainly for its health-giving benefits. It is particularly useful for increasing alertness and body awareness, and for developing concentration and sensitivity. It helps with balance and posture, and enhances a sense of "groundedness". However, all the postures can also be used when defending yourself against an attack by an opponent. Its gentleness and subtlety do not preclude its use as a very effective form of self-defence.

It is not easy to separate the physical and mental aspects of t'ai chi, as they are closely interrelated. In Chinese medicine, the interdependence of mind, body and spirit is seen as integral to well-being.

The ancient art of t'ai chi instills enormous grace and confidence.

The Theory of T'ai Chi

Like music, t'ai chi cannot be appreciated purely on an intellectual level. It also has an enormous spiritual side, and when you watch any highly experienced t'ai chi practitioners you will see how they are almost in a kind of trance, in a separate world where they cannot be touched. Correctly done, it is quite hypnotic.

For now, we must look at some of the concepts that are fundamental to the martial arts, as well as to medicine and philosophy. Although these disciplines are all treated quite separately by those in the West, they are all inseparable in the Eastern view. From thousands of years of close observation of patterns of energy, the Chinese successfully evolved a way of life that actually ropes all three ingredients together.

Chi

Chi is the prime driving force of human life, the spark behind thought, creativity and growth which maintains and nurtures us. It can be felt as movement of energy in the body, like the ceaseless flow of an electrical current. Chi flows through the body along channels called meridians.

The Tan Tien

The Chi is stored in the Tan Tien. This is an area about the size of a golf ball, located four finger-widths below the navel, and about one-third of the way from the front to the back of the body. It is the centre of gravity of the body, and in t'ai chi all movement emanates from it. Try to let the breath and the mind sink to the Tan Tien.

Yin and Yang

Yin and Yang describe the complementary yet opposing forces of nature. Their relationship has a harmony and balance: both Yin and Yang are necessary, are constantly moving and balancing each other, and this interaction creates Chi. The Chinese observed that when the balance of Yin and Yang is disrupted so too will be the body's Chi, leading to ill health.

One of the key requirements for t'ai chi is excellent balance.

warm-up exercises

Perform these exercises slowly and gently, with the mind and the breath focused in the Tan Tien. Notice any differences between the right and left sides of your body, and between the upper and lower parts. The object is gradually to enter the world of t'ai chi, and to warm up all your muscles so that you do not get any strains. The more you warm up, the better your technique will be. The movements will flow like a stream.

CIRCLING HANDS

1 Inhale and allow both hands to float upwards a comfortable distance in front of your body, palms facing downwards.

2 As your hands rise above your head, relax the wrists and begin to open the palms outwards. Begin to exhale.

3 Open out your arms to your sides. Draw your hands inwards at the bottom of the circle and smoothly begin again.

4 Inhale as your palms, facing upwards, float in front of your body. Exhale and push your right hand down by your hip and your left hand up by your temple.

5 Breathe in again, relax your palms which now turn to face each other and begin moving them towards each other in front of your body.

6 Repeat step 4 in reverse as you exhale. Breathe in again and bring your hands in front of your body in a mirror image of Step 5.

SHAKING OUT SHOULDERS, ARMS AND HANDS

1 Gently shake out any tension in your wrists and hands. Gradually work up to include your shoulders. This exercise is especially useful before, during and after long periods at a keyboard, or repetitive work with the hands.

LOOSENING SHOULDERS

1 Make increasing circles with one shoulder. Change direction and decrease the size of the circles. Repeat for the other shoulder. Rotate your shoulders alternately.

ROTATING WAIST

1 Place both hands lightly on your hips. Keeping your head up, begin by spiralling your hips slowly outwards, feeling for any restriction, tightness or lack of ease. Change direction and spiral back in slowly.

KNEE ROTATIONS

1 Bring your feet together and place your palms lightly on your upper kneecaps. Feel the Chi from your palms radiating deep into your knee joints. Circle your knees clockwise several times, then change direction.

2 Keep your legs and hands in the same position. Rotate your knees in opposite directions – one circles clockwise while the other circles anti-clockwise (counter-clockwise). Change the direction of each knee and repeat the rotations.

CALF STRETCH

1 Step forward with your right foot. Keeping the heel on the floor, pull up your toes towards the knee. Drop your body forward, keeping your right leg straight. Hold for a few breaths and release. Repeat for the other leg.

FOUR-DIRECTIONAL BREATHING

1 As you inhale, bring your hands up to chest height, palms facing upwards.

2 As you exhale, turn the palms to face away and extend your arms as if pushing something away. On the next inhalation, turn your palms back to face your body, softening your arms and drawing them back in towards your chest.

3 Exhale again, turn the palms out and extend your arms out to your sides.

4 Relax and bring your arms in towards your chest as you inhale.

5 On the next exhalation turn your palms upwards and extend your arms towards the sky.

6 Inhale and let your arms descend, palms facing downwards. As your arms pass the solar plexus, exhale and push down towards the earth. Repeat this sequence several times.

ROTATING FROM THE WAIST WITH FEET FORWARD

1 Imagine a central axis from the crown of your head, dropping down through your body to a point between your feet. Rotate your body around this axis, keeping your arms relaxed.

2 As your waist turns to the left, your weight shifts on to your left leg. As it turns right, move your weight across on to your right leg. Let your arms swing naturally.

3 Repeat the sequence for about 1 minute. As you do it, try to keep each knee over its respective big toe to avoid any strain on the muscles and ligaments.

ROTATING FROM THE WAIST TURNING ON THE BALL OF THE FOOT

1 The arms follow the same movement as above, but each foot pivots in turn on the ball. Keeping your weight in your left leg, turn your waist to the right. Lift your right heel and swivel the right foot 90°.

2 As your waist returns to the centre, straighten your right foot until your feet are parallel and shoulder-width apart. Transfer your weight on to your right foot.

3 Turn your waist to the left, lift your left heel and pivot on the ball of your left foot. Repeat the sequence for about 1 minute, keeping your head up, back straight and arms and shoulders relaxed.

OPENING AND CLOSING THE CIRCLE

1 Place your hands in front of your face, palms facing away. Turn your waist slowly to the right.

2 Drop almost all your weight into your right leg and continue turning your waist, bending forwards which in turn brings your hands around in a large circular movement.

3 As your hands cross the bottom of the circle, shift your weight into your left leg. Continue to turn your waist slowly, bringing your hands up to complete the circle.

4 When your hands reach their starting-point in front of your face, repeat the sequence and continue for several more rotations.

5 Change direction gently at the bottom of the circle to repeat the sequence. This time, join your palms together lightly at the top of each circle.

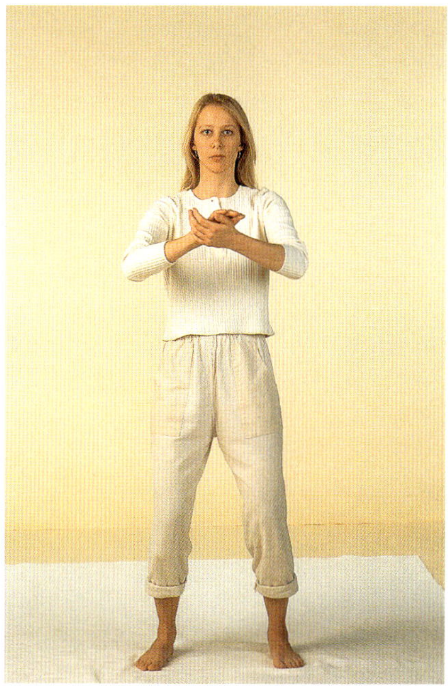

6 Keep the palms together as you turn, allowing your hands to separate at the bottom. Finish the exercise by keeping your palms connected and spiralling your hands to end in front of your chest.

SHIFTING WEIGHT

1 Place your left foot at 45° and your right foot forward, heels shoulder-width apart. Shift your weight from one leg to the other – do not tip your pelvis forwards or backwards.

2 Let your arms swing naturally. Continue for about 1 minute, then change legs and repeat the sequence again. Feel a strong root developing through your feet into the centre of the earth.

ROTATING WHOLE BODY

1 Hold both arms in front of the chest, palms facing inwards, fingertips almost touching. Turn your waist and arms and shift your weight to the right. Repeat to the left.

WAVING HANDS IN CLOUDS

1 Begin with your right hand facing the Tan Tien, your left hand directly above it, facing your chest. Turn your waist to the left, shifting your weight into your left leg. Turn your palms towards each other.

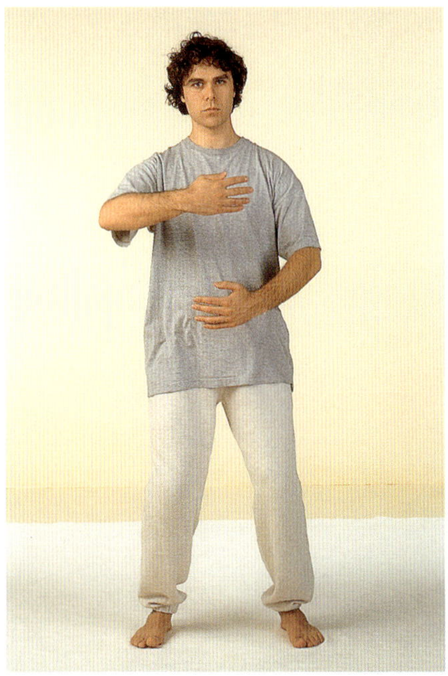

2 Bring your waist back to the front. As you do so, lower your left hand until it is opposite the Tan Tien and raise your right hand to the level of your chest, with your palms facing your body.

3 Now turn your waist to the right, shift the weight across to your right leg, and turn your palms towards each other in a mirror image of Step 1. Repeat the entire sequence several times.

PUSH TO CENTRE, PUSH TO CORNER

1 Place your right foot at 45° and step forward with your left foot. Begin with all your weight on your right leg, right hand resting palm upwards on your right hip, left fingertips in line with your mouth, palm facing diagonally forwards and to the centre.

2 Bring your weight forward on to your left leg. Your right hand turns diagonally forwards as it comes to push towards the centre of your body; your left hand turns palm upwards as it draws back to rest on your left hip.

3 Shift your weight back on to your right foot, turning your waist 45° to the right. At the same time draw your right hand back to your right hip and push your left hand towards the corner until it is in line with the centre of your body, fingertips opposite your mouth. Repeat steps 1, 2 and 3 for about 1 minute.

4 Repeat the sequence in mirror image as it is shown above. Make sure that all your movements are smooth and flowing and that the weight is gently shifted between your feet.

5 Bring your weight on to your right leg. Your left hand turns diagonally forwards as it comes towards the centre of the body, your right palm turns upwards as it draws back to rest on the right hip.

6 Shift your weight to your left foot, turning your waist 45° to the left. At the same time, draw your left hand to your left hip and push your right hand to the corner. Repeat the cycle in Steps 5 and 6.

NECK ROTATIONS

1 Keep the palms of your hands in front of your chest, fingertips almost touching. Relax your shoulders and elbows. Turn your head to look over one shoulder, then the other. Repeat several times, keeping the neck movements fluid.

HIP ROTATIONS

1 Turn out your left foot and sink all your weight on to it. Draw a smooth circle with your right knee, keeping the hip movement as fluid as possible. Repeat the same rotation on the other hip.

ANKLE ROTATIONS

1 Place your left foot at 45°, bend your left knee and sink all your weight into your left leg. Lift your right foot and slowly rotate the ankle, describing a circle with your big toe. Repeat the exercise for the left ankle.

RETURN TO CENTRE

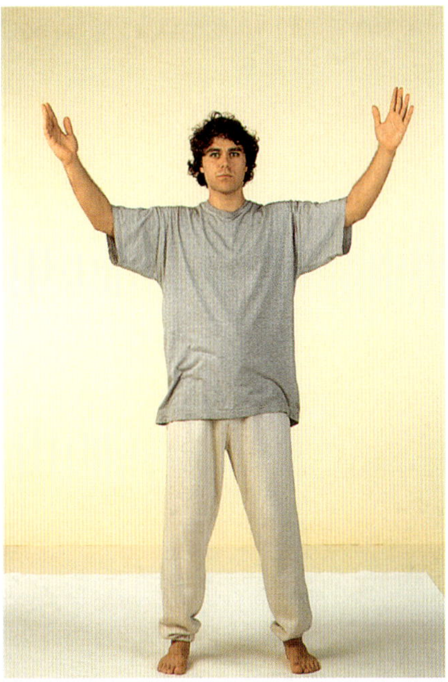

1 As you breathe in, take your hands out to the sides in front of your body, and raise them slowly in a large circle, palms facing upwards.

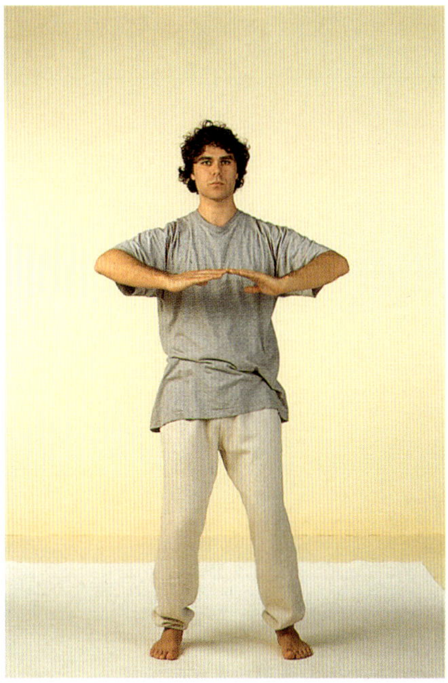

2 As you exhale, lower your hands in front of the centre of your body, palms facing downwards.

3 At the bottom of the circle, turn your hands outwards again to begin a new circle with the new breath.

KIDNEY MASSAGE

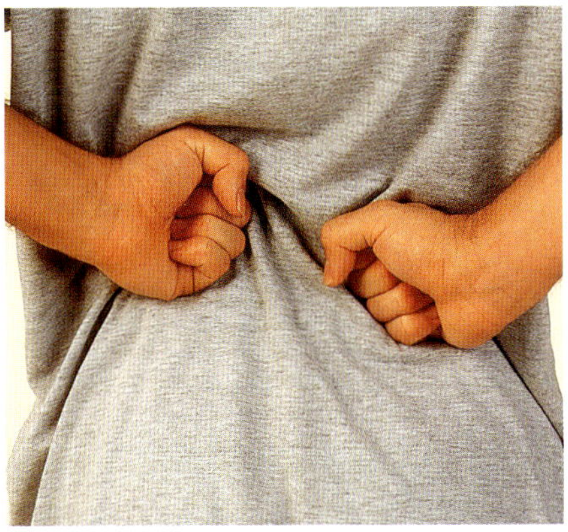

1 The kidneys are the most important organs, according to Chinese medicine, as they store the Chi. This massage provides gentle stimulation and helps to break down crystals of uric acid found in kidney stones. Bring your heels together at right angles, and massage around your kidneys with loose fists.

ABDOMINAL MASSAGE

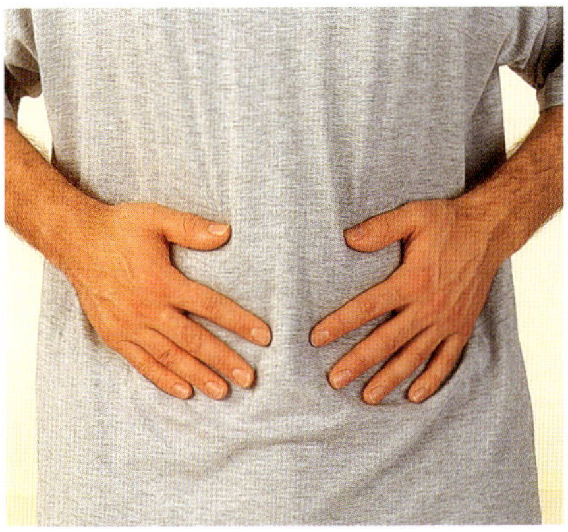

1 With your heels together, massage your abdomen in a circular motion with the palms of your hands to assist and bring blood to the digestive area.

STIMULATING THE BACK OF THE NECK

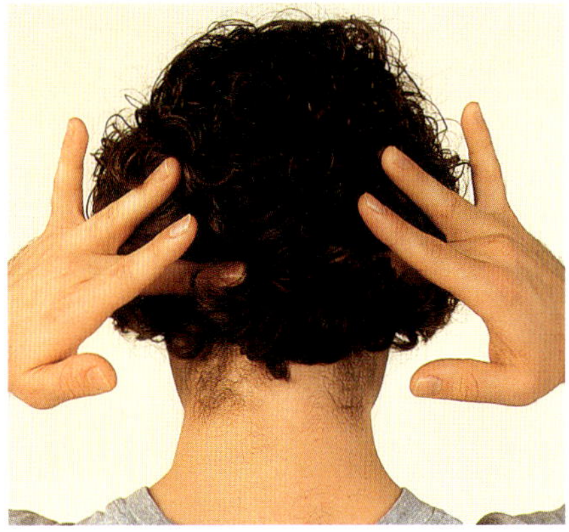

1 Lift your hands to the back of your head. Flick your index and middle fingers over each other to tap the base of the occipital ridge at the back of the skull, releasing Chi up to the top of your head. Flick the back of your head about 20 times.

FEELING THE AIR

1 With your heels together and feet at right angles, inhale and let both hands float up towards your shoulders, palms facing upwards. Feel the resistance of the air on your palms.

2 As you exhale, let both hands float back down. Try to feel resistance on the backs of your hands, and the air rushing softly between your fingers.

STILLNESS WITHIN MOVEMENT

1 Bring your heels together at right angles to each other. Try to feel where your body weight naturally lies. After a few quiet moments of standing still, you can begin some t'ai chi walking, or start the form. Notice the feelings you have, especially in the Tan Tien, and carry these feelings with you into the form.

yang-style short form

yang-style short form

yang-style short form

After completing all the warm-up exercises, and having a moment or so quietly standing to see if you can find a point of equilibrium, a few minutes of t'ai chi walking may now follow. This is known as walking with an "empty step", rather in the manner of a cat tentatively putting out its paw before committing its full weight on to the front leg.

In fact, it is well worth studying an adult cat that is gracefully walking, or gliding forwards when it has spotted its prey. Its whole movement is one of ceaseless flow, of elegant, unforced movement when every part of its body seems to be an extension of another part, and nothing is hurried or rushed.

As you progress through the form, use the following pages as an aide-mémoire for your practice, especially for the transitions from one posture to the next. Remember to keep your movements slow and smooth, like clouds drifting gently by on a summer's day, and relax. If you worry about this new exercise, you will not succeed.

In many ways that is the key problem for the new Western practitioner. Doing these exercises initially means that you will be highly self-conscious because there is nothing like it in our culture. Yet gradually, after a few lessons, and above all after watching expert t'ai chi practitioners, it becomes clear that this is something which you can do successfully, and without having to worry about what you look like.

Once you launch into the first few movements, the rest follow, and you find that an awkward state of self-consciousness is quickly replaced by an inner calm as you become less aware of the outside world, and more aware of inner ones. The key to t'ai chi is being able to make seamless flowing moves, with the emphasis not so much on specific poses as on the linking means of getting there. Ultimately, you too may be able to go into a park in the early morning, as they do in the East, and carry out t'ai chi utterly unself-consciously, gaining spiritual refreshment.

ATTENTION, PREPARATION AND BEGINNING

1 Stand in a relaxed and upright posture, feet pointing diagonally outwards, making a right angle. Distribute your weight evenly through your body.

2 Bend your right knee and sink all your weight down through your right leg into the foot, without leaning across. Then move the "empty" left leg a shoulder-width away, with the toes pointing straight ahead.

3 Transfer 70% of your weight to your left leg, simultaneously turning your waist and therefore your whole body diagonally to the right.

4 Keeping 70% of your weight in your left leg, turn your whole body back to face the front. Bring your right foot around to the front as your waist moves. Your feet should be shoulder-width apart and parallel. Your hands also move with your body, the palms facing the ground as if resting on a cushion of air.

5 Relax your wrists and let your arms float up and away from your body. When your hands reach shoulder height, gently extend the fingertips.

6 Draw your hands back in towards your body by dropping the elbows. This penultimate posture is one of relaxed, graceful ease.

WARD OFF LEFT

7 In the final position, relax your wrists and let your hands float down the front of your body, just in front of and below the waist. The bulk of your weight is in your left leg.

1 Sink all your weight on to your left leg, and turn your body to the right, pivoting on your right heel. Imagine you are holding a large ball, with the right hand in front of the chest.

2 Sink all your weight on to your right leg, as if carrying the ball forward. Pick up your "empty" (weightless) left leg and step forwards, toes pointing to the front.

WARD OFF RIGHT

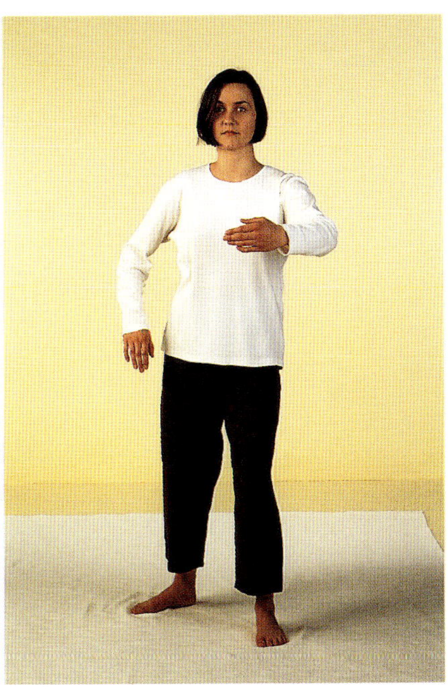

3 Turn the waist to the left, facing the front. Your left hand comes up, palm facing the chest, and the right floats down with 70% of your weight now on your left leg, as your right moves around.

1 Sink all your weight into your left leg. Turn to the right: the left palm turns face down, the right palm turns up as if both hands are again holding the large ball. The heels should be slightly apart.

2 Turn your waist to face the right-hand side and shift 70% of your weight on to your right foot, and turn your left foot to 45°. Raise your right arm so that the palm faces your chest.

ROLL BACK, PRESS AND PUSH

This posture, together with the one that follows it, "Single Whip", is also known as "Grasping the Sparrow's Tail".

1 Turn your body to the right. Point the fingertips of your right hand to the sky in a relaxed way. Your left arm moves horizontally with the fingertips almost touching the right elbow, palm facing the body. Your weight remains 70% on the right leg, 30% on the left.

2 As you turn your waist to the left, begin to shift weight to your left leg. Follow the movement of the body with your arms until your right hand is horizontal. Your left hand begins to flow down with the movement of your waist. Your weight settles on your left leg.

3 Turn your waist back to the right and let your left arm follow this movement. All your weight remains in the left leg. Bring your palm gradually across to rest against your right wrist, opposite the centre of your chest.

4 Press forward, keeping the hands in full contact. Shift 70% of your weight into your front (right) leg. Ensure that your heels are still shoulder-width apart, and that the right foot is pointing forward, and the left foot at 45°.

5 Separate your hands and sink all your weight back into your left foot. Your fingertips are now shoulder-width apart at shoulder height.

6 Move your weight forward 70% into your right leg. Your arms and hands keep the same position.

SINGLE WHIP

1 As your weight shifts back into the left leg, leave your fingers where they are in space, effectively straightening – but not locking – your arms. The palms now face down towards the ground.

2 Turn your whole body to the left and shift all your weight into your left leg. Your right heel remains on the ground while your toes turn through 120°, following the body round.

3 Sink your weight back into your right leg. Bring your left hand under the right to hold the imaginary ball in front of your body. Then form a "hook" with the fingers and thumb of your right hand.

4 Ensure all your weight is in your right leg. Bend the right knee and turn your body to the left, sending out the hook in line with, and at the same height as, your shoulder. Take an "empty" (weightless) shoulder-width step with your left foot.

5 Shift 70% of your weight on to your left leg, adjusting your right foot to 45°. Ensure that your heels are shoulder-width apart, your left hand in line with your left shoulder and your right hand hook at 90° to the rest of your body.

LIFTING HANDS

1 Place your weight on the left leg, open your hands and palms inwards, the left palm facing the right elbow. Pick up your empty right foot and place down the heel without weight, directly in front of the left heel.

WHITE CRANE SPREADS WINGS AND PUSH

2 Turn your waist to the left, your hands following the movement of your waist. Bring your right toe by your left heel, touching the ground but weightless.

3 Take an "empty" step to the right, and transfer 70% of the weight to the right foot. The left palm ends up opposite your inner right elbow. Your right arm is curved, guarding the groin, and your feet are at right angles to each other.

1 Drop all your weight into your right leg. Turn your waist to the left. As your right hand begins to rise, your left hand sweeps down in front of your left thigh.

2 Pick up your "empty" left leg and touch the toe on the ground but without shifting your weight. Bring your right hand up to guard your temple, turning to face diagonally outwards as it moves up. Your left hand floats down.

3 As you turn your waist to the left, your right hand follows and sweeps down; your left palm opens outwards.

4 As you turn your waist to the right, your right hand continues in a circle. Your left hand follows the move of your waist and faces down in front of your chest. As your waist returns to the centre, the right hand is level with the shoulder.

PLAY GUITAR. BRUSH LEFT KNEE AND PUSH

This posture is also known as "Strumming the Lute".

5 Take a shoulder-width step with your left foot, heel first. Move 70% of your weight into your left leg as your left hand brushes down across it. Meanwhile, your right hand follows a concave curve into the centre to finish by the mouth.

1 As all your weight sinks into your left leg, adjust the "empty" right foot by drawing it slightly nearer the left foot, toe first. Bring your weight into the right foot. Your left leg and arm float up simultaneously – imagine a thread connecting them.

2 Turn to the right, dropping your right hand down while your left hand follows the movement of your waist to the centre of your chest, palm facing down. As your waist returns to the front, your right hand comes to shoulder height.

STEP FORWARD, DEFLECT, INTERCEPT AND PUNCH

3 Take a shoulder-width step with your left foot, heel first. Move 70% of your weight into your left leg as your left hand brushes down across it. Your right hand follows a curve ending by your mouth.

1 Turn your waist 45° to the left and sink all your weight into your right foot. As the weight shifts back, lift the toes of your left foot and pivot 45° on the heel. Bring your hands down by your left leg.

2 Shift all your weight into your left leg. Form a loose fist with your right hand, but check that the fingers are not wrapped around the thumb. The right toes are behind the left heel.

3 Arc both of your hands and your right foot simultaneously towards the centre line, as your waist turns around to the right. The right foot now lands "empty", in line with the left instep. Check that your position is correct. Note that your left thumb should roughly be in line with your left eye.

4 Continue to turn your waist to the right, bringing the right fist palm upwards to rest on the right hip. You should now commence transferring all your weight on to your right foot. Your eyes should skim across the tops of your left fingers.

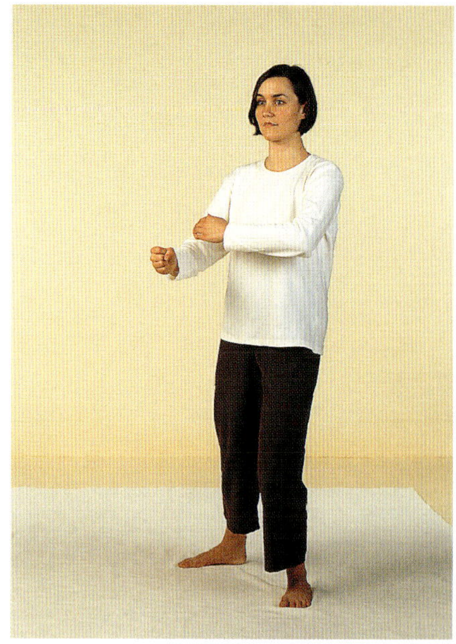

5 Place your left foot a shoulder width from the right foot. Shift 70% of your weight to your left leg and bring your right fist forward as if to punch, rotating it through a quarter turn in a corkscrew motion. Then bring your left arm across your body, with the palm facing your inner right elbow.

WITHDRAW AND PUSH. CROSSING HANDS

1 As you turn your waist to the left, your right arm follows your body to an angle of 45° and the fist opens up. Meanwhile, cup your left hand gracefully a couple of inches under your right elbow, as if supporting it.

2 Draw your right arm across your left palm as your weight sinks into your right foot, and your waist turns to the right.

3 Bring your waist back to the centre and turn both palms to face the front.

4 Move your weight forward 70% on to your left leg. Your hands remain at shoulder width and shoulder height.

5 Turn your waist to the right and simultaneously sink all your weight into your left leg. Draw your hands in towards your chest in a softly inverted "V" shape, as if holding the top of a ball.

6 As your whole weight shifts into your right leg, turn your waist to the right. Your left toes turn with your waist and your right hand travels out both diagonally and upwards.

7 Sink all your weight back into your left leg. Your left hand now travels out diagonally. Though the position might seem slightly awkward and lopsided, it actually flows naturally into the final step.

8 Finally, bring your right foot shoulder-width away from and parallel to the left, but maintain your weight 70% in the left leg. Both hands circle down and up, stopping opposite your chest, palms facing the body. The wrists are touching, with the right wrist outside the left one. Hold this stance for a few seconds.

EMBRACE TIGER, RETURN TO MOUNTAIN

1 Keeping all your weight in your left leg, turn your waist to the right. Open your hands outwards. Step diagonally back with your right foot. Move your weight 70% on to your right foot. As your waist completes its turn, move your left hand so that the fingertips are in line with your left shoulder, palm facing forward.

2 As you turn your waist slightly to the right, allow your left hand to come across so that the fingertips point to your right elbow. Meanwhile, your right hand travels upwards so that the fingertips point heavenward.

ROLL BACK, PRESS AND PUSH: SINGLE WHIP

1 Now repeat the sequence in "Roll Back, Press and Push". This time, perform this section from one diagonal corner to the other rather than from one side to the other. This picture shows your position at the end of the sequence.

PUNCH UNDER ELBOW

1 Sink all your weight back on to your right foot. Turn your waist 45° to the left, lifting the left toes and letting your left foot and both arms pivot 45° to the left.

2 Lower your left foot, gradually shifting your weight forward into it. When all your weight is on your left foot, step forward with your right foot so that the heel is in line with your left instep.

3 Rotate your upper body 90° to the left. Your arms follow this waist movement, so that the hook (your right hand) is now out in front level with your right shoulder, and your left hand is level with your face at 90° to the front. Your weight is in your left leg.

4 Transfer all your weight to your right leg, turning your waist to the right and letting your left hand move down, then up, until the fingers are in line with your left shoulder. Your left arm and leg move around simultaneously. Rest your left heel on the ground without any weight.

STEP BACK TO REPULSE THE MONKEY

1 As you turn your waist further to the right, your right hand opens and moves down by your hip, then floats up to shoulder height. The palm of your left hand turns over to face down.

2 Step back with your left foot as your waist turns to the left. Your right hand travels forward, palm facing down, while your left hand travels down towards the left hip with the palm facing up.

3 The right toes also straighten as the waist turns. As you continue to turn to the left, your left hand floats up to shoulder height, while your right hand comes forward, palm facing down.

STEP BACK TO REPULSE THE MONKEY (RIGHT). DIAGONAL FLYING

1 Turn your waist to the right, step back with your right foot and let your left hand travel forward, palm down. Your right hand moves down to rest on your hip, palm up. Your left foot turns to face the front as the waist moves. Your right hand now comes up to shoulder height.

2 With your weight on your left foot, turn your waist to the left. Turn your right hand palm upwards as it travels round in front of your waist, while your left hand, palm downwards, comes in front of your chest. Your hands are now holding an imaginary ball in front of you.

3 Turn your waist 90° to the right, maintaining the position of your arms and hands in front of your chest, as if carrying the ball.

WAVING HANDS IN CLOUDS (RIGHT, LEFT, RIGHT)

4 Stepping with your right foot, turn a further 135° to the right, and then transfer 70% of your weight into the right foot. Your waist also turns to the right and your right hand moves with it, travelling to shoulder height, arm extended and facing diagonally upwards. Your left hand moves simultaneously to just outside your left thigh, palm facing down.

1 Bring all your weight on to your right foot. Turn your waist to the right and move your left hand across near your right hip. At the same time, your right hand turns palm downwards at shoulder height. Raise your left foot and move it forward until the left heel is now level and in line with the right.

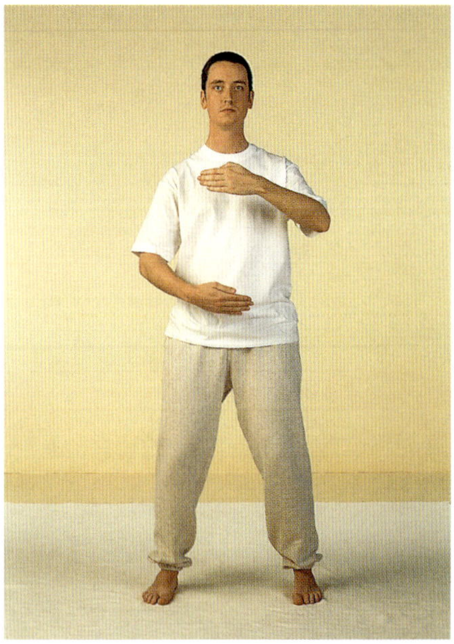

2 As your waist turns to the front, move your right hand to face it and your left hand to face your chest. The right toes swivel round to face forwards so that your feet are now shoulder-width apart.

3 As your waist turns to the left, turn your palms towards each other, as if holding a large ball to the left of your body. All your weight is in your left leg and your right foot steps in to about half shoulder width.

4 Turn your waist back to the centre. Your hands again change position, the left hand descending to be opposite and facing your waist, and the right hand opposite and facing your chest.

5 Turn your waist to the right, your hands holding the imaginary ball, with the right hand uppermost, palm facing down, and the left hand below it, palm facing up. When all your weight is on your right foot, step back to shoulder-width apart.

WAVING HANDS IN CLOUDS (LEFT, RIGHT, LEFT). THE WHIP

1 Turn your waist back to the centre, bringing your right hand down to face your waist and your left hand up to face your chest. Repeat Steps 3, 4 and 5, then Steps 2 and 3 from "Waving Hands in Clouds, Right, Left, Right".

2 Turn your waist back to the centre and form a hook with your right hand, as it moves in level with your chest, directly above your left hand. It is located in front of your waist, palm upwards.

3 Step forward with your right foot. Turn your waist to the right, then to the left as you transfer your weight to your right foot, sending out the hook at 90° to the front of your body.

4 Continue turning your waist around towards the left, and then step with your left foot to about shoulder-width apart, with your left palm now facing your left shoulder.

5 Shift your weight 70% on to your left foot, turning away your left palm at shoulder height, and turning the right toes to 45°.

GOLDEN ROOSTER STANDS ON ONE LEG (LEFT). SQUATTING SINGLE WHIP

1 Sink all your weight into your left leg, turning your left hand over so that the palm faces upwards. Simultaneously turn out the right toes. This is a nicely balanced, elegant position.

2 Move your weight across into your right leg, bringing your left palm in towards your chest. The left toes turn 45° to the right.

3 Sink down into your right leg, keeping your back straight. Move your waist to the left, brush open your left knee with your left arm and turn your left toes out 90° to the left.

4 Transfer all your weight into your left leg. Open the right hand hook, lower the hand then bring it up in front of your chest. Raise your right leg as your weight shifts forward into your left leg, so that your right thigh becomes parallel with the ground. Bend your left knee.

GOLDEN ROOSTER STANDS ON ONE LEG (RIGHT). SEPARATE RIGHT FOOT

1 Place your right foot down and move all your weight on to it. As your weight sinks into your right leg, your right hand descends to rest on a cushion of air by your right thigh. Your left arm and left leg simultaneously move up to form a mirror image of the previous posture.

2 Step out with your "empty" left foot diagonally to the left, and form a ward-off position with your left arm horizontally positioned across your body, opposite your chest.

3 Shift all your weight into your left leg, bringing your right arm up to cross in front of your left arm, with the wrists touching. Bring your right toe to your left heel. Turn your wrists, maintaining skin contact as you do so, so that your left arm now crosses your right.

4 Then turn your hands away from your body, and open them out in a fan-like action. Your eyes should be level with the tips of your fingers.

5 Keep your left hand level with your left ear, palm facing away. Open out your right hand to the corner, below shoulder height, and simultaneously kick gently with your right leg, to knee height. You should be so balanced that you do not fall over.

SEPARATE LEFT FOOT. BRUSH LEFT KNEE AND PUSH

1 Keeping all your weight in your left leg, turn to the left-hand corner, forming a ward-off position with your right arm.

2 Turn your waist to the right and step to the right with your right leg. As you transfer weight into it, bring your left hand up outside the right so that the wrists meet. The left toes come up to meet the right heel.

3 Open out your hands, the right hand this time remaining level with the head and the left hand travelling to below shoulder height. The left foot follows, kicking gently to the corner.

4 Turn your waist and left knee to the front again. Take a shoulder-width "empty" step with your left leg, toes pointing in the forward direction.

NEEDLES AT SEA BOTTOM

5 Brush your left hand across and above the front of your left leg, to just outside your left thigh. Your right hand curves in, fingertips forward, to finish with the fingers in line with your mouth.

1 Move all your weight into your left leg. Pick up your empty right foot and make a small adjustment step forward.

2 Place your right toes down, then bring your left hand across your body so that the left palm rests above your right wrist. At the same time, pick up your left leg and place the toes down.

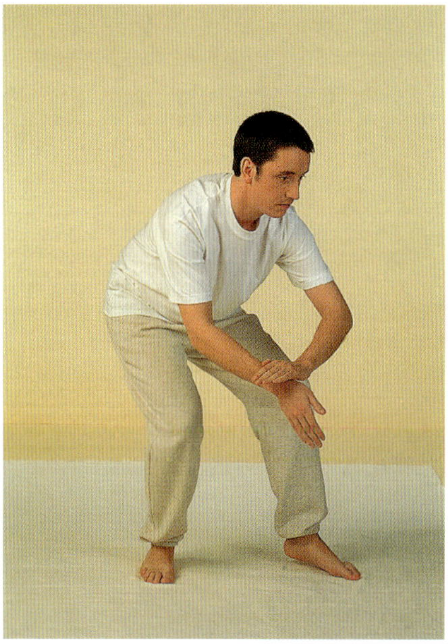

3 Move your right arm forwards and diagonally downwards with your body, then vertically downwards. The arm remains in line with your right leg, and all your weight remains in your right leg.

IRON FAN PENETRATES BACK. TURN BODY, CHOP AND PUSH

1 Your weight remains in your right leg and both hands assume a ward-off position. Take a shoulder-width step with the left foot. Shift your weight 70% into your left leg and turn your hands outwards, the left hand by your chest, the right guarding your temple.

2 Turn your waist to the right and sink all your weight back into your right leg, bringing your left toes round. Bring your left hand up, turning the palm diagonally outwards to guard the temple. At the same time, form a loose fist with your right hand, palm facing downwards.

3 Sink all your weight back on to your left leg. As you transfer the weight back, the fist descends in front of your groin.

4 Step to shoulder width with your right foot. Your right arm pivots at the elbow and your left arm folds across so that the left hand faces the right inner elbow. All your weight remains on your left leg. You are nicely balanced as shown above.

5 Transfer your weight forward 70% into your right leg. Your left arm pushes forward, fingertips in line with your left shoulder, and your right fist descends to your right hip, palm upwards. The left toes are at 45°.

STEP FORWARD, DEFLECT DOWNWARDS, INTERCEPT AND PUNCH, KICK WITH HEEL

1 Sink all your weight into the left leg as your waist turns to the left. Bring the right toe to the left heel. The right hand comes across the body, and the palm faces down by the left hip. The left hand is below the right hand, palm up. Go to "Step Forward, Deflect, Intercept and Punch" and repeat Steps 3, 4 and 5.

2 Sink your weight into your left leg, turning your waist to the right. Cross your wrists, the right outside the left. Sink the weight back into your right leg. Your waist turns left and your left foot pivots on the heel 45° to the left. Shift all your weight forward into your left leg, turning your hands palms outwards.

3 Open your hands out gracefully like a fan, the right hand to below shoulder height,the left hand at head height, palms facing away. Your right foot now comes up from the ground, and the heel kicks diagonally away.

BRUSH RIGHT KNEE AND PUSH. BRUSH LEFT KNEE AND PUNCH DOWN

1 Place your "empty" right foot on the ground, toes forward. Your right hand curves down to rest on a cushion of air outside your right thigh. Your left hand curves forward to push to the centre, fingertips in line with your mouth.

2 Sink back into your left leg, turning your waist to the right, with the palm of your left hand facing towards your body in the Yang-style ward-off position.

3 Transfer your weight forward into your right foot, with your left palm turning so that it faces downwards.

4 Take a shoulder-width step with your left foot and bring 70% of your weight onto it. Your right hand forms a loose fist, which comes over your hip and punches down the centre. Your left hand brushes your left leg and rests by the left knee.

WARD OFF RIGHT. ROLL BACK, PRESS AND PUSH. WHIP

1 Sink back into your right leg. Your left hand now assumes a ward-off position, the fingertips of your right hand pointing towards the centre of the left palm. Your right palm faces downwards. Gaze steadily and confidently forwards.

2 Turn your body 45° to the left, pivoting neatly on the left heel. Shift all your weight forward into your left leg. Your left arm should remain in this position, while your right hand now presses smartly down.

FAIR LADY WEAVES SHUTTLES (RIGHT AND LEFT)

3 Step through at shoulder width with your "empty" right foot. As you transfer 70% of your weight into it, your right hand comes up into a ward-off position opposite your chest, with the left fingertips now pointing towards the right palm, left palm downwards. Repeat "Roll Back, Press and Push" and "Single Whip".

1 Transfer your weight to your right leg as you turn your waist to the right, and turn the "empty" left toes through 90°. Bring your left hand across your body and under your elbow. Open the hook of your right hand and lower the right arm, palm turning to face upwards.

2 Sink your weight back into your left leg, turn your waist further to the right and turn out your right foot so the heel is in line with the left instep.

3 Sink your weight into your right leg, drawing your left arm across your right palm, and step at shoulder width to the left corner with your left foot. As you shift your weight forward into your left leg, turn both palms outwards.

4 Transfer your weight into your right foot and turn your waist and left foot to the right as far as possible (135°). Turn your palms to face your body, the right palm by the left elbow.

5 Sink your weight back into your left leg and draw your left arm across your right palm.

FAIR LADY WEAVES SHUTTLES (RIGHT AND LEFT)

6 Turn a further 135° right, to the corner. Step to shoulder width with your right foot, and shift 70% of your weight into it, pushing towards the centre of your mouth with your left hand. Bring the right hand up to guard your forehead, palm facing diagonally.

1 Turn to the left, sinking all your weight into your left leg. Pick up your right foot and draw it in. Transfer all your weight to your right foot, then step to the left (45°) with your left foot. Turn your palms in and draw your right arm across the left palm, left arm in a ward-off position.

2 Your left hand then moves up and turns outwards by your head, while the fingers of your right hand come into the centre in line with your mouth. Now repeat the postures described in Steps 4, 5 and 6 of the previous exercise.

WARD OFF LEFT. WARD OFF RIGHT. ROLL BACK, PRESS AND PUSH. SINGLE WHIP

1 Sink your weight into your left leg as your waist turns to the left. Both arms come round with the movement of your waist, the left hand lower than the right. The right toes come round to the front.

2 Sink your weight into your right leg as your left hand presses down, palm facing downwards. Take a shoulder-width step with your left foot.

3 Transfer your weight 70% into your left foot. Your left hand comes up in front of your chest. Your right hand floats outside your right thigh. Repeat previous step.

SQUATTING SINGLE WHIP. STEP FORWARD FOR SEVEN STARS

1 Repeat the postures described in Steps 1, 2 and 3 of "Golden Rooster Stands on One Leg (Left). Squatting Single Whip", ending by brushing open the left knee.

2 Transfer all your weight into your left leg. The right hand hook opens and the hand descends, then comes up in front of your neck, where it forms a loose fist. At the same time, your left hand rises up to form a loose fist, and connects at the wrist inside your right hand. Move your right toes forward to touch the ground without any weight whatsoever.

RIDE TIGER

1 Keep your weight in your left leg and step back with your right foot, toes touching the ground first. Sink your weight into it and turn your waist to the right. The fists open and then move down by your right hip, with the wrists still connected.

2 Pick up your left leg as your waist turns right, then place your toes down as your waist turns back to the left. Your right hand comes round to the front, fingertips level with your right ear, and your left hand rests by your left thigh.

3 Pick up your left toes, turn your waist to the left corner and place the toes down empty of any weight. Your right palm faces your inner left elbow. Your left hand is at the height of your left shoulder, elbow relaxed.

4 Lift your left toes and swing your waist clockwise, pivoting on the ball of your right foot. Your arms swing to the right with the movement of your waist.

5 Drop your left foot and transfer all your weight into it straight away. Look closely at the photograph above to check how you should be standing.

6 When your arms and waist reach the front (the arms at shoulder height and shoulder width with the palms facing downwards), your right foot lifts up and circles clockwise.

7 After circling, your right leg comes to rest with the upper leg parallel to the ground and the foot comfortably relaxed. Your left leg is bent while the arms are still pointing ahead.

BEND BOW TO SHOOT TIGER. STEP FORWARD, DEFLECT DOWN, INTERCEPT AND PUNCH

1 Turn your waist to the right. Your arms follow your waist, dropping down parallel, and your right foot is placed facing the right corner.

2 As your waist turns to the right, shift the weight into your right leg and circle your arms round to the right. As your waist turns back to the left, raise your arms and circle round with the waist. Form loose fists. Bring the right hand up to the right of your forehead, knuckles facing the right eyebrow. The left hand is at shoulder height.

3 Sink your weight into your left leg and pick up your right foot, placing the toes by your left heel. Open the left fist as your arms move across your body following the waist movement.

WITHDRAW AND PUSH. CROSSING HANDS. CONCLUSION.

4 Both hands and your right foot simultaneously arc in towards the centre line, as your waist turns to the right. The right foot lands "empty", completely in line with the left instep.

5 Continue to turn your waist, bringing the right fist palm upwards to rest on your right hip and shifting your weight to the right foot. Step through at shoulder width with your left foot. Shift 70% of your weight to the left and bring your right fist forward to punch in a corkscrew. Your left arm comes across your body.

1 Repeat the postures described in "Withdraw and Push. Crossing Hands". Ensure your weight is 70% in your left leg when crossing hands.

2 From crossing the hands, turn both palms down to face the ground as your body now rises up.

3 Bring all your weight into your left leg, turn your waist to the right and pivot on your left heel, turning the foot out to an angle of 45°.

4 Move all your weight into your right leg. Step in with your left foot so that the feet make a right angle. Bring half your weight to the left foot. Rest your arms and hands by your side with shoulders relaxed. You may now begin again.

yoga stretches

Have you ever watched a cat waking up? More often than not, it will give an exaggerated yawn, then arch its back until stretched to its limit, before loosely letting go and gracefully moving off on its way. Have you ever stopped to wonder why it makes these movements? The cat knows instinctively the value of stretching in maintaining flexibility and improving circulation to the muscles; you too can become stronger and more flexible with regular stretching exercises.

Most of us tend to hold in patterns of tension arising from everyday cares and worries, bad posture, lack of exercise and so on. These patterns make us feel stiff and unbending, and directly interfere with our movements. Inflexibility within our bodies can in turn affect mental flexibility, and we can become stuck in thought as well as in action. Regular stretching exercises not only free our bodies, allowing us to move easily, but can also help us to think and act without being so restricted. They are excellent improvers. In fact, by stretching muscles, ligaments and tendons, we make them much more efficient and stronger. The lengthening actions also help us to stand and walk taller, and even with added grace. The joints are better supported and are more able to go through their full range of movements, while the muscles are better nourished from the increased blood supply. The stretches give you that extra edge.

warm-up exercises

As any athlete will tell you, before starting to do any serious stretching or exercise, such as tennis, it is important that you first do some gentle warm-up exercises. They ensure that your muscles are nicely warmed and loosened, and will help to prevent any sudden strain or injury. The best thing is they only take a few minutes, and they can also be practised at any time if you are feeling stiff and need to loosen up.

SHRUGGING SHOULDERS

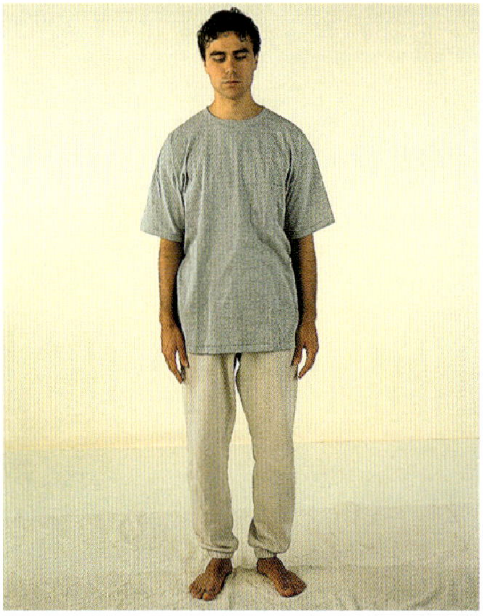

1 Stand upright with your feet slightly apart and your shoulders relaxed.

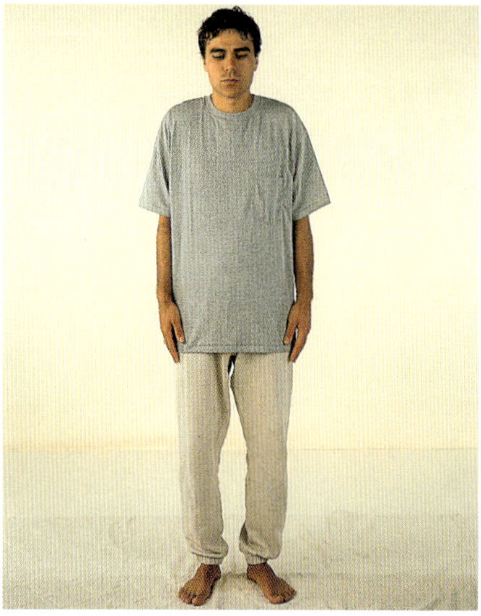

2 Lift your shoulders up as high as they will go, then let them fall down again. Stay relaxed and repeat a few times.

ARM CIRCLING

1 Wheel your arms around from the shoulders in slow, large circles.

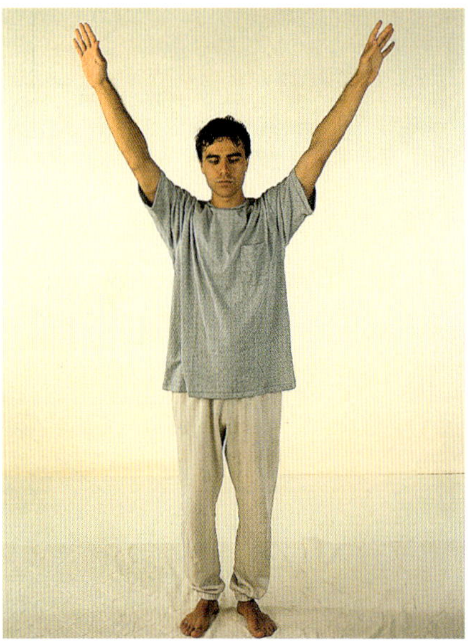

2 Do this a few times going backwards, then repeat circling your arms forwards.

SQUATS

1 Stand with your feet slightly apart, hands on hips. Go slowly into a squat.

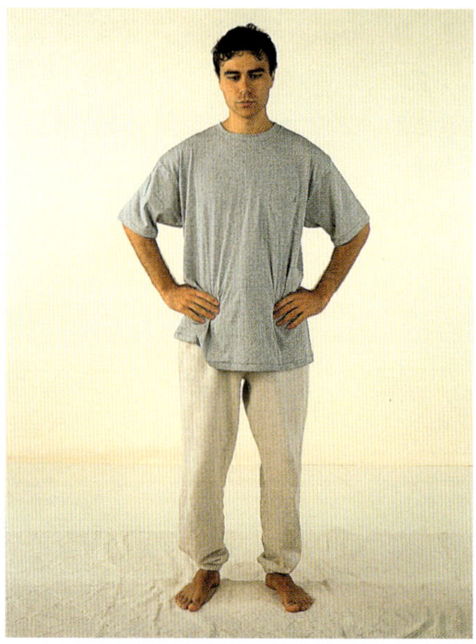

2 Slowly return to a standing position, then repeat. Your back should be upright.

LOOSE TWISTS

1 In a standing position with feet comfortably apart and knees relaxed, swing your arms loosely backwards and forwards around your body. Keep your head and body facing forward all the time, and keep your feet and pelvis still. Repeat a few times to loosen your arms and shoulders.

ARM STRETCHING

1 Stand with your arms straight out in front of you, at chest height. Take in a deep breath and exhale.

SIDEWAYS BEND

1 Stand with your feet at least shoulder-width apart and your arms hanging down at your sides. Bend down to one side, trying not to twist. Slowly return to the upright and then bend to the other side. Straighten up and now repeat.

SHAKE

1 Try to relax and let your whole body go completely floppy. Shake your limbs to release any tension.Continue for as long as you feel comfortable. If you prefer, shake each limb in sequence, starting with your right arm.

CAT STRETCH

1 Kneel on all fours, with your hands and knees shoulder-width apart. As you start to inhale, bring your head forward and slightly hollow your back.

2 Now breathe out and, as you do so, arch the back upwards like a cat, allowing your head to drop down. Repeat a few times.

therapeutic movements
therapeutic movements

therapeutic movements

One of the best things about stretches is that you can do some simple, straightforward exercises anywhere, at any time: at home, in the office, standing in a queue or even sitting in the car; there are no restrictions. However, in order to get the most benefit from regular stretching, and particularly from doing yoga practice, it is important to create a quiet, comfortable space and to give yourself plenty of time to do the movements without any pressure or interruptions from the telephone or colleagues. In fact, making this space is in itself a relaxing, unwinding step, and will enhance the effectiveness of the actual exercises.

Ideally, make an area that feels quiet and calming to you, perhaps with softer lighting if it is needed, maybe with a thick, soft mat for the floor-based stretches. If you have any back discomfort, or just need extra support when lying down, then a couple of cushions may be extremely useful. It is helpful to wear loose fitting, airy clothing so that you can move freely and easily. If the weather permits try to let in some fresh air, but do not risk getting cold. These exercises are not intended to work up a good sweat or strain the heart, but to make you feel altogether less stiff and tense, and generally much more flexible. They are great for loosening you up, releasing tensions, improving circulation, toning the body, and generally making you feel much freer and more confident with your own body. They can really perk you up. After each exercise you will also need time to relax quietly, before you plunge back into everyday life.

If you find them an enormous benefit and become inspired, and want to try out more exercises, then do find a good, local class. Yoga exercises are generally best learnt in such a class, with a skilled, experienced teacher for maximum benefit. Alternatively you could create your own class at home, inviting a yoga teacher, friends and family on a regular basis.

tension and backache relievers

In the great majority of cases back trouble is the result of chronic tensions which can build up around the spine. Tired, tight muscles are also much more prone to strain or injury. The stretches that are shown here are intended to aid flexibility of the spine, and to make you feel much more supple, but if you already suffer from back pain or an injury then you must seek professional advice.

COBRA

1 Lie on your front, with your arms bent and your hands under your shoulders.

2 Slowly lift your head and push down on your arms to help raise your trunk.

3 If you can, tilt your head backwards and stretch up and back, then relax.

SIMPLE TWIST

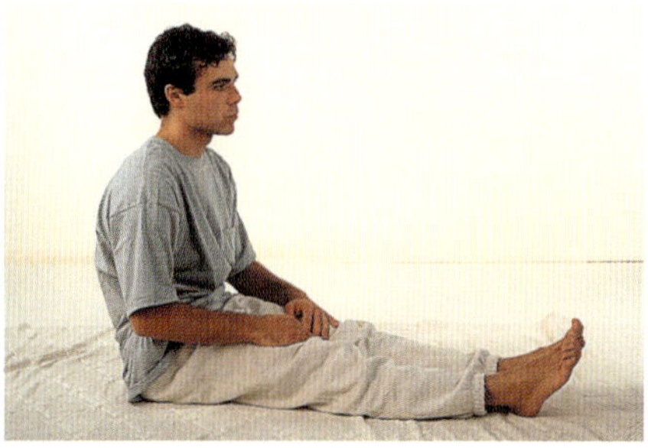

1 Sit on the floor with your legs stetched straight out in front of you.

2 Bend one leg and place the foot on the floor across the other knee.

3 Place your opposite arm in front of your bent leg and twist to look over your shoulder.

FULL TWIST

1 Bend one leg so that the foot rests on the inner thigh of the other leg.

2 Bring this leg over the first one, then grasp your foot with the other arm.

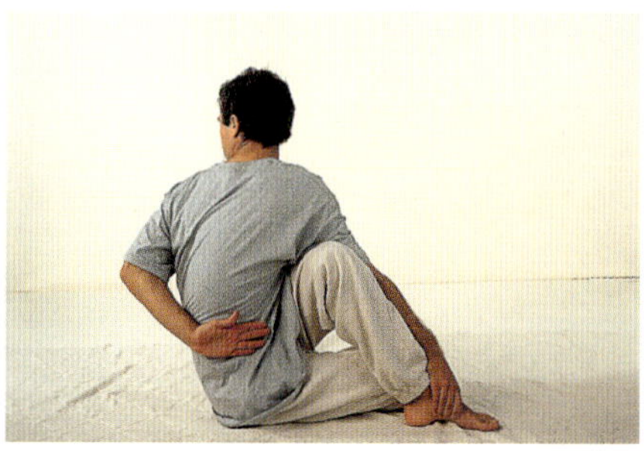

3 Twist as far around as you can, hold, then relax. Swap over your legs. Repeat.

TRIANGLE

1 Stand with your feet shoulder-width apart and your arms straight out to the sides. This should be a well-balanced, easily held position. Your head should feel like a ball balancing on your neck. Stare straight ahead.

2 Bend down to one side without twisting your body, letting the opposite arm rise in the air. If you find this awkward or uncomfortable, do not strain yourself. The object is to loosen the body, not injure it.

3 Stretch the raised arm, look up and hold. Slowly straighten and repeat on the other side. If you can, repeat several times, but be careful to move slowly into position to avoid a strain.

BENDING TWIST

1 Stand with your feet shoulder-width apart and your arms straight out to the sides. Bending forward, try to touch your foot, or the floor in front of it if you can, with your opposite hand. Slowly uncurl and return to the starting position. Repeat on the other side.

SLOUCH STRESS

1 Sit on a tall stool so that your feet are just off the floor. With your hands behind your back, slouch so that your back is rounded, with your head now lowered down towards your chest.

2 Flex one foot, and lift the leg to straighten it if possible. Release the leg, relax, then repeat a few times. Repeat with the other leg. Note that the object is to build up a slow pace, not to go fast.

soothing and removing tension

Many of us suffer at some time from tension headaches and know that they begin with a gradual feeling of pressure in the head or neck, or a taut sensation in the facial muscles. Once you are aware of such tension, tackle it immediately. A few simple stretches can help to relieve these muscular spasms and prevent them leading to a severe headache. They can be done almost anywhere.

SIDEWAYS NECK STRETCH

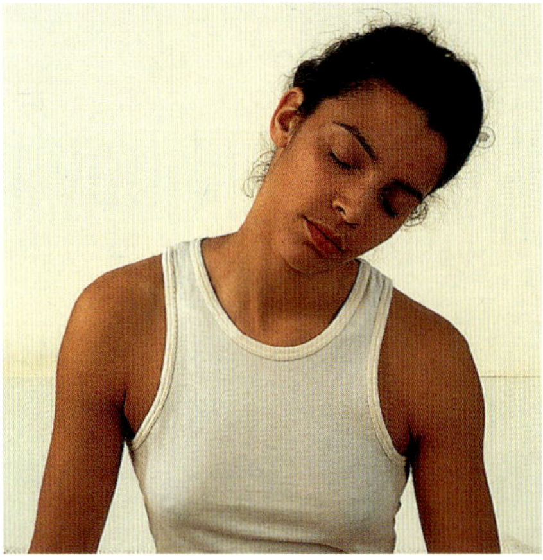

1 Slowly stretch your head down to one side, feeling the pull in the neck muscles. Return the head to the upright position and repeat on the other side.

2 To make this stretch of the neck muscles more effective, use your hands to give extra leverage. Place one hand under your chin and the other on top of your head; repeat the other side.

HEAD TO CHEST

1 Lower your head towards your chest, feeling the pull on the back of the neck. Hold at your furthest stretch before slowly raising the head again. Repeat two or three times.

LION POSTURE

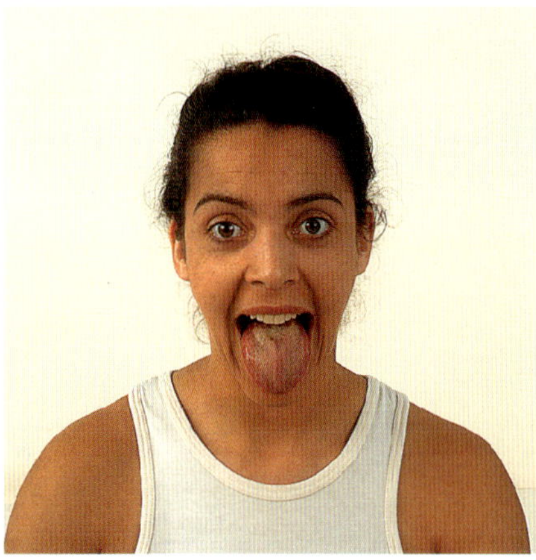

1 To stretch the facial muscles and release tension, open your mouth as wide as possible and push out your tongue. At the same time, open your eyes into as wide a stare as you can manage. Repeat a couple of times.

SEMICIRCLE ROTATION

1 Turn the head to one side, then steadily rotate it in a semicircular movement, letting the chin drop down across the chest.

2 Dropping the head backwards compresses the neck, so it is best not to make this a full circle rotation. Repeat, going back in the opposite direction.

posture enhancers

One of the great benefits of an exercise system such as yoga is the fact that it gradually and increasingly gives you considerable grace and poise. In addition it will make a huge difference to your overall posture. If it was previously a bit lax, and you ended up slouching, you will really notice the difference. In fact, learning to hold yourself properly can help you to look and feel much younger, and reduce muscle strain.

1 Stand with feet slightly apart and arms raised in front. Slowly twist to one side. Repeat on the other side.

2 Stand with your feet apart, and hold your arms out. Bend over, sliding one hand down the inside of the same leg.

3 Reach as far as is comfortable, then slowly return to the upright and repeat on the other side.

4 For the tree routine, stand on one leg and bend the other knee, as shown.

5 Either place your palms together above your head, or raise the hands.

6 For the arm and leg stance, stand on one leg and hold the other foot behind.

tired and aching leg revivers

Most of us spend too long each day with our legs stuck in fixed positions, and stiffness of the lower limbs from inactivity or tension can make you feel quite tired. Legs benefit from being stretched, keeping them toned and supple. These exercises prevent the legs, thighs and lower back from getting too tense. Since some of these positions are quite difficult, do beware of straining yourself.

ALTERNATE LEG PULLS

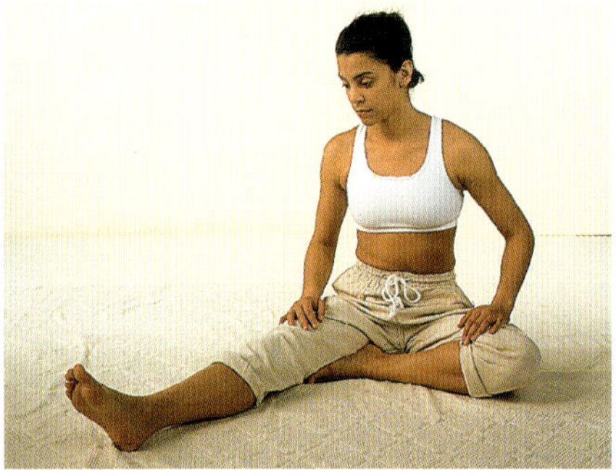

1 Sit on the floor, with one leg out straight and the other bent so that the foot rests on the inner thigh of your extended leg. Do it with care.

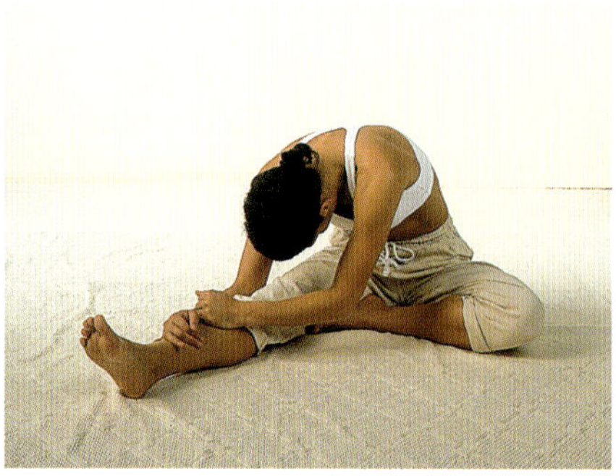

2 Lean forward and clasp the straight leg as far down as is comfortable; pull your chest down a little further and hold for a moment. Change legs and repeat.

FULL LEG PULLS

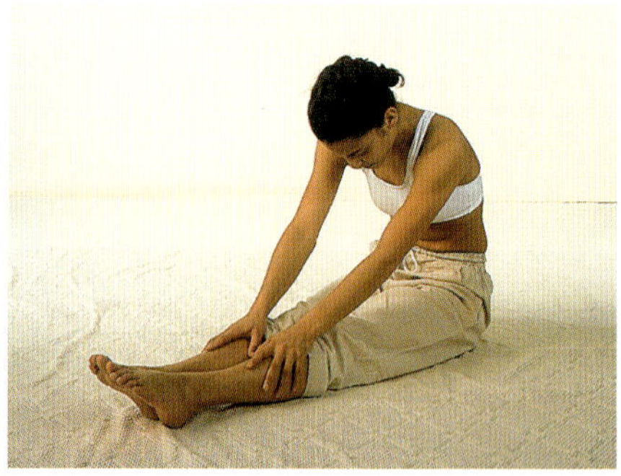

1 The previous stretch can be extended by starting with both legs straight out in front of you. Repeat as described.

2 Lean forward and hold the legs with both hands; pull yourself down a little further and hold for a moment. If this is difficult, bend the legs slightly.

SIDE LEG RAISE

1 Lie on your side with your legs and body in a straight line. Support your head with one hand and place your free hand on the floor for balance.

2 Without twisting your hips, steadily raise the upper leg as far as is comfortable. Hold, then lower slowly. Repeat with the other leg.

CAT STRETCH

1 Kneel on all fours with your hands and knees shoulder-width apart. Raise your head and look straight ahead.

2 Breathe in, and as you exhale lift and arch your back. Hold for a moment before relaxing back into the original position. Inhale, then repeat.

BACK PUSH-UP

1 Lie on your back with your knees bent and your feet on the floor, hip-width apart. Now place your hands on the floor by your shoulders.

2 Push up with your hands and feet, arching your back at the same time. Hold for a moment, then lower your body back to the floor. Do not strain yourself with this movement – it works on lots of muscles at the same time.

SIT UP/LIE DOWN

1 Sit on the floor with both legs straight out in front of you. Your torso should be at right angles to your legs, with your eyes looking forward.

2 Slowly lower your back to the floor, then start to bend the legs and raise them off the floor.

3 As you raise the legs, slowly start to straighten them until they are as close to the vertical as you can manage. Again, take care not to strain yourself.

4 Keeping the legs straight, slowly lower them to the floor.

5 Continue the movement by sitting up and clasping your legs with your hands to bend forwards. Slowly return to the original sitting position.

abdominal tension relievers

We tend to hold and lock up too much tension in our abdomen, especially if we are the kind of people who always bottle up our feelings. Even simple muscular tension can leave us feeling stiff and rather uncomfortable, and much less flexible around the waist. Consequently exercises aimed at reducing stiffness and increasing flexibility in the abdominal region are extremely useful.

LOTUS

1 For the full lotus, the first leg should be bent with the foot on top of the other thigh, and the second leg bent so that the foot goes over the other leg on to the opposite thigh. Hold if possible.

2 For an easier version bend one leg and rest the foot on the inner thigh of the other leg. Bend the second leg and place the foot on top of the opposite thigh. Keep the spine upright.

ABDOMINAL MOVEMENTS

1 Either sit cross-legged or kneel, and place your hands on your waist or thighs. Breathe out completely.

2 Without inhaling, pull in your abdomen as far as you can, then "snap" it in and out up to five times before taking a breath. Relax for a few moments, breathing freely, before repeating.

LEG OVER

1 Lie on your back, with your legs out straight. Raise one leg as close to the vertical as is comfortable, then move it across the body, keeping your hips in contact with the floor.

2 Push the leg as far over as possible, then slowly return to the original position. Repeat with the other leg.

LYING TWISTS

1 Lie on your back, hands behind your head and legs together, knees bent.

2 Twist the legs from side to side, keeping the back and hips on the floor.

SIDE BENDS

1 Stand with feet apart and hands on hips. Bend down to one side.

2 Slowly return to the upright position and bend to the other side. Repeat.

ROLL TWIST

1 Keeping the legs and hips still, roll your upper body around in a clockwise circle.

2 Move slowly and carefully, and bend only as far as is comfortable.

SIT UP/LIE DOWN

1 Sit on the floor with both legs straight out in front of you.

2 Slowly lie back, then start to bend the legs and raise them off the floor.

3 Sit up, bend forwards, clasp your legs and slowly return to the sitting position.

office tensions and stiff muscles

For people who spend their working day sitting at a desk it is very easy to get stiff, aching muscles. Badly designed chairs do not help, and as you get tired, so posture suffers and you can end up getting round-shouldered. It is therefore absolutely essential that every now and again you get up and walk around, relax your body, and try some of these excellent loosening-up exercises.

SEATED CAT STRETCH

1 Pull the chair back from the desk slightly to give yourself more room, then bend forward and clasp your ankles.

2 Carefully arch your back to stretch, then relax back and repeat.

CALF STRETCH

1 Sit fairly upright, then lift and straighten each leg alternately. Repeat a few times.

2 Flex the foot to stretch the calf muscle. Repeat a few times.

NECK TWISTS

1 Turn your head to one side, feeling the extension in the neck muscles.

2 Repeat, turning the head from side to side. Do both steps quite slowly.

ARM AND CHEST STRETCH

1 Sitting upright, link your hands together, palms away from your body, and push your arms straight out in front of you. Hold for a couple of seconds, relax and then repeat.

ARM AND BACK STRETCH

1 Link your hands together behind your back, over the top of the chair, and lift your arms slightly. Do not strain yourself. Push away from your body, hold, then repeat the exercise.

FOREARM STRETCH

1 Hold your arms straight out to the sides and stretch them. Alternately flex and extend your hands. Feel the pull on the upper and lower sides of your forearms as you do so.

BACK/SHOULDER STRETCH

1 Stretch your arms up in the air over your head. As you breathe in, arch your back ever so slightly. Relax with the exhalation and repeat the exercise a couple of times.

POSTURE CLASP

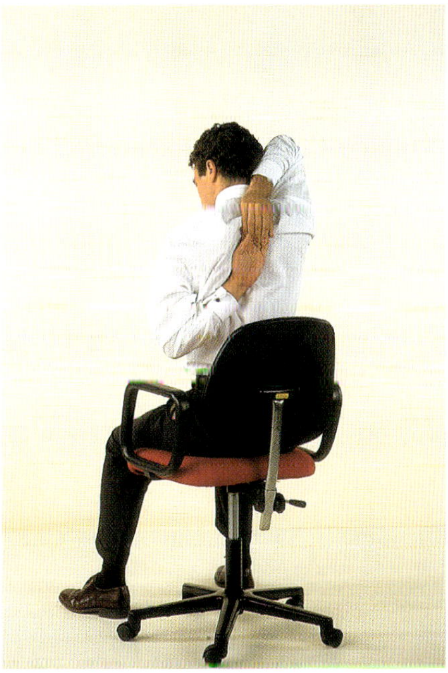

1 Put one arm behind your back and bend it up, with the hand reaching the other shoulder. With your other arm raised and bent down over your shoulder, try to clasp your fingers.

SHOULDER RELEASE

1 Link your fingers together and stretch your arms high above your head. Repeat several times.

meditation

Meditation has been in use from the beginning of time: people have always sought inner quiet and physical relaxation, whether for reasons connected with the spirit, self-realization or health. You do not have to be a physical contortionist to achieve and enjoy the benefits of meditation at both physical and mental levels.

What, then, is meditation? It has been described as just sitting and relaxing. Many people find that their lives are so full of the demands of work, family, friends and organized leisure pursuits that they have no time to "stand and stare". Many are so caught up in planning and working towards the future that they take little pleasure from the here and now. In their bustle to "get on" they miss out on the simple pleasures of life. But beauty and joy are there to be seen and experienced, even in industrial cities.

The benefits of meditation come from regular use. If you are under stress, you may find that meditating twice daily will be effective in restoring composure. Make a time and space you can call your own, and use breathing and relaxation exercises to ease yourself into the meditative state. The more you practise meditation the less time you will need to spend on these, but they remain useful in calming and preparing you. Allow at least 10 minutes, ideally 20, for meditation in each session.

the benefits of meditation

Human beings were never designed to cope with the high-pressure demands of life in the 21st century; life when you are constantly in demand, having to make vital decisions at breakneck speed right through the day, and even during the night. You might say it cannot be done, but it can, with help. Knowing how as well as when to switch off makes all the difference, and even scientists now agree.

PSYCHO-PHYSICAL LINKS

A period of meditation can often lead to a feeling of being refreshed, with a more positive attitude and a general feeling of well-being. Things that had been bothering you may now be seen in a new and more helpful way. You gain a different, wider perspective on things and feel very much more in control.

These beneficial reactions have been well known for years, but only in recent times has anyone found a physiological explanation. Detailed, extensive knowledge of brain scans and even brain wave patterns has given extraordinary new information about what is commonly called the "alpha state".

Mind and body work together in meditation to promote health and well-being in the whole person.

Meditation and Work

The tensions of modern working practices often mean that people are so bound up in meeting all the vigorous demands placed upon them that they maintain a high level of mental and physical activity right through the day. This frequently means that they are not only cutting off their extremely important emotional responses and their enjoyment of the simple things in life, but they are also pushing their physical and mental health right to the very limit. Much has now been written about the management of stress, and the significant need for periods of mental and physical relaxation during the working day.

Endorphin Release

When we are truly relaxed, both mentally and physically, there are changes in the brain wave pattern until it is predominantly located and fixed within the alpha state. Within this particular state the brain triggers chemicals known as endorphins. It is in fact this chemical trigger that has the benefits that are experienced as a feeling of well-being. Indeed, endorphins have frequently been called "nature's very own special opiates". Meditation is one of the easiest ways to achieve this, and these good feelings can easily linger for some time after the meditation has ended, the length of time varying considerably. There is also a real physical benefit, as these endorphins boost and recharge the immune system, helping you to fight off all kinds of infections.

The 20-minute Rule

One writer, Ernest Rossi, has formulated the 20-minute rule which is based on the theory of ultradian rhythms. Ultradian rhythms are biorhythms that the body works through during each day – a little like hyperbolic curves of energy which repeat every 90 to 120 minutes. Naturally, it would be best to work only at peak performance times, but this is just not possible. However, timing work breaks to coincide with the mind/body slow-down pattern every 90 minutes does ensure maximum productivity and restricts the potential build-up of stress.

Rossi suggested the pattern of working for 90 minutes and then taking a brief 20-minute break. He himself usually lies down and meditates during this period because it is the best form of total mental and physical relaxation, and is good preparation for returning to optimum mental processing.

It is important that these breaks take place every 90 minutes or so, and in such a way as to completely change the mind/body state. Ideally, you should stop all work activity and experience a change of physical status (standing rather than sitting, looking into the distance rather than close up, for example) and mental focus. A 20-minute meditation is ideal and the benefits will be felt immediately. On returning to work after the 20 minutes, you will see things afresh and deal with them more efficiently, as you are ready to climb to peak performance on the biorhythmic curve. The feeling of well-being lasts into the next 90-minute period.

To be at your best for meetings ensure you take regular breaks.

gaining the meditative state

Many religious groups, as well as adherents of Transcendental Meditation, use a sound, or "mantra", to help with meditation. The constant repetition of a phrase, word or sound ("aum" is commonly used in Hinduism) creates the alpha state by an almost hypnotic focus of attention upon that particular sound. In fact chants repeated again and again can lead to its members reaching a "high".

Sound

An effortless sound, repeated with the natural regular rhythm of breathing, can have the same soothing, liberating effect as the constant natural sound of running water, rustling leaves or a beating heart. The single sound, or mantra as it is known, is used to blot out the "chatter" of intrusive thoughts, allowing the mind to find deep repose. Speaking or chanting a mantra as a flowing stream of endless sound is a very old method of heightening a person's awareness by concentrating the senses. The simple gentle sound "om", or "aum", is sometimes known as the first mantra, which is literally an instrument of thought. The curving Sanskrit (the ancient language of Hindus in India) symbol for this primordial word represents the various states of consciousness: waking, dreaming, deep sleep and the transcendental state.

However, the actual sound need not be a special word or incantation; something simple and meaningful will be as effective. The sound of the word "calm" spoken or thought with each exhalation can be very effective, especially while imagining tension leaving your body. Any word that appeals to you will do.

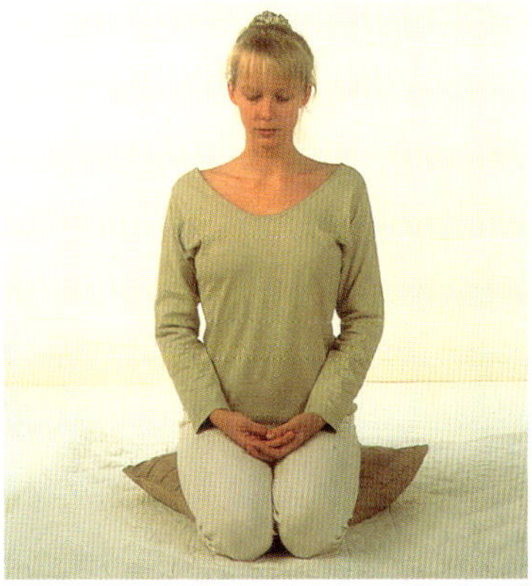

Make sure that you are sitting quite comfortably and then start breathing in the colour of your choice.

Repeating a mantra takes you into a world of peace and harmony.

Touch

You can use your sense of touch in a lulling, soothing way to induce a state of meditation at times of stress. Young children do this when they adopt a satisfyingly smooth ribbon or piece of fabric to hold and manipulate when they are feeling tense. The same technique is seen all over the Middle East, where strings of worry beads are rhythmically passed through the fingers at difficult moments to focus the mind and calm anxiety. Their uniform size, gentle round shapes, smooth surfaces and rhythmic, orderly clicking as they are passed along their string all assist the meditative state. Use one or two smooth, rounded stones in the same way, passing them slowly from hand to hand.

Colours

Some colours are associated with relaxation and can be a helpful way to clear the mind of tension and allow meditation to start. Sit with your eyes closed, and be aware of the colour that comes into your mind: it may be any colour of the rainbow – red or purple are common. Then slowly and gradually allow that colour to change to a blue or green colour, allowing it to fill the whole of your mind's eye and replacing all other colours. The colour pink is also recommended by colour therapists and this may prove helpful. You will find a feeling of relaxation growing as the new colour builds in your mind, and when the relaxed colour is complete, you will experience feelings of inner peace.

Establish a comfortable rhythm of breathing and then focus on it until your mind is completely still, relaxed and clear. Colours are associated with all kinds of qualities, so choose the best for your own particular moods and needs. Red: vitality, energy, strength and willpower (complementary colour turquoise). Orange: happiness and laughter (complementary colour blue). Yellow: intellect and objectivity (complementary colour violet). Green: cleansing and harmony (complementary colour magenta). Turquoise: boosts and strengthens the immune system, counteracts disease (complementary colour red). Blue: peace and relaxation, restful sleep (complementary colour orange). Violet: beauty, dignity, assured self-respect (complementary colour yellow). Magenta: the liberating release of all obsessional thoughts and memories (complementary colour green).

how to use meditation
how to use meditation

how to use meditation

The key to using meditation lies in recognizing that you actually need it. Once you get into the whirlpool of work and stress, they can both all too easily become an integral part of your lifestyle. In fact, they can be such a formidable cornerstone that you cannot imagine what life could possibly be like without them. But once you stand back and see clearly and exactly what is happening to you, what your life has become, then suddenly you see you actually need a way out. One of the best ways involves deep meditation.

Meditation needs to be done like regular exercise. In fact you might say you are exercising the ways in which you relax. The very first step involves switching off, like switching off a light in a room, and concentrating on what could be called the "Inner Other", that is to say the marvellous, relaxed, empty inner spaces inside your head and body. This stage, put crudely, means sweeping out all the noise and mayhem and chaos of everyday life and getting ready to enter another world.

The second stage involves being carried along what one expert teacher calls "a moving but going nowhere sound that coils round and even through itself in a perpetual state of being". Perhaps the best way of evaluating it is by hearing what people have to say after meditation. "As good as a holiday" or "like a wonderful deep refreshing sleep" is what most people say. If you are to get its full, continuous benefits then you really must make sure that meditation is something that you do regularly every day, at certain times, because like almost all forms of exercise the more often you do it, the better you are at it; the quicker you can switch off and tune in, and enter that fantastic deep state of total energizing, refreshing relaxation.

You must use meditation with care though. It is not like switching on and off a tap. It needs to be respected. Few people who meditate try, even if they could, to describe its ultimate power. That would be like divulging a wonderful private secret; to have it is quite enough.

simple meditation techniques

If you want to learn to meditate seriously, you would do well to find an experienced teacher to guide you. However, there are many simple techniques that you can practise alone, often with quite powerful effects. Try the ones described here, and see which you feel in tune with. The more you practise, the easier it will become to reach a deep meditative state.

Introduce a child to meditation by using the Numbers Game.

THE NUMBERS GAME

This is a very simple form of meditation using a blackboard, real or imaginary. It is a good "game" to use with children (or adults), giving them a taste of meditation, and they really enjoy it. It is described here as if you are leading a group, but it can be easily used on one person, and provides an excellent way to clear the mind through concentration, imagination and patterns: all wonderful ways of gaining a real experience of deep meditation.

What you must do is this …

1 Get the children to sit or lie comfortably. Once they have found a really comfortable position ask them to remember it.

2 With chalk on the blackboard, draw a diagram of numbers, making sure that there are no mathematical links, like this:

3 1 5
8 6 9
4 7 2

3 Give the children one minute to memorize this sequence.

4 Ask them to return to their relaxed position, eyes closed, and concentrate on the numbers alone.

5 Rub out the numbers, telling them to do the same in their minds. Do this slowly saying "That leaves just four numbers", etc.

6 Then rub out the last number, saying "Now concentrate on what is left" … Let them remain in silence until you notice a restlessness – this is often three or more minutes.

7 Wake them gently with an instruction to "Sit up". Ask them what the last number was and for their reactions.

THE HAVEN

Once you have managed to achieve complete physical relaxation and calm, gradually allow your mind to enter a place, whether real or imaginary, that is quite special to you. Now you can allow your mind to drift … drift to a pleasant, peaceful place. A place that you know and where you always feel able to relax … completely. A safe … secure … place … where no one … and nothing can ever bother you.

It may be a place you have visited on holiday, a beach or a place in the countryside. Or it may be a room … a room you have had … a room you do have … or a room you would like to have … an imaginary place. But it is a place where you can always feel able to let go … completely … a haven, a haven of tranquillity, unique and special to you.

In order to help you imagine this place … notice first the light: is it bright, natural or dim … is there any particular source of light … natural or man-made? Notice also the temperature level … hot, warm or cool … and any particular source of heat. Be aware of the colours that surround you … shapes … and textures … the familiar objects that make that place special. Begin to see it in all its detail. You can just be there … whether sitting, lying or reclining, enjoying the sounds … the smells … the atmosphere … with nobody wanting anything, nobody needing anything and no one demanding anything from you. Relax.

Everyone has their own haven, a quiet magical place like this.

Try to imagine your perfect country house.

A GUIDED VISIT TO A COUNTRY HOUSE

Imagine that you are visiting a beautiful country house … a really beautiful old country house or a stately home with magnificent sweeping lawns on a warm, sunny, summer's afternoon. You are standing on the staircase that leads into the entrance hall, one of those wide ceremonial types of staircase. And as you look down across the entrance hall you can just glimpse, through the open doors opposite, a gravel drive, and the sunlight on the gravel. It is a beautiful, sunny, summer's afternoon and there is no one around to trouble or bother you as you stand alone on that staircase …

Now you are moving down the last ten steps to the hallway, relaxing more and more with each step down.

10 Taking one step down, relaxing and letting go …
9 Taking another step down, feeling at ease …
8 Becoming more relaxed, letting go even more …
7 Just drifting deeper … and deeper … everything is getting darker and darker, and even deeper down still …
6 Becoming calmer … and calmer … even calmer still …
5 Continuing to relax, continuing to let go and feeling good …
4 Relaxing even more … letting go even more …
3 Sinking deeper … drifting even further into this welcoming, relaxed state …
2 Enjoying those good feelings, all those feelings of inner peace and relaxation …
1 Nearly all the way down now, feeling very good … beautifully relaxed … and **0**.

You are wandering across that hallway now, towards the open doors and the gardens beyond, soaking up the atmosphere of peace and permanence in that lovely old building. You wander out through the doors and down the stone steps outside … and find yourself standing on the gravel drive outside, a wide gravel drive that leads down to the entrance gates.

As you stand there you notice the lush green lawns, so flat and well-clipped … and there are shrubs and trees, different shades of green and brown against a clear, blue sky … and you can feel the warmth of the sun on your head and shoulders as you enjoy this beautiful summer's afternoon in this lovely old garden … There are flowerbeds with their splashes of colour so carefully arranged and neatly tended. And there's no one else about … nobody needing anything, nobody wanting anything and nobody expecting anything from you, so you can enjoy the peace and serenity and solitude of this afternoon in this beautiful garden that's been so well looked after for so many, many years.

A little way down on the right-hand side of the driveway, you notice an ornamental fish pond. So you decide to wander down and have a look at those fish. Sometimes they seem almost to disappear behind the weed and shadows, but always they reappear, with their scales catching the sunlight, red, gold, silver or black. And as you watch those fish your mind becomes even more deeply relaxed …

THE WELL

This continues from the previous visualization of the beautiful country house and is intended to take you to even deeper levels of meditation.

… As you watch those fish you notice that the centre of the pond is very deep. It could be the top of a disused well. You take from your pocket a silver-coloured coin, and toss that coin so that it lands over the centre of the pond, and then you watch as it swings down through the water. The ripples drift to the edges of the pond, but you just watch that coin as it sinks deeper and deeper through that clear water, sometimes it seems to disappear as it turns on edge, at other times a face of the coin catches the sunlight and it flashes through the water … sinking, drifting deeper and deeper, twisting and turning as it makes its way down … Finally it rests at the bottom lying on a cushion of soft brown mud, a silver coin in that still, clean water on its own cushion of mud … And you feel as still as that coin, as still and cool and motionless as that water, enjoying that feeling of inner peace and stillness.

Watch the ripples as the coin lands in the very centre of the pond. Look even more closely as it tumbles down through the water …

personal development

Affirmations are a deceptively simple device that can be used by anyone and they are remarkably effective. Try to use this method while in the meditative state, having planned and memorized the affirmations involved. These powerful, positive phrases will improve communication with all parts of your mind. All you need is a simple phrase summing up how you want to be.

THE POWER OF WORDS

To make affirmations effective, they should
- be made in the present tense
- be positively phrased
- have an emotional reward.

Now contrast the power of such phrases with what happens if you are asked not to do or think of something. The words "no", "not", "never" and so on generally have the opposite effect to that intended, and why? Yours is the most influential voice in your life because you believe it. It comes live, straight out of the personality and intellect, and is fuelled by your dreams and language. The power you have over yourself is extraordinary. That is precisely why you must be careful to avoid any negative or demeaning statements you regularly make about yourself, either to others or to yourself – "I am shy", "I lack confidence", "I cannot", "I get nervous when" and so on – they are self-limiting beliefs that you are reinforcing each time they slip into your conversation or mind. You become what you say.

The point about affirmations is that instead of running yourself down, albeit in a subtle, insidious way, you actually start building yourself up. You start creating the inner psychological scaffolding to support the new you. Such affirmations are best used while in a wonderful state of meditation.

The difference affirmations can make is extraordinary. From shy and introverted to open, confident and winning.

Thinking through what you want to be is the big key to success.

IMPROVED SELF-WORTH

We all have attributes and qualities in which we can take pride and pleasure. This exercise is about emphasizing these positive aspects to allay the doubts that only serve to limit our potential.
- I like my [physical attribute].
- I am proud of my [attitude or achievement].
- I love meeting people – they are fascinating.
- My contribution is valuable to [name person].
- I am lovable and can give love.
- Others appreciate my [opinions, assistance, a personal quality].
- I enjoy being a unique combination of mind and body.

Now imagine yourself speaking to colleagues, boss, employees or friends … See yourself behaving and looking confident, standing and looking a confident person … Notice how you stand … your facial expression … hear the way that you speak … slowly, calmly, quietly, clearly and with confidence. You are communicating your needs … ideas … opinions in a positive way. Notice how your words flow easily, and how others are listening attentively to you … valuing what you have to say. Now "climb aboard" … be there – know how it feels to stand like that … to speak like that … and to have that positive reception from others. Get in touch with the stance … expression … and feelings … and know that you can use these any time in the future to gain those same feelings or that inner strength in everything you do. See yourself in different situations: at home, in a social setting, in all the parts of your life, confident and assured, going from strength to strength.

If you want to be No. 1, then take time to concentrate on seeing yourself as the best. Give yourself the power to come out top.

VISUALIZATION

In the same way that you can utilize your voice, so, perhaps more powerfully, you can use your imagination. The imagination can stimulate emotions, and they can register new attitudes in the mind. It can be a direct communication with the deeper levels of the mind, providing a powerful influence for improvements in your attitudes, behaviour patterns and overall confidence.

Visualization requires that you imagine yourself in a situation, behaving, reacting and looking as you would wish to do at an interview, an important meeting, a social gathering, a one-to-one situation, or perhaps a sporting event. Imagine what that will mean for you, your reactions, the reactions of those around you and, importantly, feel all the good feelings that will be there when this happens in reality.

It is like playing a video of the event, on that screen on the inside of the forehead, the mind's eye, from the beginning of the situation through to the perfect outcome. Should any doubts or negative images creep into your "video", push them away and replace them with positive ones. Keep this realistic, and base it upon real information from your past.

CONFIDENCE IN FUTURE SITUATIONS

The meditative state, affirmations and visualization can be a valuable rehearsal and preparation for a future event. Athletes and other sportsmen have proved that it actually does work. We can all use these extraordinary techniques to achieve our own optimum performance during any situation. Now consider the following phrases, and how they relate to you ...

- I am quietly confident in meetings.
- I speak slowly, quietly and confidently so that others listen.
- My contribution is wanted and valued by others.
- I enjoy meetings, as they bring forth new ideas and help to renew my enthusiasm.

Imagine an important meeting that is about to happen, and see yourself there, filling in all the details that you know, and the people too; imagine yourself there looking confident and relaxed, concentrating on what is happening. Be aware of the acute interest you are giving to what is happening with complete, concentrated attention, and then imagine yourself speaking, to give information or to ask a question: hear yourself speaking quietly, slowly and calmly ...

Notice people listening to what you are saying; they wish you well and support you, as you are expressing your viewpoint or raising a question they may well have wanted to ask, too. Notice how you are sitting or standing, how you lean slightly forward when speaking, that expression of calm confidence on your face. When this is clear in your mind, just like a film playing in your mind's eye, play it back and forth. When you are feeling comfortable with it, get into that imaginary you, "climb aboard" and be there in your mind, seeing things from that perspective, hearing things from that point in the meeting. As you speak, get in touch with those calm feelings, and the attitudes that allow you to feel calm, in control, and quietly confident ... It is like a rehearsal; the more you manage to rehearse the better the final performance will be. You will acquire the right attitudes, stance and tone of voice, so that when you are in that situation all of these will be available to you, and it will be just as you imagined, as if you had done it all, successfully, before.

In short, what this technique does is take you step by step through a rehearsal. Imagine every possible scenario, and how you will deal with it. That is the key to a successful outcome.

The preparation was worth it; you went into a meeting knowing you could do it, and that is exactly what happened.

enjoyment and achievement

The mind and the body are so completely interlinked that if we keep physically fit we are also mentally alert. The one boosts the other, but it also works the other way around. If we really utilize our mental capacities we can affect and improve our physical health and performance. So it is up to you to make sure that these twin forces keep functioning at full power. Do not let either slip.

A well-tuned lively body keeps you feeling well and alert.

THE BODY/MIND LINK

Regularly say to yourself …

- I feel safe, happy and content in the knowledge that my body is constantly renewing itself. It is alive and well.
- It feels marvellous to know that every damaged cell is replaced by a healthy one.
- My immune system is strong and fights off any infections easily.
- My mind and my body are working in harmony to keep me healthy, well and alert.

Now, imagine yourself lying or sitting comfortably. As you see yourself there you notice a healing glow of coloured light surrounding your body, but not touching it. Let that colour become stronger, until it has a very clear pure colour, which is the colour of healing for you.

Now, as you watch, that healing, coloured light begins to flow into the top of your head. You can see it slowly draining into all parts of the head, face, ears, and starts its journey down through the neck and shoulders, into the tops of the arms … It continues to flow down through the arms and the chest area, that healing, coloured light, penetrating all the muscles and organs … even as you watch you can also feel a healing warmth coming into your body … NOW … as it flows down into the stomach area, the back, right the way down to the base of the spine. Then you can allow the light to disperse again and gradually return to your normal wakeful state, knowing that in those areas that need it, the healing process will continue.

STRESS REDUCTION

Stress is a factor in everyone's life and can even be a major motivator in some circumstances. Meditation can be a great help in coping with it, and combined with visualization, it can change your whole response to stressful demands. Keep saying …

- I enjoy solving problems.
- I work well under pressure.
- I am a calm, methodical and efficient worker.
- I love that feeling of having achieved so much in a day.
- I enjoy being calm when others around me are not.

Imagine yourself in a situation that has in the past caused stress. Picture the situation, and the other people involved … See yourself there … and notice a slight shimmer of light between yourself and those other people … a sort of bubble around you … a protective bubble that reflects any negative feelings back to them … leaving you able to get on with your tasks … your life, with an inner strength and calmness that surprises even you. A protective, invisible bubble surrounds you at all times. It will only allow those feelings that are positive and helpful to you to pass through for you to enjoy and build upon. Others may catch stress from each other … negativity, too, can be infectious … but you are protected … you continue to keep things in perspective … and to deal with things calmly and methodically. You are able to see the way forward clearly … solve problems … find ways around difficulties … by using your own inner resources and strengths, born of experience. In you alone lies the secret of success. You can and you will succeed.

Imagine yourself leading a healthy lifestyle and it will happen.

LIVING NOW

Although we cannot change the past, we can learn from it and build up a range of skills and useful insights from it. The future is that unknown world of possibilities and opportunities before us – but all that we can truly have any effect upon is the present. Keep saying to yourself …

- I have learned a great deal from the past.
- The future is an exciting range of opportunities.
- I enjoy laying good foundations NOW on which to build a better future.

Imagine yourself standing on a pathway. As you look around the left, right and above is brilliantly illuminated, and sounds are amazingly clear. As you check over your shoulder you notice the path behind is unclear. You hear a clock chime in the distance and take a step forward. You notice the slightest of noises, movements or shifts of light, and take pleasure even in the pure sound of silence, too. You can hear that same clock ticking now, and with each tick you can take a small step forward, effortlessly, along the path, and that illumination and awareness moves with you. At any fork in the path you can make decisions easily as you are truly involved in the moment, rather than looking over your shoulder at what might have been, or staring blindly into the future at what might happen. You enjoy being in the brilliantly illuminated, acute awareness of sound, hearing, feeling, taste and smell that is NOW.

For a complete experience, be more acutely aware of shapes and textures as well as sounds, colours and scents.

GOAL ACHIEVEMENT

A goal, in all areas of life, is vitally important in order to focus your attention and inner resources. A goal provides a sense of direction and ultimately the joy of achievement. Without it you might flounder, so keep saying to yourself …

- I direct my energies to achieve my goals.
- I enjoy directing my energies positively.
- I know where I am going and how I am getting there.
- Step by step I am moving in the right direction.
- I have the ability, I have the determination, I shall succeed.

Keep your eyes firmly fixed on your goal and you will achieve it.

Be aware of the different areas of your life: work, social, leisure activities, emotional and spiritual. Select one of these for this exercise … and be aware of what you want to happen in that area of your life, what you want to achieve … Make it realistic and clear in your mind. It may be useful to write it down and describe it fully before beginning this visualization.

While in the meditative state, imagine yourself having achieved that goal, imagine yourself there, in that situation. Surround yourself with all the things or people that indicate that you have achieved that goal. Be as specific as you can … be aware of all the senses … what are you seeing … hearing … touching or sensing … smelling … tasting. Be there … make it real … be specific … about colours … temperatures … lighting, to make it more and more real in your mind.

Now, from where you are at that moment of achieving that goal … look back … as if along a path, a pathway of time … to where you were … and notice the different stages of change … of movement towards achieving that goal … along the way … along that path … the different actions you have taken … the contacts you have made … and the people involved. Be aware of all the stages along the way … and as you return to the here and now … you remain in touch with the feelings that will make it all worthwhile … and you feel more and more determined to take one step at a time … make one change at a time … along that path to the successful achievement of your goal. And as you return from the meditative state so you are more determined to be successful in the achievement of your goal.

useful addresses

Alexander Technique

UK
The Society of Teachers of the Alexander Technique (STAT)
129 Camden Mews
London
NW1 9AH

USA
The American Society for the Alexander Technique (AmSAT)
30 North Maple
PO Box 60008
Florence
MA 01062

CANADA
CANSTAT
465 Wilson Avenue
Toronto
Ontario
M3H 1T9

AUSTRALASIA
AUSTAT
PO Box 716
Darlinghurst
NSW 2010

Alexander Technique Teachers Society New Zealand (ATTSNZ)
PO Box 3020
Wellington

T'ai Chi

UK
Tai Chi Union of Great Britain
69 Kilpatrick Gardens
Clarkston
Glasgow
Scotland
G76 7RF

Golden Rooster Tai Chi School
19 Albany Road
London
N4 4RR

Rainbow Tai Chi Kung Centre
Creek Farm
Pitley Hill
Woodland Ashburton
Devon
PQ13 7JY

British Tai Chi Chuan & Kung Fu Association
28 Linden Farm Drive
Countesthorpe
Leicestershire
LE8 5SX

USA
Mind, Body, Spirit Academy
PO Box 415
Chadsford
PA 19317

Tai Chi Cultural Centre
PO Box 8885
Stanford
CA 94309

Sarasota Shaolia Academy
4655 Flatbush Avenue
Sarasota
Florida
FL 34233-1920

AUSTRALASIA
Australian Academy of Tai Chi
686 Parrametta Road
Croydon
NSW 2132

Shaolin Wahnan Tai Chi
RSD Strathfelsaye Road
Victoria 3551

Yoga

UK
Iyengar Yoga Institute
223a Randolph Avenue
London
W9 1NL

Manchester & District Institute of Iyengar Yoga
134 King Street
Dukinfield
Tameside
Greater Manchester
M60 8HG

Edinburgh Iyengar Yoga Centre
195 Bruntsfield Place
Edinburgh
EH10 4DQ

The British Wheel of Yoga
1 Hamilton Place
Boston Road
Sleaford
Lincolnshire
NG24 7EI

USA
Satchidananda Ashram – Yogaville
Buckingham
VA 23921

International Yoga Association
92 Main Street
Warrenton
VA 20186

BKS Iyengar Yoga National Association of the United States Inc.
8223 West Third Street
Los Angeles
CA 90038

Sivanda Yoga Vedanta Center
1246 Bryn Mawr
Chicago
IL 60660

AUSTRALASIA
BKS Iyengar Association of Australasia
1 Rickman Avenue
Mosman
NSW 2088

Sivananda Yoga Vedanta Centre
409th Avenue
Katoomba
NSW 2780

further reading

Meditation

UK
Gateway Books
The Hollies
Wellow
Bath
Somerset
BA2 8QJ

Western Zen Retreats
Winterhead Hill Farm
Shipham
Winscombe
Somerset
BS25 1RS

Transcendental Meditation
Freepost
London
SW1P 4YY

The Community Health Foundation
188 Old Street
London
EC1V 9FR

USA
Greater Washington DC Association of Professionals Practising the Transcendental Meditation Program
4818 Montgomery Lane
Bethesda
MD 20814

Institute of Noetic Sciences
PO Box 909
Sausalito
CA 94966

First Zen Institute of America
113 East 30th Street
New York
NY 10016

American Buddhist Association
1151 West Leland Avenue
Chicago
IL 60640

AUSTRALASIA
Transcendental Meditation Centre
68 Wood Street
Manly
Sydney
NSW 2095

The Barry Long Centre
Box 5277
Gold Coast MC
Queensland 4217

Transcendental Meditation Centre
New Zealand
5 Adam Street
Green Lane
Auckland 5

Alexander Technique

Brennan, Richard, *The Alexander Technique Workbook* (Element Books, 1994).
Brennan, Richard, *Mind & Body Stress Relief with the Alexander Technique* (Thorsons, 1998).
Dimon, Theodore, *Anatomy of the Moving Body: A Basic Course in Bones, Muscles and Joints* (North Atlantic Books, 2001).
Langford, Elizabeth, *Mind and Muscle – An Owner's Handbook* (Garant Enterprises, 1999).
Macdonald, Glynn and Glenn, *The Complete Illustrated Guide to the Alexander Technique: A Practical Program for Health, Poise and Fitness* (Element Books, 1998).
Machover, Ilana, et al, *The Alexander Technique – Pregnancy and Birth* (Constable Robinson, 1993).
McEvenue, Kelly and Rodenburg, Patsy, *The Alexander Technique for Actors* (Methuen Publishing, 2001).
Robinson, Lynne and Fisher, Helge, *The Mind Body Work Out – Pilates and the Alexander Technique* (Pan, 1998).

T'ai Chi

Chuen, Master Lam Kan, *The Way of Energy* (Gaia Books, 1991).
Crompton, Paul, *Chinese Soft Exercise – A T'ai Chi Workbook* (Unwin Paperbacks, 1986).
Klein, Bob, *Movements of Magic: The Spirit of T'ai chi Chu'uan* (Newcastle Publishing, 1984).
Pang, Chia Siew, & Hock, Goh Ewe, *There are No Secrets: Professor Cheng Man-ch'ing and his Tai Chi Chuan* (Wolfe Lowenthal, North Atlantic Books, 1991).
Reid, Howard, *The Way of Harmony: A Guide to Soft Martial Arts* (Unwin Paperbacks, 1988).

Yoga

Bender Birch, Beryl, *Power Yoga* (Prion, 1995)
Iyengar, B.K.S., *Light on Yoga* (Harper Collins, 1966).
Iyengar, B.K.S., *Light on Pranayama* (Harper Collins, 1981).
Iyengar, B.K.S., *The Illustrated Light on Yoga* (Harper Collins, 1980).
Iyengar, B.K.S., *Yoga* (Dorling Kindersley, 2001)
Liz Lark, *Yoga for Life* (Carlton Books, 2001)
Mehta, Mira, *How to Use Yoga* (Lorenz Books, 1994).
Mehta, Silva, Mira and Shyam, *Yoga: The Iyengar Way* (Dorling Kindersley, 1990).
Phillips, Kathy, *The Spirit of Yoga* (Cassell & Co, 2001)

Meditation

Kabat-Zinn, Jon, *Mindfulness Meditation for Everyday Life* (Piatkus Books, 1994).
Khalsa, Dharma Singh, *Meditation as Medicine* (Simon & Schuster, 2001).
The Dalai Lama, *Stages of Meditation* (Rider, 2001).

a

b

c

d

e

f

g

r

s

t

w

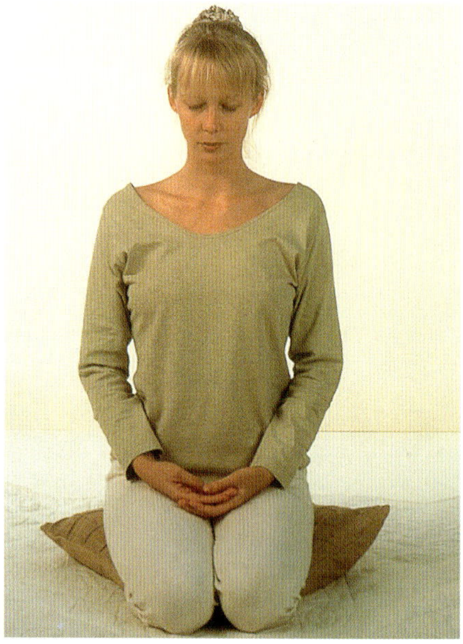

y